From MTV to Mecca

In the name of God,
the most merciful,
the most compassionate.

KRISTIANE BACKER, born in Hamburg, became one of the leading presenters on MTV Europe, where she interviewed most major artists and musicians of her time. She created her own youth show in Germany, and presented a daily guide to culture and entertainment on NBC Europe. She later studied natural medicine, qualified as a homeopath and presented a health programme on RTL. Kristiane was awarded Germany's most prestigious TV award, the 'Golden Camera', for her television work. Today, Kristiane Backer hosts conferences and gala events throughout Europe, devoting herself to promoting dialogue/understanding between faiths and cultures. She has been nominated Global Ambassador for the Exploring Islam Foundation and was the face of the 'Inspired by Muhammad' campaign in the UK. *From MTV to Mecca* has been published in German and Dutch, with Indonesian, Malaysian and Arabic editions forthcoming. Kristiane lives in London.

For more information please visit the author's website: www.kristianebacker.com

KRISTIANE BACKER

From MTV to Mecca

HOW ISLAM INSPIRED MY LIFE

Arcadia Books Ltd and Awakening Publications
www.arcadiabooks.co.uk
www.awakening.org

AWAKENING PUBLICATIONS
Uplands Business Centre, Bernard Street, Swansea, SA2 ODR, United Kingdom
P.O. Box 360009, Milpitas, CA 95036, United States of America

First published in the United Kingdom 2012
Originally published in an earlier version by Ullstein Buchverlage GMBH, Berlin 2009
Copyright © Kristiane Backer 2012

Translation from the German: Jane Paulick
Front cover photograph: Suleymaniye Mosque, Kingsland Rd, London © Heiko Prigge
Back cover photograph © Horst Friedrichs
Cover design: Salma Nafie, Ahmad Mahdy

A catalogue record for this book is available from the British Library.

ISBN 978-1-908129-81-9

Typeset in Minion by MacGuru Ltd
Printed and bound by CPI Group (UK) Ltd, Croydon, CR0 4YY

The publishers gratefully acknowledge the support of FIRD
(The Forum for International Relations Development).

Arcadia Books gratefully acknowledges the financial support of Arts Council England.
Awakening Publications gratefully acknowledges the support of the
Exploring Islam Foundation.

Arcadia Books supports PEN, the fellowship of writers who work together to promote
literature and its understanding. English PEN upholds writers' freedoms in Britain and
around the world, challenging political and cultural limits on free expression.
To find out more, visit www.englishpen.org or contact English PEN, Free Word Centre,
60 Farringdon Road, London EC1R 3GA

Contents

Foreword by Tariq Ramadan

This book recalls the journey of a woman, Kristiane Backer, who encountered Islam when she was a presenter with MTV. Hers was a world that had no association with religion, was disconnected from Christianity and Islam, far from any kind of spirituality. A world of entertainment, music and pop videos, acting as distraction in our lives, sometimes making us forget the true meaning of life. Whilst Kristiane was working at MTV she began a personal quest, which she describes in her book: how during her travels across the globe, she came across different people who believed in God, and it is through these conversations and experiences that her own spiritual journey towards God gradually began to unfold.

Throughout the book three important dimensions become apparent in the development of Kristiane's personal relationship with God. The first is when she moves her focus away from the entertainment industry, where it is easy to forget about one's self, and instead she begins to consider the true meaning of what it is to be a human being. Kristiane knew of physical and emotional love, however, when she discovered the very essence of spirituality, she found a higher love, something beyond human love – the love of the Creator. Consequently she recognises the second dimension, the quest for and the real essence of life – not only what it means to be a human being, but how each of us must deal with our own life, heart and mind. Kristiane began this journey asking questions, and along the way found new answers about how she might live a more fulfilled, contented and giving life. And finally the third dimension, whereby in returning to God, to the meaning, content and substance of life, and acknowledging the ethical teachings of our faith, one can experience a whole new beginning, start life again, with new love, new responsibility and new objectives.

All of these elements are drawn sensitively step-by-step through Kristiane's experiences – a very personal account of a conversion, a transformation of the heart, of the meaning of life and of the self.

Kristiane's story is rather like the Muslim pilgrimage to Mecca – the very meaning of which is at first an initiation, where one returns from the periphery to the centre, to God. Kristiane begins to understand that God is the Light in our lives, the essence of love. This love and its light radiate over all other aspects of our lives – marital, social, indeed everything relating to the human being, be it people of the same faith or of other backgrounds and religions. This new beginning is a return to the source and to the heart, and this, the very essence of Islamic spirituality, is reflected in Kristiane's transformation without her judging or describing what she consciously chose to leave as something which itself is bad, but simply acknowledging that it is about choosing to have a different understanding, of living a new life in closer proximity to God.

On her way, Kristiane encountered limits – in behaviour (prohibitions, commands and recommendations) and rituals (praying, fasting etc). From the outside these concepts could be perceived as rules and restrictions that inhibit freedom. Yet as Kristiane takes us through her awakening, we begin to understand that these limits and the discipline that she found in her commitment towards Islam were in fact a way for her to achieve another kind of freedom – not freedom of entertainment but freedom of being. By being free as a human being one has an understanding of the dignity needed in other areas of life such as friendship, marriage, sister- and brother-hood and in serving other people. Kristiane explains that this sense helped her to achieve inner stability and gain a better understanding of who she really is and would like to be. This was reached through developing her relationship with God, her love towards God, and understanding that with such love comes compassion – the very essence of living with other human beings.

Kristiane's memoir is interesting, indeed poignant. One often hears disturbing stories about Islam and Muslim women being discriminated against and oppressed; yet here is the journey of a woman who shows how converting to Islam gave her a sense of liberation. Liberation from appearances and superficiality towards the true and deep freedom that can be achieved through one's faith – without rejecting entertainment *per se* but giving entertainment life and love, as well as serving and participitating as a human being among other human beings – the essence of life and recognising that by serving people one serves God. Through this process of liberation one understands that true freedom is not being able to do whatever you want to do, but asking yourself what you really want and whether you really want what you think you want, if you really are where you want to be? Kristiane tells the reader that her encounter with Islam changed her life as a human being, as a woman. She had always believed that she was free, yet in fact she realised that this was not the case, so she began her quest towards true freedom and a spiritual life. This is the deepest message of the spiritual dimension of Islam and Kristiane has thoughtfully translated this message through her own story.

From MTV to Mecca is an enlightening book for the Western reader, providing one individual's perspective of Islam. Its focus is not to highlight the problems that exist within our Western societies, rather it suggests that for Muslims, both converts or by birth, Islam can be a solution not a problem – it is freedom, not discrimination; it is participation, not isolation; it is to give not only to take and yes, it is about duties as much as rights. These concepts exist throughout all spiritual and religious traditions and this is where Islam can be understood from within the heart. Kristiane Backer – a Westerner, a journalist, a woman – converted to Islam and in writing about it she is able to bring the very essence of the Islamic message to the centre of Western societies. This book is not only a bridge, it is reconciliation.

Chapter 1

Journey to the East

River Deep Mountain High …
Tina Turner

The stadium was full to bursting point. Miles of stretch limousines clogged the roads leading to the building on Westwood Plaza. Everybody who was anybody on the international music scene had turned up for what was one of the most important events of the year. And there I was, with a small group of colleagues from MTV in London and our Chief Executive, Brent Hansen. I found myself part of a massive audience surrounded by all the music industry greats: record company bosses, PR people, agents and anyone who was considered important enough to be invited to the 1992 MTV Video Music Awards in Los Angeles, known as the 'Oscars for youth'.

There was an incredible buzz, and it was my job to present Annie Lennox backstage with the MTV prize, a statue of an astronaut on the moon, for Best Female Video. It was just a photo opportunity, but as one doesn't have one's photo taken every day with 'the greatest white soul singer alive', I was looking forward to meeting her. The velvet-voiced Scottish singer was one of the few women at this event who was a natural beauty. In contrast, most of the LA starlets were flaunting their trout pouts, barely-there miniskirts and pneumatic chests. A film director's comment later, at the *Vanity Fair* after-show party, confirmed my impression: 'Natural just isn't an option in Hollywood. Not if you want to get anywhere, that is …' The guys for the most part wore jeans and T-shirts or tight leather pants, and many kept their shades on inside the venue and later at night – perhaps to look cool or to cover their doped-up eyes.

Despite the weird and wonderful backdrop, I enjoyed the show, hosted for the first time by witty comedian Dana Carvey, the star of *Wayne's World* and *Saturday Night Live*. Guns N' Roses, Red Hot Chilli Peppers, Def Leppard, Pearl Jam, The Black Crowes and Eric Clapton all performed at the awards to honour the best music videos. In true rock 'n' roll fashion Bobby Brown dropped an 'f' bomb after performing his hit single 'Humpin' around', but the censors apparently didn't catch the slip. MTV had requested that Nirvana perform their smash hit 'Smells Like Teen Spirit', while the band itself was keen to play their new songs 'Rape Me' and 'Tourette's'. Network executives had continued to push for 'Teen Spirit', but finally agreed to let the band play 'Lithium', a compromise that Nirvana appeared to accept. But when they went on stage, Kurt Cobain sang the first few lines of 'Rape Me', much to the horror of MTV bigwigs, before continuing with 'Lithium'. Near the end of the song, frustrated that his amp had stopped functioning, bassist Krist Novoselic decided to toss his instrument into the air for dramatic effect. He misjudged the move, and the bass ended up bouncing off his forehead – at least it was his own and no one else's – forcing him to stumble off the stage in a daze.

This one-week trip to 'La-La Land', as my English colleagues dubbed Los Angeles, was a thank-you gift from Brent Hansen to celebrate the success of my show, the *Coca Cola Report*. Brent had always been unconventional – it was one of his strengths and an essential part of his remarkable success. He was from New Zealand, an easy-going hippie type at heart with long curly hair – a music-lover rather than a corporate businessman. He loved Prince but was just as much a fan of country and western, which everyone teased him about.

I sat next to him during the ceremony and thought about how I'd soon be meeting Annie Lennox. But something was different that evening. It was as though the excitement was washing over me and I wasn't really there. In a way I wasn't. In my mind I was in a faraway land. Before flying to LA, I'd travelled to Pakistan and trekked through snow-capped mountains, slept beneath the stars and spent time with simple people who made a greater impression on me with their warmth, their hospitality and above all their faith in God than most of those I'd met in the entertainment business. Since returning from Pakistan, my mind had been filled with pictures and memories, and they refused to gel with the garish, over-the-top world I'd been thrown into in LA. If anything, they made the huge display of rock-chick glamour seem strangely unreal and superficial.

The show lasted almost five hours and although it was wonderful to see so many great bands, it was a long evening. There were endless breaks for commercials after every few songs, when nothing happened and we couldn't go anywhere either. The whole event began to drag on a bit. Backstage we heard that Kurt Cobain was having a fight with Axl Rose and, moments before Guns N' Roses went on stage, Kurt spat on the piano. He must have been a bit embarrassed when instead of Axl, Elton John sat down at the piano to accompany the band in 'November Rain'.

Later, some of the MTV Europe team and I hit the after-show party scene. It was a balmy evening, the champagne was flowing and the inevitable joints were passed around. There were so many parties to choose from. The *Rolling Stone* and *Vanity Fair* magazines and all the big record companies held their own. When we didn't have the right VIP passes, we blagged our way in, essentially gatecrashing. Most people I met were either in the music or film industry. No one had a so-called nine-to-five job. We chatted and danced all night and drank more and more champagne.

The next morning, I woke up in my room at the luxurious Mondrian Hotel on Sunset Boulevard with a hangover. As I lay there in the huge, soft bed waiting for my room service breakfast, images from Pakistan came flooding back to my mind.

∾

'Welcome to Islamabad!'

For the first time in my life, I was visiting a country where the population was almost entirely Muslim and there were very few tourists. As we boarded the plane, I'd noticed that my old school friend Briggite and I were the only white passengers. The cabin loudspeakers played a prayer in Arabic or Urdu and, although I couldn't understand what was being said, I gathered it was a prayer for a safe journey. We were embarking on a real adventure: we would be hiking in the Himalayas and exploring the ancient Mogul city of Lahore.

Eight hours later, the Pakistan International Airlines steward had barely opened the heavy passenger door before the heat of the Pakistani capital hit us. We stepped out at Islamabad airport, breathing in the scents of a foreign land. Everywhere we turned there were men in shalwar kameez, the national dress of tunic and loose trousers, and I felt my excitement grow at the prospect of getting to know both the country and its people. It didn't occur to me that diving into a world so different from the exciting life I was leading in August 1992 would have momentous consequences.

∾

As the first German presenter on the music channel MTV Europe, I had spent the last three years in the limelight. I had become one of the faces of MTV for a generation of kids for whom the channel was more than just entertainment. MTV made them feel as though they were part of a happening international scene that advocated fun, music, creative expression and an irreverent attitude as a way of life. Millions tuned in as I presented the *European Top 20*, a thought that took some time getting used to. My VJ colleagues and I were like friends to young Europeans – present in their living rooms and bedrooms every day. MTV was all the rage in Europe. We were teen idols and received masses of fan mail. Kids listened to what we said and copied our style.

In the months before my first trip to Pakistan, my career had taken off with my new show, the *Coca Cola Report*. Every few weeks, I was jetting off to amazing events across Europe and interviewing everyone from Neneh Cherry and Dannii Minogue to Mick Jagger and Lenny Kravitz. Bizarre as it was, wherever I popped up with a microphone, whether in Berlin, Istanbul or Amsterdam, a crowd of people would surround me and hang on my every word.

~

We had been driving for hours along the Karakoram Highway in a jeep. Centuries before, spices, fabrics, perfumes and other exotic treasures had been taken from East to West along this legendary Silk Road. Huge rock faces towered above us and the Indus River thundered far below. We had left Islamabad at dawn with a small group of friends, including the cricketer Imran Khan, who had invited us on the trip, Moby, a property developer, and our guide, Naim.

As we travelled further into the mountains, austere peaks loomed over us like crouching giants and the heat of the city was replaced by a pleasant coolness. Our drive to the base camp in Nagar, at around 3,000 metres, would take two days. With every passing mile, I felt the tension drain away and I watched with awe as the majestic landscape rose up around us. Briggite and I felt a long way from home. Dainty and tall, she had thick black hair and a face like the young Elizabeth Taylor – although her eyes were hazel brown. We wrapped ourselves in shawls and lowered our gaze modestly when we passed the many military checkpoints en route, as Imran had instructed us, so that we would look like Pakistani women. We were waved on without a problem – as soon as the control guards recognised Imran, they didn't even stop to check if we had permits, which we didn't. The higher we climbed, the harder it became to look out of the window. On one side of the jeep, there was nothing, not even a barrier, standing between us and a sheer drop of thousands of metres. The road had narrowed to a single lane and every oncoming car was a dangerous obstacle to overcome.

Imran and Naim took turns driving, skilfully manoeuvring us along the winding road. While they didn't seem fazed by the skeletons of brightly coloured trucks hanging on the rocks far beneath us, Brigitte and I were shocked. They must have skidded off the tightly curving roads, but there was no way to salvage them; it would simply have been too dangerous.

On every bend, we held our breath. There was barely time to be afraid, although there were moments when I felt like getting out of the car and walking. Now and then we stopped at little mud huts perched at the side of the road – 'restaurants'. We sat on plank beds in the shade, listening to the rush of mountain streams as we tucked into rotis – round, whole-wheat flatbreads – with cooked vegetables, lentils and chicken. We spent the night at an army station in Gilgit, the northernmost British outpost. It was the last time on the journey that we would sleep with a roof over our heads.

The next day our mountain hike began. The first stop on the way to our base camp in Nagar was Hunza, a beautiful and remote mountain kingdom which looked out across vivid green terraced fields, birches and apricot trees, all set against the breathtaking backdrop of the snow-covered Himalayas. The region is famous for its luscious apricots, which are said to possess miraculous anti-ageing properties. Many of the inhabitants of Hunza apparently live to be well over a hundred thanks to their healthy lifestyle that included plenty of physical exercise and fresh air, and the vitamin-rich apricots that make up a large part of their daily diet. Oil is pressed from the apricot kernels and used for cooking and its sweet fragrance also makes it a perfect hair and body oil.

Anywhere we stopped Imran was surrounded by a crowd of people. Some just wanted his autograph but others, often very poor people, eagerly pressed a few rupees into his hands. This money was for his greatest project: a cancer clinic in Lahore. 'It is the poor who are building this hospital, not the rich,' said Imran proudly. He was deeply touched by his fellow countrymen's readiness to help.

As we climbed higher up the mountains we came across very basic two-storey houses made from a mixture of mud and wood. 'The mountain people here live on the first floor while they keep their cattle below. The animals function as a kind of natural heating system. The rising body heat helps to keep them warm,' Imran explained. The people of Hunza were rich in faith but had almost no material possessions. Here there were no satellite dishes, no electricity and not even running water. I'd never seen such poverty and it filled me with sadness. When we stopped and got out of our jeep people with radiant eyes came out of their houses to greet us – visitors were rare in this region. With the words '*bismillah*', they offered us apricots and nuts from a shallow bowl. *Bismillah* means 'in the name of God' and, I found out, accompanies every activity a Muslim undertakes – be it eating and drinking or embarking on a long journey. I was moved by the dignity and generosity shown by these people, even in the face of dire poverty.

We left the jeep in the Nagar valley. Six Pakistani porters joined us there to carry our tents and cooking equipment. An unfortunately named goat, 'Dinner', came with us too. The poor thing lived up to her name during our hike – far from any civilisation, Dinner was our very own packed lunch. Naim slaughtered her and at first I felt so guilty that I wouldn't even taste it. I wasn't particularly keen on goat's meat anyway, but the physical exertion of the high-altitude mountain walking had made me so hungry that I soon gave in. It wasn't too bad, especially as the distinct taste of goat was masked by the curry spices. The deliciously juicy mangoes were much more to my liking, and fortunately, we'd brought a whole crate with us on the trip. A great variety of mangoes grow in the different regions of Pakistan, I learned, and the fruit is widely enjoyed. On our journey, we passed numerous families happily feasting on their mango picnics.

Luckily I was relatively fit, although not exactly an expert in mountaineering. Having been raised in northern Germany, which is completely flat, I had only ever been to the mountains proper a few times in my life. To my surprise, despite the thin air at 4,000 metres, I managed to hike for five to seven hours a day along narrow mountain paths, across icy glaciers, and through grassy meadows. Nonetheless, there were frequent moments when we had to remind Imran that we weren't all top athletes. Brigitte was a smoker and got all hot and bothered at one point, nearly collapsing. 'We're almost there,' Imran would say time and again to reassure us, before adding, 'Insha' Allah' – God willing.

Every afternoon, Naim would seek out a suitable place for us to set up camp for the night, usually next to one of the ice-cool rivers where we could bathe. Afterwards, some of the men would pray out in the open air. Using their shawls as prayer mats, they would stand straight, then bow, and finally kneel down with their faces touching their shawls before sitting back on their knees. Once they had finished, we would all warm ourselves in the last few rays of the sun. As soon as darkness fell, we would light a campfire, settle around it, enjoy a simple meal, and talk for hours until we crawled into thick sleeping bags that protected us from the freezing temperatures. We had no amenities, no showers or toilets – just Mother Nature. Surprisingly we adapted quite well. It was a minor inconvenience when Montezuma's Revenge hit Brigitte and me, but fortunately we were well equipped with toilet rolls. Being stripped of creature comforts was an exercise in humility and brought us all back to basics. It was even liberating. I'd heard that some of the other girls who had gone on hiking trips with Imran and his friends before me hadn't lasted long without their high heels and make-up, and had actually returned home early. Brigitte and I went with the flow, enjoying the breathtaking nature around us and relishing our entertaining company.

On some of the paths we were forced to clamber along on all fours, a sheer drop only inches away. Moby, who wasn't used to physical exercise at all, had meanwhile twisted his ankle and was limping along on a stick, while once or twice I came close to breaking my neck. I lost my footing and slipped on a smooth stone as we crossed a stream. Imran was quick enough to catch me at the last minute, but almost fell onto the jagged rocks himself. But he had no fear of danger and enjoyed taking risks. He moved with the confident precision of a top sportsman, though his fearlessness, as I soon discovered, had less to do with his sporting prowess than with his faith. Through him, I came to understand how firmly convinced Muslims are that our lives are in God's hands and that we have no control over when we die.

'The moment comes when God wills it: not a second sooner or later. When your time is up, there is no escape, no matter how much you try to protect yourself!' Imran exclaimed with conviction, before adding: 'God is our protector!'

While we were walking across an icy glacier one day, Imran asked us a question: 'What do you think is the purpose of life?'

I had to admit that I hadn't really thought about it. In all honesty, I was still pretty far away from my original dream of contributing through my work as a journalist to making the world just a tiny bit better. I had been charging from one show to another for MTV for a couple of years and felt like I was on a merry-go-round that never stopped turning. There simply wasn't much time for thinking about the deeper things in life. I passed. But Briggite, who was interested in spiritual matters and read tarot cards, thought for a while before replying: 'To be happy, even in adversity.'

Our answers didn't seem to impress Imran much and he began to tell us about Islam and the Muslim way of life. It wasn't a matter of finding out what led to personal happiness although there was nothing wrong with that. True happiness, however, could only be found through knowing God, he said.

'As Muslims, we look beyond ourselves to a higher goal, a greater power, namely God. To worship God and to serve Him in all we do, that is the purpose of life,' he told us. 'We humans are God's representatives on earth. We are supposed to fulfil this role responsibly.' He added that our chance to do this was limited because time is short. 'Life is a test, and at the same time a seedbed for our future lives in eternity,' he said.

Imran never wasted an opportunity to tell us about his faith. He was someone who saw God's presence everywhere. When we sat down to rest a while, he would point towards a particularly beautiful view of the mountains ahead and say it was a manifestation of the Almighty, the Creator of the universe. Here in the Himalayas, we were on top of the roof of the world.

Increasingly, I came to realise that Islam played a central role in Imran's life. It was here in the mountains on one of our walks that Imran first told me about his long-term ambition to go into politics once he had successfully built the hospital and won people's trust. He felt his beloved country had so much potential but was utterly mismanaged. Leaders were corrupt and siphoning off large amounts of money for themselves. But corruption had also seeped down to all levels of society because people simply could not live on their salaries.

It sounded like his motivations were noble and he really wanted to make a change, but his words worried me. He once mentioned that he had met a kind of fortune teller who had prophesised that it would be dangerous for him to enter politics, and that he was likely to be assassinated. When I suggested that he could be just as effective as a humanitarian and shouldn't risk his life as a politician, he disagreed. 'One can only effect real change from the inside,' he said. 'I am not afraid of death! In fact, I am happy to die for my country.' That said, he also reminded me that fortune tellers are not necessarily right anyway, and the future is ultimately in God's hands.

As we sat around the campfire philosophising late into the night, we listened to Sufi music on Imran's ghetto blaster. Brigitte and I enjoyed the passionate and emotional melodies although they sometimes dragged on a bit. The singing was an acquired taste but it wasn't long before we were hooked. Thanks to Imran's translations we were able to understand the meaning of these poetic and spiritual lyrics that often told of love – love for the beloved that turned into love for the ultimate Beloved, God. Some of these poems were written by Sufi Shaykhs, Imran explained, as far back as the thirteenth century. Bulleh Shah lived about 500 years later; he wrote this one:

> You have learned so much
> And read a thousand books.
> Have you ever read your Self?
> You have gone to the mosque and the temple.
> Have you ever visited your soul?
> You are busy fighting Satan.
> Have you ever fought your
> Ill intentions?
> You have reached into the skies,
> But you have failed to reach
> What's in your heart!

Brigitte and I both became fans of this music called *qawwali* (meaning wise utterance).

Those days in the mountains opened my heart to many things – particularly to the beauty of nature. One evening a sudden glow began to emanate from behind the dark mountains before us. At first I couldn't see where the light was coming from. Then, a vast, white, full moon emerged from behind the hills and within minutes, the whole landscape was swathed in a blaze of silver. It was almost as light as daytime, and our shadows were long and sharp. That was the night I fell in love with Imran, in the magical light of the full moon. During the day, too, the wild, untouched landscape was overwhelming, with the massive snow-covered mountain ranges towering around us; the clear-water streams winding their way down the slopes into small, turquoise pools; the green, flower-studded meadows; and all the time the brilliant sunshine, pure air and steel-blue sky. Those images imprinted themselves in my mind and made my heart leap with happiness.

On our journey back to Islamabad, I experienced first-hand how faith in God can give super-human courage and help conquer everyday adversities. As the snow had melted, part of the mountain road had become submerged. Uprooted trees and debris lay across the path, blocking our way, and we had no choice but to stop the car and climb out. The men cleared the fallen trunks and rocks as the sky slowly darkened. Brigitte and I inched our way around the tight bend on the road, trying desperately not to slip into the water or down the slope. Only Naim, our driver and resident mountain expert, remained. Frowning in concentration, he climbed back into the jeep. Clutching the wheel firmly, he recited a prayer, muttered something in Arabic that started with 'bismillah' and drove straight through the water, which came up to the windows of the jeep. Brigitte and I watched in disbelief as the men supported his daring deed with quiet prayers. Successfully.

Despite these nerve-wracking incidents, the physical exertion and the absence of any comfort – or alcohol – I felt refreshed after our trek. For the first time in years, I'd had time to breathe and think about more than just fashion and filming schedules. But, when we finally returned to our simple guest house in Gilgit, I enjoyed wholeheartedly my first warm shower in ten days. Briggite and I snuggled into our comfortable beds and she exclaimed overjoyed, 'This is heaven!' before we fell asleep like exhausted children.

～

Finally, back in Islamabad, we took a flight directly to our next destination: Lahore, in the heart of the Punjab. With its sumptuous Mogul architecture, Lahore is known as The Garden of the Moguls and its exotic flair is the inspiration for its other name: The Paris of the Subcontinent.

Lahore is one of the oldest living cities in the world. The Old City is surrounded by a medieval wall, fragments of which still stand to this day. This Walled City can only be reached through one of the ancient city gates and is home to architectural jewels such as the Red Badshahi Mosque – also known as the Emperor's Mosque, which epitomises the beauty and grandeur of the Mogul era – a majestic fort and the romantic Shalimar Gardens. I was particularly keen to visit this UNESCO World Heritage site, not only because I wore the Guerlain perfume, Shalimar, but because of the particularly beautiful Mogul designs of these famous gardens. Sadly, Lahore's precious Islamic heritage has been sorely neglected, and many of the ancient treasures there – carved marble features, for example – have been looted.

The narrow, dusty streets in the old town were full of people bustling here and there. Mostly men. Some carried their wares on their heads; others used carts pulled by donkeys. The few women we saw wore shawls to cover their hair; some even wore burkas. Briggite and I didn't want to stand out, so we covered our hair too. One of Imran's friends showed us the sights and guided us through the ancient maze of bazaars in the Old City. In one corner, craftsmen were producing picture frames, tables and dishes while praying or listening to chants of the holy Quran on a small crackling radio, thereby giving their work a spiritual dimension and transforming everyday items into objects of sacred art. The glorification of God was everywhere: in work, music and architecture.

As soon as the call to prayer sounded, everyone stopped what they were doing and rushed off to the nearest mosque. During a taxi ride through the town, our driver parked the cab in front of a mosque, gesticulated and tried to communicate something that we didn't understand and then hopped out and disappeared into the building. We sat there, lost for words in the burning midday heat, waiting for him to come back. Ten minutes passed, then twenty, and Briggite and I started to wonder where our absent driver could be. We hadn't realised that it was Friday – the day of communal prayer, which takes quite a bit longer than regular prayers. Finally, after about forty-five minutes, the driver returned. His eyes were bright and he was beaming.

In the evenings, we visited the home of one of Imran's best friends, Yousaf Salaudin. A laid-back music lover, he had been a provincial minister of the Punjab province and lived in a *haveli*, one of the private mansions in the middle of the Old City that had been built hundreds of years before in traditional Islamic style. Yousaf's *haveli* had four large courtyards with antique white marble benches, ornate wooden arches and a fountain decorated with delicate white and turquoise tiles. Small bowls of flowers floated gently on the surface of the water. I loved this ornamental, almost feminine beauty that pervaded the Islamic art and architecture in the Mogul city.

We sat together under the starry sky and enjoyed the warm evening air and the exotic ambience. Briggite and I made ourselves comfortable on a sumptuous swinging seat and drank chai, a type of tea brewed with milk and a mixture of spices, such as cardamom, cinnamon, cloves and peppercorns. For dinner servants brought us an array of exquisite curry dishes that Yousaf had prepared himself. He was renowned for being an excellent cook. Imran, who could barely make a pot of tea, showed us how to eat with our hands, using a piece of roti like a spoon. For the first time in my life I had begun to drink Coca-Cola. Somehow it went well with curries and I preferred it to Sprite and the other fizzy drinks on offer. For dessert we had the most delicious rice pudding I'd ever tasted, *kheer*, which is cooked for at least six hours with huge quantities of milk. We chatted for hours and listened to *qawwali* music, while Yousaf and Imran translated the lyrics for us, some of which had been written by Allama Muhammad Iqbal, Yousaf's grandfather, a famous poet and philosopher. One line read, 'If this earth did not exist, and there were no moon and no stars; if the secret of the truth was still unknown, and there was nothing at all, there would still be You.' This 'You' was God.

Those evenings at Yousaf's taught us something else about Eastern culture: compassion in action. Yousaf told us a story about his famous grandfather. At the turn of the twentieth century, Iqbal had studied at Cambridge and graduated from the University of Heidelberg in Germany, where he spent long hours studying the works of the great German writer Johann Wolfgang von Goethe. Not only had Iqbal become a philosopher and poet himself, he had advocated the political and spiritual revival of Islamic civilisation. With his vision of unity between state and religion he was later to encourage the creation of a state for Muslims in northern India – Pakistan.

As well as being taken with the lively intellectual debate during his time in Heidelberg, Iqbal was also impressed by German women – so much so that when he returned to Pakistan, unable to find a suitable childminder locally, he met a German woman living in Lahore who was divorced from a Pakistani and was happy to join Iqbal's family to look after the children. She stayed with them for years, returning to Germany only when Iqbal's grandchildren – Yousaf and his brother – were eleven and twelve years old. She soon became lonely in Germany, so Yousaf's family insisted that she visit them at least once a year in Pakistan, where she could benefit from the sun, as well as the warmth of the people. Later, when the frail and elderly woman had set out on her way to visit Lahore once again, she fell at the airport and broke her hip. Yousaf's brother took the next plane to Frankfurt, discharged her from hospital and took her back to Pakistan with him, where she was lovingly cared for like a member of the family until her death.

It made me think when Yousaf added, 'We don't have nursing homes here.[1] Elderly people stay with their families, where they are cherished. We value them and their wisdom, gained through their years of experience. Treating the elderly with dignity and respect is an important part of our faith.'

These stories and insights showed me clearly how religion seeped into every corner of Pakistani culture. Everything was related to God. I was equally moved by the patience with which the people I met faced their day-to-day challenges. Instead of becoming irate when there was yet another power cut or traffic jam, or losing one's temper when nothing worked as it should, they simply tolerated it more or less patiently and carried on with a gentle 'al-hamdulillah' – praise belongs to God! I liked this laid-back attitude, which seemed to draw its strength from faith. Only years later would I realise just how much effort it really took.

Chapter 2

How I Got the Job at MTV

Girls just want to have fun.
Cindy Lauper

The first time I travelled to Pakistan, I was twenty-seven years old. Back then, patience was hardly one of my main character traits. I was at the pinnacle of my career, presenting every day on MTV either from the studios in London or on location in Europe, enjoying red carpet treatment wherever our little team turned up. I was making the front pages of glossy magazines in Germany, Belgium and Sweden and it felt like I was surfing on a wave of success bigger than anything I could ever have imagined. Yet something was missing – I just didn't know what.

It had all begun in the playroom of a house in Hamburg. I was Kristiane Backer, intrepid reporter and proud owner of a toy microphone. The interviewee was my sister, a surprisingly willing target of some hard-hitting grilling. 'Hello, my name is Kristiane Backer, and I'm here today with the President of Germany. How are you doing today, sir?'

Sitting on the floor of my room, I would look up at a fairy-tale autumn forest, where wild horses with gentle eyes lingered between the trees. This wallpaper is one of the most abiding images from my childhood and sums up what those early years gave me: a sense of security and trust, and a love of nature. Much later, on an excursion to the New Forest in England, I had a feeling of déjà vu when I found myself among the same sort of ponies and trees I remembered from my bedroom wallpaper. I realised that the original picture must have been taken there.

I grew up in a semi-detached house in a leafy green suburb of Hamburg. The house had a garden and was set back from a quiet street. I had my own balcony and a bed from which I could look through the skylight at the stars. My constant companion was my invisible friend Didde, who looked a bit like a chimpanzee. I was the only one privileged enough to see him until he eventually disappeared some time after my sister came long. Susanne was nearly four years younger, but we were very close, although our personalities were quite different. I've always been of a cheery disposition, and wherever I went caused a bit of a stir. Susanne was quieter and more sensitive, and probably also more sensible. That bedroom wallpaper also expressed another part of me: my love of animals. I seemed to have a way with them, and they were usually comfortable around me. As a child, I often went horse riding at a farm on the coast, but it wasn't just horses I loved – I thought of all animals as my friends. On one of my little expeditions around the farm, I came across a shed and found a row of plucked and headless chickens hanging from a line. I was so shocked that I crept along to the chicken coop and opened the door, hoping that the remaining birds would realise the danger they were in and fly away. For that week, at least, I made sure that no more chickens were slaughtered.

I also loved the ocean. My family owned a holiday flat in Büsum on the North Sea coast. It was on the twentieth floor of a sea-front apartment block, the town's landmark, and we spent most of our weekends and holidays there. We'd go on long walks over the mudflats, do gymnastics on the grass dykes, and spend half the summer lolling around in wicker beach chairs – sun-kissed and covered in sea spray. My idea of bliss was being out in the open air, enjoying the rush of the tide and the view of the sea stretching towards the horizon.

It was a pampered childhood. Our parents gave Susanne and me everything we could dream of. My mother had a big heart, and was adored by everyone. She had the gift of bringing joy to those she met. Trained in the banking sector, she gave up her career when she had children, so that she could be there for us full-time. She was a hands-on mum. She helped us with our homework, cooked us wholesome meals, even froze freshly squeezed orange juice so that we had healthy ice pops and drove us to and from endless appointments – ballet, flute lessons, and art and craft classes. My father was a tall, handsome and charismatic man, full of charm and wit. He had both integrity and a sense of adventure, a great combination. He loved to travel and explore exotic destinations, enjoyed the theatre and had lots of friends. But he worked long, hard hours, first in the family-owned textile business and later at IBM. I inherited a large portion of his optimism and dynamism.

My parents instilled in me a sense of trust, freedom and courage. I grew up thinking of the world as an inherently good place, where anything was possible, and this positive, trusting attitude opened a great number of doors for me. However, as life went on, the same belief occasionally left me feeling let down and disappointed. Although I loved my parents, like most teenagers I wanted to break free from my well-protected home. When my parents laid down rules I considered pointless, I tried my best to negotiate my own way. I won some battles and lost others. At the age of sixteen I desperately wanted a scooter to get to school and back and also to cruise around on when going out in the evenings. I wrote down a long list of reasons why having a scooter and wearing a helmet made sense as opposed to sitting on the back of other people's scooters and not wearing a helmet. We had a long argument, but my parents stood their ground. I did end up getting my driving licence one year early though in the US.

My evening curfew was another issue. Everyone else was allowed to be out until midnight or even later. My parents were more conservative and wanted me home by ten or eleven of course. I didn't like those restrictive rules. Despite going out as much as I could, I always did well academically, so my parents couldn't really hold it against me. Good things in life just seemed to come my way. Even after I finished school, I chose a career that allowed me to treat life as a party and keep spreading my wings. The sky was the limit, I thought, and 'the only way was up'.

Religion didn't play a big role at home. My parents believed in God, and had us baptised and confirmed, but we rarely went to church as a family, and no Christian rituals took place in the home. The Bible was just one of many books on the shelf. During my confirmation classes, I enjoyed hearing about Jesus and the stories about Moses, Noah and other biblical figures, but the faith as a whole didn't quite click. Often, my friend Claudia and I – we'd known each other since we were toddlers – would sit in confirmation classes knitting out of sheer boredom. All the same, when my sister and I were tucked up in bed at night, Mum would always say a little prayer with us: 'I am small, and my heart is pure, let no one but God inside ...' I did believe in God and sometimes asked him to fulfil my innermost wishes, but that was it. Even so, I felt a certain fascination for the intangible world and sometimes dreamt things that came true, albeit fairly mundane matters. Once, I was surprised when my maths teacher, who never wore glasses, turned up in class wearing a pair of black-framed specs that were the exact same shape and colour I'd dreamt about the night before.

In school I loved philosophy and ethics. Kant's categorical imperative made a big impression on me: 'Act only according to that maxim whereby you can, at the same time, will that it should become a universal law.' I was also deeply moved by the famous speech of the American Indian Chief Seattle about the sanctity of land and the need for careful stewardship of it:

Every part of the earth is sacred to my people. We are part of
the earth and it is part of us.
The perfumed flowers are our sisters, the deer, the horse, the
great eagle, these are our brothers.

In summary:

Man did not weave the web of life – he is merely a strand in
it.
Whatever he does to the web, he does to himself.

I liked adventure and longed for new experiences. Quite independent by nature, when I was sixteen, I seized the opportunity to improve my English and spend a year in the United
States as an exchange student. In my application I mentioned
that I loved the sea and nature – hoping I'd end up in California
– and was placed on the West Coast, but in Portland, Oregon.
I stayed with two different families. My first host father was
a headmaster who loved history and philosophy and always
smoked a pipe. He lived with his wife Judith, a teacher, and
their young daughter Becky. The set-up reminded me of my
family life at home.

But before the school year even started, I nearly ended up
going back home again. I landed in jail along with some other
girlfriends I had met at the pre-school sessions. They'd taken
me out to a club and shortly after ten p.m. the police came
and raided it. We were all under age and shouldn't have been
there. I was handcuffed and thrown without my friends into
the back of a police car. As we sped off my head kept bouncing against the glass window. Fortunately I was reunited with
my new friends in the cell, along with young women who'd
murdered their parents and been charged for drug dealing. It
was a shock and not the sort of adventure I'd been bargaining
for. Calling my new host father from prison and asking him

to help was painfully embarrassing, but he was cool and took it in his stride. With his pipe in his mouth and sporting his beret, he came to pick me up smiling with amusement.

I had a lovely time with this family, took piano lessons, played with Becky, and on weekends we'd sometimes go on excursions into the vast countryside outside Portland. On Thanksgiving I helped prepare the turkey and on Halloween I joined the school party dressed up as a witch.

The Catlin Gable School I went to was special, a free-spirited private High School. I was a junior student and along with the regular compulsory courses, such as American history and American literature, I took theatre studies, pottery and painting lessons. The teacher even invited us to his beach house for a painting weekend. I learned about nutrition in a class with only three fellow students and, as part of our ornithology class the teacher took us on wonderful bird-watching excursions. Once we got up very early to watch silver birds mate at three in the morning on a lake. I loved the school, which was so different from what I knew in Hamburg. The teachers, whom we called by their first names, didn't send out formal reports, they just wrote up summaries of our progress. I did a lot of studying at home, with my huge English-German dictionary, underlining in red certain words I seemed to be looking up repeatedly. To my surprise, after about six months some people couldn't detect an accent when I spoke. Eventually I had to choose another family, to gain a broader experience, as the organiser of the exchange programme assured me. Happily my friend Dina from school invited me. She was Jewish and came from a well-to-do background. Her family lived in an imposing white villa with an outdoor swimming pool, a tennis court and a Bentley in the garage. After school and on weekends we would swim laps for about thirty minutes to exercise and then relax next to the pool. Dina and I got on fabulously. My exuberance livened things up a little and helped bring her out of her shell. In the evenings we'd often go out together. We even became blood sisters, cutting into the inner part of our left thumbs until drops of blood appeared and then pressing our thumbs together so that the blood mixed.

Dina's mother taught me how to cook Chinese noodles, prepare hummus and bake chocolate chip cookies, for which I had developed something of a passion. My hosts treated me like one of their own, and included me in everything. This was particularly nice, because I had met other parents of Jewish friends in Portland who wouldn't speak to me because I was German.

Religion played a certain part in family and social occasions, but in everyday life it was pretty much absent. On Friday evenings, we would have *challah* – braided bread made with egg – and red wine. The mother would say a small prayer over the Sabbath candles, and the father would add another blessing over the wine. I didn't notice any other rituals, though my host mother retired to her room once a day for a long session of 'transcendental meditation', as she called it. She followed the teachings of an Indian guru, Maharishi Mahesh Yogi, the man who'd inspired the Beatles. I watched her once as she sat in the Lotus position with her eyes closed, just breathing deeply for at least half an hour. I didn't really know what she was doing or hoping to achieve, but her silent contemplation fascinated me.

Curiosity led me to experience other spiritual traditions I'd never encountered in Germany. A few times I visited a gospel church, where the pastor delivered his sermon with so much soul and passion that he had me gripped, and the singing was amazingly rousing and groovy. I remember it felt strange to be one of the only white people there but I loved the warm feeling of those services.

Another time, a school friend and I visited the Bhagwan ranch in the hills of Oregon, just a few hours' drive from Portland. We noticed that everyone wore red or orange-coloured clothes, with many of the women in just bikinis or sarongs. Free love ruled, and we saw same-sex couples walking arm-in-arm and openly kissing. I got chatting to an attractive, suntanned woman who told me she'd worked in advertising and had suffered an identity crisis before moving to the ranch. She said there were quite a lot of successful business people, many former advertising and media types who'd quit the rat race to find their inner peace. Out of gratitude they all voluntarily gave Bhagwan, or Osho, as he called himself later, huge amounts of money. My schoolmate Chris and I had a healthy lunch at the vegetarian restaurant and I bought a Bhagwan book for inspiration. I flicked through it, but was repelled by the sexual orgies that were meant to be part of the path to spiritual enlightenment. In the afternoon we watched the followers form a long row and bow down as Bhagwan drove by in one of his many Rolls-Royces, a ritual that we were told took place twice a day. But I asked myself why a spiritual leader needed a huge collection of Rolls-Royces and Rolex watches. After all, the money could perhaps have been better spent on good causes. Apparently, his devotees saw it as a spiritual teaching of a special kind, a way of challenging them with their prejudices. I wasn't convinced.

I thoroughly enjoyed life as a carefree guest student in the US, including the Independence Day Parade on the 4th of July – when huge figures covered in flowers rode on floats fronted by dancing cheerleaders in micro skirts – and the many student 'keg parties'. It basically meant hanging out in a field around a keg of beer – one keg was nearly sixty litres – chatting and listening to music. Although I was never a beer drinker, I could just about handle some of this watery American version – a bit like the American coffee, it was fairly tasteless – and it was great to have parties outdoors in the summer. What I found off-putting in the States, though, was the commercialisation of Christmas – they began playing carols and Christmas ads on TV as early as September. And some people asked me the most bizarre questions. 'Is Berlin in London?' for example.

I often went with friends to San Francisco, where I got to know about the origins of the hippie movement. I learned about the beatniks, the romantic literary scene made up of poets and rebels that had inspired the hippie movement. On one occasion I helped out in a second-hand bookstore that stocked a lot of beatnik literature. As payment I was given a tattered old book with gold binding called *The Rubaiyat of Omar Khayyam*, a masterpiece of Persian literature. I didn't realise at the time that there was something prophetic about this gift.

All in all, I was very happy in the US and, when my year as an exchange student came to an end, I didn't want to go back home. I'd learned how to cope on my own in a foreign country and I cherished my new-found independence. I was no longer the sheltered little girl I'd been. I'd grown up, I thought, and was loath to lose the ground I'd gained. So back in Hamburg, I did what one does when seventeen, full of energy and yearning to break out: I threw myself into the club scene.

It was a happening time in Germany back then. London Punk had inspired what was called the '*Neue Deutsche Welle*' (New German Wave). Its rebellious, raw energy captured the zeitgeist, and one of the anthems of the era was called 'Floor it, I Wanna Have Fun!' That was exactly how I felt. My friends Nora, Briggite and I loved going out and dancing the night away in the most fashionable Hamburg clubs of the time – Cha-Cha, After Eight, Madhouse, Bsirs and Gala. I loved dancing and I loved music: Prince, David Bowie, Iggy Pop, Talking Heads, The Cure, U2, Simple minds, Depeche Mode, Pet Shop Boys, Simply Red, Eurythmics, Billy Idol, Pretenders, Sinead O' Connor and Grace Jones … The list was endless.

∾

One day during my final year of school as I was on my way home I was approached by a photographer. He told me he worked for a newspaper that was running a modelling competition, and asked if he could take my picture. I didn't know whether to believe him or not, but when he showed me his ID and later called me at home to explain everything to my parents, I gave it a go. I posed by a lake in a T-shirt and black leather skirt, without make-up, and, to my great surprise, the paper voted me 'The most beautiful girl in Hamburg'. Shortly thereafter a model agency called. We shot some so-called tests but I quickly realised modelling wasn't for me. I didn't enjoy the photographer ordering me around to pose this way and that, telling me to drop my top off my shoulder, pout into the camera and lean forward to show my cleavage. Nonetheless, I was thrilled with the prize for winning the beauty competition: a five-star trip for two to San Francisco and Maui, including a hire car. My mother thought it was all very irresponsible of the paper, particularly the hire car. After all I wasn't even eighteen yet, and had passed my driving licence during my exchange year after only six lessons by answering a simple multiple choice questionnaire. She called up to complain – to no avail.

Briggite came with me and we flew to San Francisco and then to Portland, where we visited some of my old school friends before flying on to LA and Maui. We had a fabulous time and met all sorts of interesting characters along the way, including an African American who spoke fluent Bavarian German and turned out to be a crackhead, as well as a Native American who lived with his dog in a cave on Maui beach. One evening when we went out in San Francisco we got a bit lost and asked a policeman for directions. Right in front of him, a joint fell out of my pocket. I quickly put my foot on top of it, but it didn't help. 'I saw that,' he said. Blushing furiously, we explained that we'd just come from Oregon where pot was allowed for personal use. He not only let us off but asked for our telephone numbers, which we didn't give him. My parents were worried about us because, long before our postcards arrived, they'd received a string of letters from the American police listing the eleven parking tickets we'd amassed in San Francisco.

Back in Hamburg, once I had my 'Abi', the German equivalent of A-levels, in the bag, I wasn't sure what to do professionally and began an internship at an advertising agency. I
thought it could be fun, but I quickly became disillusioned. I
just couldn't get to grips with the idea of having to spend my
career wholeheartedly promoting anything and everything
in order to make money. A particularly crude example was a
campaign for a brand of cigarettes that used a classic quote by
Goethe – 'Linger a while' – to convey the message that these
smokes were the best ever. Even though I was a smoker at the
time, ads like this didn't seem right, so I gave it up. The advertising career, that is.

A chance opportunity while working at a café where Hamburg's media types came for their cappuccinos led to an interview at Radio Hamburg. I pictured myself digging for the truth
and uncovering political scandals and loved the idea of going
round, microphone in hand, interviewing people. Working
with music was an added attraction. I applied for a two-year
traineeship – and got the job.

∾

I worked in every department of the station, from the news
desk and the youth section, right the way through to police
radio, service programmes, on-location reportage, in-depth
features and human-interest stories. Every day brought challenging new projects my way and I interviewed countless
people, from mayors to market stall owners.

Although our training was structured, we were encouraged to pursue stories close to our hearts, and for me these
were usually arts- and culture-related, or about other worldly
matters. One of the features I produced was about witch-
craft in Hamburg schools, based on reports that students
were slaughtering chickens, trying to summon the devil and
praying to inverted crucifixes. For 'Kids and the Occult', I
interviewed Briggite's sister and her classmates, who claimed

to have summoned spirits by 'playing' with Ouija boards. The kids actually started weeping with fear while I was interviewing them. It seemed that the whole game had worked a little too well. I added a sound bite from the priest and another one from the Institute for Paranormal Studies. When the story was broadcast, *Bild*, one of Germany's largest tabloids, got in touch to see whether they could publish it.

My bosses were pleased with my work and were soon sending me to bigger events, for instance to cover the Luna Luna Park, a massive outdoor exhibition located near Dammtor train station designed by André Heller. Gigantic sculptures by the late American graffiti artist Keith Haring and other New York artists Kenny Sharp and Roy Lichtenstein were positioned on the lawn in front of the station and another installation featured music by the composer Philip Glass.

While I was wandering around the sculpture park taking everything in, a New York photographer approached me. He mentioned that he was friends with some of the artists and invited me to a press dinner, which some of them would also be attending. I went along, of course, sensing there might be a chance to interview Keith Haring, one of my favourite artists.

And that's how I landed my first celebrity interview. After the main course, I led Keith into a side room and posed my questions. With his small, slender frame, his glasses and his shocking yellow T-shirt, he reminded me a bit of a young Woody Allen. It was an open and interesting conversation and even though I was quite nervous to begin with, Keith put me at ease and chatted away about the universal appeal of his artwork and how it spoke as much to native Brazilians in the rainforest as to businessmen from the urban jungle of New York.

I enjoyed my work at Radio Hamburg, but the city had gradually started to feel too small and I was getting itchy feet. I wanted to go out into the world again, although perhaps not as far as I'd ventured during my exchange year. So London became my new dream destination. I'd already visited the

UK capital once or twice and had really enjoyed it. Anything seemed possible there. In 1988, my friend Briggite and I had gone over by bus for the legendary Nelson Mandela tribute concert. It was a sunny June day and we were among a crowd of some 80,000 fans at Wembley Stadium, watching great bands from Bryan Adams to Simple Minds protest against apartheid and rally for the release of Nelson Mandela, who was still in prison in South Africa. It was an amazing atmosphere. We saw Tracy Chapman play live for the first time. She was an unknown artist at the time but shot to international fame with her captivating performance that day of her track 'Talkin' 'Bout a Revolution'. After a long, hot, sweaty day at the concert we had some Chinese dinner and fell into our beds in a very simple students' bed and breakfast. The next day we met up with Dom, who was the brother of Ben from the band Curiosity Killed the Cat. We knew him from Hamburg where he'd lived for a while. Dom and Ben took us to Covent Garden, a pretty market square in the centre of town with shops and cafes where people hung out and street artists performed. London was an exciting, international city, with a vibe that suited me perfectly. I decided it was to be my new home. The only question was how to make that happen.

My first attempt failed. My boss at Radio Hamburg had heard I was going to London and had offered to arrange an interview for me with Capital Radio. I was very excited and had every intention of following through. But our bus journey to London had been so strenuous that we couldn't face doing it again on the way home. So Brigitte and I booked the only plane we could afford back to Hamburg, which left on the day of the appointment. When I turned up at Capital Radio for the interview one day early, the boss wasn't too impressed and declined to see me – understandably. As so often in life, something then happened that seemed to be a coincidence but was really an act of providence. A friend who knew how much I wanted to move to London noticed an ad in a city magazine.

MTV Europe wanted 'a breath of fresh air'. The music station, still fairly unknown in Germany at that point, was searching for young, bubbly presenters to help establish the channel in Europe and follow up on the success it had achieved in the USA since 1981. They were hiring new faces to work as video jockeys or VJs. At that time, music videos were unheard of in Germany. The idea of creating a film to accompany a pop song was a completely new art form. The best thing about the job, though, was that whoever got it would be contractually obliged to move to London! I couldn't believe it. Good English skills were essential for the role and, since that wasn't a problem for me, I decided to apply. Brimming with excitement, I tapped out my application on a good old typewriter, popped it into the envelope along with my mock introduction to one of the only video clips I could dig up at the time, a Michael Jackson impersonation, and sent it off to London with a quick prayer for good luck.

This was followed by months of silence, and I soon forgot all about it. But one day, out of the blue, a telegram arrived at my house, inviting me to go to Berlin for a VJ audition. My heart leapt.

When the initial thrill had worn off, I realised that the audition fell on the morning after a Prince concert I had been looking forward to for ages. Prince was in the middle of his 'Love Sexy' tour in Europe and I was a die-hard fan. I loved his music – the beautiful ballad 'When Doves Cry', the classic 'Purple Rain,' and his funky rock tunes 'U Got The Look' and 'Sign of the Times'. The concert was a must for me, and missing it wasn't an option. Moreover, I was also really looking forward to going with friends to the after-show party in the Hamburg nightclub Große Freiheit 36 off the Reeperbahn right next to where the Beatles used to perform regularly. We'd heard that Prince would be playing a small, private gig there – but that it wouldn't start until long after midnight. My audition was scheduled for nine o'clock the next morning. To get to Berlin on time looking even half human would be impossible. The journey through communist East Germany, from Hamburg to Berlin, took four hours.

On the spur of the moment, I called MTV and explained my dilemma. I told them that I had to report from the concert and the after-show party for my job at Radio Hamburg. It was almost true – I really was planning on sharing my experiences of the Prince show and the private party with the station's listeners. To my surprise, the people at MTV completely understood and rescheduled my audition for a couple of days later. Brent Hansen – still just an MTV news editor at the time – would be holding my audition and he was as big a Prince fan as I was.

The concert in Hamburg's Volkspark Stadium was amazing, and so loud that afterwards a new law on acceptable sound levels was passed. The after-show party was the icing on the cake. Ron Wood, the Rolling Stones guitarist, ended up jamming with Prince until he was thrown off the stage, and Mavis Staples, the American rhythm and blues artist, joined Prince for a duet. Although I'd been up since five in the morning, working the early shift at the station, I was still dancing my heart out in a flowing red dress twenty-two hours later. During a short break, I felt a tap on my shoulder and turned around. A man of about forty was standing in front of me and introduced himself as Roland Fackel – the tour promoter. 'The manager would like to meet you,' he said. I figured it was just a random chat-up line. 'Well, he can call me at work, then, can't he?' I said, handing him my business card.

I didn't imagine anyone would ring but to my surprise Roland actually did. He invited me to see the show again that same evening and of course I accepted immediately. I had no idea what the manager wanted from me, but a front row ticket at a Prince concert was an opportunity not to be missed. That evening, a huge limousine with darkened windows arrived to take me to the stadium just when I'd finished with Casey

Kasem's American Top 20 at the station. When we arrived, a tall, slightly overweight man dressed in a casual dark blue jacket and jeans, black framed glasses and salt and pepper hair approached me. He introduced himself as Steve Fargnoli, Prince's manager. He was very friendly, and even seemed a little shy. He suggested we meet after the show as he was a bit busy.

So just before the last song had ended, I was ushered into a waiting limo and taken to the hotel where Prince and his entourage were staying. Everyone met in Steve's suite – a bunch of music bigwigs, promoters, photographers, models, managers and TV executives. We all waited for Prince to get ready to go on to the Madhouse, a nearby night club. Steve and I had a chance to briefly chat, and when he asked me what I did, I told him about my audition in Berlin in a few days' time. He mentioned that he was friendly with Mark Booth, MTV's chief executive at the time. Steve was himself in the process of moving to London, because he loved the city and because one of his artists, Karl Wallinger of World Party, lived there. He told me a bit about himself, that he'd managed bands like Earth, Wind & Fire and Sly and the Family Stone, and how when he'd taken on Prince, he'd helped him get his big break with 'Purple Rain'. As we said goodbye, Steve and I promised to keep in touch.

A couple of days later, en route to the audition in Berlin, I cast my mind back over the last few evenings in Hamburg. Aside from Prince's manager, I had met half of the entourage and at the Madhouse I had even been introduced to Prince himself. He was quite short but looked amazing in high-heeled boots, a long well-cut blazer and white gloves. We'd only exchanged a few words – his voice was deep and soft. The whole event had been a real trip and I was on cloud nine. I was so excited by the experience that when Brent Hansen asked me to give an off-the-cuff summary of the concert on camera, it all came spilling out of me. Any nervousness and uncertainty disappeared in that instant and I almost forgot that I was at a job interview.

I returned to Hamburg and resumed work at the station. Months passed and I didn't hear a thing from MTV. But then suddenly I was invited for a second interview, this time in London. I was put up in a small boutique hotel near Holland Park, a favourite with rock stars, where the channel used to accommodate their guests. The next morning, I jumped into a spacious black cab and was driven to the MTV studios in Camden, a funky area with cafes, bars and market stalls selling leather jackets and T-shirts. Hip clubs and stylish bistros serving Mexican, Italian and French food were scattered all around the neighbourhood.

As soon as I stepped out of the car in front of the MTV offices, I was greeted by two young men, Henrik from Sweden and Justin from Australia. They were both excellent hosts and complimented me on my outfit, a red T-shirt mini dress by Jean Paul Gaultier Junior, black and white striped tights and a denim jacket. Their easygoing manner and many jokes soon helped me to relax and enjoy myself. I had to introduce a couple of songs, talk to the camera and host an interview. Everything went fairly smoothly. That evening, Hansen and his wife Pip Dann, one of MTV's presenters, invited me to dinner. It felt like I was having sushi with friends rather than potential employers as they told me all about the history of MTV and what it was like to work for the company and meeting so many famous musicians.

It had all started in the US in 1981, with the famous Buggles song 'Video Killed the Radio Star'. At that time, music videos were still a rarity and the channel started out with only six video clips, which had to be played over and over again, all day long. Sometimes, when the staff were changing tapes, there would even be a few seconds of dead silence between songs. But things took off in a major way when Billy Idol, Madonna, Eurythmics and Michael Jackson came on the scene with their stylish videos. In 1988 MTV launched in Europe with the Dire Straits track 'Money for Nothing'. As the world's leading youth channel, MTV had become a global phenomenon.

I flew back to Hamburg and, once again, heard nothing for months. My traineeship was coming to an end and I had to seriously start making plans for my future. I applied to work at *Spiegel TV* – a programme made by Germany's most influential political weekly. Just as I was about to accept the offer of a position as producer, London called.

I recognised Brent Hansen's voice. 'Would you like the job?' he asked. I was thrilled, and answered straight away that I'd like nothing more.

As soon as my traineeship came to an end, I was to travel to London. The editors at Radio Hamburg were pleased for me and really proud. I didn't know it at the time, but a door had been opened for me. Still, it was up to me to prove myself – if I didn't, I would be out again in the cold before I knew it.

Chapter 3

Life as an MTV VJ

The only way is up.

Yazz

London was fabulous from the very start and I never regretted my decision to move there.

Home for the first month in my new city was a tiny room I rented from a photographer I had met on Prince's Love Sexy tour. With the help of Brian, a colleague at MTV who hailed from New York, I soon found a lovely flat around the corner in Notting Hill, where large houses with high ceilings lined the leafy streets. My flatmate, Caroline, was a graphic designer from Switzerland who worked for *Melody Maker*, the top music industry magazine at the time. I felt instantly at home in Notting Hill, a multicultural and bohemian district in West London that was popular with artists, filmmakers, musicians, models and journalists, as well as an African Caribbean community. This vibrant mix gave the neighbourhood its unique flair.[1]

On my first day at MTV I took the underground – or the 'Tube', as Londoners call it – to Camden. Everything was new – the city, the job, the people and, of course, the language. British English was my new means of communication and although I managed fine at the casting, I was wondering whether my English was good enough to be a TV presenter. I could hardly believe my eyes when the two most senior managers at MTV boarded the train. I felt like jumping into the next compartment to dodge them but they greeted me with warm smiles. Bill Roedy had taken over from Mark Booth as head of MTV Europe. One of Mark's last decisions had been to hire me. The other was Tom Freston, one of the young whizz kids who together with Mark launched MTV in the USA. He later became Chief Executive of the entire MTV group. He was a tough businessman and a huge music fan at the same time. And it turned out one of his favourite artists was Prince.

Bill Roedy was a great boss. He did everything for his employees, encouraging us when things didn't go according to plan and ensuring we got into all the VIP music industry parties. Long after my official departure from MTV, when I was called back to present the show *Greatest Hits*, Bill sent me a postcard. '*Greatest Hits* was never greater!' he'd written.

But that morning on the Tube, I felt somewhat intimidated when Bill and Tom sat down beside me – all smart in their business suits while I was in jeans. Nevertheless, they both seemed pretty chilled and their witty banter soon helped to overcome my nerves. Perhaps it was an auspicious sign that on my first day at MTV I entered the building smiling in the company of the two top bosses.

MTV was based in a loft building split into offices of varying sizes. Press, marketing, admin, production and management were all housed under one roof, but the studio where we recorded was ten minutes away on foot. We VJs each had a tiny dressing room, with a huge mirror ringed with light bulbs, a phone and a wardrobe. That was where I kept my outfits and make-up, as well as fan mail and good luck charms. This little room became like a second home to me until 1993 when MTV moved to the former TV-am building – a silver-coloured, post-modern complex down the road where we no longer had private dressing rooms. The advantage was that the offices and studios were all in the same place.

I spent the first month in the news department, where I learned the basics of the production process and how to write scripts. Three weeks after I started my job, I was thrown in at the deep end when MTV went to the Berliner Funkausstellung, a huge communications fair in Berlin. I was to do my first TV interview in front of a live audience. My interviewee was Heino, of all people, a schmaltzy German singer popular with a much older generation and an icon of the *Schlager* scene. *Schlager* are sentimental ballads sung in German – hardly cutting-edge stuff – and I was mortified having to conduct the interview with a crowd of people watching me. Thankfully I survived my MTV debut without any major hitches.

A few weeks later I was put to the test again and asked to present my first show, *Awake on the Wild Side*. It was MTV's breakfast programme and aired for a couple of hours every morning. The concept was simple: easy-to-digest pop music – rather than heavy metal or indie – such as Snap's 'I Got the Power', Seal's 'Crazy', Chrissie Hynde and UB40's 'Breakfast in Bed' and the Boomtown Rat's 'I Don't Like Mondays' – all interspersed with me chatting about early-morning topics such as hangover cures, and updates on musicians, bands and videos. Luckily it wasn't live because I had no idea what I was doing, and getting up at the crack of dawn for a breakfast show wasn't my idea of fun. Ahead of the big day, a professional make-up artist taught me how to apply TV make-up and then took me shopping to a specialist film and stage make-up shop in Notting Hill. She then taught me how to apply the different lotions, powders and colours, which I kept in my room. After that, I did my own make-up for years because MTV didn't have a professional make-up department until shortly before I left.

I was excited about going on air and presenting my own show, but nervous at the same time. After all, MTV broadcast all over Europe – a scary thought. Initially I was quite shy and felt awkward standing in the empty studio behind a blue screen and in front of the camera. I didn't know what to do with my hands and to make matters worse, I sometimes forgot even the simplest everyday terms in English. We recorded the links one after the other the day before the broadcast without watching the videos in between. The producers were very sweet and helpful, and when I made a mistake I could just do it again – although taking up too much time recording links didn't make you popular since it delayed the recording of the next show.

In time I got to know the camera and sound crew better and began to feel at home in the studio. But it took me a while to get used to constantly speaking and joking into this black hole that was the camera, no matter what else was going on in the studio. When the little red light went on, potentially half of Europe was watching, and I had to be ready. The trick I needed to learn was to try and give each and every viewer from London to Lisbon, and Munich to Milan the impression that I was talking to them personally.

Brent Hansen advised me to relax. 'Just be yourself, kiddo,' he'd say casually – but it was easier said than done when standing there under bright studio lights, linking one clip after the next for hours at a stretch, trying to be witty and charming. Ray Cokes, MTV's number one presenter, who went on to host the legendary live show *Most Wanted*, was a big help in those early days. He borrowed a camera, invited me to his place and cooked me a delicious meal. He was actually a trained chef. Then we practised in the garden.

'Make friends with the camera and flirt with it, have fun!' he said. 'Look right through the lens – that's how you'll reach into people's living rooms.'

It took a lot of practice, which fortunately I had as I was presenting every single day, and soon was also given additional VJ shifts in the afternoons and late at night. I loved being on the forefront of popular culture, listening to music for work, hearing the inside scoops on bands, meeting all kinds of interesting people and talking about it all on air. We were sent to different parts of Europe for press interviews or to participate in music shows. The job was fast-paced and, when on location, we'd stay out late partying but get to work on time the next day. I'd always been the energetic type and I thrived on the adrenaline. On Ray's recommendation I bought some Guarana to keep myself going, stocked up on Alka Seltzer for hangovers and Vitamin B for my nerves. But despite all the precautions I took, I developed a ringing sensation in my ears, probably from the noise and the sheer exhaustion of working all day and living it up at night.

Another major challenge for us VJs was that we were expected to look edgy and stylish at all times. That meant we needed an endless supply of hip and trendy outfits that also had to work on TV – they couldn't have small patterns or be red, blue, white or black. Sometimes we'd flout the rules on colour and get away with it, even though the lighting men would complain. Our clothing allowance was nowhere near enough, but I soon discovered some inexpensive and funky stores such as Hyper Hyper, a fashion haven in Kensington, and I'd also go to Portobello market to check out the street fashion that inspired leading designers of the time such as Katherine Hamnett or Jean Paul Gaultier. After a while I also found out about the when and where of the best designer sales. Sometimes I would blow my entire budget for the year on just two outfits. Eventually I managed to persuade some designers including Vivienne Westwood, Arabella Pollen and Rifat Ozbek to lend me their latest creations.

It was great fun to work at MTV and a totally unique experience. It was rock 'n' roll TV made *by* young people *for* young people. The average age was twenty-four and that was one of the most important ingredients in MTV's recipe for success. It was also a truly international company, with staff from all over the world: New Zealand and Australia, New York, Paris, Amsterdam, Stockholm and Copenhagen. In those pre-globalisation days, this mix of backgrounds was unheard of and we all felt part of a boisterous, international family, where everyone could contribute their ideas. At night we'd often go out for drinks or a meal in one of the many Camden cafes, bars and restaurants. But I also had an active social life outside of work thanks to Steve Fargnoli and my flatmate. Caroline was a Swiss beauty with a voice that drove all the boys wild, and she had a lot of friends in the music industry. Platinum-haired Neil X from the future cyberpunk rock band Sigue Sigue Sputnik was one of her closest buddies and we went out a lot with him and his friend and band colleague Tony James, who masterminded Sigue Sigue Sputnik in the eighties. Tony had ditched his wig but still wore his hair long when I met him. He knew everything about the workings of the media, marketing and the fame game, and became a great friend and adviser. We hung out with a crowd of stylists, event organisers and sometimes the actresses Elizabeth Hurley and Patsy Kensit as well as other musicians – including Gavin Rossdale, who went on to become lead singer of Bush. If we didn't go to private parties we went clubbing, often starting out at Fred's in Soho for drinks and moving on to go dancing at Quiet Storm, which was run at the time by Davina McCall who later became a colleague at MTV, to Cafe de Paris or the legendary Browns. There we'd bump into pop stars like Boy George and George Michael, whose cousin owned Browns. As the 'new chick in town' I could have gone out on ten nights a week. A lot of guys were after me and swore they were in love but I soon had two new nicknames coined by Neil and Steve: 'Iron Maiden' and 'The Kraut that doesn't put out'.

But now and then I felt defeated by the all-English environment. Thanks to my exchange year in the US, I could speak the langauge fluently, but I just wasn't familiar with the various British accents and dialects – Scottish, Irish, Welsh or cockney, to name but a few. People would be chatting away and if it took me a moment or two to understand a joke, they'd say 'Germans have no sense of humour'. But things soon improved and when I eventually started to dream in English, I knew I'd arrived. It amazed me that everyone I met in London was into music.

The knock-on effect of this national obsession was that most people were impressed by my job and asked me so many questions about it that I often ended up talking shop all evening, which could get a bit boring. Back in Germany people generally looked down on pop music, but the Brits loved their rock and pop. Whether businessman or taxi driver, everyone had a favourite band and knew a fair bit about the music scene.

As much as I loved living in London, a few things seriously surprised me. Even though it was one of the world's most important capital cities, the bars closed at eleven p.m. If you wanted to go for a drink with someone after dinner you either had to be a member of a private club – access to which could take years – or go to a noisy night club. In Hamburg I was used to going out 24/7 if I wanted to. In the summer there were hardly any places to sit outside and restaurant food generally tasted bland. Not only that, I often couldn't even find the ingredients I needed for cooking. Once I invited Brian over to thank him for finding the flat-share, and wanted to cook a special salmon pasta dish with a creamy sauce and chives, but I couldn't find the herb anywhere. I drove around Kensington in a taxi from one supermarket to another, and a forty-five-pound fare later, I gave up and went home empty-handed. Back then, London was light years away from the international gastro heaven it has since become.

After a year, I moved out of the flat-share and into my first apartment, near Regent's Park, just across the road from London's Central Mosque and a few hundred metres away from Lord's Cricket Ground. Every Friday I would see a stream of people pass by my house on their way to the mosque – women in veils and men in long flowing robes. On the other side of the road, men in navy blue blazers, straw hats or linen suits made their way to the cricket ground, their cooler boxes in hand. A mosque and a cricket ground – a prophetic combination if ever there was one.

I settled into my new neighbourhood quickly. In the

mornings, I rode my bike through the park to Camden, and, at night, I invited friends and colleagues back to my place or hit the town with them. On the weekends, I would meet up with Caroline and browse Portobello market before stopping off for lunch at 192, a popular hangout at the time where we would always bump into friends. On the way home, we meandered through art galleries, bookshops and boutiques. Steve Fargnoli, who split his time between London and Los Angeles, often came along too. He was fun company, of Italian and American heritage, and a generous friend who gave advice to anyone who asked. He even negotiated a new record deal for Tony as a favour, and was always inviting huge groups of friends out for dinner. He knew everything about the industry and loved good food. By then he'd had a dispute with Prince and been fired, but his eyes would still light up whenever he talked about his former artist. He described Prince as a musical genius – 'the Mozart of our times' – and told me that Prince had written hundreds of songs that were tucked away in a vault and had never been heard. Sometimes, he'd wake in the middle of the night and call his band in for an impromptu session at his Paisley Park studios in Minneapolis, where they would work on one of his new ideas. Managing this special artist came with special challenges though. In Hamburg, for example, he had asked that a hairdresser be brought to his room at four in the morning – on a Sunday, no less. But Steve loved his artists and forgave them everything. Yet he did suffer when the fame he had helped create went to their heads – not an uncommon story.

Steve had an amazing feel for talent and a knack for discovering artists whom he helped to commercial success. One of them was Sinead O'Connor, a remarkable, if opinionated, young lady. With her petite, slender build, strikingly beautiful face, shaved head and huge eyes framed by heavy lashes, she had something otherworldly about her. I'd loved her album *The Lion and the Cobra*, and had often played tracks from it during my time at Radio Hamburg, so I'd been looking forward to meeting her and I was finally introduced to her one day by Karl Wallinger, the lead singer of World Party and one of Steve's artists, at a picnic on Hampstead Heath. Sinead turned out to be a Sagittarius like me. That same day she told Steve she wanted to record the song 'Nothing Compares 2 U', which at that point had only been released as a b-side by Prince. Steve had always loved the song and had wanted to bring it out properly for a long time. He believed in Sinead, and took her under his wing. 'Nothing Compares 2 U' was to be her big break.

Working at MTV was special and I was well aware that I was living what most people would consider an enchanted existence. It wasn't just a job, but a way of life. I identified with the company motto, 'work hard and play hard' – it was what I'd always done anyway. Music was the language of youth, and MTV transcended national boundaries. In a way, we were uniting young people across Europe and creating an important part of European youth culture. That, at least, was how it felt.

Back then, the channel was setting new trends not only in music but also in TV production, whether it was with the sets – often works of art in their own right – or the brightly coloured blue screen animations that served as backdrops. The camera work was radically different, dynamic, fast-moving and forever switching angles. Numerous other channels started taking their cues from MTV. Ray Cokes played with the camera like no one else – he'd move in close, then step away again, pull funny faces and duck in from weird angles. The whole team would end up getting involved, sometimes answering from off stage or giving just the thumbs-up in shot. Our cameraman Rob ended up being famous across Europe as 'Rob the Cameraman'. MTV also invented new formats, including the first ever reality show – *The Real World*.

But of course it wasn't just the VJs, programmes and

aesthetics that made MTV so popular. Video really had killed the radio star. It was no longer enough for people just to listen to their favourite artists. They wanted to see them. MTV had set this ball rolling, establishing an almost global monopoly and revolutionising the music industry. In the nineties, MTV was instrumental in making or breaking a song. Music videos had become the key to success for the artists themselves. The image of a band became almost more important than their musical or singing skills, and to land a number one hit in the charts musicians needed a catchy video that MTV would play in heavy rotation. This of course was a double-edged sword because not every talented musician was equally as gifted visually.

And music videos had become a new art form. Budgets with the major labels were often sky-high, allowing directors to really go to town and set their creativity loose. They played a vital role in creating a band's image and some video directors became stars in their own right. One of them was John Landis, who directed Michael Jackson's groundbreaking 'Thriller' video. It was actually a short film, and catapulted Jackson as the first black artist onto MTV and to super-stardom. Other sought-after directors included David Fincher, who shot slick videos for almost all the great artists of the time – including Madonna and George Michael – and the Dutch photographer Anton Corbijn, who made a name for himself with his grainy black and white videos for U2 and Depeche Mode.

As MTV grew more and more powerful in the music indus-try, Ray Cokes, Paul King, Steve Blame, Rebecca De Ruvo, Simone Angel, Davina McCall and I became famous in the countries where MTV broadcasted. For the kids who were watching we opened a window onto a seductive world of fun and dreams. In the beginning we were able to choose a few videos per hour during our own shows, but as MTV became more commercially driven, we were no longer allowed to select our personal favourites and no amount of protesting from our side could change that. From then on, the videos played were determined entirely by local charts and the MTV A&R colleagues who had the relationships with the record companies and sat in the playlist meetings. Of course ratings counted on the channel – MTV was a business.

After less than a year, I was given one of the flagship shows to host – the *European Top 20*. This came as a relief, since I'd previously presented the hard-rock show *Headbangers Ball*, decked out like a rock chick with backcombed hair and a studded leather jacket I'd bought from a shop on Kensington High Street, where apparently all the rockers got their leather gear. I'd reported on heavy metal music and interviewed Metallica, Thunder and White Snake. Some of them were a bit scary and I remember the lead singer of the rock band Warren sticking out his tongue at me during our interview. Other musicians quite liked me; the lead singer from Thunder once took me out to the rock club St Moritz in London. But however much enthusiasm I managed to muster while on air, it just wasn't my scene.

The worst event I had to attend for *Headbangers Ball* was an Alice Cooper concert in Rotterdam. I didn't like the music and to get near the band, I had to fight my way through a crowd of greasy-haired fans in green parkas, not my kind of crowd, and when I was finally face-to-face with them, it was quite an experience. They'd obviously lived their life to the full and it showed, but, despite the gruesome stories of them having eaten live hamsters on stage in their heyday, they were actually very friendly and charming during the interview. My team and I flew back to the UK with the band and, although the musicians looked like the living dead, I was the only one who had trouble at customs. All washed-out jeans, long leather coats, dark glasses and bloodshot eyes, the band filed through one by one but, when it was my turn, the customs officer examined my various cosmetics for ages.

Back then, you were allowed to take a full beauty case on

board a flight, and she laboriously inspected every single lipstick, pot of cream and powder box. Eventually I lost my patience. 'Careful with that,' I said. 'It's heroin.' The customs officer wasn't amused, and sent me off to be strip-searched while my producer, Vanessa, waited outside the airport with the team in a pre-ordered cab, with the meter running up a huge fare. She didn't know whether to laugh or be angry.

Presenting the *European Top 20* was definitely a springboard in my career. I was introducing the most popular hits to a prime-time audience. Things could hardly have been better, and I began to realise what it meant to be famous. Whenever I walked down the street – particularly in Germany, the Netherlands, Denmark, Belgium or Ireland – people recognised my face. At the time, cable TV wasn't widespread in England, so we were much better known on the Continent. I was invited onto chat shows, asked for my autograph and given the best table in restaurants. When interviewing pop stars I was less star-struck by now, and of course they knew me from the channel, too. We usually had fun doing the interviews, and there was always time for a chat and a laugh before recording. It more or less felt like we were meeting as friends and it never occurred to me to ask any of the musicians – no matter how famous they were – for an autograph or a photo with me. When we were on location in Europe, we'd sometimes go out together or meet up at the hotel bar after the shows. And when I bumped into musicians anywhere else, we stopped for a chat. Even Prince, who had no doubt forgotten meeting me in Hamburg, once said to me in the nightclub Tramps, 'Hey, you're on TV, aren't you? See? I know.'

At my first birthday party in London, which Steve had organised, Dave Gilmour from Pink Floyd approached me. 'Hey, how's it going?' he said. 'You're in my living room every day – I feel like you're my friend and I've known you forever!' We'd never met before.

I once went Christmas shopping with Bryan Adams. We

tried on different kinds of hats and he gave me one as a gift. Another time, he invited me to his place for dinner with some of his friends. He was a committed vegan with a personal chef who conjured up tasty vegan dishes. Twice I had dinner with Eric Clapton, an interesting and deep thinking man who happened to be one of the greatest guitarists of all time, nicknamed 'Slowhand' after one of his classic albums. I just thought it was a bit strange that he and his friends were tee-totallers. They'd all been to AA or NA and were unbelievably clean-living, unlike everyone else I knew. I got on well with Seal, too. Once, when Briggite was visiting me, he came round and played the guitar. The babysitter we'd hired for Briggite's daughter was completely gobsmacked when the three of us walked in after our night out. Seal was good fun and very pro-fessional – he had a healthy lifestyle and didn't stay out late if he had to be on tour or in the studio early the next morning. He was really good with Briggite's daughter and even shot a little film of her.

It was great to have a job that involved meeting so many interesting people, but I sometimes wondered if I was really on the right path. At Radio Hamburg, I'd had the chance to cover a wide range of subjects, whereas at MTV it was all about video clips and bands – pop music. I'd actually had my first crisis after only three weeks into my job but persevered because I was given new shows to present. One of the biggest challenges for VJs was to come up with new and exciting ways to announce the same old clips again and again. Whenever a new song charted somewhere in Europe, we played it a lot, and then it would enter the charts in different countries at differ-ent times. That meant we ended up playing the same songs for months on end, until we were all completely sick of them. So we'd seize on topics like the racy lingerie Kylie Minogue was wearing in her new video, the Queen/Bowie bass line Vanilla Ice sampled for a track, any kind of gossip about the bands, or the colours in the new Neneh Cherry clip. Sometimes I seriously doubted if these were the kinds of issues I wanted to be thinking about long-term.

At one point, my parents suggested I join them on holiday in Morocco. It was a very different environment, my mother told me, and a change of scene might do me good. When she mentioned how women there were completely covered up, I retorted that I saw women like that on my doorstep every day. But I agreed I needed a break from the crazy world that was consuming me and I welcomed the invitation wholeheartedly. So as fate would have it, I joined my parents on our last family holiday together with my sister in Agadir, Morocco. My family were already there and came to the airport to pick me up. My mother was taken aback when she saw me in my huge sunglasses, tight black leggings and a long black sweat shirt with a big silver A for anarchy printed across the front. She'd specifically told me to wear long clothes and was embarrassed by my get-up. I felt like I'd made an effort, but my mother pointed out that everyone was staring at me. Luckily I had brought a long, flowing skirt as well and some linen trousers, so eventually she relaxed. My parents weren't particularly impressed by my work on MTV and couldn't really see the merit in it. They wished I'd chosen a more solid career or at least a more serious line of work within the media. On the other hand they were proud that I was doing well, even though they couldn't relate to the world of pop music and video clips. By a strange coincidence, the parents of one of my colleagues, the blonde Danish bombshell Maiken Wexo, were staying in the same holiday resort as we were. They felt similarly about their daughter's work and shared my parents' concerns. It was lovely to spend time together as a family, even though – as anyone who has flown the nest will have experienced – old family dynamics suddenly re-emerged and it was as if nothing had changed. I was Kristiane the daughter and sister – rather than the MTV presenter – with a lot of energy and bursting to play tennis and go sightseeing, while the others were a bit more reluctant.

However, in my sister's case, there turned out to be a more serious reason behind her slight lack of enthusiasm. Susanne and I were planning to visit the ancient royal cities of Marrakech and Fez, when she suddenly fell ill with acute appendicitis that got so bad that she couldn't take a plane home and had to have an operation in Morocco. It was a shock for us seeing her so ill and pale in hospital. Eventually my mother and I had to return home for work and my father stayed behind to look after her. She didn't get better and when she contracted an infection after the operation, she needed further surgery and was flown back to Germany immediately. I had no idea all this was going on, but that night in London, a photograph of Susanne I had on my wall fell on the floor and the glass broke. Minutes later, my mother called me with the bad news: my sister was in an emergency helicopter en route to Hamburg. I was desperately worried and wished I could help. I felt very bad that I couldn't even go and visit her in hospital because I wasn't able to get any more time off, but had to keep ploughing on with work in London and abroad, doing my best to look happy and not show how upset I was. Fortunately, Susanne recovered after two operations and it wasn't too long before I saw her again in Hamburg. The experience of being so close to death and the prolonged time in different hospitals had taken its toll and made her more thoughtful. She even ended up doing community service in a hospital afterwards. I felt guilty I hadn't been able to be there for her.

This whole episode increased my doubts about the point of my job and the nature of show business. Being professional was tough sometimes, because it seemed inevitably to entail personal and emotional sacrifices. My private life always had to come second. Every evening I was told what time I was to record the following day, and often ended up cancelling private engagements when I was either working on camera first thing the next morning or late in the evening. But that was life in the media. People who weren't in the business couldn't always understand that, and I had come to realise that I could only be friends with those who did.

Aside from that, MTV was a completely apolitical channel. So many important events were happening in the world – the fall of the Berlin Wall in 1989, the Gulf War in 1991 and, a year later, the war in Bosnia. But we presenters were asked not to comment on anything political because MTV was an entertainment channel, full stop. People saw enough of politics everywhere else, we were told. I could understand MTV's philosophy, but it felt frustrating at times – we had so many viewers across Europe and were in a perfect position to spread a message of peace, mutual respect and understanding.

Steve Fargnoli, who'd become a friend and a mentor to me and readily advised me in all questions relating to my career and indeed any others for that matter, would reassure me. 'There's a time and place for everything – even entertainment,' he said. 'If you want to make a contribution, first invite people to your party!' – meaning make a name for yourself and become known, only then can you effect change. He firmly believed that people want and need escapism into a world of fun, especially in difficult times. 'You're giving them a chance to be happy,' he'd say. And one day he told me an incredible story he'd heard from a friend of his who worked as a war correspondent in Bosnia. Apparently he observed the opposing forces laying down their weapons for a few minutes when my show came on in the afternoons. If true, purely by chance, that may have been my biggest contribution.

I was always grateful to my fans. When everything got too much for me and I missed my family and friends back home or felt overwhelmed by the daily grind, the small mountain of fan mail that awaited me every day at work never failed to cheer me up. Reading about the joy I brought to someone's world and the poems they wrote me touched my heart. Once I was sent a teddy bear. Just for fun and because I thought it was sweet, I thanked the viewer on air and showed the bear on camera. A few days later, there was a whole zoo full of stuffed animals waiting for me. I gave them all to charity and reminded the viewers that Marilyn Monroe had famously said: 'Diamonds are a girl's best friend!' Amazingly, De Beers got in touch a little later and actually gifted me a precious stone that my friend Caesar, a jewellery designer from Hamburg, turned into a piece for me to wear on MTV.

However, the adoration couldn't take away the loneliness I sometimes felt. And despite all the highs, I still needed to escape the world of music and videos every now and then and experience some normality. At work it was a matter of leaving my brain at home and just having fun. I was missing intellectual stimulation at MTV, so in my spare time, I started taking evening classes in film studies, European and art history, macrobiotic cooking and Italian.

Everything was moving so fast and suddenly I was given a new show to present that seemed tailor-made for me: the *Coca Cola Report*. It was a mix of live music, retro clips, tour guide and travel show. The best thing about it was that the team and I were able to jet around Europe once a month to interview artists and musicians and report from events like the Cannes music festival or a major football tournament in Istanbul. We would fly out as a small team made up of our laid-back, savvy producer Ed, and his funky assistant Vlad, who changed his hair colour and style every few weeks. We hired cameramen on location and shot several programmes a day. Between shows I would change wherever possible, usually in a small van we'd hired. I'd restyle my hair and make-up using just a little hand mirror, before it all started again. After the shows were in the bag we'd have a nice meal and hit the local nightspots in whichever city we happened to be in, Barcelona, Bruges or Berlin. Once around Christmas we were in Paris. I got stuck in an Alaia outlet store and due to the terrible traffic turned up forty-five minutes late for my interview with France's biggest pop star at the time. The record company people and MTV weren't too happy when I arrived so late but I had managed to pick up a few great outfits and the interview went well anyway. Later we partied the night away at the Bain Douche, a trendy nightclub at the time where the dance floor was covered in little white Styrofoam balls that came up to my waist. I felt like a kid messing round in snow. Mini Styrofoam balls stayed in our clothes and luggage for months to come. Wherever we went, we were treated like VIPs. At the opening of Eurodisney other journalists struggled through crowds to find a suitable place to film the red carpet, while my little team was in pole position right at the front. I could relay everything to the camera without a hitch, while stars like Eddie Murphy, Tina Turner and Luc Besson walked up the red carpet right behind me. I interviewed Bob Geldof the morning after the grand opening, which was a breathtaking event with fireworks, light shows and overflowing buffets of mouth-watering food and champagne galore. Needless to say, we were both pretty tired and hung-over – Bob had attended the party with his wife and children. Even so, he was charming and came across as eloquent and soulful and it turned out to be a great interview.

And so it went on, one highlight chasing the next. The Eurodisney opening was followed by the Olympic Games in Barcelona, which were a real treat for me because I got to spend a whole week in Spain reporting from different locations.

I was also given the honour of carrying the Olympic torch in the amateur run through Saragossa. It was an important event. Everything had been planned down to the tiniest detail, and Coca-Cola, one of the main sponsors, had spent days briefing us on what to do minute by minute so that everything would go smoothly. Of course, nothing went according to plan.

To start with, I was handed the torch too early. I turned around and as arranged spoke into the camera, which was set up on a car behind me. Then I turned back again and jogged off with the torch. Suddenly, I saw Ed running next to me gesticulating wildly. I didn't have a clue what he was trying to say, so carried on running and passed the flame to the next person. Later, a panic-stricken Ed told me that I'd been speaking into the wrong camera, and that MTV hadn't got any of my link on tape. It was a total disaster. All the trouble and expense had been for nothing. Our entire week-long trip to Spain hinged on this one link and the footage of me carrying the flame. In the end, though, Ed saved the day. It turned out that the camera I'd spoken into belonged to Coca-Cola, and he managed to get hold of the footage. However, the saga didn't stop there. I was allowed to keep the torch as a souvenir, but when we tried to pass through the Spanish customs, the officer on duty wanted to know what was in it. We tried to convince him that there was nothing, but he continued to regard it suspiciously. Suddenly, Ed had an idea. 'Light it!' he suggested. That's exactly what the customs officer did, and a huge flame shot up into the air. The torch had been filled with gas to keep the Olympic flame burning during the run. We'd assumed that all the gas had gone and had even checked and emptied it at the hotel. Luckily, the customs officer didn't hold a grudge, and sent the torch on to me a couple of days later. Back home I thanked the man on MTV and have kept it ever since.

As fun and exciting as my life was, I also began to realise that behind the scenes of the music industry, creativity met commerce in a way that wasn't always comfortable. Not everything was as rosy and glamorous as the glossy videos had audiences believe. George Michael, for example, was dissatisfied with the record contract he'd signed as a complete unknown at the age of eighteen, which committed him to agreed terms until 2003. In late 1992 he launched a lawsuit against his record label Sony Music. He claimed that his contract constituted a restraint of trade and, alleging that Sony regarded artists as 'little more than software', he sought to sever it. His lawyer in court pointed out the unfairness in the recording contract – apparently Sony Records made six times more profit out of George Michael than he did – and complained that the concentration of power among the six companies that dominate the music industry amounted to their stars being 'fettered'. David Fincher's video for 'Freedom 90' symbolised the singer's wish to break free and move away from the squeaky clean George Michael image the company promoted towards an identity as a more serious artist. The video showed his leather jacket burning, with top models Naomi Campbell, Linda Evangelista, Tatjana Patitz and Cindy Crawford lip-synching the lyrics, but there was no sign of the star himself. Around the same time Prince's relationship with his record company Warner Brothers also deteriorated. He claimed they couldn't put up with his prolific artistic output and didn't market his material properly. Infuriated, he renamed himself 'symbol' or TAFKAP – 'the artist formerly known as Prince' – until his contract ran out, and he performed with the word 'slave' written across his face.

When I spoke with Steve, he had a lot to say about the challenge of bridging the chasm between commercialism and creativity. The gap between sales and art was growing steadily. The manufactured boy bands put together by business managers were also symptomatic of this trend. Steve was ambivalent about MTV: on the one hand, the channel offered artists an amazing platform to make their name on the world stage, but on the other, MTV was known by some industry insiders as the curse of the music business. The fact that the image of a band and a cool video was more important for commercial success than musical talent was seen by many as a betrayal of music itself. Another complaint was that everything had started moving faster, and the shelf life of artists was becoming shorter all the time. Young bands were being thrust into the limelight by the media, only to sink back into obscurity soon afterwards.

Steve's artists, though, were not one-hit wonders. They were old-school musicians with staying power – like Jim Kerr, the singer from Simple Minds, another star I met who shared his rise to fame with me. He was a friend of Brian, my colleague from MTV, and we were introduced at an MTV Unplugged concert given by Paul McCartney. Jim was witty and spoke with a charming Scottish lilt. Simple Minds was the very first band I'd ever seen live in concert, when I was fourteen years old back in Hamburg and they were the support act for Gary Numan. And now I was meeting their lead singer in person, and what's more, he told me he was a fan.

Jim invited me out to dinner – he loved sushi and Thai food – sent me flowers when I was sick and asked me repeatedly to visit him in Scotland. I liked him a lot, but was just too shy to accept his invitation. It turned out to be for the best because, shortly afterwards, Jim fell in love with Patsy Kensit.

But in those early days of our friendship, he told me all about how he'd become a musician and worked his way up right from the bottom. Before their big break, Simple Minds had played endless gigs in pubs and clubs up and down the country, gradually learning how to play live and deal with the audience and the ensuing fame.

I'd seen how young musicians who'd experienced instant fame had no time to come to terms with stardom, worldwide success and the pressures of public life. Nirvana was a good example. They were nothing more than a cool young band in Seattle's grunge scene when MTV put their song 'Smells Like Teen Spirit' on heavy rotation and they became overnight superstars. Everyone knows how sadly it all ended for Nirvana and their lead singer, Kurt Cobain. His suicide shocked an entire generation of kids, and indeed everyone in the music industry.

The band Take That were another example of how random the ascent to stardom could be, and how fragile the nature of fame. I was invited to present a music award ceremony on one of the big German TV channels. A young girl had won a meeting with her favourite band, New Kids on the Block. For some reason, the band bailed out at the eleventh hour and

Take That – complete unknowns at the time – were drafted in as a last-minute replacement. After I announced the band, the cameras pointed to the little girl in the audience and it was obvious that she was disappointed to see some nameless band on stage instead of her idols. She didn't realise she'd just witnessed what was to become one of the biggest boy bands of all time.

We had dinner with the band and the record company people afterwards. The boys were all very likeable and good fun and extremely keen to get on MTV. I crossed paths with Take That quite a few times after that. At several big music shows in Germany I introduced them on stage and we always had a little chat backstage. I got on particularly well with one of the singers, Robbie Williams. He was not only an outstanding entertainer, but a really sweet and funny guy. When I first met him, he was a young, unknown artist, full of zest and drive, and was just as charming when Take That became famous. That set him apart from other up-and-coming artists, who would start out all smiles, probably because they wanted to get on our shows, but when they became famous, turned rude and arrogant.

In contrast, major stars like the Rolling Stones, Peter Gabriel, Dave Stewart and Lenny Kravitz, who had not only made the big time but managed to stay there, were unfailingly kind and polite. That's quite an achievement, because life in the music industry is tough – musicians have a heavy workload. They tour from one city to the next for months, doing endless shows and making countless PR appearances. They often find themselves both adored and demonised, trying hard to strike a balance between their own need for creative expression and fulfilment, and the pressures of being contractually obliged to churn out hits. They live a life of extremes. What with nights on stage in front of thousands of screaming fans and mornings alone in an anonymous hotel room, their lives are an emotional roller coaster that many only coped with by drinking heavily or turning to drugs.

I myself experienced that treacherous contrast between highs and lows, albeit on a smaller scale. But the feeling was the same – a constant to and fro between chasing something and being chased. It was a cycle that never let up. However, I did manage to avoid overdosing on drink, drugs and egotism, at least most of the time.

We once spent a week on tour with Prince. Our little team reported from backstage for the *Coca Cola Report* and I interviewed the individual band members. Shortly before a gigantic concert at the Rock am Ring Festival kicked off, I heard someone yell, 'Kristiane! Go on stage and tell them about the Prince competition!' I thought I was hearing things. Out there was a heaving mass of fans and they wanted me to go out in front of them? As it happened, I had no time to think or to feel nervous. My colleague Judith from the press department just shoved me straight onto the stage. I took a deep breath and a few steps forward. The sight that greeted me can hardly be described – an ocean of 70,000 wildly cheering music fans as far as the eye could see. I guess they recognised me from MTV and were excited to see what was going to happen next. They didn't care what I told them about the competition and were just screaming and clapping regardless. The sheer strength and positive energy coming from those thousands of people sent me soaring. I understood how musicians could get addicted to the rush of adrenaline, though it must be so much more intense for them when playing a gig. And yet, when the magic was over and I was back in the quiet of my hotel room, the noise still in my ears, I felt empty inside.

Of course, such a way of life can't possibly last forever. I was living in a bubble, cut off from the real world. It was as if I was surfing on the crest of a massive wave which I didn't realise could crash any minute on the shore of a world I'd almost forgotten. Once embroiled in this kind of life, it's hard to escape – even if you want to.

In 1991, the inevitable happened. I fell into a black hole of depression. I suppose I'd just run out of energy. I was constantly stressed and didn't know why I was doing what I was doing. I was at the peak of my career and yet I felt like a hamster in a wheel. The only thing that seemed to matter was the next show.

As a presenter, for all the glamour and fame, I was under huge psychological pressure, having constantly to improvise in front of thousands or hundreds of thousands when things went wrong, which they did all the time. The info and scripts were forever turning up late; at live music shows bands would drop out or change plans at the last minute; the sound system would go haywire; and the make-up artist would turn up just minutes before I had to go on stage. And I was the one who had to fill in the gaps. The memory of the pressure has stayed with me, and to this day I occasionally have nightmares that I'm late for going on stage and am searching frantically for my script or dress while everybody is waiting for me.

Also, being a well-known presenter didn't guarantee job security. MTV made sure their stars kept their feet on the ground and didn't start believing they were irreplaceable. Every contract I signed with the channel was fixed term – twelve months at first, but later only six – and with a four-week notice period. I had to live with the fact that it could all be over tomorrow. That year I was told that my future at MTV was shaky. The announcement came out of the blue and I wasn't given a reason. Video jockeys were replaced all the time, I was told. I think it was my friendship with Jim Kerr that saved my skin. Jim agreed to get involved with an MTV competition that offered the prize of a backstage pass to meet Simple Minds at their concert in Rome. The advert featuring the band and me ran for six months on MTV and everyone was really pleased. I guess it gave my career a second wind. However, reading my diary from around that time, I discovered the following entry:

I feel so ill – much worse than I've felt in a long time. Sick, dizzy, weak, no energy or drive, irritable and jaded. When is this low going to come to an end? It's work, work, work and then I'm alone again. When am I going to fall in love again? I don't want to work just for myself any more and I can't stand the pressure any longer. Tonight I'm supposed to entertain 2,000 Belgian farmers. Horrendous! I can't think of anything worse. Somehow it's all too much. I just don't know where all this is supposed to be leading to.

In dark moments like those, there was only one remedy: retail therapy. I'd head out and buy myself a new dress or a pair of shoes and, for a while, I'd be happy. But the thrill didn't last. It wouldn't be long before I felt like buying something new again. Ultimately, I felt lonely and wanted a partner, a soul mate to share my life with, but where would I meet someone serious?

I didn't have an answer, but someone else did. Miserable as I felt, I was about to have an encounter that would change my life forever.

Chapter 4

Higher Love

Think about it, there must be higher love,
Down in the heart, or hidden in the stars above
Without it life is wasted time
Look inside your heart, I'll look inside mine …
Bring me a higher love
Where's that higher love I keep thinking of?

Steve Winwood

I had a great job, was travelling a lot for work and play, and was inundated with invitations to go out in London. But somehow, I couldn't shake my feeling of dissatisfaction.

One evening, Susannah Constantine, a friend at the time, asked me at the last minute to attend her birthday party at the Groucho Club where she'd hired a private room. I hesitated at first but then agreed, asking her if she could seat me next to 'a nice man'.

Susannah had once dated Viscount Linley, the son of Princess Margaret, and later became a high-profile TV presenter. 'I know who,' she replied amused. 'Funnily enough, another guest said he would come only on condition that he would be seated next to a beautiful woman.'

And so I met Imran Khan, the man who inspired me to change my life for good. He was tall, dark and handsome, although on first sight, I thought he looked a bit old. I'd been told that he was a famous cricketer but I didn't know anything else about him, certainly not that he was a national hero in

Pakistan or an international heartthrob. His team's historic win in the recent World Cup had completely passed me by – I had never followed the sport; cricket is virtually unknown in Germany and wasn't remotely part of my upbringing. Imran wasn't in the least offended when I said I didn't know who he was. He admitted that he didn't know the first thing about the music business either and had no idea I was a VJ on MTV.

It was a relief for both of us not to be quizzed about our careers. Instead, we happily chatted about other topics – for example the movie *Basic Instinct*, a major box office hit at the time. Imran criticised the film's explicit sex scenes, telling me that they would be censored in Pakistan and other Muslim countries. He argued that the West had lost an essential part of its moral compass: a sense of shame. Such films, he believed, were symptomatic of a wider spiritual and ethical malaise. His comments were seized upon by the other guests. Most of them thought that the movie was good precisely *because* it was explicit and broke taboos. I told Imran that I wasn't sure if he was right, but that I had a mosque and Lord's Cricket Ground right outside my flat. He laughed and began to tell me more about himself.

Imran came from Lahore and was proud of his Pathan heritage. He explained that Pathans were known as the 'warrior race' and consisted of different tribes living primarily in Afghanistan, in the North West Frontier Province[1] of Pakistan and the lawless area in between, called the Federally Administered Tribal Areas (FATA). Imran came to England to study politics and economics at Oxford before launching his career as a professional sportsman in the seventies. He started playing for the Pakistani national cricket team at the age of eighteen, and after finishing university he played county cricket for Sussex. England became a second home to him. Nicknamed 'The Lion of Pakistan' – although I found out later that he was actually mad about tigers himself – he was eventually appointed captain of the Pakistani national team, which contained a bunch of talented but individual players. With his leadership qualities, motivational skills and charisma, he managed to turn them into a unified team and in 1992 led Pakistan to win the World Cup, defeating England in the final. This sparked tumultuous celebrations in his homeland – and shortly afterwards we met. It was some time before I realised just how famous an athlete Imran really was. An exceptional all-rounder, starting out as a fast bowler who could deliver a ball at over 90mph and developing a technique called 'reverse swing'; he later became an equally skilled batsman. Cricket cogniscienti considered Imran ever since to be one of the All-time World 11.

That first evening at Susannah's birthday party, he talked about his success and attributed it to a higher power – to God. I told Imran about my job as a VJ on MTV Europe, but unlike most people he wasn't terribly impressed when I said I interviewed rock stars for a living. I asked him about his future plans, now that he'd won the World Cup, and he explained that he was building a cancer hospital in Lahore, in memory of his mother, who had suffered terribly before dying of the disease a few years earlier. Imran described how painful and frustrating it had felt to be powerless to help her, despite all his contacts and connections. Now, at the height of his career, he said he was ready to give it all up and use his fame to raise funds for the construction of the first cancer hospital in Pakistan, 'where poor people would be treated for free,' he said. 'God was helping us. The victory will be an immense boost for the hospital,' he told me.

He sounded idealistic and serious, and deeply committed to his cause. 'You really want to give up cricket at the peak of your success to do charity work?' I asked him. He replied he'd had a long career already and wanted to contribute more to life than cricket. 'It's to do with faith,' he said. 'The essence of Islam is to believe in God and do good deeds.' He upped and left soon afterwards.

Sometime later, I returned home from MTV to find a message on my answerphone from Imran, inviting me to join him for dinner with some friends. The host was Andrew de Candole, a property tycoon. Imran didn't pick me up at home, but asked me to meet him at his Chelsea flat. He came down as soon as I rang the doorbell and we drove off to dinner in his metallic-blue sports Mercedes. This time, we weren't seated next to each other but at opposite ends. Imran looked deep into my eyes from across the table. The next invitation followed soon after, and this time he took me to Annabel's nightclub in Mayfair. I turned up at his flat in a buttercup-yellow Azzedine Alaia mini dress and a light summer coat. Looking dashing in his pale blue shirt and navy suit trousers, Imran complimented me, but then, to my astonishment, asked me if I could keep my coat on throughout the evening.

'Why?' I asked, mystified.

'In Pakistani culture women don't show skin,' he explained. 'They dress modestly, and so do the men. And, as you are accompanying me tonight and there is going to be a mixed crowd, it's better this way,' he said.

OK, I thought and pulled my coat over my legs. If it meant that much to him, why not? So I left the coat on all night – even on the dance floor.

Later, Imran told me something else that threw me. He said that he didn't like women to wear much make-up in public, and that the only person a woman should really beautify herself for was her husband. When at home, a wife could wear revealing clothes and red lipstick but when going out she should look conservative and demure. An unusual attitude, to say the least. The opposite was the norm in my experience. Western men generally liked women to look pretty and alluring, after all. And of course I was used to wearing make-up and dressing up every day for work, although in private I actually preferred a more natural, casual look.

I carried on being myself, and Imran and I hit it off anyway.

We were soon seeing each other regularly and he gradually introduced me to his crowd, which was even more glamorous than MTV's and also more multicultural. Whether they were Bollywood stars, writers, aristocrats, scholars, models, bankers, businessmen or sportsmen from Pakistan, India and the UK, they were mostly interesting people that I enjoyed meeting with Imran by my side. Sometimes our worlds overlapped. Imran knew Sting, for example, and was also great friends with Mick Jagger and his then wife Jerry Hall. Mick was a huge cricket fan.

It was summer and London's social season was in full swing – a relentless whirl of dinners, garden parties and charity events. The season traditionally kicks off with the Chelsea Flower Show, followed by Royal Ascot, the famous horse-racing event attended by the Queen. Then comes the Cartier Polo tournament, in which Prince Charles and his sons often participate, the Glastonbury Music Festival, Elton John's White Tie & Tiara Ball and, of course, Wimbledon.

Imran would spend the months of June and July at his penthouse flat in Chelsea, and lead an active social life as a sought-after guest at all the A-list events. He also had a small office in Kensington, which served as the headquarters of the Imran Khan Cancer Appeal. From there he oversaw the organisation of numerous fundraising events around the world for the hospital. Imran was a unique blend of East and West, dynamic, with a sense of humour, and a magnet for the opposite sex. Women threw themselves at him wherever he went. Initially I found this irritating, but I got used to it, and eventually accepted it as a vaguely amusing by-product of dating this unique man. I managed to get Sinead O'Connor's best friend, who'd also become a friend of mine, a job at his office and even she couldn't resist falling for him.

Tracy Worcester, who was married to Imran's good friend Harry Somerset, the Marquess of Worcester, adored him and named her horse after him. Harry, known as 'Bunter' to his friends, and his younger brother Johnson were passionate about music and knew me from MTV. Harry has a beautiful voice and is the lead singer of The Listening Device, while Johnson has worked as a music producer on albums for Steve Winwood and Bryan Ferry amongst others and used to play percussion in his own band, Ramshackle.

On the one hand were Imran's fun Western society friends and on the other his hospital project, for which he worked very hard, and his Islamic faith, which he was in the process of discovering for himself anew. After the death of his mother, he'd begun exploring his religion more deeply, he told me. During a rare quiet moment over lunch at a French restaurant near his flat, I explained to Imran that I'd had practically no contact with Islam in my life and had never really given it much thought. A few years earlier I had travelled to Malaysia with friends and had once visited Morocco with my parents, but that was the limit of my experience of Muslim countries. I assumed that Muslim women had no freedoms and were oppressed by a patriarchal system and I imagined the Quran to be a strict, antiquated book of rules. But I was happy to be enlightened.

'The Quran is actually not written by man, but is the word of God,' Imran explained. 'Belief in God is the basis of Islam,' he said. Okay, so far so good, and I did believe in God. 'But how can the Quran be God's word?' I asked him. 'The Quran was revealed over a period of time by the archangel Gabriel (as)[2] to Prophet Muhammad (saw)[3] who is the last Prophet,' he explained. I didn't really understand, and I thought he believed in Allah and not in God. 'The Arabic word for God is Allah,' Imran retorted. 'Allah is the same God that all people believe in. Islam actually means "surrender to the will of God". And it has a second meaning that is "peace". In other words, those who submit to God and place their trust in God will find inner peace.'

What exactly did it mean to submit to God, I wondered.

All I knew was that in my world, there was neither God nor peace. I had no connection with religion as such, and God meant little more to me than distant childhood memories. My parents had just got divorced, and I felt as though I was emerging from some kind of existential crisis. If I was honest with myself, I couldn't remember the last time I'd felt inner peace, even though I had all the success a young person could have wished for. Deep down I felt empty and a bit lonely, and I thought that what I needed was a partner. But the truth was that no human being could have filled my inner void.

Imran helped me to realise this. He made me aware of another dimension to life altogether, one that I had always been vaguely interested in, but which I had never seriously pursued. Life had been far too hectic to even think about it. 'The material world is not all that exists,' Imran said. 'There is something more important that is not really tangible but is definitely there. In the East people were very open to the spiritual dimension and they even experienced it, whereas in the West it is more or less buried.' I was intrigued. Spirituality had always interested me: I just didn't know anything about it. I remembered that when I'd met the singer Terence Trent d'Arby, he'd said that spirituality meant a lot to him. The remark had stuck in my mind and I'd wondered what he actually meant, but never had a chance to ask him. So now that Imran was mentioning it, I took the opportunity to find out more.

He spoke to me of the Sufis in Pakistan who were apparently very spiritual people and could master the greatest challenges through sheer spiritual power. One, he said, survived with a lethal bullet in his body and lived happily ever after because of his elevated spiritual state – through prayers. And Ali, the Prophet's cousin, is said to have been operated on while in a state of prayer, and didn't feel the pain. I wasn't sure if I believed him, but I was captivated and wanted to hear more. He told me about his encounter with a simple but pious man called Mian Bashir. 'He was blessed by God with extraordinary wisdom and insight. So many people turn to him to seek his advice,' he said. 'Do you also consult with him?' I asked, amused that this sporting giant would sit with a humble man to discuss his problems. 'Yes, and so far he's never been wrong!' Imran answered, much to my surprise. Mian Bashir either saw the solution straight away or, if not, he would stay up all night praying and contemplating until he had an answer. 'He is a devout and truthful man who has the gift of clear vision and is definitely no charlatan,' said Imran. The fact that he never accepted money reinforced his belief in Bashir's integrity.

I would have loved to have met this man. Not that I had any burning questions on my mind, but I was curious and wanted to find out more about Imran's religion. Pleased by my open-minded attitude, when he next left London to raise funds for the hospital he gave me a small book. I would read it whenever I had a free moment in between working and socialising. *Man and Islam* was written by the Iranian sociologist Ali Shariahti, who died in England in 1977. He had long been a university professor in Tehran but was imprisoned several times because his religious theories did not conform to the ideology of the Shah's regime.

Shariahti did not write about dogmatic rules or female oppression but focused on philosophy and ethics. He criticised modern society, asking how civilised and advanced a society can really be if it promoted capitalism and materialism while failing to prevent poverty, the destruction of the environment and social ills such as mental depression. He diagnosed the fundamental problem besetting the Western world as an absence of spirituality, of faith in God. 'Man can free himself from the prison of nature and history with the aid of science. He can free himself from his social order with the aid of sociology. But in order to free himself from the prison of his self ... he needs religion and love,' wrote Shariahti. He believed that love could help us transcend our ego and find true freedom. This love, he believed, came from God and was for God. It was beyond our rational faculties and ultimately led us to sacrifice some of ourselves for the sake of helping others to serve a higher purpose – namely God. And this state of servitude, he wrote, was the most exalted level of becoming a true *human* being.

Something resonated in me when I read those words. Perhaps he was right. Perhaps what I was missing in my life was this love that would make me serve a higher purpose. Deep down I had always been idealistic, but somehow had never had a chance to put this into practice. In my world the purpose was entertainment, everything was ephemeral, every trend fleeting.

I talked to Imran about my first impressions of the book and it felt as though a door had been opened. Soon we were discussing the differences between his culture and mine, between the East and the West, and how faith and tradition provided a set of values unlike those that are forever changing, depending on the whims of the zeitgeist. We spoke about how globalisation was promoting Western consumerism and secularism and undermining traditional societies such as Pakistan's. We discussed the tyranny of fashion, and how the less figure-hugging clothes worn by Muslim women positively affected the way they were perceived and their own self-confidence. Our discussions were often heated. For me, it was an intellectual awakening, although sometimes I felt Imran's views were a bit too black and white.

However, when it came to his critique of the way women were portrayed in the Western media, I didn't take much persuading. When we drove down the street and passed a large placard, he would rant about advertisements featuring half-naked women selling anything from car tyres to men's perfume. He found it degrading for the women who were allowing their bodies to be exploited like this. 'That is precisely why Islam asks women to dress modestly,' he told me. 'To preserve their dignity as human beings.'

I sometimes teased Imran and called him 'mullah' when he went on a bit, but, as I had witnessed throughout my career, 'sex sells' is a key principle in the media and I questioned its merit. Women in the entertainment industry often resort to the old trick of 'if you've got it, flaunt it' and to a degree I did as well, but I didn't really make the 'less is more' philosophy a deliberate strategy for career advancement as others did, dressing as daringly and provocatively as possible to attract maximum media coverage. And I didn't like the way that ninety per cent of the time, the portrayal of women in commercials wasn't based on their personality or intellect, but their body shape and sex appeal. So I saw Imran's point that, regardless of what people said about the perceived subjugation of women in Muslim cultures, the Western world's way of objectifying women was undeniably an insult to their dignity and a form of exploitation.

Those early days in my relationship with Imran were undoubtedly among the most interesting and intense of my life. Our discussions about morality and ethics, politics and the meaning of religion were the antidote to my job that I'd been craving, and I started questioning everything I thought I knew. At the same time, as a presenter on MTV Europe I was busier than ever before. If I wasn't introducing videos in the studio in London, I was flying around the world to do interviews, to be interviewed or to host music shows.

I was also getting offers from other TV stations. In 1992, a German producer asked me if I'd be interested in creating and presenting a new nationwide music show. I was thrilled by the offer. MTV had pretty much swept away all competition in Germany but I was given my own music show to host, *Bravo TV*, a platform for up-and-coming talent. Once a month, a camera team would come to London and we'd film at a studio in Soho. After one year *Bravo TV* started flying me out to Hamburg on a regular basis. It wasn't long before the show became a success and my status as a pop icon in Germany was consolidated. Among the many bands I interviewed was East 17. Tony, the lead singer, was entertaining and eloquent but when I asked Brian about his motivation, he responded monosyllabically that he was 'just in it for the girls'. Another time some of the band turned up drunk for an interview. That sort of attitude contrasted with the soul-searching debates I was having with Imran, and contributed to my growing disillusionment with the world of celebrity.

All in all, Imran and I spent a wonderful summer in London. However, somewhere in the back of my mind I knew that he didn't feel completely at home here. He hosted and attended lots of dinner parties, but even though he quite enjoyed the glitz and glamour, he knew it wasn't the be-all and end-all. His roots were everything to him, and he often spoke passionately about Pakistan. Imran loved his country and was proud of its people, its culture and its potential. He told me that once he started a family, they would live in Pakistan. He showed me stunningly beautiful slides of lush, wild nature and the Himalayas and invited me to go on a hiking trip with him and some of his friends. I hesitated at first. Pakistan seemed like a world away and it wasn't exactly an obvious tourist destination. Plus, I had noted the remark about his future family. But he kept insisting and eventually I accepted. Imran was delighted, and confidently stated: 'In Pakistan you will fall in love with me.' We'll see about that, I thought.

So in August 1992, three months after we'd met, we set off together with Briggite on a two-week trip through Pakistan. When we visited Lahore, we stayed at Imran's father's house in the leafy suburb of Zaman Park. I noticed the respect he showed his father, addressing him with the polite form comparable to '*Sie*' in German and '*vous*' in French. It seemed a strange thing to do with a family member, but he explained it came down to the Islamic principle of showing respect for the elderly, which Yousaf Salaudin had mentioned as well. 'The Quran teaches us to be kind and loving to our parents, because they took such care in raising us,' he said. I wondered if this traditional way of addressing parents also created a boundary and a distance, which balanced the closeness I observed amongst Pakistani families who often lived with all the generations under one roof. I was just as surprised, though, to see how unfailingly polite Pakistani children and teenagers were to their parents – so unlike some Western children, including myself when I was younger.

During our three weeks there, we hiked across snow-covered mountains, slept in tents and brewed tea over open fires. We also travelled to Islamabad and Karachi, and at various functions, lunches and dinners we met Imran's friends, who were all open-minded, modern and mostly well-to-do. Once we went on a boat ride under the stars in the vast Karachi harbour and drove back to the house with Nusrat's catchy hit 'Must Must' blasting from the speakers, stopping at a set of traffic lights where Imran bought Briggite and me sweet-scented bracelets of jasmine flowers. I enjoyed the colonial architecture of the Sind Club in Karachi, built by the British in the 1860s and which locals were only allowed to join after partition. The atmosphere still evoked the grandeur of the Raj. Alcohol was generally not served in public, I was only offered it at a few private houses – but usually the wine wasn't terribly good and I didn't drink hard spirits, which were popular amongst some men. Imran didn't drink at all. It probably did Brigitte and me good to abstain for a few weeks.

It was an incredible journey, my first visit to Paksitan, and one that left me with many unforgettable memories. I thoroughly enjoyed the sensuous, Eastern atmosphere and was deeply touched by the gentle, hospitable people I encountered – people who carried God in their hearts. It was all in such stark contrast to the weird and wonderful world of entertainment – a world I was unceremoniously catapulted back into immediately after that first visit to Pakistan. The trip fresh in my mind, I flew to Los Angeles for the MTV Video Music Awards.

∽

The razzmatazz of this showbiz spectacle was unreal and over-the-top. The surgically enhanced rock chicks in their micro outfits seemed utterly fake, and some of the supposedly cool dudes in their undershirts and dark shades at night just looked ridiculous. (What were they trying to hide?) I drank champagne for the first time in weeks at the after-show parties, which gave me a terrible headache and made me feel hung-over the next morning. The following week I stayed with Elizabeth Hurley and Julia Verdin, a film producer friend of hers. They were keen to see my holiday pictures and were fascinated by this very different world I'd been to with Imran. We went out on the town together, and often bumped into celebrities; at one party Nicolas Cage was amongst the guests. Another night I spotted Billy Idol with platinum blonde hair, all dressed up in rock gear and shades. Tony James also happened to be in LA and we all hung out together. Tony and Billy were catching up at length – they knew each other from their Generation X days. I met many people who were all on the make in the film industry. 'What do you do?' was usually the first question I was asked, followed by 'What does your father do?' People were extremely career-minded and goal-oriented but somehow removed from reality. The energy couldn't have been more different from what I'd encountered in Pakistan. I missed the warmth, the hospitality and the authenticity of the people I'd met there.

When I saw Imran back in London, he started making references to our future. He didn't formally propose, but began wondering aloud whether perhaps we should get married. He gave me a beautiful gold pendant depicting the word Allah. I was touched and wore it most of the time. He also asked me to move in with him. This came as a bit of a surprise, because I knew Imran had never lived with a woman before. His religion didn't allow men and women to live together unless they were husband and wife, but it appeared that he was seriously contemplating marrying me and perhaps he wanted to test things out first. Marriage was a difficult issue for Imran. For years, the Pakistani nation had been wondering when he was going to marry, and above all, whom. A Western woman or a Pakistani? It was a question the country's tabloids never tired of asking, and the hope was clearly that he would choose a bride from his own country. For this reason, Imran was keen to keep our relationship discreet and out of the public eye. I went along with it out of respect for his culture, although I didn't feel great about the fact that the man I was with was unwilling to stand by me publicly. But then again, I certainly didn't want to jeopardise his hospital project. There was still a lot of work to do and he was worried about whether marriage to a Western woman would have negative repercussions on his fundraising efforts in Pakistan. He suggested we marry after the hospital opened. I understood his concerns and wasn't really focused on getting married anyway – after all, we'd only known each other for a few months. So we did our best to keep a low profile. We'd try to trick the paparazzi, not showing up at public events together and leaving separately. But it was hard going and inevitably we were being snapped together on our way to a restaurant or the gym. The pictures were hardly incriminating, because he never showed affection in public anyway. 'Muslims just don't do that,' he explained – something else I had to get used to – but we were obviously a couple. To Imran's horror, the photos were immediately published in huge articles in the Pakistani press and he worried about the consequences. But nothing terrible happened, and support for his hospital never flagged.

Imran had given up playing professional cricket by now but I accompanied him to some of the charity tournaments he participated in outside of London, including the annual cricket matches in Groombridge, at Andrew's amazing country retreat and in Gloucestershire at the estate of the Duke of Beaufort, father of Bunter and Johnson. Whenever we were invited there, we would stay either at Tracy and Bunter's cottage nearby, or at Badminton House, where the Duke and his wife lived. It was a glimpse into another world, one where butlers and gourmet chefs would wait on us day and night. A select mix of rock stars, businessmen and writers, filmmakers, models and friends of the Duke and his children were invited for lunch and dinner, and afterwards the younger guests would retreat to the library and carry on partying into the early hours of the morning. I grew to understand that cricket is synonymous with English country life – players in spotless whites on manicured lawns, munching cucumber sandwiches and sipping glasses of Pimms. I must admit I never developed a great passion for the game itself, but I learned a lot about it over the years and was enchanted by the theatre of it all.

Imran was at his most relaxed when he was with a small circle of friends, having dinner in a restaurant or entertaining at home. He used to order the most delicious curries from a special cook in the East End and we would chat and listen to music until late into the night. His all-time favourite artist was the Pakistani singer Nusrat Fateh Ali Khan, but he also listened to Western bands such as U2 and Pink Floyd. I particularly enjoyed the compilation CDs that Johnson used to make for him.

Imran's closest friends were all easy-going types and fun to be with. Jonathan Mermagen, a fabulous raconteur, was a sports manager with a shock of silver hair. He would amuse us for hours on end and was always teasing Imran about his attempts to Islamise the 'MTV chick'. Then there was Oliver Gilmore, an orchestral conductor who had just returned from Bulgaria and confessed that he'd often stayed up late to watch me on MTV; Mark Shand, an adventurer, elephant lover and brother to Camilla Parker Bowles; Shariah Bakhtiar, a descendant of the former Iranian Prime Minister, and king of London nightlife, incidentally one of the first people I had met in London with my flatmate Caroline; Charles Glass, a handsome American journalist and writer who'd spent two months as a hostage in Lebanon; P.J. Mir, a cricket friend from Lahore, who loved all kinds of gadgets and used to ask me for tips on how to get into TV; and of course Bunter and Johnson. Imran's loyal helper was Akram, a cab driver who chauffeured him wherever he needed to go. There was a large group of Pakistani businessmen who were on the cancer hospital committee and regularly met at the flat to discuss business, and then there was Dar, Imran's hair stylist and close confidant. Dar idolised Imran. Posters and articles of him were plastered all around his salon and he attended every TV interview Imran gave to make sure his hair was just right, using some very special, ingenious tricks. He was always inviting 'Immy', as he called him, to Indian fashion events, which sometimes annoyed me because we had so little time as it was. That said, Dar was a sweet man and an excellent hairdresser.

When Imran celebrated his fortieth birthday, everybody came. Mick Jagger showed up with Jerry Hall and Marie Helvin, and he and Imran got into a discussion about how hard they worked for their success as cricketer and rock star. It all looked so easy and effortless to their fans, but both stressed that their success was not just down to talent but also hard work. Imran used to train for hours every day and Mick told us about his gruelling workouts before going on world tours. It was a treat to hear the two speaking so frankly about one of the keys to success, and I was also delighted to note that they both scoffed one piece of birthday cake after another. For the first time ever I had baked my mother's special hazelnut cherry cake that afternoon. She helped me with a few tips over the phone, and I served it with cinnamon whipped cream. Thankfully it was a hit. Even Mick couldn't get enough of it.

However, it wasn't Imran's famous friends that really impressed me. What drew me to him was his idealism and his tireless work on behalf of his hospital project, which was costing more than 20 million pounds to build. Imran raised funds all over the world – from the US and the UK to the Middle East, India, Pakistan and Australia. He loved Pakistan and always said he wanted to serve his country and to help move it forward, rather than leading an empty life of luxury in the West. Imran was supported by an army of volunteers and VIPs, including his friends in London, Amitabh Bachchan, the King of Bollywood and India's most popular actor, and Pakistani music legend, the late Nusrat Fateh Ali Khan. He organised umpteen charity events, persuading as many friends and potential sponsors as possible to 'buy' tables at his dinners. In between courses he went on stage and spoke passionately about the need for this hospital due to the terrible state of the Pakistani health system. The country lacked any kind of public health care or insurance scheme and provided no adequate treatment for cancer sufferers at all. Then he showed a video clip to illustrate the squalid conditions of public hospitals and the progress his hospital was making, and asked the guests to donate generously.

One of these fundraising events took place at the Intercontinental Hotel in Hyde Park, and it was there that I first saw Nusrat Fateh Ali Khan perform live. I was utterly blown away. He was known as the Pavarotti of Pakistan, and his concerts were among the most moving shows I'd ever experienced. Nusrat was a very large man and sat cross-legged on the stage with a couple of tabla players and several backup singers next to him. As he sang, his voice swelled with passion and he gesticulated wildly, conducting with his hands. His voice seemed to come from somewhere deep inside him and could allegedly soar over eight octaves in one breath.

The audience that night in London was mesmerised. Everyone was swaying in their seats, even Mick and Jerry were tapping away. The atmosphere grew increasingly charged the longer he performed. Some Pakistani fans whirled about in circles, their arms outstretched while showering Nusrat with pound notes. 'In Pakistan, people get into a real trance,' Imran told us. Concerts there were spiritual experiences for both musicians and audiences alike. 'According to Sufi tradition, *qawwali* music can give wings to the soul and carry it towards God,' he said. Actually I was given my first Nusrat CDs by the director of the American *SPIN* magazine a couple of years previously at Pink Floyd's The Wall concert in Berlin to celebrate the fall of the Berlin Wall. I had never listened to them, but now that I'd come across this extraordinary artist again, I found myself enthralled and wanted to know more about him. I learned from his manager, Anjim, that Nusrat was born into one of Pakistan's oldest musical families, and with this ancient form of mystical Sufi music he became the most famous *qawwali* musician in the Indian subcontinent, praised as *Shah Shaheen,* the brightest star in the *qawwali* heaven. Peter Gabriel introduced Nusrat to the West through his WOMAD Festivals and, inspired by the remarkable singer himself, he went on to produce a few albums with Nusrat for his label Real World. *Rolling Stone* magazine once wrote that Nusrat had the best voice in the world, and many famous Western performers such as U2's Bono and even Luciano Pavarotti were keen to collaborate with him. Jeff Buckley, another artist who died far too young, covered several of Nusrat's compositions and once famously exclaimed: 'I have no food in my refrigerator, but I have every single Nusrat album in my collection.' Jeff obviously found the nourishment he needed in Nusrat's devotional music. Hearing all this, I resolved to introduce Steve to this special artist as soon as an opportunity arose.

After a rousing concert, Imran circulated amongst his guests, attempting to speak to everyone. Amitabh Bachchan, the Indian movie star, supported him, going from table to table asking for donations. Their efforts paid off and, years later, the Shaukat Khanum Memorial Cancer Hospital & Research Centre, named after Imran's late mother, became an established institution, where only the patients who can afford it have to pay, and seventy-five per cent of the treatment given is supposedly free of charge. Imran continues to raise about 20 million US dollars annually to cover these costs. A second cancer hospital in Karachi is in the pipeline.

I thoroughly enjoyed Imran's fundraisers. They were for a good cause and had little to do with the hedonism and networking for personal gain that I was used to from music industry events and all the other parties I attended. Alcohol was only drunk in moderation, if at all, and the guests would still dance, talk and enjoy themselves well into the night.

Imran organised Nusrat concerts all over the world and worked hard day and night for his project, ultimately 'to serve God' as he said. He credited his faith for giving him the courage and strength to pursue his 'mission' over the course of so many years. He didn't just talk about Islam. I saw him praying daily on his prayer mat, which pointed south-east in the direction of Mecca, and sometimes I heard him talking loudly and at length to God in Urdu. He fasted during Ramadan and read voraciously, seeking answers on Islam. We often visited a specialist bookstore near Regent's Park Mosque, where he stocked up on Islamic literature. Back home we sat for hours reading those books and also studied some of the Quran together. When I first looked at the text, it felt a little strange because it was so different from anything I'd read. But I could sense the power behind the words. God. I was surprised to discover similarities between Judaism, Christianity and Islam. For one, Muslims, Jews and Christians all believe in God, but I knew that already. Now I also came across the same prophets I recognised from the Bible – Abraham, Moses and Jesus.

'God conveyed the same message through different Prophets at different times,' [4] Imran explained to me. 'Muhammad was the last in a long line of these Prophets – Muslims call him the Seal of Prophets. He clarified and completed God's message'. I hadn't realised that. Christian concepts that I'd always found hard to get my head round, such as the trinity or original sin, don't exist in Islam, I learned.[5] Instead, it teaches that every human is born in a primordial state of purity, the so-called *fitra*, the way God originally made us. And rather than being born with an inherited sin, Islam promotes the idea of personal responsibility. *Each soul is responsible for its own actions,* says the Quran. *No soul will bear the burden of another* (6:164). I thought about all of this and found it to be logical. I liked the concept of individual responsibility and took it further when I mulled over this verse. I remembered how during my exchange year in the US some Jewish people of the older generation didn't speak to me because of the Holocaust. I understood their resentment, of course, and was appalled myself by this dark chapter in German history. But surely, it couldn't be right that I should be punished for what had happened before I was even born. Or was I guilty simply because I was German? Reading about Islam opened my eyes to the possibility that justice is not compatible with collective guilt and punishment; at the same time, we are well advised to learn from past actions of others and strengthen our resolve to prevent and oppose injustice and cruelty from happening anywhere in the world.

Chapter 5

Adventure, Discovery and Realisation

Free your mind and the rest will follow.
En Vogue

Every few months over the next two years, I returned to Pakistan, getting to know the country better and learning to love it. The trips were adventures into another world and a feast for the senses, what with the heat, the colours, the sounds, the scents, the spicy food and the lush landscapes where big black water buffalo bathed in pools by the roadside. I always enjoyed the drive from the airport into town, which felt like the gateway between my other life and this warm and welcoming exotic environment. I would gaze out of the car window, taking it all in and looking forward to immersing myself once again in this very different culture that was becoming more and more familiar to me.

On one trip we visited Kashmir, which has to be one of the most beautiful regions in the country, with snowy mountains, turquoise streams and wild meadows covered with flowers. We also went to the Tribal Areas in north-western Pakistan, home to the incredibly hospitable but occasionally fierce-looking Pathans. Tall, slim and with big green eyes beneath dark eyelashes, the men and the few women we saw were striking. Most of the men had moustaches, like those in Punjab, some also had full beards, and they all wore shalwar kameez with different coloured turbans – I particularly liked the ones made from a shiny black and silver fabric. Many of them also sported ammunition belts and Kalashnikovs slung over their shoulders, even the boys. I saw hardly any women at all, except for a few working in the fields in bright pink and deep red traditional tribal dresses. I was given a beautiful, brightly coloured dress as a gift. It had a wide, pleated skirt and was weighed down with embroidery and sewn-on silver-coloured bells and coins. The terrain was rocky and near impassable, and the mud houses looked more like small fortresses, with windows so tiny that only a gun could fit through. Although the Tribal Areas were part of Pakistan, state law did not apply, and it was the tribal leaders who ruled there. They discussed regional matters at assemblies called *jirgas*, where decisions were made by consensus. The Pathans adhered to their own law, a code of honour and ethics that governed individual and communal conduct called *pakhtunwali*. Later years saw the rise of Taliban insurgents in the Tribal Areas, and certain extremists were said to have exploited the fabled Pathan hospitality to find succour there. It became far too dangerous for anyone to visit and even then, it was only thanks to Imran's fame and his Pathan heritage that the border soldiers allowed us in, as part of an armed convoy. On our way, we visited the frontier town of Peshawar, which lay on the edge of the tribal belt and where you could buy anything from large slabs of dark hashish to handcrafted antique Afghan silver jewellery with lapis lazuli stones, any number of emeralds, guns and even uranium. Here I saw more women wearing burkas: thick, greyish-blue tent-like garments worn predominantly by women in the North West Frontier Province and in Afghanistan, which looked exactly the same from all sides. Out of curiosity, during a tea break in the village of Banu, I tried one on myself, slipping it over my head on top of my own shalwar kameez. I was hot and couldn't breathe very well. The grille over the eyes blurred my vision and I could only see directly in front of me. This walking prison is not my cup of chai, I thought.

Nothing, however, could spoil my enjoyment of browsing through the bazaars wherever we were, observing the *hakims*, the herbal medicine practitioners, selling all kinds of exotic and bizarre remedies such as snake venom and an aphrodisiac powder made from dried tiger testicles – despite the creatures being nearly extinct – and the most popular natural medicine in Pakistan, *kalonji* or black cumin seed oil. 'There is a healing in it for every disease except for death,' the Prophet said of this seed, as everyone told me. Donkeys and cattle would roam along the dusty roads with bells round their necks, and the air was fragrant with the aromas of frankincense and curry powder, as well as all the other spices that were piled high at the market stalls next to exquisitely engraved gold jewellery, hand-embroidered cashmere shawls, and rolls of natural silks, cotton and lace.

In the Sindh Plain we spent a night in a romantic, oriental luxury tent complete with shower and toilet, and went buffalo hunting the next day, although to my relief we didn't find any to actually shoot. We also visited a Sufi shrine in Multan, which served as a home to many poor people. I saw a woman with long black hair, eyes wide open, running around the sacred sanctuary in circles in a seeming frenzy and was told that she was possessed by *jinn*, spirit creatures made from air and fire, and was undergoing an exorcism. We ate a simple meal in a neon-lit run-down room and carried on with our journey. In Sindh we stayed in a palace belonging to a feudal lord, where the living room was as large as a ballroom and decorated with thousands of tiny hand-painted flowers in ancient Mogul style. It felt as though we were in a spring meadow. The feudal lord told us that the artists had been working for his family for over 300 years. At dinner he offered us the local aphrodisiac, camel's milk. I tried a sip but didn't like it, the consistency was quite thick and it had a strong taste. The feudal landlord himself lived in typical Sindhi style in the lap of luxury, waited on by an army of servants. Most of them would have worked for the family for generations. The local villagers were almost equivalent to his serfs: the land they worked on belonged to the feudal landlord as did their votes, and everything else, which was something I found hard to digest. Every morning he would hold court, with hundreds of them coming to him to seek help in solving their problems. We had stepped into a medieval world where democratic institutions, social justice and human rights as we know it were non-existent and a very different system of protectionism, patronage and kinship was in place. But the basis of Pakistani society was the family. And witnessing how family members looked after one another, unconditionally and without hesitation, touched me. It was all very different from European society.

We stayed in the best places, and wherever we went – except for the mountains – we enjoyed red-carpet treatment. Every day in Pakistan, when fans approached Imran, I saw what it meant to be a national hero and understood why Imran felt at home here in a way he never would in London. His roots were in Pakistan, and I could see how the country and its people helped fuel his faith, which inspired him to use his status and make his contribution there – wholeheartedly. Imran very much opposed the general brain drain; the well-educated leaving the country for a cushy life in the West.

We would go for walks when the sun started to set, and he loved to watch the farmers bringing in the cattle and goats from the fields. He admired the way they lived in harmony with their animals and nature, and felt that theirs was an example worth following. We are meant to treat nature, animals and humans – in fact all of creation – with respect and compassion, he told me, and not to abuse them or waste resources, because as the Quran says: *God does not like the wasteful* (6:141). For the same reason Imran heavily criticised the deforestation that went on everywhere in Pakistan. Pointing to the piles of logs we could see below naked mountains that used to be covered in pine trees, he vowed to put a stop to it if ever he got into politics. Nature and animals had always been important to me and I liked the fact that protecting the environment, along with care and respect for all creation, was an explicit part of his religion.

Imran also explained that the local farmers never took more than they needed from the earth and always gave away any surplus produce. 'As a Muslim, you decide what you need and give the rest away to the poor,' Imran explained. Hoarding was un-Islamic and, regardless of how much wealth we might amass in this life, we couldn't take it into the next. 'Life is transient,' he said, 'we should be in this world like a stranger or a wayfarer,'[1] he quoted the Prophet, meaning we shouldn't cling to this worldly life or material things. 'When you stand before God, or when you're lying in your grave, all that matters are your good deeds,' he said.

If someone else had talked to me in this manner, I would have probably considered it a little over the top, but coming from Imran, I knew he meant it. Beyond his immediate needs, he really did spend everything he earned on the hospital.

Later, after the sun had gone down, we gazed at the stars and snuggled together under Imran's enormous eggshell-coloured shawl, which he took with him wherever he went and which doubled up as a blanket. One evening, he drew me into his arms and said, 'This is where you belong!' adding, after a small pause, 'now'. I registered his meaning, but still felt butterflies in my stomach. Perhaps to comfort me, Imran went on to recite a poem by Mian Muhammad Bakhsh, who lived in the nineteenth century. His poetry was revered and loved by the educated classes as well as the simple people from the villages:

> Destroy the mosque, knock down the temple,
> Break everything you are able to break
> But don't break another's heart,
> For God – the Beautiful – lives in hearts.

However moved and fascinated I was by everything I heard and saw, the thought that one day I might actually live in Pakistan was a daunting one. 'Your children will be Muslim,' Imran said to me one day while we were having a picnic lunch near a stream. I was touched by the implication and I knew I wanted to be with him. I believed in his goals but at the same time I wasn't sure what it would be like to actually live in Pakistan. I put his comment to the back of my mind, but subconsciously paid attention to how I was treated as a Western woman, and indeed to how women in general were treated in his country. In truth, no man ever showed me contempt, hostility or disrespect. On the contrary, I was warmly received wherever I went, and the men I encountered were unfailingly polite and courteous. It was only now and then, in the more remote areas, that men would avoid looking at me and ignore me. It was a sign of respect, Imran told me. A strange concept that would take some getting used to. I paid no attention, and would read one of my Islamic books rather than participate in the conversation. Others would show their respect by addressing me as 'sister'.

Nonetheless, there were aspects of Pakistani culture that I continued to question. Women were not allowed into many of the mosques, and segregation of the sexes was practised pretty much throughout the country except by the Westernised elite. In the Tribal Areas, for example, I was left alone in a special women's room while Imran went to pray and chat with the men. I often had to wait for him while he took care of apparently important matters. Once in Kashmir, after a day's drive, we finally arrived in an army guesthouse and I couldn't wait to stretch my legs and go for a walk with him, which he promised immediately after greeting the hosts. But he disappeared and I waited for over two hours by myself with not so much as a cup of chai. By the time my patience finally ran out, it was already getting dark outside and I decided to go and look for him, only to find him in a men-only room, watching cricket with about thirty others. My bursting in and speaking to him in front of everybody proved to be a huge embarrassment for him, but he dragged himself away for a short walk, saying half-seriously that no woman had ever set foot in that room before.

Segregation of the sexes wasn't a question of geographical region or indeed social status. In Sindh, at the palace of another feudal lord, the wife of our host lived in purdah. She was always covered and never mixed with men, so I only saw her when I visited the separate ladies' wing of the palace where she lived with her daughters and her female servants. It was a bustling place, full of laughter and activity. The wife relaxed and joked with the other women, who spent their time embroidering, folding the laundry and chatting away while the children ran around. Whenever the feudal lady stepped outside the walls of the palace, she would wear a head-to-toe black chador, and the villagers she passed would avert their eyes and even turn away out of respect. On leaving, her husband gave me a generous present – a pair of hand-crafted gold earrings. I wore them for years, until sadly I lost one.

Something I noticed wherever we went in Pakistan was that the photographs and pictures adorning the walls of our hosts' homes only ever showed men, never women. When I pointed this out to Imran, he told me that the idea was to protect women like precious jewels and that they shouldn't be seen by just any men. I thought of all the photo shoots I'd done over the years and the family portraits I knew from Europe, and wondered about the point of this kind of 'protection'.

The women I did get to meet in the villages were all very warm and welcoming, but few of them spoke English, so our communication was hampered by my very limited Urdu – a few words of praise and some swear words I'd picked up from Imran.

The poverty I witnessed upset me. Sometimes I even saw children working, but Imran claimed it was by no means as bad as in India where people slept and even died on the streets. 'Poor people usually have as many children as possible as a form of insurance for their old age,' he explained on one of our many long jeep drives through the country. Traditionally the men were responsible for the care of their parents and any unmarried sisters as well as their own wife – or wives – and children; hence it was important that education for the boys was prioritised over female education. The girls were expected to get married at a young age. Once again, I thanked my lucky stars for the privileged life I'd led.

The plight of some of the young Pakistani girls from poor families saddened me in particular, and I wanted to do something to help them. Imran, who was already doing his utmost to improve conditions in the country, took me to a senior school in the breathtaking Chitral Valley, which was co-founded by a friend of his from London called Sophia Swire, who had a soft spot for Pakistan. With her London charity Learning for Life, her goal was to improve schooling in Pakistan. She had brought to the country over 200 kilos of schoolbooks and other teaching equipment, and, with the help of the deputy commissioner and a few teachers from London, had set up several schools in remote areas. I chatted to the English teacher in one of the schools, now known as the 'Eton of the Hindu Kush' due to its high educational level, whilst she showed us around the classrooms. Nearly 250 students – both boys and girls, though segregated – were studying all the subjects on the British national curriculum, with some additions that were relevant to their local culture. For example, they learned about the nearly extinct snow leopards, about conservation and deforestation, and basic health care and hygiene. Sophia proudly told me years later that many former students, particularly girls who might otherwise have entered into early marriages, were now pursuing Masters degrees and PhDs abroad. So at least she'd helped to improve some of those girls' lives.

Overall, the experiences in Pakistan left me with mixed

feelings. I found it hard to get used to the segregation of the sexes and it seemed a bit boring to only speak and hang out with women who hadn't seen much in the world. Imran assured me again and again that the ethos behind it was to protect women and the sanctity of marriage, stressing that it was mostly practised in conservative and rural regions and that things were more liberal in the cities. He was adamant that it didn't amount to subjugation of women and insisted that Muslim men very much respected women – not only did the Quran command them to, also Prophet Muhammad, every Muslim's role model, loved and honoured women and treated them in an exemplary manner. 'The best among you is the one who is kindest to his wife,'[2] he quoted the Prophet. Muhammad himself was apparently always loving and attentive to his wives, helping with household tasks, joking with them and often seeking their advice.[3] They accompanied him on his travels and looked after the community. He loved his young wife Aisha (r)[4] so much that when he shared a drink with her, he would put his lips to the glass exactly where her lips had just been. I was touched and suggested Imran follow the Prophet's example, especially when it came to sharing household chores. Imran loved talking about Muhammad. It saddened him that Westerners were sometimes so dismissive of the Prophet, despite being ignorant about his life and teachings.

We always took a few Islamic books on our travels to read and discuss. On one trip we went on a jeep safari, driving from Islamabad for a couple of days and stopping in the village of Chilas, then heading further into the mountains and glaciers to the spectacular, turquoise-blue Lake Rama where we stayed in a guest house for a few nights and explored the area before moving on to the Deosai Plains, also known as the playground of the devil, at nearly 4,000 metres. This vast area was said to be the highest plain in the world. After a soul-stirring morning walk to the lake we got comfortable on the grass under the shade of a tree and Imran immersed himself in a biography of

Muhammad. Written by the English scholar Martin Lings, it was called *Muhammad: His Life Based on the Earliest Sources*. Imran was so moved by Muhammad's death that he shed tears, which was really saying something. He wasn't the sort of man who was in touch with his feminine side and often joked about those who were. 'You might want to try it some time,' I teased him. But he wouldn't have it – he was too macho for that. Although he loved the Prophet from the bottom of his heart, probably more than he loved anyone else, which was nothing unusual. Every Muslim loves the Prophet deeply, he told me. 'Anyone who speaks or writes about the Prophet always adds "may God's peace and blessings be upon him" out of respect and love,' he explained. 'Even when they mention other Prophets like Jesus, who is considered a Prophet in Islam (rather than the son of God), Muslims utter a similarly respectful greeting.' This deep love and respect for Muhammad explains why Muslims take insults against the Prophet so seriously, I realised.

Lings' biography brought the Prophet to life and described his noble character in all its guises, from caring husband, loving father and loyal companion to wise teacher, benevolent statesman, judge, and Prophet of God who guides people towards salvation. Many of the stories I read and heard were an illustration of his magnanimity and kindness. I liked this one in particular:

Every day, when the Prophet set off to the Ka'ba, a Jewish neighbour would throw litter in his way to show her disrespect for him. But one day when Muhammad left his house, he was surprised to find no litter scattered on the path. He thought the woman must have been taken ill. Concerned for her well-being, he paid her a visit. When she saw the Prophet at her door, the woman was afraid. She wasn't ill; she just hadn't managed to sweep up her own litter in time to throw it outside. She asked him what he wanted. The Prophet told her he was worried about her, because he hadn't seen any litter on the path that day and had come to make sure she was alright. Muhammad's words melted the woman's heart and convinced her that the Prophet truly was God's messenger.

The Quran actually states that the Prophet was sent as a mercy to all creation, not just to humans (21:107), but also to animals, plants and angels. What I read was so different from the little I thought I knew about Muhammad before, which really was just hearsay, and I was glad to be able to correct my preconceptions. We often passed on books to each other and discussed what we were reading. Our conversations engaged me intellectually and raised my spiritual awareness, enabling me to delve deeper into the religion. My curiosity awakened I encouraged Imran to tell me more about Islam and its Prophet, which he happily did. 'There are many stories that relate Muhammad's mercy and kindness to all, something remarkable for his time and that part of the world, and this is why he was loved even by the animals,' Imran told me. Once, for example, the Prophet and his companions were travelling and while he was busy the companions saw a small bird with two chicks. They took its chicks away, and the mother bird started flapping her wings vigorously. When the Prophet came back, he wanted to know who had harmed this bird and asked them to return her chicks to her.[5] And then he told me another famous story about a prostitute who showed kindness to a dog. She saw him panting, dying of thirst next to a well, took off her shoe, tied it with her scarf and drew out some water for the dog. The Prophet informed the woman that God forgave her because of that.[6] Muhammad always asked his companions to treat animals well, not to let them go hungry, exhaust them or upset them in any way. In contrast to these wonderful teachings I sometimes found the reality to be a bit different in Pakistan. For instance I heard donkeys or other animals cry out loudly. I began to realise that I needed to distinguish between the essence of the religion and certain cultural practices and traditions.

Every day new questions arose and we talked about them during our hour-long hikes. The intellectual stimulation made up for the rather basic accommodation in the mountains, which I didn't mind in the least. At one guest house near Lake Rama, the staff boiled hot water and poured it from a bucket into a tub that was large enough for one person to sit in. I mixed extra boiling water with cold water in a separate bucket to pour over myself and even managed to wash my hair. At least we had beds at night and were served hot food every day rather than sleeping in tents and cooking on Bunsen burners. The magnificent mountainous landscape was magical and more than made up for any lack of comfort. I enjoyed my adventurous holidays in Pakistan immensely and as I got used to the environment, I acquired the stomach of a horse and even Montezuma gave up his revenge.

∾

From Lahore we went on a shoot in the Salt Range, where Yousaf Salaudin had a small hunting lodge. It took us a few hours to drive there from the city into the mountains. Imran and Yousaf went round trying to shoot partridges and I accompanied them for the exercise and to take in the scenery. 'Shooting in the wild like this requires far more skill than English shoots, when birds are set free in a field right in front of where everyone stands with a gun,' Imran explained proudly. They actually managed to catch a few, but because they had to be hung to bleed out properly – since Muslims, like Jews, are not allowed to eat blood – dinner was usually a curry made with partridges that someone else had shot earlier. They had a slightly sweet taste and I found them quite delicious. In the evenings we chatted and joked for a while and then I retreated to my room with a book borrowed from Yousaf's shelf while the men carried on gossiping in Urdu.

I read some interesting facts and found out that Islam was apparently the only religion that actively encouraged the abolition of slavery. I mentioned this to Yousaf and Imran and they enthusiastically agreed, explaining that it was Muhammad who encouraged people in order to atone for a mistake, to set free a slave. Moreover, mechanisms were put in place to integrate them into society. Bilal, for example, a slave at the time of the Prophet, became the very first *muezzin*, someone who calls for prayer because of his beautiful voice. Entire dynasties arose from former slaves, such as the Mamluks who reigned in Egypt from the thirteenth century. But even Yousaf and Imran had to admit that in the Pakistan province of Sindh something akin to slavery actually still existed. Both men complained bitterly about the feudal dynasties, like the Bhuttos, who were firmly holding on to power and their ancient traditions – including serfdom and blood feuds – and they blamed Pakistan's failure as a democratic state to a large extent on the feudal system still dominant in the south of the country.

Politics, cricket and religion were everyone's favourite topics of discussion. The next morning we boarded a small wooden motor boat crewed by men in electric-blue waistcoats with matching turbans and white shirts with Nehru collars. We chugged down the Indus, passing the ancient village of Kalabagh nestling in the mountains. For breakfast we were served *doodh* chai cooked with milk, freshly made wholemeal rotis and a delicious Pakistani omelette of chillies, potatoes, onions, tomatoes and cheese topped with coriander. The temperature was pleasant, a little cool from the water and mountains, but sunny. I shared with Imran and Yusuf some more of those intriguing facts I had discovered in the book. It said the Quran contained all kinds of scientific facts that were not known at the time of revelation and were discovered by scientists only centuries later, for example that the planets moved in elliptical orbits around the sun. 'Yes,' Imran proudly confirmed, 'your German scientist Johannes Kepler only discovered in the seventeenth century that planets move around the sun in ellipses.'

Yousaf added that the Quran also described how mountains had roots as deep as the mountains themselves. We were looking at the hills of the Salt Range as we were gliding past and I imagined just how that could be possible. 'None of those facts mentioned in the Quran have so far been disputed by scientists,' Imran exclaimed emphatically. It made me think. 'Clearly these are signs of the Quranic miracle!' Imran exclaimed. Then the men broke into Urdu again. I switched off and made myself comfortable on the boat, closing my eyes to sunbathe while thinking about what they'd said and letting their voices wash over me. I was looking forward to continuing reading when we got back to the house later.

We could debate different aspects of the religion for hours with anyone we met. No matter where we were, everyone was enthusiastic when the talk turned to Islam – from women's issues and religious practice to the greater responsibility of those who are privileged. People explained that Islam was a flexible religion, easy to practise. I had never experienced such love for religion before as I did with the Muslims I met in Pakistan. In London, people usually weren't interested in organised religion, and both religion and politics were generally deemed subjects not to be discussed at dinner parties. Here, everyone talked about them morning, noon and night.

Something else that I learned was the major difference between the Quran and the Bible: when God revealed the verses of the Quran to Muhammad, his companions immediately wrote them down on parchment, papyrus, or even palm leaves and bones, depending on what was available. The text is unchanged to this day. That means the Quran is viewed by Muslims as the direct revelation of God rather than a compilation of inspired stories or reports that were written down by different people decades after he'd passed away.

Later in London I wanted to look through the Bible to

see how it compared and I came across some passages in the Old Testament that made it clear to me that faults must have found their way into the Book. It said that certain Prophets got drunk and committed incest with their own daughters. I was appalled. I couldn't imagine any Prophet behaving like that. This is why Muslims, while required by the Quran to believe in 'earlier Scriptures' such as the Bible, believe that there was an original version of the Bible that was altered to such an extent that the text presently available is no longer the exact word of God. This is one reason that the final Revelation of the Quran upon Muhammad summarises all other revelations that came before and ties up loose ends.

∽

Over time I noticed Imran was getting more and more serious-minded. His work for the hospital was taking its toll, ever new challenges arose, the hospital opening had already been delayed several times and he had to invest ever more time and energy to meet his targets. Gradually, he began to lose interest in social events, especially big parties, however exciting they promised to be. But he made an exception for Mick Jagger's fiftieth birthday bash. The theme was 'French Revolution', and the party was held in a fabulous stately home with sprawling lawns. Guests dressed up as Napoleon, Robespierre or Madame Roland to celebrate with Mick. Hordes of paparazzi had gathered outside, including the notorious duo Dave and Richard. If they were there, you knew you were in the right place. Imran and I arrived separately, as usual. 'He's already there,' Dave whispered knowingly when I passed him. Unfortunately, we were the only two guests not in costume. Imran had refused to dress up, even when I suggested we coordinate our outfits to represent the French national colours.

The party was great, and so was the music courtesy of Jeremy Healy, a DJ I knew from MTV. I headed into the fray, and was soon having such a good time I would have happily stayed all night. But even though Imran knew lots of people, he was ready to leave by midnight. He no longer felt comfortable at raucous parties, surrounded by people drinking, flirting, taking drugs and generally letting their hair down. Instead he longed to be in Pakistan, he felt his country needed him. His stays at home had become prolonged, and he also travelled a lot to India and the Middle East. Although I missed him, I didn't mind his frequent absences but admired his tireless work on behalf of the hospital, as well as his passionate and infectious idealism.

I was travelling a lot myself. I was still presenting for MTV every day, and once a month I reported from various European locations for the *Coca Cola Report*. I also regularly flew to Hamburg to record new episodes of *Bravo TV*, as well as hosting live music shows, giving interviews and doing photo shoots. I was getting increasing recognition for the work I did, especially in Germany.

One of the highlights of my career came in February 1993, when I got to pick up two awards in Berlin on the same evening. First I hosted the *Bravo Supershow*, where I introduced numerous pop bands, and was then presented with a trophy called 'Goldener Otto'. Minutes later I was whisked away with a police escort to the Golden Camera Awards, Germany's equivalent of the Baftas. A make-up artist freshened me up in the car and I headed straight onto the stage to be handed the prestigious television award by German rappers Die Fantastischen Vier. The ceremony was broadcast live to the audience I'd left behind at the *Bravo Supershow*, and as soon as I came off stage I rushed back there to continue hosting.

Imran was very pleased for me and gave me a warm welcome when I got back to London, but I knew he really couldn't relate that much to my work. He'd told me before that in his view most of the videos shown on MTV had a corrupting influence on young people and were especially harmful when broadcast in traditional societies like Pakistan. He did have a point. My very own show aired there too and to my great surprise I was once even asked for an autograph at Islamabad airport. Another time when we were driving through the semi-desert of Sindh, we stopped for a tea break with some people Imran knew. They guided us to a tent in the middle of nowhere. I saw a few blindfolded men with their hands tied behind their backs, sitting on their knees, and when I asked about them, Imran said they were 'decoits', bandits who robbed travellers in remote areas. They'd been caught and were going to be shot without trial. People here believed they had to take the law into their own hands because there was no justice system and as Imran would always complain, the common man was the one who suffered most. It was a very different world and one that scared me at times. As we were having our chai and biscuits in the tent, the host switched on a TV and I couldn't believe my eyes when I suddenly saw presenter Pip Dann on the screen, standing in for me on the *European Top 20* chart show. I was astonished that MTV Europe had even managed to invade this faraway desert that seemed to belong in another century. It felt bizarre to be in the tent watching bright and flashy pop videos with scantily clad girls seductively skipping around, while 'decoits' waited outside to be executed.

As a rule, there was no way round the fact that most videos revolved around sex and seduction, and even if they stopped short of showing the actual act, the basic underlying message was that this was the goal of interaction between men and women. Imran maintained that this was a form of cultural imperialism that undermined traditional values and drove a wedge through society. 'Shouldn't the role of youth TV be to teach values such as modesty, respect and responsibility?' he asked me repeatedly.

Admittedly, Imran came from a different culture, as I had witnessed with my own eyes, and although I could understand his point of view, he was probably exaggerating a little, too. 'MTV is entertainment,' I told him. 'You can't take it too seriously – and anyway, some of the videos are actually quite artistic.'

However, I had to admit that I increasingly felt the futility of it all and began to view some of the content shown on MTV with a much more critical eye. I was particularly turned off by the hip hop videos, all macho posturing and gangsta look, flashy cars and lyrics glorifying violence and misogyny. What kind of a message did they send to the millions of teenagers watching all around the globe? It wasn't as though I disliked hip hop as a genre, and I enjoyed listening to old-school rappers like The Sugar Hill Gang and De La Soul, but while the best videos were about respecting women and 'sisters' who were strong and go-getting – some of which, as I later found out, were actually made by Muslim rappers like Afrika Bambaataa, A Tribe Called Quest or Queen Latifah – in general it tended to be sexist stereotypes that prevailed.

Then there was *Beavis and Butthead,* an animated series that aired on MTV about two socially inept, monumentally moronic, rock-loving teenage boys. These asinine characters communicated in monosyllables and routinely left havoc in their wake. 'What exactly is so great about *Beavis and Butthead*?' I once asked my boss Bill Roedy. 'However much fun it may be to be non PC and subversive, they're hardly a positive example for young people,' I argued.

'It's a very popular show,' was Bill's amiable but emphatic answer. And the ratings were particularly high in Germany, the biggest market for MTV. Apart from a campaign to raise environmental awareness called 'Don't be part of the problem, be part of the solution' and the 'Rock the vote' campaign that ran in the US, I don't remember many distinct messages on MTV. Predominantly MTV was a music station that gave artists a new platform; it entertained and set new trends in the music industry. Of course every video that aired had to meet British broadcasting standards, and some were only shown at night.

Despite his views, Imran always supported my career. He was proud of my achievements, and would boost my confidence before I hosted important events. 'Go on stage like a tigress,' he encouraged me when I was to host my first major awards ceremony, broadcast live on German TV. Or he'd quote the great poet Allama Iqbal, who wrote: 'Oh hawks, don't be afraid of the winds, they are only there to make you fly higher.'

He knew only too well how to deal with professional challenges, the media and the public. 'Who is the most interesting star you've ever interviewed?' journalists often asked me. It was a difficult question to answer because the man I went out with was far more interesting to me than any of the musicians I met through MTV, but of course I couldn't say that. Even reading the Sunday papers together was an educational experience. He would point out terms and euphemisms that he felt showed the anti-Islamic filter through which the Western media processed world news.

'Palestinian freedom fighters are called terrorists, while the Israeli army – an occupying power – are referred to merely as soldiers,' he would complain. He was outraged by what he saw as the UN's failure to help the Muslims during the war in Bosnia; by the massacres taking place; by the siege of Sarajevo; and by the fact that, for a very long time, the international community simply stood by and watched. I learned to view world events from a different perspective.

All the while, Imran was reading the Quran and continuing to study Islam in depth. He was inspired by what he learned and wanted to share it with everyone, and especially me. Unlike most of his other Western friends, my curiosity had been ignited, and I just couldn't learn enough about Islam. Moreover, whenever we had an argument, Imran would reason from an Islamic perspective. Regardless of what we were debating, the only way of getting anywhere was to counter what he was saying with a point equally based on Islamic values. He had no time for mere personal opinions. What mattered to him was the word of God.

Meanwhile I bought my own copy of the Quran, and before long I knew enough to beat Imran at his own game now and then. When I told him I wished we could spend more time together, I would cite the Prophet's advice on time management – from an Islamic book I had found at Imran's in Lahore by a scholar called Dr Seyyed Hossein. I had read that one third of the day should be spent on work, one third on prayers, family, and social activities, and one third on sleep and relaxation.

However, I had to understand that for Imran his 'mission' was always going to be his first priority, no matter what, even if it meant working far longer hours and spending much less time with family than the Prophet recommended. But I believed in what he was aiming to accomplish, so I tried to be accepting and supportive and in my spare time continued my studies.

Some of the things I discovered in Islam seemed relevant even to my own life. The 112th chapter in the Quran, which is very short and one of the last, states that *He is God, the One. The eternal. He has neither begotten, nor was begotten, and comparable to Him there is none.* I found out that the belief in one God, who is the source of everything that exists and the end to which everything returns, who is all encompassing and intimately present, all seeing and all hearing, is one of the central ideas of Islam. The concept is called *al tawhid,* the Oneness of God. 'Anyone who is serious about practising Islam bows down before nothing and no one but God – not before riches, power, social expectations, class, fashion, fame or people,' Imran told me. 'And *that* is *true* freedom.' This notion did seem liberating.

Something similar is actually written in the Ten Commandments. *Thou shalt have no other gods before me,* states the first (Exodus, 20.3). I had never spent much time thinking about this notion, but gradually I began to grasp what it meant. Whoever worships something other than God, believes in anything else but God, or devotes and trusts himself to anything but God, will only suffer from its imperfection and be disappointed by its ephemeral nature and its ultimate powerlessness to create anything or to provide protective, loving care and hope for eternity.

These ideas cast a new light on my work and the scenes of mass hysteria I regularly witnessed when hosting live music shows. Young girls with teeth still covered in braces would sometimes pass out from excitement when they saw their favourite pop star on stage. Was this level of adoration bordering on idolatry? And more importantly, was I facilitating it?

Then there was the obsession with youth that dominated the entertainment industry, even among people well over forty. In pursuit of eternal youth, so many women and even some men in showbiz and London society would go under the knife – have 'boob jobs', liposuction or collagen and Botox injections. Surely, surgically altering their bodies to conform to a certain image that the media had created seemed to be a sign of grave insecurity. No surgeon, toxin or technology in the world can prevent the passage of time. That much I knew. Only in Paradise are we said to be forever young and only our soul is everlasting, therefore it made sense to work on beautifying that.

Fashion was another factor. Imran found the loose-fitting shalwar kameez worn in Pakistan far more feminine than the tight, revealing numbers worn by young Western women. And because they hid any physical imperfections, he argued, Pakistani women were under less pressure than Western women to constantly diet and be slim. Instead, they drew their sense of security from their faith and their families. 'Islam values women for their inner qualities, their character and their faith,' he maintained.

His words chimed with me and made me realise that I had spent years over-preoccupied with my appearance due to the nature of my work. I wanted to make a conscious effort to try and focus more on inner values: to *be* good rather than just look good – although that still remained part of my job. But I began to ditch my mini skirts; my hemlines became longer and my tops less revealing. No one at MTV even noticed – it was the grunge era and short skirts were passé anyway. Once grunge had run its course, everyone else started showing more leg again. But I no longer believed in it and didn't want to attract that kind of attention. Who needs to be whistled at in the street for their long legs? I actually felt more dignified and comfortable as a result, although some of my girlfriends complained that it was a great shame I didn't show my legs any more.

My social life was beginning to change as well. Instead of going to parties and clubs with colleagues or friends, I usually headed home after work to bury myself in books or go to a dinner or an event with Imran. If I did end up at a club or a concert, I quite often felt a bit bored and even out of place because most people weren't there to have good conversations but to get wasted or laid. They'd take pills, which made them suddenly overly affectionate, or they'd start talking like waterfalls after returning from the loo, or acting silly and flirting ferociously when they'd had too much drink. I also drank a bit. It was unthinkable to go out and remain completely sober, and I quite enjoyed the slightly euphoric feeling from drinking champagne. It gave me confidence as I was quite shy by nature, and I felt I was funnier, but I didn't enjoy talking to people who were out of it from whatever substance they'd been consuming. It just felt fake and I knew that most of what they said would be forgotten the next day. I often ended up telling myself I was having a good time, but I wasn't really. It was as though I was putting on a shiny and polished mask, and many times I regretted ending up somewhere I didn't really want to be, just because everyone else was going. 'Kristiane has joined the Pakistani cricket team!' announced my boss Bill Roedy once during a speech at an MTV party. Everyone laughed, but no one could understand my burgeoning interest in Islam. When I told Imran how I felt, he quoted Jalaluddin Rumi, the thirteenth-century Persian poet, theologian and Sufi mystic. 'Hell is surrounded by fun, beauty and seduction, Heaven by poverty, suffering and ugliness,' he wrote. When I thought about it, that was exactly the world I found myself in – one of fun, beauty and seduction. It might not have been hell, exactly, but I could see what he meant. I was definitely starting to outgrow my work and my lifestyle.

Imran and I were still talking about marriage, but the date of the hospital opening continued to be postponed – and was now already a year overdue. Imran took it in his stride. 'It shows that we have no control over our fate,' he said. 'We can only do our best, and leave the rest to God. He rewards our efforts but the outcome is up to Him. *God is the better planner*, says the Quran.' The delay allowed me to deepen my knowledge further before making any major decisions.

I was well aware that Imran wanted to marry a Muslim woman, despite the fact that his religion permitted him to also marry a Christian or a Jew, and in fact Islam does not require the woman to convert. As far as I was concerned, it was anything but certain at this stage that I would convert to Islam. I wasn't exactly a practising Christian either. I had been christened and basically believed in God, but that was it. For me, the real question was whether I, as a Western woman, could adopt Islam as a way of life. It seemed pretty full on. I was definitely looking for some kind of deeper fulfilment. I knew that a TV studio, a happening party or a new Prada dress could not give me the inner satisfaction I longed for; but work was work, and I wanted to continue doing my job as well as I could. Even so, I knew it had its limitations; MTV was never going to take me where I really wanted to go. I was intrigued by this religion that extolled values I could believe in, which transcended this world and gave me guidance on how to live a meaningful life. But I needed more time to figure it all out.

The thought of living with Imran in Pakistan still unsettled me. What would I do if he was always away travelling on behalf of his projects? He was planning to enter politics as soon as the hospital had opened, to fight for greater social justice, the common man, a better education and health care system, and the protection of the environment. He was also determined to fight all forms of corruption. I believed in all of these causes, but there were practical issues that concerned me. I couldn't quite imagine what life would be like in a largely segregated, male-dominated society. Nor was I sure whether he could look after me, and possibly a family, alongside his other commitments. And being so far away I wondered how often I would be able to visit my own family. Imran had always mentioned that he would like his wife to support him in all his activities, which I would have loved to do. But whilst he was in favour of women being educated and pursuing careers, like most of his sisters, he explained to me that the Islamic stance on family life was unambiguous: when a woman had children, they were her first priority. It was her role to bring them up, rather than sending them to day care or having staff look after them. 'It's far better for the children and gives them an emotional security that serves them later in life,' he said. 'Children are our future.' He lamented the fact that the institution of the family was being eroded in the West. 'In Pakistan the family is the fabric of society,' he stressed. 'There are no insurance policies or other state organised help, the family is it and because all the generations live together under one roof, there's always an auntie somewhere who can take care of the children when you need her to. And in turn, the younger generation looks after the older generation.'

I loved the close family bond I saw in Pakistan and I couldn't help but reflect on the difference in attitude in the West, where most families take it for granted that young people will move out at eighteen, as I had, or if they stay with their parents they often have to pay rent. My experiences in Pakistan and reading the Quran did a lot to convince me of the central importance of family, and I vowed to try and make a better effort with my own. I had greater reservations about the gender roles in Muslim families, which I felt entailed huge sacrifices on the part of women. Imran countered that raising the next generation was not only a woman's responsibility but also a privilege. The role of a mother commanded the greatest respect in Islam and was even seen as a path to God, he said. 'Paradise is at the feet of the mother,' the Prophet Muhammad had famously said.[7] Even the most educated and independent women never perceived raising their children as a burden in Islamic societies, Imran told me. 'On the contrary, it is a privilege and the most honourable task there is for a woman,' he said, 'whereas in the West, the role of mother and housewife is undervalued and de-glamourised. It's almost considered uncool to be "just" a housewife and mother.'

I had to admit there was some truth in what he said. I knew women whose self-esteem was flagging because they were 'just mothers', even though they often worked harder than anyone else I knew, from the moment they woke up until the moment they fell into bed. Imran and I discussed the role of women in Islam time and again, and sometimes we also debated the issue with my girlfriends. Patricia was an old friend from school who had moved to London to work for *Bravo*, the youth and music magazine that later co-created my show. A feisty young woman with long curly reddish hair, she was quite opposed to Imran's traditional theories regarding women. Her own mother had worked while raising her and she thought this to be the best way. Another argument was that many families couldn't otherwise afford a decent lifestyle. Imran retorted that Muslim families had other priorities and simply cut back on expenses instead of being slaves to a high-end lifestyle. He used to call her and my friend Brigitte 'the Hamburg women's lib brigade'. I myself doubted that staying at home as a full-time mother was as easy and fulfilling as Imran made it out to be, and felt that it also depended on the husband's support.

But I couldn't entirely dismiss what he said about some of the advantages of traditional gender roles either. After all, he wasn't the only one who'd grown up in that sort of family. I had too, and his words reminded me of the security, care and love my upbringing had given me. It was also refreshing to hear that in Islam women are cherished for their role as mothers and looked after financially by their husbands, rather than being expected to work, run the family, do all the household chores and completely exhaust themselves in the process. According to Imran these were the roles decreed by God, and were in keeping with our nature.

Nevertheless, I still had certain doubts when it came to the issue of women and respect. I reminded him of an evening we'd spent with Yusuf Islam. Formerly known as Cat Stevens, he had converted to Islam in the seventies. Imran and I both loved his music, which was also very popular in Pakistan. Imran invited him round so I could meet him and talk to a convert who came from the same world as I did.

Yusuf arrived with a friend from the mosque, an Islamic scholar. Both had big beards and wore long white robes. Neither of them shook my hand in greeting, but I was familiar with that attitude from Pakistan and didn't take it personally. The two sat down opposite us and after the men had indulged in a bit of small talk and exchanged a few pleasantries, they began talking about Islam. It was all very interesting and polite, and I recognised much of what was said. I would have loved to have talked to Yusuf about his music and his journey into Islam but it felt inappropriate, so I asked them an Islamic question that had been troubling me. *Surah* 4:34 in the Quran says: *If you fear high-handedness from your wives, remind them (of the teachings of God), then ignore them when you go to bed, then hit them.* This seemed to be giving Muslim men licence to beat their wives, and I wanted to know what they made of it. Yusuf's friend explained that it applied only to very serious situations, such as infidelity, and not to harmless disagreements.

'Ideally, a man and his wife should do their best to reconcile, but if this fails, then a man may hit his wife, symbolically, with a newspaper or a toothbrush, but not hurt her and certainly not in the face,' he said.

I was speechless. This attitude was a million miles away from the Islam I had been studying and which Imran had conveyed to me. He saw how taken aback I was and recommended that I shouldn't try to find flaws by taking verses out of context. 'What matters is the overall spirit of the book, and that is one hundred per cent egalitarian. God loves both men and women, and they are equal before God, although they may have different functions in the world,' he insisted. 'When you come across verses in the Quran you don't understand, just leave them aside and return to them another time.' He later suggested that our guests obviously subscribed to a strict, literalist school of thought.

Be that as it may, I'd had enough. I wanted to talk to open-minded, undogmatic Muslims who believed in a more enlightened or relaxed form of Islam. I was sure they must exist as well, and indeed, it wasn't long before I met one. Imran and I had been invited to a party at the home of Ramola Bachchan, the brother-in-law of the Indian film star Amitabh Bachchan. I soon noticed among the guests a charismatic woman with a certain Eastern flair, who instantly struck me as likeable. She wore an elegant black shalwar kameez but had her *dupatta* draped over her shoulder rather than over her head in the customary style. Ruby and I soon got talking. She was a TV producer from Pakistan and had also directed the video clip about the hospital project called 'Let's bowl out cancer', which Imran was showing during his fundraising dinners.

I liked Ruby. She was also born in Lahore, and had grown up with her grandmother because she was quite a naughty child, her father was often away travelling, and her grandmother, who had more time, was the only one who could deal with her. Later, at the age of seven, she and her parents moved to London. She told me that she was raised as a Muslim, and grew up with two cultures. She spoke of her religion in clear, simple terms, and basically told me to relax. 'Everyone is free to practise Islam their own way, regardless of their gender,' she told me. 'We answer to God and no one else. Whether a woman wears a headscarf or not for example is her own choice. It is between her and God.'

It was a weight off my mind. Ruby was the first woman to show me how a Muslim in a Western society can combine faith, tradition, career, a social life and self-fulfilment. Ruby's attitude was on the liberal side but she obviously loved God as well. Whenever she recounted a successful personal experience she finished up with the words *shukr, al hamdulillah*, which means 'Thanks All Praise to God'. She was an inspiration.

Chapter 6

Over

And if you make it through the trouble and the pain,
That may be the time for you to know His name.

Yusuf Islam

I'd become a traveller between two worlds. In one I was the queen of teen, a high-profile presenter of music shows with record ratings, hosting events and travelling widely, recognised wherever I went; in the other, I was gradually discovering a completely different world: the culture and religion of Islam that I had got to know in Pakistan and through Imran's friends in London.

Even though I was more critical of my work and it sometimes irritated me, by and large I still enjoyed it. At the same time, my fascination with Islam was growing. I was learning to appreciate the perspective the religion taught and understand the idea that we serve a higher goal and must be patient and accept our destiny. And it was Imran who showed me what this could mean in practice.

Shortly after I'd spent the Christmas of 1993 with my family in Hamburg I flew back to London to make the final preparations for another trip to Pakistan. My sister and I were planning to fly to Lahore to visit Imran and travel through Sindh. Imran was waiting for us in Lahore at his father's house and looking forward to our arrival. His London flat was freezing when I came through the door. I tried to switch on the heating but it wasn't working, so I had a go at lighting one of the gas fires. While I was trying to get it going, a huge flame suddenly shot out at me. I leapt back in shock, and in seconds it had caught the bunch of dried tiger grass next to the fireplace. Before I knew it, the fabric that covered the low ceiling and gave it a tent-like feel was also on fire. I ran into the kitchen to get a bucket of water, and by the time I got back the whole room was in flames. Luckily I had enough presence of mind to shut the door and, with shaking hands, to dial 999. It was the holiday period and it took an eternity for the fire services to turn up. They also got the address wrong, and I had to call several more times, eventually having to run down to the end of the road to fetch them. But when they finally arrived, they had the situation under control in no time. On their way out they patted me on the shoulder and the nightmare was over.

What was left was a blackened shell of a room, a dreadful stench and complete chaos. Among all the charred clothes, melted CDs and singed papers, the one book that appeared to be undamaged was the Quran. I paced around desperately, feeling relieved that nothing worse had happened and that I was alright. But I was in a state of shock. It took me a while to come to my senses and realise that I needed to tell Imran what had happened. It was his apartment, and he was fond of it. It was his personal haven when he was in London and just about all he owned. Everything else he'd possessed, he'd given to the hospital.

I went to stay with a friend and, when I finally got through to Imran in Lahore, expecting him to be angry, all he said was '*al hamdulillah*, my sins have been burned! Come to Pakistan quickly, I miss you!' Not a word of reproach, no questions as to the extent of the damage and insurance claims. Imran accepted the whole episode as fate. Nothing happens without the will of God. 'Money comes and goes, we cannot hold on to it when we die,' he said. 'Don't worry about anything, just get on the next plane and come to Pakistan.' I was impressed by his calm reaction, but, like many Muslims, Imran was able to process and accept fate – God's will – no matter how challenging, with dignity and without losing his cool.

Getting on the next plane wasn't an option, though. I spent the following days dealing with the damage. The services sent two men round to inspect the gas fires. They sealed them with hazard stickers adorned with skulls and told me the heaters were death traps and didn't even have extractor fans, nor had they been installed properly. I carried on tidying up and throwing things out, and took all the clothes to the dry cleaners.

I also had to look for somewhere to live, since I obviously couldn't stay in the flat, so I phoned Steve Fargnoli's secretary. When she came round and saw the devastation she immediately invited me to stay in Steve's home office, which was also in Chelsea. I turned up with a huge pile of smoke-ridden clothes that desperately needed washing, which I hung up to dry on every spare surface, including radiators and lamp shades. A neat and tidy Virgo, Steve couldn't believe his eyes when he returned from his holiday. Initially I only planned to stay for a month, which was the length of time I thought it would take to sort out Imran's apartment. But instead I ended up renting the room for a whole year.

After all that stress, the holiday in Pakistan with my sister was just what I needed. Imran had the top floor of his father's house to himself, and while he was working I spent hours with my sister on the balcony, drinking chai and chatting. Susanne and I hadn't seen much of each other since she'd moved to Milan where she worked as a design duo with her husband. Her job, like mine, was demanding. But despite both of us being busy and living far apart, our relationship remained strong and close. When we'd met up for Christmas at our parents' house a few weeks before, we'd been amazed to see that we were both wearing the exact same coat – she'd bought it in Milan, I'd found it in London.

We could tell each other everything, and as the elder sister

I was always protective of her. Later during that visit we went to Sindh, and when it turned out that there was a shortage of space in one of the guest houses, it was suggested that she share a room with two single beds with Imran's friend Zak, another former cricketer. 'Treat my sister the way you'd treat your own,' I snapped. A Pakistani woman sharing a room with a man she's not married to would be unthinkable. Imran realised the suggestion was a mistake, and his friend ended up sleeping on the floor in the hallway.

Once again, I had to wonder how much respect women in Pakistan really enjoyed, especially Western ones. Susanne wondered too. She wasn't sure that Imran was really the right man for me and had her reservations about how supportive he would be once we were married and living together in Pakistan. She saw how much I needed to rely on him there. I wasn't the independent Kristiane she knew.

On that visit I got to know three of Imran's sisters, who were strong, confident women, just as he'd described them. They came over to the family house and we chatted over tea and samosas. One of them was a surgeon, another was studying economics, and the third had been to university but was now a housewife. Their husbands supported their choices. I asked them about the role of women in Islam, and they all stressed how many rights Islam had granted women as early as the seventh century. A husband had to protect his wife, feed, clothe and house her. Even if he was poor and married a queen, it was his duty to look after the family. A woman could keep the money she earned during marriage for herself; she was not obliged to spend it on her family. If she decided to do so, it was considered as charity. At the same time, a wife had every right to acquire, own and dispose of property, and to represent herself independently in court.

As a Western woman, I took the latter for granted. To me, these were basic human rights. But I learned that in fact, along with the right to vote, these rights had only been won by women in the West relatively recently, whereas they had always existed in Islam.

However, I felt that until now I'd got by perfectly well without male protection and had to ask myself what exactly this 'protection' entailed – and at what point it turned into oppression. All the women I met in Pakistan assured me that oppression of women and infringement of their rights was essentially un-Islamic behaviour. Muslims are supposed to base their attitudes to women on the Prophet's own family, they said, and, without exception, all his wives were strong personalities, who played active roles in society and contributed to the greater good of the community.

One of the most notable women in Islamic history, they told me, was Khadija, the Prophet's first wife. She was a successful businesswoman and fifteen years older than him when *she* proposed to *him*. She believed in Muhammad when he had his first revelation. She soon became the first Muslim and supported him until the end of her life with her wealth and her energy. After Khadija died he eventually married Aisha, his youngest wife but another strong lady. She later became one of the main teachers of the community and, after the Prophet's death, taught his followers about his practices and ideas. A lot of her reports became officially part of the religion of Islam and a significant portion of the Shariah (Islamic code of conduct) is based on the collection of *hadiths* (the Prophet's sayings and actions) narrated by her. She was never shy about correcting some of the Prophet's companions if they misquoted his words or misrepresented his behaviour.

'That's all well and good,' I said when I heard this. 'But that was 1,500 years ago. What about today?' 'The Prophet's wives were role models for all Muslim women, then and now,' Usma, the surgeon, replied. 'They taught women to be strong and dignified; to fulfil their role both in society and the family. Women like men should both seek education from the cradle to the grave,' she added, quoting Muhammad.

I got to talk at length to some of the women I met on that visit and found many of them inspirational. Imbessad was the young wife of Yousaf, Imran's good friend. She had no children and supported him during his election campaign to become governor of Lahore. While I was there she was busy rallying for him and giving speeches in front of crowds of women, and she still found time to run the huge *haveli* where they lived and oversee its renovation. Despite an army of servants, it wasn't easy for her. They were mostly illiterate and simple people, and she lost her temper with them many times because 'none of them understand anything', she complained. Then there was Moby's wife Samina, a well-to-do businesswoman who ran the factory that her late husband had left behind. She became my dearest and closest friend in Pakistan. She took wonderful care of me and on occasion even stood up to Imran on my behalf – she didn't let any man tell her what to do.

Imbessad and Samina were interesting personalities in their own rights and couldn't have seemed less oppressed. In public they wore shalwar kameez with a matching *dupatta*, which they would either throw over their shoulders or over their heads to cover their hair if they were in a conservative environment or out on the streets of Lahore. When it got cold, they would wear large cashmere or woollen shawls. My sister and I loved going with Samina and Imran's sisters to the bazaars in Islamabad and Lahore. They took us to places that only insiders knew, and we stocked up on beautiful hand-embroidered pashmina shawls.

On my many trips, Samina and I used to chat at her house while Imran was out on appointments. She had a great set-up with maids and servants who had worked with her for decades and looked after us while we were deep in conversation. They served freshly squeezed juices, chai and snacks whenever we wanted and, of course, cooked all the main meals and cleaned the house. They even did my laundry, so I always came back from Pakistan with my clothes freshly washed and ironed.

Samina put the Quran's teaching about modest dress in context for me. What exactly it meant depended on the environment and the culture. In the West, 'modest dress' might mean jeans and a longish blouse, whereas for women in Pakistan it might be a shalwar kameez or even a burka. I also asked Samina about certain women's issues such as 'forced marriages'. She admitted that they happened but maintained they were completely un-Islamic. She also told me about the cult of virginity, explaining that it was very important in Pakistani culture for a woman to go into marriage as a virgin – so much so that many women who'd defied this rule would go to a doctor before marriage to have themselves 'stitched up' so their husband would think their virginity was intact on their wedding night. What a bizarre type of cosmetic surgery, I thought to myself.

Truth be told, I also met women on that trip who seemed far from headstrong and self-determined, although they were clearly not suffering from poverty. When we were having tea with one of Imran's acquaintances, I noticed that his wife had blank eyes and didn't take part in the conversation at all. She seemed apathetic and depressed, and her husband was somewhat dismissive of her. In fact, most of the time when I was travelling with Imran, we didn't meet women at all, because they didn't mix with men and the ones I did meet only spoke Urdu. Amongst the educated elite, however, most people spoke English and were quite relaxed. There was an international scene in the country's capital Islamabad where all the diplomats and government officials were based. Karachi was known as a business centre or party city, while Lahore had the culture and the flair. But living the high life wasn't Imran's sort of thing any more and he largely avoided it.

When I was alone with Imbessad in Lahore or Samina and her friends in Islamabad they often complained bitterly about Pakistani men. Husbands are selfish, they come and go as they please, they said. Women would wait for hours with dinner on the table only to be told by their husband on his return that he'd already eaten. They blamed their mothers-in-law, who adored their sons unconditionally and spoiled them – that's why they all turned out to be such machos, they grumbled. But I had heard similar complaints back in Europe and therefore shrugged them off.

Selfish men and oppressed women exist all over the world, I realised, and the reasons are manifold – from culture, upbringing and religious background to personal shortcomings, and sometimes a combination of them all.

∾

I had become a bit of a bookworm and was devouring Islamic literature by both Eastern and European writers. Imran arranged for us to meet some of them. Gai Eaton was the author of *Islam and the Destiny of Man*. It was considered the definitive English-language work on Islam and we both enjoyed it immensely. It explored many different aspects of the religion, from Islam's roots in Eastern and European history, to its political, cultural and spiritual aspects.

I was curious but didn't know what to expect from this scholar – after all, the book was quite a serious read. We went to meet him for lunch on a sunny summer day and I dressed for the occasion in a white shirt and long skirt. Gai Eaton was already at the restaurant and stood up to greet us. Tall, elegant and formal in his grey suit and tie with a handkerchief in the top pocket, he smoked a cigarette with an old-fashioned cigarette holder and had such an air of refined eccentricity about him that I wasn't surprised when he told us drily that at one point he had trained as an actor. He had led a very full life. Born in Switzerland, he joined the British Foreign Office after studying at Cambridge and spent time in Jamaica, Egypt and India. When he retired he busied himself working in the Cultural Centre of the London Central Mosque on Regent's Park, guiding Muslims who sought his advice, editing the *Islamic Quarterly* and translating the *khutbas*, the sermons during the

Friday prayers, into English, usually adding his own twist. 'I get away with saying things that born Muslims couldn't,' he confessed with a twinkle in his eye. 'They consider me a bit of a rebel in the mosque, but somehow they feel they can't get rid of me.' We all smiled – it wasn't hard to imagine. Gai had the understated humour of an upper-class English gentleman and, even though he was already over seventy when we met that first time, he seemed young at heart. 'The mosque is Saudi influenced,' he explained. 'They usually follow a rather austere version of Islam which is opposed to Sufism, the spiritual dimension. I'm the unlikely but tolerated Sufi in the mosque, who's become irremovable. Anyone asking about Sufism gets sent straight to my room.'

I liked Gai immediately and my initial shyness soon dissolved. Imran explained how he was in the process of rediscovering Islam himself since his mother died, and asked him how he had come to Islam. 'I was always interested in philosophy and studied the great philosophers in the hope of finding guidance and wisdom relevant to my own life,' Gai recounted. 'But eventually I realised that what they wrote were their personal thoughts and subjective philosophies. Therefore, their opinions could never help me in my quest for a higher, absolute truth. Not only that, I realised these philosophies also failed to offer me concrete guidance and practical instructions for my daily life. It was at this point that I began to study the sacred Scriptures and eventually I found the answers I was looking for in Islam.'

'So when you converted how did your life change?' I asked.

'Initially, it didn't, really,' he laughed. 'I converted in 1951 in Cairo with a teacher I met, Martin Lings, before leaving for my beloved Jamaica again where I didn't even know any Muslims. I was thirty years old at the time and by no means a good Muslim. But the seed had been planted.'

I was enthralled. As a journalist, Gai Eaton had a wonderful ability to explain complex ideas in a succinct and accessible way and it was a pleasure to listen to him. I felt I could trust him, and I confessed that although I was also fascinated by Islam I wondered whether I would ever be able to grasp the full depth of the religion – and, more worryingly, keep to its rules. On this score he set my mind at ease. 'No one becomes a true Muslim overnight,' he said with a smile. Delving into the depths of Islam was a process that lasted a lifetime. 'What's more important is to reflect on your behaviour every day anew and to keep asking yourself how you can become a better person,' he told me. 'The Quran was revealed to the Prophet Muhammad over a period of twenty-three years, so the people around him had plenty of time to get accustomed to the Divine commands. God never demanded that people put everything into practice at once.'

Gai's words were reassuring. He also encouraged me to see Islam not so much in contrast to Christianity but as a continuation of it. His own cultural background was Christian, although 'the religion never attracted me,' he said. 'It is important to realise that Islam does not negate Christianity,' he explained. 'On the contrary, many of its central values are also found in Islam, such as belief in God and the principles of charity and compassion.' In his opinion, 'the advantage of Islam is that as the youngest revealed religion, it summarises and completes earlier Divine messages. And its sacred knowledge is relatively easy to access.'

After this conversation I realised that, above all, Islam was not merely an intellectual exercise, but a way of life and a path to God. I felt inspired to try and put some of these ideas into practice, however I could. For a start, I tried to introduce some substance to my presenting work and began to include Nusrat Fateh Ali Khan on my show on MTV when we publicised bands' tour dates. And on my German show I mentioned green issues in between the usual youth topics and suggested to the viewers they might want to think about visiting their grandmothers. It seemed to strike a chord – the environmental features actually became really popular. Not so sure about the grandmothers though.

Some time later, Imran and I went to the Caribbean together accompanying a cricket tournament through the West Indies, which was a fabulous experience. Imran commentated on the matches and, wherever they took place – in Jamaica, Saint Vincent or Guyana – it was a national holiday and party time. Some of the locals arrived in big hats and funky outfits, and carrying huge ghetto blasters or enjoying family picnics nearby. The whole island was involved. Those who didn't get seats climbed on trees and watched the matches from up there. In Trinidad, Imran and I made the big mistake of sunbathing in the midday sun without protection because the wind felt so nice and cool. We both had such bad sunburn that we suffered for the rest of the trip. The former English player Ian Botham, who was also commentating, made matters worse – when we told him about it he found it so amusing that he slapped me heartily on my thigh. We stayed in the shade from then on, reading our Islamic books whenever we could. But suddenly a rumour started circulating that some of the Pakistani players had complained I was reading the Quran in a bikini. It wasn't true, and I wondered what they were doing peering into our private balcony in the first place, when the Quran tells men – and women – to keep their gaze lowered. Luckily such judgemental attitudes were the exception to the rule; most of the Muslims I met welcomed my interest in their religion and were extremely helpful.

Imran and I were still planning to get married and on our next trip to Pakistan we started dreaming of living on a farm with lots of animals in Skardu, a very airy and particularly beautiful mountainous region near Kashmir in the north of the country. The sight of pink cherry blossoms against a backdrop of snow-capped mountains in the bright blue sky was heart-stopping. We went on long walks in the vast dried river beds and in the foothills of the mountains, where I collected the most magical stones and fossils I had ever seen: bright neon green or shiny silver ones, clear crystals, and perfectly preserved shells turned to stone. I was so enamoured with all of them that much to Imran's annoyance we had to carry a whole collection back to Lahore in two heavy bags, where I decorated his jacuzzi with my special collection.

But soon after that the preparations for the hospital opening began to gather momentum, and Imran was fundraising all over the world, which meant we gradually saw less of one another. He had more and more to do in Pakistan, travelling up and down the country rallying support. He left it pretty much to me to sort out the renovation in his apartment, which was a huge responsibility. I was helped out by a team of architects and my friend Lynn, an interior designer. Imran insisted he was under a great amount of pressure in the run-up to the opening of the hospital and I just had to bear with him. I appreciated how much he was doing for the project and was ready to support him and make all the sacrifices necessary. But when I visited Pakistan in September 1994, I felt for the first time that something was wrong. On a trip to Lake Rama he was a bit quieter than usual, but when I asked him what was on his mind, all he did was drop mysterious hints, but wouldn't elaborate. At one point he disappeared for a few hours and I didn't know what to make of it all.

Straight after that trip I flew to Boston to interview the Rolling Stones and Lenny Kravitz, a highlight in my career. Lenny was the Stones' support act and I had announced him many times on stage before, so we had a good chat before doing the interview. The Stones were good fun as well. We took photos with some competition winners, and the band couldn't have been more helpful. Mick invited me for dinner with him after the show. I was flattered, but because I was there with my team I asked if I could bring my producer. He looked at her, and despite her scary dominatrix attire of tight black PVC pants, platinum blonde hair, silver chains and multiple piercings, he agreed. The trouble was that when I told her about our invitation, she simply said no and strictly forbade me from going too, insisting we have dinner at a Chinese restaurant with the crew instead. I couldn't believe it and protested that this was a once-in-a-lifetime invitation, but she dug her heels in and suggested we go for a drink after dinner. We finally made it to Mick's hotel around midnight. He was tired by then but politely invited us in. 'I've been waiting all evening and ended up having dinner alone,' he said when we entered the suite, gesturing to a very long dining table. I doubted Mick had been stood up by many girls in his life, but he graciously offered us a glass of wine and we chatted for a while. When he asked about Imran, I told him I had just got back from Pakistan and that Imran had been talking about marriage for two years but wanted to wait until the hospital had opened. Mick just looked amused. He warned me I should give it some serious thought and that, with my European mentality, I would no doubt find life in Pakistan very hard.

'I've had my share of fun, so why not experience something different,' I replied. He obviously wasn't convinced. 'It's one thing to visit a country like that but quite another to actually live there,' he said. A note of concern crept into his voice. 'Don't you know what sort of a reputation Imran has?' he asked me. Of course I knew but I genuinely thought he was serious about marrying me. When I said so to Mick, he answered with a look that spoke volumes.

Mick's words were somewhat of a reality check, and when I thought about what he had said the next day, I felt like I was slowly coming down from cloud nine. I walked around Boston checking out the shops, but ended up rushing out of a mountaineering outfitters suddenly feeling sick from the food I'd eaten the evening before.

That year, Imran and I spent New Year's Eve apart for the first time. He didn't celebrate it at all, since he was in Pakistan and it is not a traditional Muslim day of celebration, and I went to the Baltic coast with my friend Nora, her small son and a couple of her friends. I felt desperately lonely, and she and I went on long walks by the sea, pushing her son's pram against the wind. Our long talks did me good. But it was icy cold, foggy and dark, and my thoughts kept drifting to Pakistan, where I knew it would be warm and sunny. On New Year's Eve, one of Nora's friends cooked a nice meal and everyone drank and smoked. I didn't want to be there and felt deeply unhappy. I managed to speak to Imran just once, only for him to tell me how busy he was with the fundraising campaign.

So that was how 1995 began. It was an appropriate start to what turned out to be one of the toughest but most important years of my life.

In spring, Imran called me to announce out of the blue that one of his spiritual advisers had told him that our relationship couldn't last. My world was turned upside down. I felt completely out of my depth. I hadn't seen him for months, was working flat-out, supervising the renovations in his flat and still living in Steve's guest room. I was devastated, confused and deeply hurt. My feelings fluctuated between hope and despair – one minute I missed him and felt lost and disorientated, the next minute I would have a flash of optimism. The pressure was making me ill. I developed a skin rash, lost my appetite and often couldn't keep down the little I did eat. A friend recommended I see a specialist in Harley Street.

The practice had high stucco ceilings and was stylishly decorated, with shelves of books and Eastern-looking ornaments. It felt more like a private home than a doctor's practice and had an instantly calming effect on me. I noticed a lot of artefacts from the Middle East, bottles of Arabic perfume, and calligraphy on the wall, and when I complimented the doctor on their beauty, she said they were gifts from her Arabic patients. Not only that, much to my surprise, it turned out that

Dr Anne Coxon was a Muslim convert. Blonde-haired, blue-eyed, gentle and empathic, she was the classic English rose. She took her time talking to me and soon established that the cause of my ailments was largely psychological. When I told her about Imran's spiritual adviser, she recommended I talk to one myself. She suggested I accompany her to a mosque, where she would introduce me to Shaykh Nazim, her Sufi master. It can't hurt, I thought to myself.

The mosque was housed in a building that used to be a convent on St Ann's Road in Tottenham, a district of North London with a big Turkish community. It was called The Priory, and from the outside it looked nothing like a Muslim place of worship. Instead of a minaret, it had gables and several entrances. We walked into a large room full of people, most of whom looked Turkish, but there were also Pakistanis, Arabs and European Muslims there, including children and many women wearing headscarves. They were all gathered around a man leaning on a walking stick and dressed in a long grey robe and a green turban, with big laughing, blue-green eyes and a longish, grey beard. This was Shaykh Nazim. Every Sufi group has a Shaykh, I found out, who assumes the role of teacher, spiritual guide and counsellor. Shaykh Nazim was kind enough to give Dr Coxon and me a private audience. He listened to my problems and advised me to be patient and to pray to God. He also suggested I come to one of his lectures when I had time. I thanked him. Although I wasn't sure I would come back, it felt like I had taken an important step: for the first time, I had entered an Islamic environment alone, without Imran.

∽

So far, I had kept my interest in Islam quiet and never spoke about it to the press. In March I presented the 100th anniversary edition of *Bravo TV* in Hamburg, a milestone marked by a carefully orchestrated media fanfare, and I gave a lot of interviews. One reporter with the daily *Bild* newspaper – the equivalent of the *Sun* in Britain – must have done his homework, because he asked me outright if I had already converted to Islam for my boyfriend. I answered truthfully that I hadn't converted but that I was a Muslim 'at heart'. The next questions were about my relationship with Imran, about which I had never spoken in public. Even though my response was guarded, the paper carried a story the next day with the headline 'Kristiane Backer – The Next First Lady of Pakistan?'

Nothing could have been further from the truth. A week later, Imran called from Pakistan to accuse me of betraying him with another man and to tell me it's over. I had been seen one night leaving a man's house in the early hours of the morning, he said. It was an absurd suggestion, and completely unfounded. In floods of tears, I tried to convince him that someone had made a mistake. If we were going to break up then we should be able to talk about it like adults, I argued. Circumstances seemed to be conspiring against us, and I couldn't do anything about it. I was so sad. Imran was my love. And his accusation was untrue.

In the meantime I had become friends with Dr Coxon, whom I now called by her Muslim name Dr Amina. When I told her over dinner what had happened, she just shook her head. In Islam, malicious slander was a great sin, she said, and Allah sided with its victims, especially when they were women. 'Don't worry,' she comforted me. 'Every time someone slanders you, you receive a blessing from God.' Then she told me a story:

Whenever the Prophet Muhammad left Medina, he was accompanied by one of his wives. They tended to the wounded and kept guard at the camps. On such trips, the women would travel in palanquins carried by camels, seated behind curtains and hidden from the beating sun and prying eyes. One morning, after the party had rested and the camels had been reloaded in preparation for moving on, the Prophet's youngest wife Aisha realised that she'd lost her necklace and went to look for it. Nobody noticed she was gone and the procession set off. When Aisha found her necklace and realised the caravan had left, she decided to stay exactly where she was, waiting for someone to come looking for her. Soon, a young man named Safwan, who was travelling on his own behind the caravan, came along. When he recognised Aisha, he helped her on to his camel and proceeded himself on foot. They finally caught up with the others, who were all greatly relieved and welcomed Aisha back. But some people who had seen her arrive in Medina with Safwan began to talk ill of them, making intimations that she had committed adultery. Initially, Aisha was unaware of this, since she had fallen ill and was staying with her parents to recover. She was upset and saddened when she heard the rumours.

Of course, the Prophet had also heard them. In an address to the people, he called on them to think well of both Aisha and Safwan. But many took the opportunity to ridicule the Prophet and incite disagreement amongst the Muslims. So the Prophet went to talk to his wife, who was still with her parents.

'If what they say is true, then you should fear God,' he said. 'If you are guilty of what people say you did, then seek God's mercy. He accepts his servants' repentance.'

When Aisha heard these words, her sadness was transformed into anger. She looked to her parents, expecting them to support her, but they remained silent. 'Have you nothing to say?' she cried. 'By Allah,' replied her father Abu Bakr (r),[1] the closest friend of the Prophet's, in despair. 'What should we say? We do not know.'

Aisha began to weep, but soon regained her composure. 'I have no need to repent for any of the things you accuse me of,' she said. 'By Allah, were I to admit to doing what I have been accused of – and Allah knows I am innocent – then I would be telling an untruth. If I deny these accusations, then no one will believe me. By Allah I can only say what the father of Prophet

Yusuf said, *Patience is beautiful and Allah is my protection against what you describe'* (12:18). The Prophet sank into deep thought and verses of the Quran were revealed to him:

> *Why did not the believing men and the believing women,*
> *when they heard of this slander, think well of their own people,*
> *and say: 'This is clearly a false accusation'? Why did they not*
> *produce four witnesses? If they do not produce the required wit-*
> *nesses, then they are the liars in God's eyes.* (24:12,13)

Abu Bakr was relieved, and kissed his daughter, while his wife told Aisha to take her place by her husband's side. 'By Allah,' responded Aisha, 'I will not stand by his side, because I have only Allah to thank for my acquittal.'[2]

When Dr Amina had finished telling me this story, she explained that according to the Quran malicious slander is something very serious, and is punished nearly as severely as adultery. I felt a little better now that I knew that God protected and honoured women, and that it was the truth that counted. Still, when I went home to my parents in Germany I couldn't stop my tears at dinner in a restaurant one night. I told them everything. They knew I had adored Imran and would have gone through everything and anything with him. He had always told me that anything could happen once he entered politics and that it wouldn't be a cushy existence. I never imagined he would one day let me down like this. But there was a lesson in this as well for me: not to put a human being on a pedestal – God is the only one worthy of worship! My parents understood my grief and did their best to console me, but at the same time they were relieved that I wouldn't be moving to Pakistan. My mother had been terribly worried and had even gone to find out about mixed marriages at a marriage advice centre, where the clerk had asked her to please let her know if the marriage was a success because, in her experience, mixed marriages generally didn't work out in the long term and it was usually the woman who suffered. I dismissed this as a provincial attitude; I had seen many happy mixed marriages in London. But Imran had often told me that in Pakistani culture, love marriages were regarded with a degree of suspicion because the fear was that they wouldn't last – whereas the customary arranged marriages were seen as far more promising and were the norm. At this point, I wondered whether he wasn't just trying to convince himself.

A while later, Imran and I talked again and managed to clear the air a little. It was important to me that he accepted that I hadn't done what he suspected, and in the end I think he did. But our relationship was still over, even though we continued talking regularly on the phone. I thought he shouldn't pay such heed to his spiritual advisers and should listen to his heart instead, but I was powerless to change his mind.

Dr Amina and my other friends did their best to cheer me up, but they all agreed I was well out of it. In all likelihood, Imran would never have been able to spend much time with me. His personal mission was always going to be his first priority. At that point, it was his hospital project, and later it would be politics. Although I didn't mind that because I believed in his mission, I had to accept and submit to what was obviously God's will.

Chapter 7

Becoming a Muslim

If you don't have
This Die and Become,
You are just a sad guest
On this dark earth.

Johann Wolfgang von Goethe, 'Blessed Yearning', *West-Eastern Divan*

The period that followed was a time of heartache but it was also the beginning of a new phase in my life. I soon found a small flat for rent above a restaurant in Chelsea. It was good to be in my own space. After a period of hibernation I started to feel over the worst and optimistic that life could only get better. But instead, I was in for another shock.

When the *Bild* newspaper quoted me saying that I was 'a Muslim at heart', it triggered an avalanche of media coverage, much of which made it appear as though I had lost the plot. 'Kristiane prays five times a day while the cool crowd goes to rock concerts,' read one headline. I could live with that, but other journalists went so far as to suggest I supported terrorism. My parents and the *Bravo TV* team were constantly faxing me the latest reports that had appeared in Germany and everyone seemed to find it objectionable that I had spoken so openly about the religion of my heart. I regretted ever having made this innocuous remark. I never imagined there would be such a negative public reaction in my country and I was pretty sure it wouldn't have happened quite like this with the media in England, particularly in London, where tolerance and acceptance of other people's beliefs are taken for granted. Not one journalist had actually bothered to ask me the reasons for my alleged conversion and what that meant for me. I was stressed out and upset, and I missed Imran and the welcoming warmth I had encountered in Pakistan. Above all, I missed our discussions about spirituality and Islam. Of course, I had numerous friends and acquaintances with whom I could talk about religion, sometimes even in depth. But these conversations tended to be exhausting and even argumentative rather than uplifting and nurturing. I was constantly having to battle negative preconceptions. What I longed for was contact with like-minded people.

On weekends I sometimes went for country walks with Tony James, who had become my walking partner. His glamorous girlfriend Penny, who was great fun and also had a motherly side, didn't mind. She was my friend too and wasn't into hiking. Tony was a sensitive listener with a feeling for spirituality and, like Penny, he said to me that Imran obviously didn't deserve me. I talked to all my friends and it helped to get things off my chest. Whenever I needed to seek refuge from the world at large or just wanted to be in the company of Muslims, I would go to the mosque that Dr Amina had taken me to. The group, led by Shaykh Nazim, belonged to the Naqshbandi *tariqa*, one of the major spiritual orders of Sufi Islam that originated in Central Asia and also became prominent in Russia, Turkey and the Balkans. *Tariqa* means 'way, path, method', and in a spiritual sense refers to a group of people who are travelling together on the path to God.

Initially, I sought out the company of the Sufis because they welcomed me with open arms and gave me a feeling of acceptance and security. They had no idea what had happened to me and were just friendly and warm-hearted. I didn't need to say anything, I didn't need to justify myself, I could just *be*, and that did me a world of good.

The group consisted of quite a cosmopolitan mix of people

from all walks of life, including doctors, politicians, British aristocrats, a Persian prince, even the former king of Yemen and many simple, down-to-earth people as well as some slightly crazy ones. The women I met there were also kind and helpful. They showed me how to wash before prayer, wrote down particular prayers for me, and generally welcomed me into their midst. Before a lecture from the Shaykh – he would often turn up late – or afterwards, we would sit in small circles and chat amongst ourselves. Sometimes I opened up and spoke about my troubles. Then the women comforted me and told me that I needed to trust: trust in God who is infinitely good and trust that everything that happened was by the will of the almighty and merciful God. 'According to Islam, whenever we are struck by illness or misfortune or someone hurts us, there is a higher purpose behind it, which we may not understand at the time,' one of them said to me. 'That's where trust comes in. Through suffering, God helps us to better ourselves and make good our mistakes. It is a form of purification and also God's way of testing the strength of our faith and the goodness of our character.' Another lady suggested I look on the bright side. 'Suffering draws us closer to God and that is our aim in life,' she said. Then she quoted Rumi who had said, 'It is pain that draws man to his Lord, because when he is well, he doesn't remember the Lord.' I tried to look at the positive and believe that there was a higher, spiritual perspective on what I had just been through, and all the advice I was given helped me a lot. But it took quite a while for my heart to catch up with my mind. Rumi, I learned, likened suffering to the boiling water in which chickpeas cook until they become soft and delicious.

Speaking of chickpeas – the Sufis would occasionally invite me to join them for a meal they had cooked, most often a tasty curry, and I loved the atmosphere, partly because it reminded me of Pakistan. I watched with interest as they prayed and I joined them when they sat in circles on the floor and sang

God's praises, repeating the beautiful names of God and honouring the Prophet. These devotional practices, almost like chanting, are among the key forms of worship for Sufis, and are known as *dhikr*. I enjoyed these sessions and also liked to sit and chat for a while with the others afterwards.

Dr Amina was particularly kind and caring and took me under her wing. One evening we went to a lovely Persian restaurant in Notting Hill that had become our favourite place whenever we wanted to talk in peace. I asked her how she actually came to Islam. 'I was a Catholic attending a convent school,' she said, 'but I felt something was missing and kept praying to God for guidance. My work as a doctor took me to the Middle East, where I was part of a team of doctors looking after the mother of the Sultan of Oman. On one occasion the Queen was very ill, but against everyone's advice insisted on continuing with her full schedule of appointments all day without a break. At the end of the day, the Queen lay down exhausted and I asked her, "You give so much to everyone, who gives to you?" The Queen sat up with great difficulty, raised her right hand with the finger pointing to the sky, and with an enormous energy, almost with anger at the stupidity of the question, she said, "Allah!" I was awestruck. Whatever it was that had given this very ill woman such strength, I wanted it too.'

'So you converted in Oman?' I asked.

'No, it took a while longer,' replied Dr. Amina. 'Sometime later, I was on holiday in the South of France on a boat, and dreamt that I'd returned to London in my car, and saw my flat in flames. The car then turned on to a road, fifteen degrees to the left of an existing road, Kensington Park Road. No other cars were on this road, which led straight across London, over the river, through woods, and then through the desert, with a straight track to the horizon, where there was a light. Gradually in that light I saw the Arabic letters for Allah. I woke up and knew this dream was telling me I had to become a Muslim.'

Much later, she said, when she was in her flat working out the direction for prayer, she found Mecca actually was fifteen degrees to the left of Kensington Park Road.

How extraordinary, I thought. I knew Dr Amina to be a very well-read and informed person, but her conversion was 'an intuitive realisation', as she put it. 'An intellectual understanding of Islam only came much later.'

I soon became friends with another inspiring woman in the Naqshbandi group called Zero, a great devotee of the Shaykh, who was Swedish but spoke perfect German. About ten years older than me, she had huge green eyes and always wore purple. One afternoon, when the Shaykh was busy seeing people in private, we sat together on the floor at the back of the mosque and had a chat. She told me she'd lived in Berlin for many years and was a founding member of the German Green Party. She'd been a close friend of Rudi Dutschke, the leader of the German student protest movement who survived an assassination attempt in 1968 but died eleven years later of related health problems. She was the last person to have spoken to him and his passing had upset her enormously. She'd heard about it in Egypt and, when some friends saw her crying, she told them of her grief. They consoled her by saying that in their culture, when someone dies, people were grateful and glad because they knew this person was now with God. Zero was deeply moved by the idea of a religion that was more powerful than death and wanted to find out more. I mentioned to her that I had actually come across the same idea in Pakistan. 'There they celebrate the death anniversary of a saint in what is called *urs*,' I said. 'Sometimes tens of thousands of people gather at the shrines to celebrate that meeting with God, which they call the wedding with the Beloved.' *Qawwali* musicians sing people into a trance with their songs of devotion, and these events are said to be wonderful ecstatic spiritual experiences for everyone. 'I'd love to witness an *urs* one day,' I added. 'I like the way that the dead are not perceived as gone, so people continue to pray for them because their souls are alive.'

'Death really has a very different meaning in Islam,' Zero agreed. 'It is not the end but eternal life.'

Zero then spent time soaking up Islam in Egypt and other parts of Africa, reading key works by great Islamic scholars such as Imam al-Ghazali and absorbing Arabic culture. Eventually she went to live for six months in a famous Sufi centre near Hamburg, of all places. I had never even heard of it. It was there that she converted. Later she found her way to Shaykh Nazim's Naqshbandi order, and as a journalist, wrote a number of books for him.

During his speeches Shaykh Nazim reminded us to pray regularly. 'Prayer will carry you to Judgment Day; it is your nourishment and your protection. In prayer you are closest to God. It is then that you develop your own personal relationship with God,' he told us.

It was clear to me by now that studying Islam was one thing – and absolutely worthwhile, because it helped me grasp the meaning of the religion and how it all fitted together. However, I felt as though I was standing in front of a shop window full of lovely things, and all I could do was admire them from afar. I was still separated from them by the window, or, as Muslims might say, a veil. In order to lift this veil, there was only one way forward: to get down onto the prayer mat and start living according to Islamic principles.

One weekend, I visited a friend in Cornwall and went on some amazing walks along the coastline, filling my lungs with the bracing sea air. Back in the house, I spent most of the time engrossed in a little book I had brought along called *What is Sufism* by Martin Lings, who had written the biography of Muhammad that Imran and I had enjoyed so much. I couldn't wait to get back from our walks to continue reading. In it, Lings describes Sufism as the spiritual fruit of Islam, a foretaste of Paradise in this world. By doing things in the name of

God, we could sanctify every day and every deed. Reading this book made me finally decide to convert.

I knew now that Islam was the path I wanted to follow, and especially the inner, spiritual dimension practised by the Sufis. All I had to do was place my trust in God. He would always be there, and I was accountable to Him and Him alone. The message of *tawhid*, the absolute Oneness and Sovereignty of God, was clear and ultimately irresistible to me. I knew I was ready, from the bottom of my heart. The sense of independence and security this realisation brought me was an extraordinary source of strength to me, and one I couldn't wait to tap into. There in my room in Cornwall, I stood and prayed to Allah for the first time.

But once I was back in London, my doubts that I would be able to keep to all the rules returned. Dr Amina and Zero reassured me that it wouldn't be hard, and repeated what Gai Eaton had said – it takes time, patience and endurance to become a devout Muslim. No one, not even God, expects anyone to become an angel overnight. That's fortunate, I thought, because I sensed that the road ahead might be a long one.

My friends also helped banish my last remaining reservations regarding the status of women in Islam. Men and women are not the same, they told me. They have different qualities, but the same ethical values and religious duties apply to both, and they share the same responsibility for their respective tasks in the world. As it says in the Quran: *The believing men and the believing women are protectors of each other* (9:71).

This sounded good enough to me, and I felt I just had to take the plunge. I knew I would continue my reading and find out everything I wanted to in the course of time.

So I asked around at the mosque about the process of taking the *shahada*, saying the declaration of faith, which would make me a Muslim. One morning in April, before the midday prayers, there would be quite a few people converting with Shaykh Nazim I heard and, if I wanted to, I could come and witness the process. If I felt ready, I could join them. There was just one practical matter in the back of my mind, and I decided to ask the Shaykh himself about it.

When the day came it was cool and grey. I dressed in a long skirt, a loose top and a coat, and took a headscarf along as I always did when going to the mosque, because all the women there were covered. I put on the scarf when I parked the car outside the *dirgha*, as the Sufis called the mosque, and entered.

After greeting the Shaykh in an upstairs room, I asked him how I would need to dress in order to please God if ever I went on a beach holiday. He smiled and quoted the Quran:

We have sent you clothing to cover your private parts, and for adornment. But the garment of conscientiousness is the best.
(7:26)

Keep God in your heart and mind, whatever you do, and wherever you are, that is number one.

Otherwise he recommended I dress modestly so as not to attract undue attention, but that I needed to decide for myself what to wear. I thanked him, left the room and joined everybody else downstairs in the mosque area and thought about it for a while. For some Muslim women, dressing modestly may mean not going to the beach at all, or only going fully dressed from head to toe. But there were also women who wore perfectly normal swimsuits or shorts and covered themselves when they came out of the water.[1]

For the time being, my last questions of conscience had been cleared up. I was ready to convert.

When Shaykh Nazim arrived, we all followed him into a room adjacent to the main mosque where he sat down in front of us. There were about fifty people all sitting on the floor, men on one side, women on the other. His cousin and some of his helpers sat down next to him. The Shaykh spoke a few general words about the meaning of embracing Islam and stressed that we needed to do it with all our hearts and minds. From now on a new life was beginning for us, which also meant that all our sins from the past would be forgiven and forgotten, he said. What a relief, I thought. I wasn't nervous at all. In fact, I felt relaxed and happy about taking this step and officially becoming a Muslim as my heart and mind had already felt Muslim for quite a while.

Each of us held on to the shoulder of the person in front of us while the one closest to the Shaykh clung to his walking stick, so we were all connected to him. The Shaykh murmured a few Arabic formulas that I didn't understand and then he asked those who wanted to embrace the faith to repeat the *shahada,* the Muslim declaration of faith, one after the other: '*Ashhadu an la ilaha illa, Llah, wa ashhadu anna Muhammadar rasul Allah* – I declare there is no god but the One God, and I declare that Muhammad is God's messenger.'

The Shaykh thought for a while and gave me a new name as a symbol of my new beginning: Yusra. It derives from the Arabic word *yusr*, meaning 'ease'. I didn't really like the sound of the name in English and said so. He gave me another name, Bushra, meaning 'good news' or 'glad tidings'. That sounded even worse, so I decided to stick with the first one. Everyone congratulated me, saying '*Mabruk*, welcome, may God protect you and bless your path.'

That was it. I was now a Muslim. That also meant no more alcohol, no sausages when in Germany and no more Spaghetti Carbonara, which I loved. Never mind, I was prepared to make sacrifices.

Then I took part in my first ritual communal prayer. It was the noon prayer, recited in silence punctuated only by the Imam's exclamations of praise to God, which signalled a change in praying position. I joined the women at the back of the room and simply copied what they did without actually reciting anything because I didn't know what to say.

Afterwards Dr Amina explained to me that my name was mentioned in the Quran. It appears in chapter (*surah*) 94 and she wrote it out for me in English and in Arabic English so that I could actually learn it in Arabic to recite it.

Did We not relieve your heart for you, and remove the burden that weighed so heavily on your back, and raise your reputation high? So truly where there is hardship there is also ease. Where there is hardship there is also ease. So when you are free, work on and direct your requests to your Lord.

I wanted to memorise the *surah* as soon as I could, but first I had to tackle the basic one, called the *Fatiha*, which I now needed to recite a minimum of seventeen times a day. There was a lot to learn and so much to remember.

On Dr Amina's advice, I went straight from the mosque to the Islamic bookshop near Regent's Park and bought a children's book that described the different prayer positions in *salah* (formal prayer) and transcribed the prayers phonetically.

The first proper prayer I did on my own was back home in my living room. I had been given a prayer mat as a gift, and I rolled it out reverentially. The question was: which direction should I face? I first had to work out where Mecca lay. Specifically for the purpose of showing me the *qibla*, the direction of prayer wherever I was, I had bought myself a compass. A friend before had pointed out that Mecca was to the southeast and as the river was south, it was just to the left of it.

With the children's book in my hand, I stood on my prayer mat facing Mecca and read *al-Fatiha*, 'The Opener', the first chapter of the Quran, which consists of seven verses. Then I bowed down, repeating a formula of praise three times, stood up again with another formula and prostrated with my forehead touching the ground. I was supposed to recite something else while in that position but logistically that was impossible, so I straightened up again to read the formulas, and put my forehead back on the mat afterwards as a gesture. I then got up and did the whole ritual again before sitting down on my knees reciting praises of Prophet Muhammad and Prophet Abraham and their descendants – all of course in broken Arabic. Two *rakat* of the afternoon prayer were done and I had to do another two. Initially, it felt strange to stand and prostrate before God, not understanding the meaning of what I was saying and at the same time trying to feel God's presence, which I couldn't. But I made an effort to pray every day, and in time it all went a little smoother. I also learned a few small verses to recite after the *Fatiha*. As I became a bit more practised, I tore out the most important pages from my book and kept them in my filofax. Whenever I travelled, I took along those prayer notes, together with my compass and, as usual, some books.

Shaykh Nazim had recommended that I start slowly and concentrate on doing one or two of the obligatory prayers, the *fard*, regularly every day, and build it up from there. I began with the morning and evening prayers recited at dawn and sunset. If I overslept, I made up for it when I got up. Sometimes, though, when Shaykh Nazim was in town, Dr Amina would drive totally out of her way to pick me and a few others up in the middle of the night, when it was still dark outside, and we would all go to the mosque in North London for morning prayers (*fajr*) with the Shaykh. Surprisingly, many people turned up at that unearthly hour as if it was the most normal thing to do. Once I managed to get out of bed I actually enjoyed these visits. The quiet of dawn supposedly makes it the best time to pray, because it's a time when a great many angels are believed to be around, carrying our prayers to Heaven. The city was still asleep when we set out, and I always had a strong sense that I was doing something only for myself and for God. Usually a great day would follow such a blessed start. Smiling inwardly, I'd think to myself how, not so long ago, I would have been coming home from a big night out at this time of the morning.

My friends were a bit surprised when I told them I had converted, but they respected my decision. Of course, they couldn't really understand my reasons for taking this step, but they were open-minded enough to ask me questions and learn a bit about Islam. Most of them were now in their thirties and also beginning to discover their spirituality, asking themselves about the purpose of life and how they could make it more meaningful. Others simply took it in their stride – my friend Johnson, for example, once told me: 'I like you whether you're a Muslim or an MTV presenter, Kristiane, because I like *you*.' My aunt, who was my godmother, was also very supportive. She followed everything I was doing and collected all the articles I featured in. When she read the news and spoke to me on the phone, she said: 'We are all brothers and sisters, and Abraham is our father.' She also sent me a book, and even though I know she meant well, I doubt she'd read it. It was called *The Sword of Islam* and was a study by the German journalist Peter Scholl-Latour of the dangers of radical Islam. Then again, this and other negative issues were the subject of most writing about Islam on sale in Europe's bookstores.

But unlike my godmother, my parents were initially taken aback by my decision. They thought I was acting on a whim, or somehow trying to escape reality. They had some serious prejudices against Islam and especially Muslim men – prejudices that Imran's way of ending our relationship had only confirmed. Now my parents simply couldn't understand why I needed to embrace his religion. We weren't getting married, so why convert? I tried to explain to them that I had discovered the religion for myself and had made it my own. Imran had merely opened the door for me. On my next visits home we had long and in-depth discussions and I tried to explain to them the basic concepts of Islam and that converting wouldn't actually change *me*, I still loved them the same, and if anything, trying to submit to God would probably help me to become a better person. My parents weren't convinced since their opinion of Islam was shaped by what they read in the media, and that version of the religion was something very different from what I believed in. My father even mentioned the word pantheism – in his view, Muslims wanted to take over the whole world. He eventually asked me to stop talking about Islam, and from then on the topic became taboo in his house and we focused on family matters instead, which was probably just as well.

Ultimately, though, the worst hostility I encountered didn't come from family and friends but from the German media. I was invited to appear on a chat show about Islam, *Die Menschen hinter den Schlagzeilen* (The People Behind the Headlines) on one of Germany's main private TV stations, Sat 1, hosted by Ulrich Meyer, a slick presenter who wore a lot of mascara. The other guests were to be Peter Scholl-Latour, a political journalist who had spent a long time in the Arab world, and Betty Mahmoody, author of the bestselling memoir *Not Without My Daughter* about her flight from Iran and from her Muslim husband. I was going to be in Hamburg to record my show anyway, so I accepted, imagining it would be a good opportunity to set the record straight and explain to the German public why I had chosen to embrace Islam. I prepared myself by talking at length on the phone with Dr Amina in London and Imran in Pakistan. Both helped me with key points they thought I should convey. I suggested to the producers that they might want to invite someone who was born and raised as a Muslim – surely that made sense in a talk show about Islam, I argued. They hadn't thought of that but, after some hesitation, they agreed. However, they were unable to find anyone at such short notice, and I ended up proposing they invite an acquaintance of mine from the Sufi group, Prince Faradudin, who lived in both London and Paris.

On the day of the show, the producers suddenly announced they needed to start a little earlier than planned, and Faradudin didn't get to take part after all because his flight landed too late. He ended up sitting in the audience, without a microphone. The show began with a report that featured heavily veiled women dressed in black, edited together with armed men screaming *Allahu akbar* and images of recent attacks. 'Fear of Allah!' intoned the narrator. 'Holy war is raging all over the planet. Islamic fundamentalists are waging a war of terror against the infidels. How dangerous is Islam?' he asked.

I started to wonder what I had got myself into. The report alone was an example of extreme Islamophobia and complete ignorance of what Islam really stood for. For a start, women in most Muslim countries, as far as I knew, didn't necessarily wear black, but a rainbow of colours. More importantly, 'holy war' was a mistranslation of the term *jihad*, which actually means 'exertion or struggle in the path of God'. A Muslim is allowed to take up arms in defence alone and, even then, only under strict ethical conditions – this much I knew. Basically, the whole report was geared first and foremost to panic-mongering. If it had been shown in England, there would have been an outcry from Muslim organisations claiming religious discrimination, and rightly so.

After the gory introduction, the presenter turned to me and asked what on earth it was that fascinated me of all people, an MTV presenter, about Islam. 'The warmth and kindness that I've encountered amongst the Muslims I've met,' I answered. 'And their willingness to selflessly help others.' Referring to Imran as my 'ex-boyfriend', I talked about what he and thousands of volunteers had achieved with the hospital project, which was an expression of faith and a way to serve God. The energy and the strength for this monumental task came from his faith, I said. I also explained that I found Islam to be the truth; that the word Islam actually meant peace; and that violence perpetrated in the name of Allah contradicted the religion. 'Is that the sort of thing you say on your shows?' the presenter asked me then. Dumbfounded, I couldn't grasp what he was getting at. He seemed to be suggesting that I was

using my position at MTV and on *Bravo TV* to try to Islamise young kids. I was speechless. 'I talk about music on my
shows, not religion, you obviously haven't watched,' I eventually managed to say.

Next, Ulrich Meyer asked Betty Mahmoody to talk about
her experiences in Iran. To begin with, she too had seen only
the good in Islam, she said – until her Muslim husband began
making her life hell. Meyer asked me to comment. 'I'm sorry
she had to go through this,' I said. 'But we can't judge a religion
by the bad practices of some of its followers.'

The words 'Fear of Allah' were beamed on the wall in the
background and a huge image of a woman in a burka popped
up on a video screen behind us. This eventually morphed into
a picture of Mahmoody's little daughter wearing a tight headscarf, followed by a photo of Imran and myself at a ball, then
back to the woman in a burka. It was getting ridiculous. I gestured to the image, and said that burkas were by no means
an Islamic obligation: nowhere in the Quran did it say that a
woman must cover her face.

Then it was Peter Scholl-Latour's turn. He agreed with me,
acknowledging the point. But he went on to accuse me – somewhat patronisingly – of talking about 'Islam light', a version of
Islam that was a utopian ideal. 'A lovely dream, that's all,' he
maintained.[2] In the West, in London, I might be able to practise this kind of Islam, he said, but it wouldn't be possible in a
Muslim country. 'You wouldn't be making music shows over
there, or many other things you enjoy here,' he said. Meyer
seized on this and asked how I would feel in a Muslim country
if I had to give up my career. 'I'm not planning on moving to
one at the moment,' I answered. 'What makes London great
is that I can live there, work there, and still be a practising
Muslim.'

Inwardly I actually thought that it would be pretty interesting to live in an Arab country, learn the language and maybe
host a different kind of programme.

The longer this ghastly show went on, the more I realised that none of the participants had a genuine interest in discussing Islam. Whenever I said anything positive about it, they barely let me finish my sentence before all three of them would start bombarding me with counter-arguments. They weren't taking me seriously, and I felt belittled. All in all, it was a deeply frustrating experience, and it left me feeling utterly miserable. I comforted myself with the thought that I'd at least tried to get the audience thinking.

Afterwards, Prince Faradudin and I discussed the show. We both felt the agenda was unfair, and as we were walking along the studio corridor chatting to Betty Mahmoody, even she admitted her experiences could have happened anywhere in the world. The evening ended well, with a dinner invitation from the Naqshbandi Sufis of Berlin. We all watched the show, which had been pre-recorded, and it did me a world of good to be with people whose hearts were in the same place as mine. They lifted my spirits with their empathy and spiritual support, and, at the end of the evening, they gave me a silver chain with a pendant that contained prayers for protection.

Boosted by their support, I flew back to London, and in subsequent weeks received all sorts of letters from Muslim viewers who congratulated me on my courage in standing up to two notorious Islamophobes and wished me God's blessing. The general consensus was that I'd done a good job. Nonetheless, I resolved not to talk about my faith on German TV again in the foreseeable future – a decision I stuck to for some time to come.

∽

Back in London I soon received more bad news from Germany. I found out reading the papers that my show *Bravo TV* was to be fronted by a new presenter called Heike Makatsch who later dated Daniel Craig. It was the first I had heard of it, and I immediately called my manager in Hamburg to find out what was going on. For the past few months the show's producers had been begging me to sign a contract as presenter for another year. I had scooped any number of TV awards, and at the 100th anniversary show of *Bravo TV* all the big bosses had been praising me effusively for my work, telling me that I had written TV history in Germany. So what had happened to make them drop me? It didn't take much guesswork. The producers – who were also my management – feigned innocence and maintained their information only came from the papers too. But a few weeks later in a meeting to which I brought a new manager, they suggested that there was no signed contract. Fortunately I had a copy with me and pointed to their signatures. Lawyers got involved, and since the producers had contractual obligations to me, I was eventually offered a job presenting a show about environmental issues. Perhaps I should have accepted, but I felt betrayed and had lost my trust in the company. Further, I didn't want to look like a dilettante, presenting music one day and environmental issues the next.

It was obvious – to me, at least – that the sudden annulment of my contract was down to my conversion to Islam and my appearance on the chat show. Taki Theodoracopulos, a columnist at the *Sunday Times*, made the same connection and called on the German TV producers to give me back my job. In England, no one could believe that a TV personality could be so publicly denounced and then dropped because of her private beliefs. It wasn't as if I was wearing my religion on my sleeve – or in this case, my head. But there was nothing I could do. The *Bravo TV* chapter of my life was over. It wasn't a tragedy – I had been presenting the show for three years and that was long enough. Even so, the way they ditched me before the ink had even dried on my latest contract was a bitter pill to swallow.

I was left feeling insecure and in need of advice. I recalled my first conversation with Gai Eaton and how he had helped me overcome my doubts about converting. On the spur of the moment, I rang him at the mosque in Regent's Park, where he worked. He remembered me and suggested meeting up at the Travellers Club on Pall Mall, a street lined with gentlemen's clubs and close to St James's Palace, home to the Prince of Wales. I told him about the fallout from my conversion. He wasn't surprised and said it seemed that new Muslims were inevitably 'tested', and how they dealt with this showed their degree of commitment to their faith. It was a form of initiation. When I explained what had happened with Imran, his response was dispassionate. 'Boys will always be boys,' he said. 'The relationship obviously wasn't meant to be.' He told me I should trust that the break-up was for the best, even if I couldn't see that yet. As with every form of suffering, heartache brings with it catharsis, and turns us into better human beings. 'It is like an iron in the furnace that is beaten into shape,' he said. These bad experiences were ultimately a good sign because God tests the ones He loves. That might be why He has so few friends,' he added dryly. His words cheered me up a bit.

Then Gai told me about the famous cup of the heart, which I should now begin to empty. The Sufis compare our spiritual heart, the seat of God within us, with a cup into which the love of God flows. This cup, however, needs to be emptied before it can be filled with Divine love. This emptying is a long process that requires courage, strength of character, determination, and, above all, sincerity. It is a process of reining in and eventually extinguishing the ego, of letting go of material needs, bad and unhealthy habits and emotional attachments in order to make room for God. Sufis often likened it to the process of dying and being born again. 'Die before you die' is a famous Sufi saying. This was the essence of every spiritual path, Gai told me.

I remembered his words and a few days later, I was even happier that we'd had this talk. Imran called and told me out of the blue that he was getting married. It was an arranged marriage, he said. I was taken aback. We had been in regular contact until now, and I didn't really know what to say. When I asked him if he had actually proposed, he said of course he had. But then, two days later, I got a call from Dr Haroon, the Pakistani cricket team's doctor whom I had met through Imran and who had become my doctor too. 'Have you heard that Imran is getting married to Jemima Goldsmith?' he asked me. Apparently, Imran had been seeing this young, beautiful and well-connected English heiress for a while. I was shocked. In my mind's eye, I saw Imran tumble off his pedestal and crash to the ground. Why hadn't he just told me the truth? No sooner had I hung up than the phone rang again. It was the *Sunday Times*. The reporter had just seen the news come in on the wires and wanted a statement from me. I was at a loss for words and had nothing to say.

When I left the house a few hours later, I was confronted with a mob of journalists camped out on my doorstep, all thrusting microphones in my face. I was still digesting the news and said 'no comment'. The idea of saying anything about the matter in public was anathema to me. But the press wasn't prepared to give up that easily and managed to extract snippets that they then fabricated into headline articles.

The next morning I was woken up at eight a.m. by the sound of my neighbour yelling 'F… off!' out of the window. The pack was back, and someone had rung his doorbell by mistake. When I finally left the house they shoved newspaper articles at me with headlines screaming 'Love Rat' and 'Liar', demanding a comment. I avoided them as best I could – without succumbing to my neighbour's choice of words. It was days before they dispersed. At one point, a newspaper offered me a lot of money for a kiss and tell. I refused, of course, and left Imran to God instead. I had a clear conscience and was determined to keep my dignity.

Talking badly about others, slander and gossip are considered sins of the tongue in Islam. And if we uncover people's mistakes, God may uncover our own. Hard as it was, all I wanted was to let Imran go so I could concentrate on my own path. I had plenty of support, empathy and comfort, including from Imran's friends, most of whom were no wiser than I was about the whole affair. Vimla, who was known as the Indian Yoga Queen, told me she had read the news in a plane and was so shocked that she dropped her glass of champagne. Imran's close adviser for the hospital called to say that something had gone wrong with the public announcement, it wasn't meant to be like that. I was given a lot of good advice from everyone I met during that time. 'The challenge is to turn a crisis into an opportunity and become better rather than bitter,' someone said. That was precisely my intention.

Zero talked to me at length on the phone about forgiveness. The path of faith is a path of forgiveness, she said. If I forgave others, God would forgive me. She told me an anecdote from the life of the Prophet. When a man once asked him what he should do to ensure God's mercy and forgiveness, the Prophet answered: 'Allah will show mercy to those who are merciful to others.'[3] She also said that one shouldn't judge anyone before looking for at least seventy excuses for their behaviour first.[4] Eventually I was genuinely able to find it in my heart to forgive Imran, even though the pain lasted for a long time. I trusted that God had His reasons for making things happen the way they did. Somehow, it must have been a blessing in disguise. I was grateful for the gift of faith. It was as though God had used Imran as a tool to call me to Him – in which case, he had served his purpose. Had Allah sent a strict imam with a long beard, I would probably never have become a Muslim. And as soon as Imran had fulfilled this role and faith had taken root in my heart, God took him away. God took human love from me so that I could discover a higher love – God's love. This way of looking at what had happened helped me to move on.

I prayed regularly and practised reciting simple verses from the Quran. I also went to the mosque frequently, listening to spiritual teachings and joining the meetings where we praised God together, reciting certain formulas in a melodic and repetitive way (*dhikr*).

On the day of Imran and Jemima's wedding, which was a huge media circus, I wanted to be as far away from London as possible. However, it didn't work out like that, and I ended up spending some time with Dr Amina in the mosque, praying for their happiness. 'You may have lost someone, but you've found something immeasurably more valuable: God,' she told me. 'And God's love lasts forever.'

∽

It was a while before I started going out again. When I did, one of the best parties I went to was in Badminton House, the grand home of the Duke of Beaufort in Gloucestershire. The game of badminton took its name from this house, and one of the halls in this imposing seventeenth-century estate was exactly the size of a badminton pitch. Bryan Ferry, Mick Jagger and Jerry Hall, Steve Winwood and his wife Gina were there, as well as numerous interesting personalities and friends of the family.

The Duke himself arrived in style – in a helicopter. I went for a long walk across the grounds where the famous Badminton Horse Trials, which used to be attended by the Queen, are held every year. I was joined by the friends I'd taken along with me, Lynn, and Agenta, a bubbly Italian journalist who interviewed actors and musicians for Italian magazines. Just like the other girls, we too were enamoured with the dashing Duke. In the evening we all dressed up for dinner served by the family butlers, who had been working there for decades. A bit like Sindh, I thought.

I sat next to the film director James Dearden. We had a lively conversation, and soon he was asking me about being a Muslim. He knew Imran and the entertainment world I worked in, and he just couldn't see how I could possibly cope without drink, drugs and sex. I told him I preferred clean living these days and was saving myself for the right man to marry. He looked baffled. He had written the screenplay for *Fatal Attraction* and was proud of the movie's risqué scenes.

After dinner we all moved into a ballroom for the more raucous part of the evening. Steve Winwood sat down at the piano and anyone who wanted got to choose a song. We boogied away to 'Spanish Dancer', 'Higher Love', 'Dancing in the Streets' and a few songs by Bunter, the Duke's eldest son, who was on top form and sang his heart out. Johnson, Bunter's younger brother, played percussion with his little boy and Mick danced with Gina, Steve's wife – who later bonded with Agenta in the small hours of the morning, making my friend very happy because she was such a Steve Winwood fan. Meanwhile, Lynn – who had never played an instrument in her life – leaned over the percussion kit in her little black dress and drummed up a storm. It was an unforgettable night.

The next morning, I got up to join Tracy, Bunter's wife, and the kids, the Winwoods, who are practising Christians, Agenta and Lynn, and a few others who had managed to get out of bed, for prayers in the house chapel. I had done my morning prayer already but felt like enjoying this moment for God with the others. I silently recited the *Fatiha*, and added some prayers of my own.

∼

By now I was regularly attending Muslim cultural events, lectures and seminars. Dr Amina invited me to the annual Calamus Dinner, attended by a who's who of London's Muslim society. Scholars such as Karen Armstrong, John Esposito and Gai Eaton spoke about God, inter-religious dialogue and various aspects of Islam. At sunset – a prescribed time for prayer – we interrupted our dinner and joined Shaykh Nazim, who led the *maghrib* prayers in the hallway. Dr Amina and I covered our heads with scarves and stood in a row amongst the other women behind the men, before we all bowed and then knelt in unison on tablecloths. I felt a wonderful sense of belonging and an inner connection with the others. Afterwards we returned to the dining room and the evening continued. I enjoyed these communal breaks at Muslim events when we prayed together and then carried on with the programme. It gave an event an extra dimension and forged a spiritual connection between people.

My German youth show had finished, but I was still working for MTV Europe and had started a voluntary job on the side. I joined the charity organisation Learning for Life, which funded schools in Southeast Asia. It was founded by Sophia Swire, whose school in Chitral I had visited with Imran. She had called me up and asked if I would like to support the project. I went to her office in Chelsea and agreed immediately – charity work was God's work, after all. At our next meeting she introduced me to two other new colleagues over lunch, Ruby and Dani. To my delight, it was the same Ruby I had met years before with Imran. We had lost touch, but now we were both thrilled to discover that we would be working together. Ruby and Dani soon became my new best friends. Along with Sophie, we called ourselves the A-Team. Unlike the boys in the TV show, we didn't hunt down criminals, but raised funds for the charity. We organised dinners and parties that drew a great mix of society, including rock stars and artists. Our events were covered in glossy magazines and funded the education of thousands of children – particularly girls – in Pakistan, Nepal and even Afghanistan. As Malcolm X once said, 'To educate a man is to educate an individual, but to educate a woman is to educate a nation.' It was my job to invite the celebrities. And it seemed that God was helping me, because I had no trouble getting people on board.

One day, walking around my neighbourhood with a friend, I bumped into Bob Geldof. I had not seen him since interviewing him many years previously, and now we became friendly, bonding over the similar experiences we were going through. His wife Paula Yates had just left him for a more famous rock star and it was all over the papers. Bob was the guest of honour at several of our LFL charity events. Another time I was waiting at an airport in Germany for a delayed flight and found myself sitting next to Liz Mitchell, the voice of the seventies disco band Boney M. She was delighted when I asked her to perform at one of the charity events. It was a fab night, everyone danced and she kept the party going for hours. I also enlisted the help of the band Right Said Fred and Simply Red frontman Mick Hucknall, who had once asked me out. Because I knew Dodi Al Fayed through Dr Amina, we managed to persuade Harrods to donate a mountain of raffle prizes. Ruby, Dani and I became like sisters and went on several holidays together. I regularly took them along to various showbiz events, Sufi concerts, exhibitions and lectures, and in return they introduced me to their crowd.

Ruby had a lot of friends of Indian and Pakistani heritage, including Fa, whom I already knew because she worked at Imran's office; a young lawyer called Renna, who was enthralled by glamour and movie stars; and many other women from Pakistan who spent their summers in London. She even knew the late Benazir Bhutto, the former Prime Minister of Pakistan. Ruby and all her friends still lived with their parents, even though they earned good money and were over thirty years old. They may have thought about living alone, but it was out of the question because of their conservative backgrounds. Their parents would never allow it. In their culture, women only moved out when they got married. It was a concept hard for me to imagine and I think it made some of them lead a bit of a double life – all prim and proper when at home with the parents, only to escape whenever possible and hit the town with a vengeance, putting on their dancing shoes and lipstick in the car and taking off their demure long tops to reveal something more racy underneath. Nonetheless, these girls were all strong personalities and fiery spirits, and I loved their warmth.

They radiated an inner strength that came from their unshakeable faith in God. This was a great inspiration to me. And to these young ladies, my long relationship with Imran – their national hero – made me something of a celebrity.

I told Ruby about Sufism, and she was intrigued by this path I'd chosen to follow. 'The Islam of the heart' was unfamiliar to her. Even though she was born and raised a Muslim, she was taught the fire and brimstone version of Islam by long-bearded mullahs and strict teachers in London mosques and Islamic centres. There was no warmth in these teachings, just rules and regulations, rote learning and discipline. Needless to say, she had found it all scary as a child and tried to escape it as much as she could.

Now she was keen to find out more. I took Ruby to my Sufi group, and Shaykh Nazim gave her a new name. We often went together to the North London mosque to learn from the Shaykh and receive blessings – *baraka*. We called ourselves the 'Sufi groupies', because during that brief phase we would show up everywhere the Shaykh went. As our friendship grew, we developed a kind of a spiritual bond, and sometimes Ruby dreamt messages for me or I deciphered dreams for her, however strange that may sound. For example, she dreamt that her grandmother recommended she read a certain chapter of the Quran, but had no idea what she meant. When she told me, I knew immediately she was talking about the short protection chapters at the end of the Quran I had just learned. Other times, Ruby actually dreamt messages for me about certain things that would happen, prayers I needed to recite or charity I had to give. She told me that it was through my quest that she got to know the spiritual dimension of Islam and also began to look at the religion on an intellectual level. It was Sufism that opened Ruby's heart to Islam. In turn, she taught me many things about Eastern culture, about reaching out to others, making sacrifices for family and friends and being there for them unconditionally.

In the summer of 1995, I went on a Mediterranean cruise along the Amalfi coast with friends from Hamburg, Briggite, who had become a skilled fortune teller, Sylvie, a jeweller who was into Buddhist teachings, and her husband Caesar, a jewellery designer with a soft spot for the Middle Ages. We didn't have much in common with the other passengers, a bunch of European socialites and party people who were into techno music even first thing in the morning. Rather than partying, we preferred to sit on deck, discussing the meaning of life.

I was fascinated to discover that there seemed to be universal principles at the heart of all spiritual traditions, principles that are found everywhere and can be reached via various different paths. Briggite and Caesar told me about The Seven Cosmic Laws of Hermes Trismegistus, which I had also found in Islamic philosophy.[5] They include the Law of Correspondence, based on the hermetic principle: 'As above, so below – as below, so above …'

For everything that is in the world, there is a correspondence on every level of existence. The macrocosm is a reflection of the microcosm, and the way we experience the outer world is a reflection of our inner state: it is our mirror. If we are in harmony with ourselves, then we will be in harmony with the outer world, i.e. God. If we change from within, then everything around us also changes. I certainly knew how true this was.

When Briggite suggested reading my cards, I thanked her but declined. 'I can't,' I said. 'My religion doesn't allow me. According to Islam, the future is known only to God, not even to the Prophet.' Briggite didn't mind in the least. 'You don't need it anyway,' she said.

However, a little later, I wondered if she'd had an inkling that my fortunes were about to take another dive. After coming back tanned and uplifted from our holiday I found out that my show, the *Coca Cola Report*, had been cancelled because much of its content had been taken over by other formats. As a consolation prize, MTV offered me the same chart show I had presented when I first joined the channel. It felt like a step backwards. During my time at MTV Europe I had presented so many different programmes, and I now knew that the channel could no longer offer me new challenges.

But I still had fun at the opening party of VH1 in Hamburg, an MTV channel for the older generation that played more sophisticated music than the latest charts. We all stayed in the Atlantic Hotel, an old-fashioned grand hotel overlooking the lake that is popular with rock stars – including Mick Jagger, who once told me that he had a bit of a soft spot for the waitresses who used to come to the room wearing uniforms of white lacy aprons over black dresses and matching lacy bonnets. I went to the party with Brent and Ray, and hung out a bit with them backstage. At some point Brent passed me a joint, but I declined, 'Can't do that any more, I'm a Muslim now,' I explained. 'Imagine I get snapped.' 'It would probably do your image a world of good,' he laughed. But he couldn't convince me. I told him I felt bad enough that I was drinking a glass of champagne. I don't think he understood that either.

Shortly after, I was approached by Alan Edwards, an influential London music PR I had met over the years at music events with the Pet Shop Boys and other bands. 'David would like a picture with you,' he said. I was staggered. To me David Bowie was one of the greatest and coolest rock stars of all time and even though I had always loved his music I had never managed to interview him. And now he was asking if we could have our photo taken together! I was so flattered that initially I didn't know what to say to him. But then I remembered that David had spent time in Berlin with Iggy Pop in the seventies, so I broke the ice by asking him about those years. He hadn't been back since the Wall came down and Berlin had become the capital, he told me. Incidentally, he had married the Ethiopian model Iman, who is a Muslim. Her name means 'faith'. But I only remembered that later. As fate would have it, David also has a sister called Iman. She apparently changed her name when she converted to Islam after falling in love and marrying an Egyptian man. I didn't know that at the time.

I hosted my last *Coca Cola Report* from Glasgow, where I interviewed the first band I had ever seen live, Simple Minds. It felt like I had come full circle and it was the first time I had seen Jim Kerr in a long time. He was curious to know what I had been up to – especially in Pakistan. He had been following what had happened in the press and said he admired my courage and adventurous spirit. He was divorced by now and we exchanged numbers. It was an emotional last show for many reasons and speaking the last link into the camera felt like the end of an era.

I had been at MTV for seven and a half years, and when my contract ran out in November 1995, it wasn't renewed. The station was in the process of restructuring, launching a number of small national spin-offs rather than continuing to broadcast a pan-European programme from a central location. Soon after I left, MTV Deutschland and MTV Italia evolved, and various other MTV branches focused on particular musical genres. This allowed the station to respond more flexibly to local music scenes and to give the viewers what MTV thought they wanted. Apparently, part of the new philosophy was to ensure that VJs didn't become stars – in the eyes of MTV, Ray Cokes, Steve Blame, Rebecca de Ruvo and I had ended up wielding too much power. We were the faces of the channel across Europe, and that made MTV dependent on us. These days, VJs get replaced frequently, and they rarely build up a cult following. But now the Internet and iTunes have changed the entire music industry so much that MTV has lost its power and status.

I often asked myself why, of all the candidates, I had got the job in the first place. After all, thousands of young people from all over Germany had applied. Only much later, at a reunion party held long after we had all stopped working for MTV, did Mark Booth tell me that someone quite influential had put in a good word for me. It was Steve Fargnoli. 'The arrangement had worked out well for everyone concerned,' Mark said, adding that my shows had attracted some of the highest ratings on the channel. No one had ever told me that in all the years I had worked there. I left MTV on very good terms. I had achieved everything there was to achieve at the channel and I had stayed for a record length of time. In truth, though, I had outgrown video clip culture long ago, not least because of my faith. All in all, working at MTV – with its highs and lows – had been an amazingly exciting experience and I didn't regret it for a second. But I was ready for new challenges. MTV gave me a huge leaving party at a bar in Soho and as a farewell gift presented me with a beautiful Moroccan mirror. A prophetic present.

The strange thing was, the good feelings I left MTV with were not echoed in Germany. *Bild* ran a headline saying I had been fired and of course that was copied by other papers. It was complete nonsense, especially as MTV kept asking me back to host the show *Greatest Hits* for another half year after my departure, but it no longer bothered me. I wanted to have a break and relax, so I accepted Jim's invitation to visit him in the Scottish Highlands. He showed me around the area – we drove to the picturesque seaside town of Oban, and the Kintyre Peninsula, which inspired the Paul McCartney song. Another treat was a visit to the famous Simple Minds studio right in the middle of the Highlands with amazing views from the very large windows. The extraordinary energy of this spectacular setting must have seeped into all the tracks Jim and Charlie recorded here, I thought, which was no doubt one reason they were so fabulous. We went on long walks through rugged countryside and across desolate mountains. At times it felt like we had left civilisation behind and I was reminded of the mountains in Pakistan. We caught up with each other's news. He too had learned a few (important) lessons the hard way and advised me to develop a thick skin, to ignore the headlines and the stories, both the good ones and the bad ones. I told him about my adventures in Pakistan and how they had led me to change my religion. As an artist with a poetic streak he was fascinated by my spiritual path and by the Sufi music CDs I played for him. He wanted to know everything about Sufism and told me I would get on really well with his first wife, Chrissie Hynde, because she too was interested in spirituality.

In December my friend Tony James invited me to the Chrysalis TV Christmas party. He knew a lot of people in the media and introduced me to Tom Gutteridge, the CEO of the entertainment TV production company Mentorn. 'Today is your lucky day!' Tom exclaimed as he gave me a Chinese fortune cookie. He then told me that NBC Europe had asked him to develop a daily culture and entertainment show called *The Ticket* and that he was looking for a presenter to host it. He thought I might be perfect for the role. I would be covering arts and culture events and interviewing designers, directors and musicians.

Although it had been a turbulent year, it couldn't have ended on a better note. So many doors had been slammed in my face, but new doors had opened as well. When I sat down with Dr Amina and looked back on all that had happened, she quoted an ancient Japanese saying: 'My house has burned down, now I can see the rising moon …'

Chapter 8

Learning for Life

Come, come, whoever you are, it doesn't matter
Whether you are an infidel, an idolater or a fire worshipper.
Come, our convent is not a place of despair. Come even
If you have violated your oath a hundred times
Come again.

Jalaluddin Rumi, *Diwan*

After leaving MTV I had more time to devote to Learning for Life. To me, the charity's name was a statement of intent and became my personal motto. I had put a lot behind me and was facing a future in which everything seemed new and anything possible.

In December 1995 I celebrated my thirtieth birthday at a restaurant in Notting Hill with friends, including some I had met through Imran. Bunter and Johnson were there, along with Shariah, Tony James and his girlfriend Penny, Ruby and Dani, Lynn and Agenta. I had recovered my energy and felt I had emerged stronger and a little bit wiser from a turbulent year. I still felt some lingering sadness but my life had taken a new direction, even though I still had some way to go before I could empty the proverbial cup of the heart, the Sufi symbol of spiritual purity. I tried to pray regularly, to be calmer and more patient – and to drink less alcohol. The ascetic lifestyle that my faith required of me entailed a thorough adjustment, which I knew would take some time to implement fully. My first, ignominious attempt to observe Ramadan made it glaringly obvious what a challenge this was. Through a friend I had started going to an Islamic teacher in Tooting, a sweet lady who once a week taught me the basics of the faith at home over a cup of tea.

As Ramadan approached, Mrs Khan – a very common name among South Asians as I discovered, actually meaning 'ruler' – began to prepare me for this important pillar of Islam, my first month of fasting. Ramadan is a time when Muslims refrain from food, drink and sexual relations from dawn until sunset, she explained, the point being to deny ourselves what is normally permitted in order to help us resist what is prohibited during the rest of the year. Fasting serves to strengthen our willpower. But there is more to it than that. All negative impulses are also to be avoided during this month: there should be no cursing and no talking or even thinking ill of others.

This is the one month in the year wholly devoted to God, and that means cutting back on socialising and spending more time reading the Quran and praying. My teacher also told me that I should break the fast with friends, because Ramadan is a month not just of self-control and purification but also of generosity, kindness and charity towards others. I listened to everything she said, but it didn't really sink in.

On the eve of Ramadan, I went out for dinner with friends to San Lorenzo, a popular Italian restaurant I had gone to regularly with Imran, and a few of us headed off to Browns for a drink after dinner. There I had two more glasses of champagne. The next morning I woke up dehydrated and with a pounding headache. With the prospect of no food and drink until sunset – not even a sip of water – I decided to stay in bed, something I never normally did. I felt dreadful and, after suffering for hours, by the afternoon I decided that Ramadan wasn't for me, and gave up. May God forgive me. The cup of my heart appeared to be full to overflowing. I realised that I couldn't really carry on like this on my path to salvation. If I didn't want to give up Islam, my only option was to give up alcohol.

The Quran prohibits alcohol, as well as any other intoxicants that impair our judgement. Their effects alienate us from our higher selves and from God, and make us more susceptible to temptations and passions we only regret later – hence even a state of 'drunkenness' induced by anger and rage is not permitted in Islam. The injunction not to drink alcohol came down in the Quran in three stages, probably for good reasons. First, it was stated that there was some good in alcohol but that the sin outweighed the benefit (2:219). Then people were asked not to pray when drunk (4:43), and in a third phase, alcohol was forbidden altogether (5:90). So far I had 'mastered' the second phase. However, I was still struggling with the third.

As it happened, giving up alcohol was easier than I thought it would be. I wasn't drinking much anyway at this point in my life because I was always driving and, even during my days at MTV, I had subscribed to Catherine Deneuve's theory that champagne is the only alcohol that doesn't ruin a woman's beauty. During recordings I had often seen on the monitor how bad I looked the morning after a night out, especially after drinking red wine, which appeared to make my face look swollen. So for years I had stuck to white wine or champagne and since becoming a Muslim, I only drank on special occasions. The biggest obstacle in my attempt to be completely teetotal – or so I told myself, at least – turned out to be other people. They were constantly offering me drinks, and I really had to fight for my right to a glass of water at dinner parties and social events. 'Oh come on, make an exception', 'Don't be boring', and 'Allah isn't looking tonight' were just some of the comments I had to put up with. It was strange. I always had to explain myself, and people seemed disappointed by my refusal to drink. I began to realise what a central role alcohol plays in our society. Working in the entertainment industry, I could have got drunk at some event or another every single night, and it seemed that most people, including myself not so long ago, couldn't imagine a party without alcohol.

Another somewhat tedious aspect of going out was that at dinner parties friends who meant well would often introduce me with the words: 'Meet Kristiane, she's converted to Islam.' It was slightly embarrassing being put on the spot like that. Most people had terrible preconceptions that they would then project onto me. Inevitably, they would approach me about the topic late in the evening, when the music was louder, they'd had a few drinks and felt like being confrontational. To begin with I tried to explain myself and answer their questions but I found that it rarely led anywhere. It felt out of place talking about Islam or even spirituality for that matter at dinner parties, bars and nightclubs. I once mentioned to a film producer that I was drawn to people who were humble and spiritual. 'But who wants to be humble and spiritual?' she replied. 'I don't!' I guess those qualities were rare in the ego-driven entertainment business. After a while, I got used to not drinking and realised that I could still have as much fun as ever. But I went home as soon as others started slurring their words or became obnoxious. I would wake up the next day feeling fresh as a daisy, and I was more energetic than ever. I felt like I gained time and got more out of life this way.

Whenever I did manage to have deeper conversations with people, I noticed that I could usually argue quite well from a Muslim perspective, whether the discussion was about social issues or philosophy, and that my faith gave me a way of seeing things that some people seemed to appreciate. At one dinner party the woman next to me told me that for years her life had been overshadowed by guilt over her grandfather's death. She had called him one morning when she'd had to go to work but her car wouldn't start. Even though he had other things to do, she persuaded him to drop everything and help her because it was urgent. While she was waiting she tried to start the car again. This time it worked, so off she dashed. When she later phoned her grandfather, it turned out that while rushing to pick her up he'd had a car crash and died. I could see she was still upset. She said she'd felt so guilty and suffered for years. 'Let me try to relieve you of your guilt,' I tried to comfort her. 'What I've learned from my religion is that life and death are in the hands of God and no one else,' I told her. 'We die when we are meant to die and not a moment later or earlier. It was his time and if your grandfather hadn't died on his way to you, he would have died some other way.'

I hoped I had helped her. I was happy to have my faith and felt it gave me strength and clarity to deal with the deepest of issues; it empowered me.

Whenever I needed company but didn't want to head out into the London nightlife, I visited the Sufis. In the last few months, Shaykh Nazim's group had become a kind of refuge for me, and a source of tranquillity and inspiration. The group prayer, the communal *dhikr*, where we praised God, the shared meals – it all did me good. But unfortunately I soon found out that not even Sufi groups are always havens of purity. Now and then, I would share my enthusiasm for Sufism with my friends. Ruby was hooked immediately and called it the 'true Islam'. But others were less impressed, for example Dani. She believed in God and quite liked Sufism, even coming with us to the Shaykh Nazim Mosque a few times. But she had deep-seated prejudices against Islam and Muslims. The worst thing for her was that Muslims were generally not keen on dogs, which they see as unclean, and Dani loved her dog. Gai loved dogs too, I pointed out, and Muhammad loved all animals. But however much we discussed things, nothing could really change her mind. We still connected on other levels though, and simply tried to avoid the subject.

Bob Geldof was another sceptic. He was pretty low when I met him and I thought that spirituality might help him the way it was helping me. But he told me he was a committed atheist, even though he mentioned that his sister had experienced a profound healing miracle at Lourdes. Still, he couldn't believe in God. I found that a bit sad considering he was such a great humanitarian who had raised enormous amounts of money with his Live Aid Concerts for Africa. So I gave him Gai Eaton's book about Islam to see if it could open his mind and heart, and I also invited him to hear Shaykh Nazim speak at a dinner that I had organised with friends for non-Muslims who were interested in Sufism.

I don't know if he ever read the book, but he eventually agreed to come along to the talk. He was interested enough in meeting a 'holy man', he said. Dani, Ruby, Andrew, Dr Amina and Prince Faradudin were among the guests, together with a few of Shaykh Nazim's followers who had gatecrashed. Bob listened to what the Shaykh had to say, but later told me he was 'utterly bored' and thought Shaykh Nazim 'talked rubbish – cliché after cliché' and 'he is a fraud, a fake Shaykh'. He even called him a cultist. Well, Bob isn't known to mince his words and his criticism seemed a bit harsh, although I had to admit that Shaykh Nazim wasn't at his best that evening. I felt embarrassed by how wrong the encounter went but still, I thought it was worth a try. Or I did until I heard what happened next. A few weeks after the talk, Bob came round to my house and handed me a newspaper article. 'You terrible woman,' he said half in jest. It was a clipping from a Turkish newspaper: an article about his supposed conversion to Islam and his acceptance into Shaykh Nazim's Sufi community. His new name was allegedly Abdullah. The proof was a picture of the two of them together at our dinner – obviously, one of Shaykh Nazim's followers had secretly taken photographs that evening and leaked them to the press. I was mortified. Bob said his PR company and record label were being inundated with calls asking for confirmation of the story. Fortunately, he took the incident in his stride and managed to laugh it off, although it was the last thing he needed at that difficult time in his life. I felt terrible and found it impossible to shrug off the episode. I called the Sufi group and vented my anger. This was a betrayal of trust, I told them – not only had one of them taken pictures of Bob and published them without his agreement, they had also spread deliberate lies about his interest in Islam and his alleged conversion. It was obvious that they had wanted to use a famous star to boost the image of Islam – but to call people to the truth with lies? I didn't know if the Shaykh had approved of what happened, but it didn't matter. Despite my complaints, the group wouldn't remove the entry from their website, and soon they had posted new reports that suggested even Prince Charles had converted.

I never went back to that mosque, which meant I lost my Sufi group. Or rather, they lost me. Dr Amina also left shortly afterwards, for equally valid reasons. As the Sufi community's treasurer, she was in charge of finances. The group often collected money for projects such as the renovation of the premises or for charitable donations, and the sincere, open-hearted followers who were there to seek guidance and purity gave generously. However, at one point Dr Amina told me, she had found 'irregularities' in their financial affairs, of which Shaykh Nazim was fully aware, and when he wouldn't remedy the situation, she felt obliged to report them to Companies House and the Charity Commission. Not only that. A deputy of the Shaykh accused her of theft in front of everybody in the mosque, when in fact she had donated a lot of money to the group. I was sad to hear it, in addition to my own disappointment. We had liked Shaykh Nazim and enjoyed feeling part of the community. But our trust had been destroyed, and I felt it was necessary to make a clean break. Once again, I had to remember how wrong it is to put my faith in mere mortals. Humans are flawed, we both agreed. Only God should be trusted unconditionally. He was the One I wanted to find and worship, and I remained on the lookout for signs that would illuminate the path to Him.

Most of the signs I found were in my books. One of my main inspirations had become the work of Annemarie Schimmel, an outstanding German scholar of Islam and an expert on Sufism. She had written over eighty books on Islamic literature, mysticism and culture and was highly regarded in the Islamic world. In 1995, she was awarded the Peace Prize of the German Book Trade.

The first book of hers I read was *Mystical Dimensions of Islam*, an in-depth exploration of Sufism. I attended her lectures whenever she was in London. Prince Charles's Temenos Academy often invited her as an honorary speaker, and she gave deeply moving talks on aspects of Sufism, including one on the spiritual master and poet of love Jalaluddin Rumi, to whom she had dedicated much of her work. When she spoke, she would shut her eyes and hold forth without notes. She would often spontaneously switch languages, reciting poetry in Persian, Arabic and even local dialects such as Pashto. After one of these lectures, I approached her and we got talking about Pakistan. She lived in Bonn, but described Pakistan as her second home. There is even a street in Lahore named after her. And we had friends there in common, including Yousaf Salaudin, with whom I had stayed in contact; she too had enjoyed dinner at his *haveli* in Lahore.

When I first read her work, I was on holiday in Tobago with my friend Sylvie from Hamburg. I really needed the break. As if life wasn't challenging enough at the time around my conversion, I'd had some terrible arguments with my father's new wife and was feeling pretty down. I had brought along Schimmel's *Mystical Dimensions of Islam* and read how the Sufis used to be criticised and ridiculed but never retaliated or fought back, instead returning any attack with a smile and going on their way. I liked the idea of winning people over not with poison but with honey, acting with forbearance and generosity of spirit. I promised myself on my return to extend a few olive or aloe vera branches to my stepmother as soon as the occasion arose.

I talked to Sylvie about my difficulties and in turn she

shared her problems with me while we went on some lovely walks along the island. It was good to get it all off our chests. We also talked about spirituality and our need for it. Sylvie was following a different spiritual path from mine, but we discovered that we shared many essential values. At the heart of both Sufism and Buddhism are the principles of morality, nobility, virtue and transcendence of the ego through spirituality. Both religions describe the state one seeks to achieve as bliss, but Sufis believe this is achieved through *fana*, 'extinction' of the ego, and *baqa*, 'subsistence through God', while Buddhists attain it through nirvana, which actually means 'extinguish' and is thought of as passing into another kind of existence. As the Dalai Lama put it, 'a state of freedom from sorrows' or 'freedom from cyclical existence'.

It was an inspiring and relaxing holiday. Early in the mornings Sylvie would meditate and I would pray. After a healthy breakfast we went to the beach or drove around the lush island, sightseeing and hiking. Often we just relaxed and read. Once, when I was sitting in the garden with my book and a virgin cocktail, a friendly hotel gardener started talking to me. He turned out to be a devout Christian. He told me about the signs of the end of times – some of which, he said, were already apparent. I agreed and said Muslims believed in them, too. The common denominator among faiths seemed to be the general reversal of values – good behaviour appeared boring while being bad was exciting. We both concluded it was a shame that most people had moved away from a spiritual way of life and a worldview with God at its centre towards more selfish and even destructive behaviour. It was as though people had been uprooted from the source. The gardener then carefully dug out a small aloe vera plant and gave it to me as a gift to take home. Later, when I got home, I put it in my kitchen and it blossomed magnificently. In Tobago, aloe vera is used not only to heal burning pains on the skin, but also for inner cleansing. And that was exactly what Sylvie and I wanted.

So Bryan Ferry's invitation to party didn't exactly fit our agenda. He happened to be holidaying in Tobago at the same time. We ran into him one night at a restaurant where he was having dinner with his wife and children. We said hello and Sylvie and I sat down at another table. Eventually they left but he reappeared by himself less than an hour later. Bryan joined us for a drink and a chat, then invited us along to the famous Sunday School, a weekly festival of local steel bands, which sees the audience drinking rum and *rhyming* – dancing raunchily in a tight row one behind the other – to steel pan, reggae and calypso until dawn. We were on a very different trip, so politely declined and had an early night instead.

Our holier-than-thou phase didn't last very long, though. Back in London, we celebrated Sylvie's birthday in style when we met up again with Brian, Johnson, Dani, Lynn, Shariah and some other fun friends for a fabulous dinner at San Lorenzo, everyone's favourite Italian restaurant in Knightsbridge.

On the surface, at least, things were beginning to look up in my personal life. A big photograph of me appeared in the much-talked-about annual *Little Black Book* compiled by the glossy society magazine *Tatler* – a list of the 100 most eligible singles in London. It was flattering to have been included, even though the magazine's comment was: 'You better talk mosques.'

I soon had a few ardent suitors who, by all the usual criteria, were highly eligible men – including musicians, businessmen, aristocrats, TV personalities and filmmakers. Most of them became friends. But that was it. I felt that however much I liked these men, there was something missing – that inner flame, the love for God that motivated me and was the prism through which I now saw and experienced the world. In its absence, I knew the friendship was limited without that deeper connection I was longing for. I often asked myself if I was looking for the impossible. Girlfriends advised me to remain open and not to narrow my options to Muslim men only. Where was I going to meet them, they asked, and worried that they were too culturally different from me, especially with the kind of experiences I'd had. But I couldn't change the way I felt and had to be truthful to myself, even if it meant staying single. Inadvertently, I would send my suitors packing anyway the minute I played the Muslim card and told them a fully fledged relationship wasn't an option. It was also a pretty good excuse when I didn't like someone that much. If the gentleman in question wasn't deterred, I would explain that ideally I was looking to marry a Muslim, who would share my values and my faith. And if they were still interested, I would give them a book or two about Islam so that they could gain a basic understanding of the religion. With some of these friends I even had deep and meaningful philosophical discussions, but if they didn't believe in God or were dismissive of the idea of a Higher Power, I knew we would never be able to share a dimension of life that was so important to me. On the one hand it was liberating to see how my religion helped to set things straight right from the beginning, but on the other, I came across a problem that would stay with me for a long time to come: no Western man could even imagine marriage after a purely platonic relationship and I didn't meet anyone who would consider converting either. I knew that none of the men courting me was Mr Right, and I had started to realise that finding him may take a while. I trusted that God would send him to me when the time was right. I did hope, though, that He wouldn't take too long over it.

I was busy enough with my new job at NBC Europe, presenting a daily show called *The Ticket NBC*. It had launched in autumn 1996, and the producers were hoping it would be watched by millions across Europe, the Middle East and North Africa. I got to cover a much wider range of subjects than at MTV, and the work was infinitely more interesting. I interviewed classical stars such as Yehudi Menuhin and Placido Domingo, as well as film directors Peter Greenaway and Michael Radford, the actor Ben Kingsley and the singer Ute Lemper.

The good thing was that I could set up a lot of fun shoots myself: a report, for instance, from the Festival of Speed held on the Earl of March's estate, as well as interviews with Peter Gabriel and Steve Winwood. I also covered a wonderful exhibition of Islamic art – Princes, Poets and Paladins – featuring a private collection by Prince Sadruddin Aga Khan from the Persian, Mogul and Ottoman Empires. And when the legendary Sufi singer Nusrat Fateh Ali Khan died in London at the age of just forty-nine, I produced an obituary. It was wonderful having the freedom to contribute ideas and to explore my own interests.

However, the downside was that many times I had to present topics that I felt conflicted with my new-found values and made me feel uncomfortable. Extremely violent films directed by Quentin Tarantino, for example, satanistic hard rock videos and so-called 'shock art' that had pornographic elements, to name but a few. This meant that I found myself grappling with my conscience. I enjoyed my job with NBC Europe a lot and, after all, it paid the rent. But deep down I was beginning to realise that I wouldn't be working in the entertainment business forever should my faith continue to grow. And it did.

Ramadan came round again, and even though we were only a few months into the show, this time I was determined to see it through. I did my best to psych myself up for it and mobilised all my energies.

It was particularly challenging because Ramadan coincided with the pre-Christmas period, and we were producing twice as many shows as usual so that we could all have a two-week break during the holiday season. I was in front of the camera all day every day, and also had to record endless voice-overs. Normally, I would boost my energy levels with a snack or two and sip water between takes to keep my mouth and vocal cords moist. But for a whole month I wasn't going be able to eat or drink between dawn and sunset. Despite my good intentions, I really wasn't sure that I would manage.

The first day or two, I had a headache, but then my body seemed to adjust and it actually wasn't as difficult as I thought. After a while, I even enjoyed my Ramadan. In the afternoons, I felt a little light-headed and as though I was in an altered reality – sober, but on a different plane. Fasting just seemed to make my heart and soul more receptive. And it heightened my sense of smell and taste when I got to eat at about four-thirty p.m. The discipline gave me a sense of achievement. Not least, fasting is a test of willpower and, whenever I felt my willpower weakening, I would tell myself that I could eat as much as I wanted after sunset. But then the strange thing was that after fasting all day long, I tended to feel full with just a small snack. Traditionally, Muslims break their fast with a few dates, as the Prophet did. I liked to have one or two large and succulent medjool dates with a glass of milk. I usually took some to work with me. My colleagues at NBC were very sweet and support-ive. Once one of my producers suggested getting me some lunch because I had to work straight through, but then he remembered I was fasting and apologised profusely for offer-ing. They were quite impressed by my stamina, and some even complimented me on how radiant I looked, perhaps because fasting is a process of purification on many levels, both physi-cal and spiritual. As well as renouncing food and drink during the day, I also tried to avoid gossip, impatience and anger, and instead tried my best to be polite and kind to one and all: not sure I always managed but I made a conscious effort. I read a little bit of the Quran every day, which was nothing com-pared to many who finish the entire Book during Ramadan. On a few occasions I joined Dr Amina for *tarawih* prayers in the evening at a mosque in South London. Perhaps all these things do give a person a special radiance. All in all, despite the hard work, I was sailing through my second Ramadan unexpectedly smoothly. I was further encouraged by something else my teacher Mrs Khan had told me: Ramadan was a time of intense blessings, especially the last ten days, because that was when, on one of the nights, the Quran was first revealed to Prophet Muhammad. And whoever fasted was protected throughout the whole month, she had told me. Nothing bad could happen to them. 'When Ramadan comes, the gates of Paradise are wide open and the gates of Hell are closed,' for those who fast, was a saying of the Prophet.[1] In this sense, fasting was like a spiritual shield. Knowing this gave me extra strength and confidence. Now and then I felt quite weak and went to bed much earlier than I normally would. It became particularly exhausting towards the end of Ramadan but, when it was over, a certain euphoria set in. I felt cleansed, fulfilled and closer to God. It was a wonderful feeling, and it lasted some time after I had finished fasting.

When one can see the crescent of the new moon in the sky, the month of Ramadan is over, and Muslims celebrate *Eid al-fitr*, the festival of breaking the fast. The word *fitr* is related to *fitra*, which means primordial nature. It is the pure state we are born in and which we aim to move back to through the spiritual discipline of fasting in Ramadan. Ruby called in the evening to wish me *Eid mubarak*, but I didn't see her the next day because she was busy celebrating with her family, as was everyone else I knew. *Eid al-fitr* is a bit like the Christian Christmas, except that it is linked to the spiritual practice of fasting for one month. Muslim families the world over dress in their finest clothes and meet for a festive feast, and children receive presents. Everyone congratulates one another and looks forward to savouring all those favourite dishes they have denied themselves for the past month. So, on my first proper Eid I felt a bit lonely. As a new Muslim, I didn't have a family to celebrate with. Nevertheless, I wanted to mark the day, so I went to the Regent's Park Mosque in the morning to join the communal Eid prayers. It was completely full, but even though everyone was jostling for space, the atmosphere was wonderful. I loved the way people from all different backgrounds had come together to pray to God. Everyone had spent the past month fasting, practising self-restraint, and doing their best to purify themselves spiritually and to come closer to God. In the mosque we were all given a printout so that the non-Arabic speakers could understand what was being said. I loved the melodic Eid prayers blessing the Prophet and his family. Then we warmly wished each other *Eid mubarak*. I felt connected to everyone there and part of a community. It was a bit of an anti-climax, though, to then go to work for business as usual. Luckily, Dr Amina, who also had no family to celebrate with, took me out that evening to our favourite Persian restaurant for dinner. Even though life soon returned to normal and that wonderful sense of purity eventually disappeared, I felt that by fasting throughout the month of Ramadan I had passed a milestone in my life.

∾

The following spring, in 1997, I packed my books again and flew to Granada. Friends had told me about a Sufi group in southern Spain, and I was keen to meet other European Muslims. For the first night they had organised a room for me in the wonderful Alhambra Palace hotel, a grand hotel with fabulous Moorish architecture, and then I moved to a more modest place nearby with a charming outdoor restaurant. Andalusia fascinated me for both historical and cultural reasons. I had once spent a weekend exploring the Alcázar Palace in Seville with Imran, and ever since then I had longed to return to visit Cordoba and Granada, the two other major centres of Islamic culture in Europe. I couldn't wait to take in Granada's famous landmark, the Alhambra Palace, hailed as one of the finest examples of Moorish architecture in the world.

Al-Andalus, which is the Arabic name for the region, exerts a special allure for every Muslim. It was here that Islamic civilisation flowered in Europe between 711 and 1492. During the Muslim reign in southern Spain, which lasted for nearly eight centuries, Andalusia became a leading centre of knowledge and learning. This Golden Age of Islam witnessed an intellectual flourishing in the areas of science, mathematics, medicine, pharmacology, theology and philosophy, commerce and art. It was a period of high culture during the European Dark Ages. Today *al-Andalus* is a region that still attests to Islam's deep roots in Europe not least through the Moorish architecture. Arab influences are also apparent in flamenco music and dance, the exclamation 'Olé' is said to derive from 'Allah'.

My friends had given me the phone number of an American woman called Bashira, who had converted to Islam many years ago. She had been living in Granada for a while and was married to her Sufi group's *muqaddam,* the local representative of the Shaykh, who lived in Scotland. I visited Bashira on my first day in the city. We talked for hours and she told me the story of her life. Like me, she loved Sufi music and played me some fantastic Arabo-Andalusian songs. I was entranced by these deep male voices singing God's praises, accompanied by a wonderful orchestra of traditional instruments such as lutes, ouds, tambourines and violins, and I later bought a few CDs of the music for myself.

I was looking forward to meeting the other Sufis in Bashira's group, with whom we had planned a visit to the Alhambra. We met up in the centre of town at eleven in the evening and walked up the hill to the Moorish citadel. It was lit up and completely empty. By this time of night the tourists had long since disappeared, and we could marvel at the elegance and grandeur of this architectural masterpiece at our leisure. An elderly gentleman from Algeria, who was there with his wife, explained to us the history and the symbolism of the architecture. We visited the Court of Lions with the water fountain at its centre, surrounded by sandstone columns and lined with round arches with such ornate filigree they looked like delicate lace; we admired the *murqanas*, the small, pointed niches stacked in tiers like honeycombs from the walls up into the dome, catching the light and symbolically linking Heaven and Earth.

I loved the typical Moorish mosaic tiles with their geometric designs all leading to a centre, which stands for God. The elegance of this architecture overwhelmed me. Not only exceptionally beautiful, it was also deeply symbolic; an aesthetic expression of religious principles, such as the Oneness of God. Many of the walls in the Alhambra are covered with floral arabesques that reflect plant motifs in nature, God's creation, and beautiful calligraphy with verses from the Quran. The most common proverb I noticed that was carved into every wall and pillar was the motto of the ruler at the time: 'No victory except with God.'

The hermetic principle – 'as above, so below; as below, so above' – was apparent everywhere I looked. I was struck by how eloquently this architecture reflected the sacred, reminding us with every pattern of the highest level of reality. The artists who had created this perfect beauty had done it as a form of adoration or worship, for 'God is beautiful, and He loves beauty', as the Prophet famously said.[2]

While I found the Islamic art and culture in Andalusia stunningly beautiful, I also came across one aspect of the religion that troubled me. A few men in the group lived in polygamous marriages, and in a way that didn't make all parties involved happy at all. Bashira, for example, told me that after she had been married for twenty years, her husband had taken a second, much younger, wife and brought her to live with them in their apartment, which I could see wasn't exactly spacious. Bashira witnessed how they flirted and disappeared into the bedroom together on a regular basis. Soon the second wife had a child from her husband, which only added to Bashira's unhappiness. I felt very sorry for her, especially because she had nowhere to go when she needed space. Yes, the Prophet had several wives, but they all had their own homes, even if they consisted of just one room. Muhammad also made sure he spent the same amount of time with each of them and tried to pay them all equal attention.

It transpired that many of the Sufis in Granada were looking for a second wife. Apparently, the Shaykh had told them that polygamy was a good way of spreading Islam in Europe. I was perplexed as I hadn't expected this kind of attitude amongst European Muslims. After all, polygamy is not exactly part of Spanish culture. Though I did like the Sufis I met in Spain very much. But thoughts of Bashira and her marriage kept haunting me and I felt that I couldn't just dismiss the polygamy issue. A Muslim man is allowed to take up to four wives and I asked myself whether I could seriously imagine living in a polygamous marriage. My instinctive answer was of course not. When I came home I decided to ask Gai Eaton about it. He had become a good friend and was always happy to discuss any Islamic issue with me.

Gai lived with his dog in his family home in Purley, south of London. So I went round one afternoon and, over tea and homemade sponge cake, showed him my holiday snaps and asked him about the polygamous relationships I'd come across in Andalusia. Before he answered he put a cigarette in his cigarette holder and lit it. Upper-class English gentlemen always used to have mistresses, he stated bluntly. He had a point, and I knew that mistresses were even occasionally invited to the family home, where they would sleep in the 'mistress room'. I had stayed in one myself at Badminton once – though not as anyone's mistress. 'In France, having a mistress was even more common than here,' Gai added. 'Not even Monsieur le Président was worth his salt without one. Men are polygamous, and that is a fact.'

'But there are also plenty of faithful men,' I countered.

'Yes, but then what we see in the West is a system of serial monogamy,' he retorted. 'In Islam, if the man wants another woman, he gives her respect and marries her. Their children will be legitimate. The first wife retains her status and is not out in the cold but always looked after. There is an argument for saying that with more women in this world than men, polygamy offers a solution that may be far better than secret affairs, as long as it is done with full transparency to all family members. Of course, jealousy still rears its head. It's a human emotion but the Quran says it needs to be checked and controlled. This, however was difficult even for the virtuous wives of the Prophet.'

I could understand Gai's argument, but I was glad he also mentioned that the injunction regarding polygamy was there to restrict the number of women Arabs were marrying. It was common in Arabia before Islam was revealed, during the so-called age of ignorance (*jahiliya*), to have over ten wives. And the orientalist idea of the Prophet marrying more than one wife as a perk was absurd. A life of promiscuity hardly started in a man's mid fifties. Moreover, Muhammad could have easily married and divorced four women at a time, had he wished to, and people would have gladly given their daughters to him. But he didn't. He married in order to support those women or to benefit the community; through one of his marriages an entire tribe was saved from captivity. Except for one, all his wives were divorcees or widows; some weren't even beautiful or young. Still, since I thought that the whole issue might well one day concern me directly, I continued my research and asked my girlfriends how they felt about polygamy.

Zero was all for it and told me that 'Muslim women, particularly in Africa, consider it an honour to marry a man who already has a number of wives. They see it as a sign of strength, and comfort themselves with the thought that sharing a great man with other women was better than having a boring one all to themselves. It also means they have less work to do in the household and more time to spend doing their own thing.'

Dr Amina told me she could imagine it 'only within an

Arabic context' and Ruby recounted that her *chacha* (uncle) in Pakistan had two wives, each had her own separate house and everyone was perfectly happy. 'It used to be very normal in Pakistan,' she explained. An Arabic girlfriend of mine, on the other hand, said she couldn't imagine it and that, when her husband joked about taking another wife, she told him that that would be a reason for divorce as she wasn't going to tolerate a co-wife. Her fear was that jealousy would distract her from Allah. But she also explained that polygamy was originally introduced as a way of solving social problems and to provide for widows and orphans after wars, assuring me that one option was to include a clause in the marriage contract saying that if the husband ever took another wife, it would be grounds for divorce. Some women even did this hundreds of years ago.

I still wanted to know what the Quran said about it and found out that it permits polygamy only on certain strict conditions, all of which must keep a man pretty busy. For a start, the husband alone has to provide for each woman and treat all of them equally, which, when it really comes down to it, is far from easy. Even the Quran admits that it's an almost impossible task. *If you fear that you cannot be equitable (to them), then marry only one (4: 3).* Later in the same chapter it says: *You will never be able to treat your wives with equal fairness, however much you may desire to do so (4: 129).* As I found out, many modern scholars therefore believe that the Quran actually promotes monogamy. With this comforting thought, I was able to lay the topic to rest – for the time being.

That afternoon with Gai Eaton we also talked about spirituality, which I wanted to learn more about. He told me that it was actually Sufism, the spiritual dimension of Islam, which had brought him to the religion in the first place. It meant being in touch with one's inner heart, the higher self, which is the gateway to God. Over the years he had found that Sufism was generally more accessible for Westerners than other, more formalistic, interpretations of Islam. Sufism was considered the heart of Islam, he explained. I had actually read in Martin Lings' book *What is Sufism* that the Arabic word *sufi* literally means 'woollen' and, by extension, 'wearer of wool', and that simple, woollen dress was always associated with spirituality, even in pre-Islamic times. According to Gai, the term *sufi* was also linked with the word *safi*, which means 'pure'. Basically, the Sufi keeps his heart pure.

I told Gai what Imran had said about some of the legends surrounding the extraordinary spiritual power of the Sufis. 'Yes, and many of them were women, especially in the early days,' he said. 'Take the example of the famous Rabia al-Adawiyya, also known as Rabia of Basra. She devoted her life to God and believed that everything – good and evil, beauty and ugliness – was an expression of God's omnipotence and perfection.'

When I left, Gai gave me a book about her called *My Soul is a Woman* by Annemarie Schimmel. Rabia was born to impoverished parents in the early eighth century in Basra, Iraq. She was orphaned at an early age, sold as a slave, and had to work hard for her master. One day he saw that she was surrounded by light during prayer. Realising that she was a saint, he feared for his life if he continued to keep her as a slave and freed her. She left Basra for the desert, where she lived a life of self-denial – spending the nights in prayer and fasting during the day. Many miracles are attributed to Rabia. She was believed to have levitated on her prayer mat and, on her way to Mecca, was said to have seen the Ka'ba coming to meet her. In time, people sought her out to listen to her teachings, and she had discussions with the most renowned religious people of her time. Though she received many marriage proposals, including one from the Amir of Basra, she refused all of them, saying she had no time in her life for anything other than God. When asked if she felt lonely, she responded: 'My Beloved is always with me.' According to the best-known legend about her, she was seen running through the streets of Basra with a torch in one hand and a bucket of water in the other. When asked what she was doing, she said, 'I want to put out the fires of Hell and burn down the rewards of Paradise, so that these two veils disappear and no one worships God from fear of Hell or from hope of Paradise, but solely for His own sake.' Rabia was the first to have initiated a higher form of worship, namely the idea that God should be worshipped out of love alone. This became known as the concept of Divine Love.

I loved immersing myself in the works of the great spiritual teachers and one key figure was Jalaluddin Rumi. He lived in the thirteenth century and was born in Balkh, in what is now Afghanistan but at the time belonged to the Persian Empire. He and his father migrated to Konya in Anatolia, where Rumi became a renowned scholar of the Quran and *hadith*, Islamic jurisprudence, as well as history, philosophy, mathematics and astronomy. But Rumi's life changed when, in the year 1244, he met the mystic Shams-al-Din of Tabriz. A deep friendship developed between the two of them and gave rise to an outpouring of inspired love poetry and lyrics that lasted until the end of Rumi's life. Today, his work is admired in the West as well as the East, and, ironically, this Persian spiritual master has become the most popular poet of all time in the United States, where he is seen as something of a New Age guru. His wisdom is timeless and universal. Anyone can understand it, anywhere in the world, regardless of culture and religion.

At first glance Rumi's poetry is about human love but, when looking deeper, the subtext is always Divine love. To Rumi, love was the only reality, and he saw it manifested in everything – from the desert, to fire and water. He describes the lovers' desire for one another as follows: 'Not only do the thirsty seek water; water seeks the thirsty.'

Rumi's magnum opus, the *Mathnawi*, a series of six books of poetry amounting to about 25,000 verses, begins with the words: 'Listen to the reed, how it tells a tale, complaining of separation.' The reed flute is a symbol of our soul, which longs to be joined to its source, God. For as long as we live on earth, we will only be able to soothe the pining of our soul with prayer and *dhikr* – the perpetual remembrance of God which is the key to Paradise.

Later that year, I went on a pilgrimage to Italy with my friend Agenta. She was a warm-hearted Catholic whose faith in God and kindness to less privileged people I had often admired. She regularly took an old man in a wheelchair to the pub, for example, and had been a great support to me after Imran and I had split up. She was very sociable, gave lots of great dinner parties and we often hung out together in London. She had invited me to stay with her at her holiday home on the coast of Italy. From there we went on an excursion to the sanctuary of Santa Rita, who lived at the convent of the Augustinian nuns at Cascia in the late fourteenth century. After the death of her husband and sons, she had become a nun and dedicated her life to helping the sick. Her love for God was infinite. Legend has it that, shortly before her death, Rita asked a cousin to bring her a rose from the garden of her old home in Umbria. It was January, and her cousin did not expect to find anything because of the snowy weather. But much to her surprise, she found a single blossoming rose and brought it back to Rita at the convent. This was the famous rose miracle, which made the rose a symbol of her sanctity. After Agenta and I had prayed in the chapel of Santa Rita and went to the nearby shop, I was suddenly struck by a faint scent of roses, which I mentioned to Agenta. She didn't notice it and, sure enough, there were no roses to be seen anywhere. I was perplexed – the fragrance had been quite unmistakable. Was it an illusion? Sometime later a Catholic priest who was a friend of hers told us that the scent of roses is considered sacred and that holy people, prophets and saints were felt to be carriers of the rose scent, just like Jesus and Mary, Solomon, Joseph and also Santa Rita.

In a book on Sufi healing I read that the rose also plays a significant role in Islam. Muhammad is believed to have admired the flower, and they say that his beads of sweat carried the fragrance of roses. The Sufis' arduous path to God is often described as the thorny stem of a rose, at the end of which awaits the flower itself, signifying Paradise. I was fascinated by the symbolism of the rose – heavenly perfection, love and death, eroticism and passion, the heart and femininity – and was also enamoured with its scent and its beauty. The rose became my favourite flower.

Later, I thought to myself that the different religions were all facets of the same truth: different windows through which we all look at the same sky, or, to use a German saying, different jugs with which we fetch water from the same well.

Chapter 9

Awakening

We shall show them our signs on the far horizons and in themselves.
(Quran 41:53)

The Ticket was taking up all of my time, and at some point the
German TV station RTL came to London to find out what I
had been doing since leaving MTV. The weekly *Stern* magazine had also been in touch. Both reporters sent to interview
me started out politely asking a few questions about my show
and the charity Learning for Life, but it soon transpired that
they really were interested in something different: my conversion to Islam. I was wary of this line of questioning, having
learned the hard way – from the deliberately sensationalist
coverage I had attracted in Germany – that discretion was
advisable. I still hadn't quite managed to figure out a way of
talking about Islam in Germany that wouldn't inevitably result
in negative headlines, and I was also worried about the effects
on my career.

It was different in London. There I had the feeling that
people were accepted for themselves and, when asked, I never
shied away from giving interviews about being a Muslim.
In fact it was a pleasure, because naturally I wanted to talk
about a topic that meant so much to me and I was keen to
try and build bridges. I once appeared in a very positive two-
page spread in the *London Evening Standard*, the feature was
reprinted in other newspapers, and eventually in Germany.
There it led to more prurient media interest, which I tried to

respond to by being as vague and non-committal as possible. On a chat show, when asked about Islam I simply said that it was a private matter, but that I believed in the truth of all religions.

All in all, it was a time when I often found myself struggling to reconcile my faith with the expectations of the professional world I inhabited. Even though I met many interesting people through my work at NBC and enjoyed having my own input, I became increasingly uneasy about having to paste a smile on my face and promote issues that were at odds with my religious beliefs. But I had come to realise that inner processes of change always manifest themselves externally, and that these external 'reflections' bounce back and change one even more. So it was probably no coincidence that in late 1997 something happened that completely broadened my horizons. It was just before Christmas when an acquaintance asked me if I wanted to get involved with a charity project in Bosnia and Herzegovina. The Pavarotti Music Centre was opening in Mostar, a divided city where the eastern, Muslim part had been under siege for nine months in 1993 and had been largely reduced to rubble through the shelling carried out by Croat and Serb forces.

The Bosnian War ended in 1995, officially claiming 200,000 lives all over former Yugoslavia. For the three years the war lasted, the international community stuck to a policy of non-intervention beyond a mandate to deliver humanitarian aid, while people were murdered or used as human shields, thousands of Muslim women were raped and millions of innocent civilians displaced. For four years, the city of Sarajevo was surrounded by Serb forces in the longest siege of a capital city in the history of modern warfare. Nearly 10,000 people were killed, and most of them were Muslims.

Meanwhile, in July 1995, the Army of Republika Srpska continued their mission of ethnic cleansing and captured the town of Srebrenica, where they massacred more than 8,000 Muslim civilians, mostly men and boys, while the 400-strong contingent of UN peacekeepers did nothing to stop them. It was the worst massacre on European soil since the Second World War and was later classified as a crime of genocide by the International Criminal Tribunal for the former Yugoslavia in The Hague.

I had followed the events in Bosnia and Herzegovina, feeling powerless to help. As a Muslim I feel an affinity for the fate of my fellow Muslims around the world. The Prophet compared the *ummah*, the 'community of believers', with a body: if one part of it hurts, the whole body suffers.[1] So I was thrilled to be invited to the opening of Pavarotti's music centre in Mostar by this friend of mine who was an adviser to War Child, an international charity that protects children living in the world's most dangerous war zones. It was a fantastic project. For years, the Italian tenor had been donating a large part of his earnings towards building a centre for music, hope and reconciliation amongst the ruins of the city. Brian Eno and David Bowie were the patrons.

The War Child offices were close to the MTV Europe studios in Camden, and I was happy to join them in helping raise awareness of the situation in Bosnia. Through my friend Janine di Giovanni, who was a war correspondent and knew Bosnia well, I set up a few interviews with bands and local activists in order to write about the situation in the German press.

There was another reason I was keen to visit Mostar. For over 500 years, while Bosnia was part of the Ottoman Empire, Jews, Christians and Muslims had lived there together in peace and harmony. Due to both its geographical position and cultural roots, Bosnia's identity is deeply European, making it a unique bridge between East and West, Christianity and Islam. Perhaps, I thought, the country might prove to be my own personal bridge between my European and Muslim identities.

The opening of the Pavarotti Music Centre was a moving

event attended by journalists from all over the world. Amidst the ruins of Mostar, the freshly renovated and gleaming white building served as a striking symbol of renewal and optimism. Inside, it boasted state-of-the-art sound studios – which the organisers hoped would soon be used by top international artists – as well as rehearsal spaces for music and dance classes designed to help children and young people work through the traumas they had experienced.

Various high-ranking politicians from around the world had sent messages, and cameras were flashing thick and fast as Bosnian celebrities and politicians greeted the host of international stars involved with the project who had arrived for the launch. Pavarotti was there, Tom Stoppard, Bianca Jagger, Zucchero, The Chieftains, Jovanotti and, of course, Bono. The U2 frontman addressed the crowd and proudly showed off his honorary Bosnian passport given to him earlier that year by Alija Izetbegovic, the Bosnian president, in recognition of the singer's support during the Bosnian War. 'Even though it's become uncool to be associated with charity functions, I am very happy to be here and to be part of this media event,' said Bono. 'Because in Bosnia, it was the media that shouted against the deafening silence of the international community.'

Bono did everything he could to highlight the plight of Bosnia. During their Zooropa world tour in 1993, U2 regularly broadcast live from Sarajevo when it was under siege, and screened footage of the war to their audiences. Another feature of the tour was the phone calls Bono would make during the shows to Western politicians to grill them on what they were doing to stop the violence.

When I visited, it was plain to see that normality still hadn't returned to Bosnia. The people I spoke to were all warm and friendly, but whenever I dug deeper in my conversations with anyone, it was as though their masks would slip, and their eyes would fill with such sadness that I was often moved to tears. So many of them had lost family, friends, and all their worldly goods. Others had been displaced and persecuted, forced to hide or to witness people – often their loved ones – being murdered or raped before their very eyes. 'Children turned grey overnight,' the writer Ozren Kebo told me. I was shocked to hear these stories and started to see that the bombs and damaged cities were by no means the worst effects of the war. Far more terrible was the way it destroyed people's souls and their faith in humanity and in the meaning of life. I soon realised how much work, commitment and support would be needed to give the survivors back this faith and to convince them of the need to build bridges of reconciliation between one another and towards a better future.

It was no coincidence that Mostar was chosen as the site for the music centre. Apparently, Mostar was named after the 'bridge keepers' (*mostari*) who guarded its famous landmark, the Stari Most. This literally means 'old bridge', and this six-teenth-century feat of Ottoman engineering spans the Neretva River and connects the western Croat part of the city with the eastern Muslim part. Traditionally, it was seen as a symbol of the bond between peoples and religions, the occident and the orient. It was destroyed by Croatian artillery during the war specifically because of its symbolic value – and for this same reason, UNESCO pledged to rebuild it. The reconstruction work was already well underway; workers were fishing one stone after another out of the river, replacing missing stones with stones from the same quarry as had been used 450 years ago. It was a hugely ambitious undertaking that took years to complete. In 1997, the only bridge connecting east and west Mostar was a rickety rope and wooden plank suspen-sion affair. The banks of the river were lined with romantic-looking cafes and restaurants beneath picturesque canopies of trees, and I could see that Mostar must once have been a very beautiful place. But for the time being, the cosy atmos-phere was blighted by the traumas of the war. The damage was mainly in the eastern, Muslim sector. The western, Croatian side of town was relatively intact. As I wandered around what remained of the Muslim quarter, I saw the words *Allahu akbar* (God is greater) graffittied on one of the many facades laced with bullet holes, a declaration of faith that opened my eyes to its eternal meaning. God is indeed greater than anything; compared to Him, everything in the world is relative – even the destruction, suffering and death the war inflicted on the people of Mostar will ultimately be judged by God and compensated according to His Divine justice. Knowing this gives hope even in the darkest of times.

One of the people I met at the opening of the music centre was Enes Zlatar Bure, the short, dark-haired lead singer and lyricist of the Bosnian band Sikter. I first noticed him and a blonde punk – who was his fellow band member – deep in conversation with Bono. The last time I had seen Bono was only half a year previously at his home gig in Dublin, the night Princess Diana and Dodi Al Fayed had died. Jim Kerr had organised backstage passes for my friend Dani and me. Bono had told me that evening that he had desperately wanted to record an album with Nusrat Fateh Ali Khan but that, sadly, he had died before it could happen. And as a man of faith, he gave my religion the thumbs-up, saying that he saw the rituals of Islam as a tremendous support in the faith and respected Islam as a 'commendable' path to God. 'It really is a full-on religion,' he said, 'not a hobby.' He was happy to support the music centre in Mostar and had a great affinity with the country.

Bure, meanwhile, was a funny and clever young man with a poet's soul. He reminisced about the U2 concert in Sarajevo just after the war had ended. The atmosphere in the city had been fabulous, and 'just as festive as it was when the Winter Olympics were held there in 1984. Suddenly the power was back on and the trains were running,' he said. 'Everyone who had come to the concert embraced each other regardless of religion and ethnicity and sang along together to hits such as "One" and "With or Without You".'

He reminded me how much music can move people. 'The best thing was that they'd come from all corners of the country and, once the show was over, they all returned to their villages as ambassadors of peace and reconciliation. Rock 'n' roll achieved far more than politics ever did,' he exclaimed. I thought back to my days at MTV and how I had often felt that what we were doing was superficial and meaningless. But in fact, as Bure had pointed out, music is a universal language and a force for good.

With typical Bosnian hospitality, he offered to take me on a tour the next day around Sarajevo, his hometown. Surrounded by hills, Sarajevo's traditional Ottoman kiosks stood side by side with grand family mansions, mosques, imposing art nouveau houses and churches dating back to the Austro-Hungarian Empire, while gigantic concrete housing and office blocks built in the 1950s were the legacy of the country's communist era. In the old city, we passed by typical dark wooden Bosniak buildings, mostly shops selling local arts and crafts. Sarajevo's history was palpable, but scattered all across town were also countless bombed-out ruins.

The city had long been home to four religious communities: Serbian Orthodox, Croatian Catholic, Bosniak Muslim and Jewish. Bure told me that the population had lived together in peace for centuries and the communities frequently intermarried – so more than one faith within a family was by no means an uncommon phenomenon. But since the war, mistrust had spread like a disease, spawning aggression and violence. Everyone felt under attack, he said. It was as though madness had descended on the population, and even members of the same family began turning on one another.

Bure also told me how – bizarrely – some of the best parties he had ever been to had taken place during the war. Everyone had so much pent-up energy, he recalled, and with their futures uncertain, they lived every day as though it were their last. They lost their inhibitions and for a time life felt wild and anarchic.

But fear cast a long shadow in Sarajevo. Bure recalled being painfully aware of his own mortality every day, 'but when 100 people feel like that, you have a party,' he laughed. I was amazed to hear that they had often danced all night to none other than Nusrat, letting loose to his rousing brand of *qawwali*.

According to Bure, many of his friends had embraced creativity as a way of releasing their energy, and lots of young people used to watch MTV to distract themselves from the horror of the war raging around them. I was happy to hear that, and as we wandered around town, people actually approached me asking for autographs. Steve may have been right after all when he told me that I had served a valuable purpose on MTV.

When I asked Bure where he drew his inspiration for his song lyrics from, I was surprised by his response. 'Sufi poetry,' he answered, and said that in the song 'Tonight is Forever' he quoted Rumi's words: 'Everything and everybody you love, one day you have to be prepared to lose.' The poem was recited to me again and again while I was in Bosnia, and, as true as it is, it made me sad.

Bure's grandfather was a devoted Rumi fan and would often read to him from the *Mathnawi*. 'Rumi was always close to the hearts of the Bosnian people,' Bure told me. 'We have a special tradition in Sarajevo: for the past 100 years a group of Sufis meet every week to read the *Mathnawi* for one hour. Usually Shaykhs and scholars give the reading and anybody is welcome to attend this circle. It takes them seven years to get through the entire work.'

Bure's grandfather was a Sufi himself and belonged to the Qadiri order, which still met for *dhikr* in a 400-year-old *tekkje,* the traditional Sufi place of prayer, in Sarajevo. The Qadiris apparently derive their name and their teachings from the famous twelfth-century Sufi Shaykh Abd al-Qadir al-Gilani, who was born in the Persian province of Gilan and later moved to Baghdad, where he brought thousands of people to

Islam. Abd al-Qadir al-Gilani was known to be the first official Sufi Shaykh.

I was fascinated to hear about Bosnia's Sufi roots. Reading about Sufism in London was one thing but it was something else to discover more about it in a place where it actually had a living history. I asked Bure if we could visit the age-old Sufi *tekkje*. Normally only initiates were allowed in but, thanks to his grandfather, he was able to arrange it for us.

From the outside the place looked unassuming and much the same as all the other white brick houses around it. Inside, however, it was a temple of tranquility. The keeper of the mosque led us into a large prayer room with a wooden floor and high ceilings; the walls were decorated with only a few exquisite pictures of Islamic art and two swords that crossed each other. This was where the Sufis had been meeting and meditating for centuries, I thought to myself as I breathed in the majestic and beautiful atmosphere. We walked through the hall towards the garden and came across an unexpected gem. On the white wall of the *tekkje,* which faced the garden and the cemetery, was an extraordinary example of sacred geometric Islamic art: a large flat stone circle measuring about two metres in width, decorated with straight lines forming a six-cornered star. When viewed from one side the lines crossed each other in such a way that calligraphic writing appeared – the names of God and Muhammad. On the rugged stone walls near the entrance to the garden, I could see countless phrases of Arabic calligraphy written in black, a bit like graffiti. The keeper of the mosque explained that every Shaykh who had resided at this *tekkje* had expressed his own realisations on these walls, insights he had gained through his devotions. The dervishes still meet in the *tekkje* today, he said, and while they don't actually whirl, they do rituals of *dhikr,* which sometimes result in a trance-like state and supposedly bring them closer to God. Seeing and sensing this tradition of Sufism – what's more, in Europe – felt extraordinary.

Although Sufism was deeply rooted in Bosnia, it had always remained underground, Bure told me. But it was this flame of faith in the hearts of the people that helped keep Islam alive during the communist era, when many mosques were deliberately destroyed. The same was supposed to be true of the Soviet Union, where religion was greatly suppressed and thousands of mosques closed, but faith could never be erased from the hearts and souls of the Sufis. 'Not a lot of people know about Sufism,' said Bure, 'although it has been practised here by different orders for over 500 years.' The first Sufis in Bosnia were the Mevlevis, the order linked to Rumi, and as we were leaving to go back to town, Bure pointed out a petrol station. 'There used to be a beautiful Mevlevi mosque here,' he said. 'Look what the communists have replaced it with.' I was appalled. 'Yes, and that's why the Mevlevis disappeared from Sarajevo,' he added. 'But now we have other orders here, such as the Naqshbandis, Qadiris and some Rifa.' I wondered aloud how the Bosnian Muslims felt about the Sufis. 'They are respected by all believers, and I too respect them,' he said. 'Those people are on a very high spiritual level and are gentle and wise. They are not like ordinary people.'

But as much as Bure respected the Sufis, religion didn't seem to play much of a role in his daily life, nor in that of his friends. They were all young artists, writers, filmmakers and musicians, and even though they described themselves as Muslims, most of them drank alcohol and didn't pray. Communism had eroded the influence of religion, especially amongst the younger generation, they all told me.

However, when I spent Christmas Eve in Sarajevo, I discovered that faith did matter to them more than it seemed. I had arranged to meet up with a journalist called Boba who had once helped out my friend Janine. Boba's mother was a Croatian Catholic and her father Serbian Orthodox – so some of the fault-lines of the conflict ran right through her family. Tall, dark-haired and fashionably dressed, Boba had reported on the war for the international media. She invited me to join her with some friends at the main Christmas mass in town. We found the church so crowded that there was standing-room only and we could barely get through the door. Bure and his friends were there too. When the priest greeted the Christian congregation, the response was lukewarm, but then, after a brief pause, he welcomed everybody else. His words were met by cheers and applause, and the atmosphere was like nothing I had ever experienced at a Christmas service. It was a true celebration of joy and love. Everyone – Christians, Jews and Muslims – had come to this church simply to celebrate and pray together.

Boba told me afterwards that during the war, the churches and mosques – faith in God in general – had become more popular. People needed God in those terrible times to find comfort and not lose hope. The younger generation in particular had discovered their religious identity and some of them had started to explore it.

Everything she told me was confirmed by Dr Mustafa Ceric, the Grand Mufti of Bosnia Herzegovina, when I had the chance to interview him a few days after Christmas. I went to meet him at his mosque. In his long grey coat and a tall white brimless hat that signified his position, he cut an imposing figure, but had a kind face, snow-white hair and a well-trimmed beard. 'When you see that earthly powers are not listening to you, that you are under siege in this city for four years and shot at without the international community doing anything to help, what should you do? Die?' he asked me in the course of our conversation. 'No, you pray to Heaven for help.' During the war with the Serbs and Croats, Ceric represented the defiance, dignity and God-consciousness of the Bosnian scholars, the *ulema*, who led their people in the face of international apathy and acquiescence. He was head of the Muslim community in Bosnia from 1993, and six years later he assumed the office of Grand Mufti, *rais-ul-ulema,* a position that combines religious leadership and political authority. Ceric is a member of various local and international organisations and societies, including the Council of 100 Leaders of the World Economic Forum and the Executive Committee of the European Council of Religious Leaders, and he is widely seen as one of the most important voices in contemporary Islam. His reputation in the Islamic world is as positive as it is in the West and he has received a number of awards for his efforts to foster understanding between faiths. To my surprise he echoed Bure's remarks when he described the U2 concert just a few months previously in September 1997 as the greatest step taken in Bosnia and Herzegovina towards reconciliation after the war.

But I really wanted to speak to this scholar for personal reasons. As a European Muslim I was still trying to reconcile these two identities of mine that sometimes seemed to be at odds with one another. How should I balance my life as a member of London society with being a Muslim? This was just one of the issues I needed to work out. Most non-Muslims seemed to believe it was a losing battle. So I asked Dr Ceric if he thought there was a conflict between European values and Islam. 'Not at all,' he said. 'Respect for other religions lies at the heart of Islam. And the principle of democracy is even anchored in Islam.' When I looked surprised he explained: 'Go right back to the origins of Islam. After Muhammad died, how did his followers seek his successor? They consulted with each other and chose his closest friend Abu Bakr in a democratic vote. Democracy is absolutely Islamic.'

But I needed more personal advice. I wanted to know if he thought I could make a positive contribution to cross-cultural understanding while working as an entertainment presenter, and what he said gave me hope: 'When you accept Islam, you don't cease to be the person you were before in your identity and culture,' he told me. 'The only thing that Islam does is make you stronger in your identity in terms of actualising your personality, and in understanding who you are, what you're supposed to do and what the purpose and meaning of your life is.'

I was still trying to find out why exactly God had called me to Islam and what my role on earth was to be. But for the time being, I was happy to ask questions and seek answers – of which Ceric had many. 'We can adopt the good aspects of Western culture, such as education, creative expression, a high standard of workmanship, honesty, reliability and punctuality, and at the same time we live according to Islamic principles,' said Ceric. 'But I don't agree with expressing Islam in Europe just by changing your clothes and wearing flowing robes, which belong to Eastern culture but not to Islam.'

Although I quite liked some of those clothes myself, I agreed that they could look a bit out of place, especially in small-town Europe. Ceric went even further and said he thought it was counter-productive when new Muslims in places like Frankfurt, Nice or Glasgow started wearing *jilbabs* or shalwar kameez. 'It makes them recognisable as something different or strange, and maybe even scary. Some Muslims are unconsciously damaging Islam by imitating certain cultural customs rather than Islamic ones,' he stressed. 'Instead they should be concentrating on the essence of the faith.'

Needless to say, I couldn't resist asking him about the hijab, the much-debated Muslim headscarf for women – a symbol of dignity and liberation for those who wear it, despite the discrimination they often experience in the West. But to certain non-Muslims, it can symbolise the oppression of women. Most classical Islamic scholars have declared the wearing of hijab an obligation for a Muslim woman. So what was this European scholar's view?

'I wouldn't tell you whether to wear it or not, you will have to decide that for yourself,' he said. 'But in my knowledge of Islam there is no statement in the Quran which says that in order to become a Muslim you must wear hijab. I know the principles of Islam, to believe in one God, the angels, God's revelations, the Prophets, and the Last Day, and to believe that whatever is happening here is determined by God. You have to say the *shahada*, the declaration of faith, you have to pray five times a day, and you have to pay the alms tax for the poor, fast and go to Hajj. These are the principles of Islam.'

I was relieved to hear that. After all, the Quran is the first source of Islam and I'd encountered enough problems merely telling people I was a Muslim in Europe. I felt that I would draw far more attention and an enormous amount of controversy to myself if I suddenly started wearing the scarf in Europe, which would defeat the objective. I promised to keep looking into the issue, but for now I was content with the answers I'd been given.

It was an inspiring discussion and I liked what the Mufti said. As a European I felt comfortable with his vision of Islam.

∾

Once back in London I needed time to process my experiences. The trip to Bosnia had given me plenty of food for thought and affected me deeply. I wanted to get involved, do something to help. And I felt a growing need to meet more European Muslims with whom I could share my thoughts and experiences. What I liked in Bosnia was that Islam was a natural part of everyday life. People understood each other without needing to resort to lengthy explanations. In one way we were all on the same wavelength – they looked like me and felt like me. They were European Muslims. In London I had met mainly Pakistanis, Persians and Arabs, and many of them were either very Western-leaning, not really practising Muslims, or very pious and strict. Most of them seemed weighed down with cultural baggage. Men in particular tended to seesaw between two cultures, unable to decide what it was they wanted: a housewife at home who cooked, looked after the children and obeyed her husband, or a woman with a mind of her own, who was an equal partner and had her own career.

The various Muslim ethnic groups I had encountered were quite hermetic in their social lives: they pretty much tended to keep to themselves. I didn't feel like I belonged to any one of them, nor did I really feel part of a larger, more open Muslim community. Very few Muslims I knew ever crossed over into my Western circle of friends, except for maybe Ruby, and most of the Muslims I knew stayed in their respective neighbour- hoods and mosques but wouldn't really mix with Muslims of other ethinicities. They even began Ramadan and celebrated Eid on different days, depending on which calculation they followed to mark the beginning of Ramadan – the local, physical sighting of the moon, the calculated time of the new moon, or Saudi Arabia's declaration to determine the start of the month. I couldn't understand this disunity.

Fortunately, London was nonetheless home to a growing Muslim cultural and intellectual scene that was modern, open- minded and sometimes even hip. I would often see these kinds of Muslims at cultural events and lectures. For a brief period in the late nineties, the scene even had a home in a private club called ArRum. It was the brainchild of Reedah Al Saie, a successful former lawyer. ArRum was hailed as the Muslim answer to the Groucho Club, with a restaurant, cocktail bar, chill-out zone, gallery and lounge – all divinely inspired – with a contemporary, yet Islamic feel. The interior had been designed by students at the Prince's School of Traditional Arts in Shoreditch, a trendy part of London's East End. They knew how to express sacred principles with a contemporary twist, creating amazing arabesques and geometric designs out of frosted glass, clay, wood or metal.

I loved ArRum. It was exactly the sort of social setting for Muslims that the community needed and of course every- one else was welcome, too. The atmosphere was relaxed, and women and men were able to mix and talk in a respectful way

– unlike in normal bars and pubs, where alcohol is served and flirtatiousness is the norm, which is the reason practising Muslims generally don't feel comfortable in such places. I felt the same by now and tended to avoid clubs, bars and pubs. Although I had never really frequented pubs much anyway. I had always found the mentality of getting drunk after work and eating packets of crisps instead of having a good meal and a glass of wine rather unappealing. I also thought it was off-putting that, shortly before eleven p.m., when it was last orders, people would ask for several beers at once.

Yet, I also didn't feel at home at traditional Muslim events in London, where men and women were strictly segregated. At certain talks, men would sit on one side and women on the other, which was nonetheless better than the events where men sat in front and women at the back, which I had also witnessed. I never really understood these attempts at segregation in London, where Muslims, like everyone else, studied and worked in completely mixed environments, and were often squashed up against fellow travellers on public transport. I always felt that Muslims are so aware of the ethical code of conduct between the sexes that they automatically keep to the boundaries of respect. They even call one another 'brother' and 'sister' to show that they are off-limits, as it were, and yet share a certain connectedness as brothers and sisters in faith. I understood that interaction with the opposite sex among Muslims wasn't as casual as between non-Muslims, and I even liked that. But sometimes this 'respect' could be taken a bit too far.

ArRum became *the* place to be. Yusuf Islam was a regular, as was former rock photographer Peter Sanders, who had snapped most of the major stars in the music business, including Jimi Hendrix. He and his wife Hafsa, a healer from Scotland, both used to belong to the sixties hippie scene and had developed an interest in Islam, and specifically in Sufism. Gai Eaton spoke there many times, and, when he launched his book *Remembering God*, he asked me to introduce him. We also held a few fundraisers for Learning for Life at ArRum, and the popular American scholar Shaykh Hamza Yusuf chose it as the venue for the launch of his CD collection of the *Burda, The Poem of the Cloak*, the most famous and beautiful poem in praise of Muhammad. Other frequent guests included Dr Amina, Abdul Latif Salazar, an American actor and film-maker, and his wife, who founded Archetype Publications, a publishing house specialising in books on spirituality. Sadly, ArRum lasted only a few years. It closed down when Reedah got married, because she wanted to devote herself fully to her husband and future family. We all missed it terribly.

But there were always interesting events happening in London. I enjoyed going to art exhibitions, the theatre, world music and Sufi concerts, and I found lectures and conferences a great way to educate myself, to learn more about Islam and other topics of interest. Fortunately, London attracted some of the best scholars from all over the world – East and West. One special lecture that I went to shortly after my trip to Bosnia was given by the renowned Persian philosopher and scholar of Islam and Sufism, Dr Seyyed Hossein Nasr. He had published over fifty books and hundreds of articles on subjects such as cosmology, ecology, Islamic art and philosophy, and was included in *The Library of Living Philosophers* along with Einstein, Sartre, Russell and other luminaries of twentieth-century intellectual life. Nasr was also one of the world's leading proponents of *sophia perennis*, the perennial philosophy, which is based on the idea that there are certain universal truths on the nature of reality, humanity and consciousness that are found in Divine revelations or philosophical teachings from different traditions, independent of time or culture. I was attracted by this idea as I had found it to be true in my own discoveries, and was keen to learn more from this leading scholar.

The lecture hall was jam-packed and Dr Nasr, dressed in

a black suit and Nehru-collared shirt, was a distinguished-looking gentleman. He appeared serious and humorous at the same time. As it turned out, he shared with us the keys that unlock the doors that lead to the Divine: religious practice, the cultivation of virtuous behaviour and knowledge of God. He explained how human existence took place on two levels, the horizontal and the vertical: the horizontal was the worldly, material, day-to-day life, and the vertical, the spiritual, transcendental dimension. 'Anyone seeking to draw closer to God needs to curb the horizontal and ascend to God vertically,' he said. 'And this means giving oneself fully to God – with all one's heart, body, mind and soul. There mustn't be any dark corners.' Skimming the surface wasn't an option, he stressed. 'People often tend to merely skate around the edges of religion, but what they really need is to plunge into its depths like deep-sea divers looking for treasures. Too many people nowadays make selective choices from various faiths – the New Age approach, but never embrace any one of them fully,' said Nasr.

It was true, so many people didn't believe in organised religion but liked to take the best from every religion or spiritual teaching. 'The most direct means of communication with God,' he concluded, 'are prayer and *dhikr*.'

As usual I saw many familiar faces in the audience, including Dr Amina, but I never expected to bump into someone I knew from the music industry. As I left to attend a film premiere party, I brushed past Chrissie Hynde, the lead singer of The Pretenders and Jim Kerr's first wife. I did a doubletake when I recognised her and we said hello. We had seen each other at various music events over the years, but had never spoken, even though Jim had recommended I seek her out and predicted we would get on really well. I had always been a fan of her voice and her poised performances. To me she was the ultimate Queen of Rock, and looked it even at the lecture that evening – amazingly youthful in boots, jeans and T-shirt, which she teamed with a well-cut, elegant black blazer.

Jim's hunch proved right. We had a nice exchange and when we met again backstage at a Bryan Ferry concert a few months later, we swapped phone numbers and became friends. After that I never missed any of her London concerts, which were always memorable occasions. Her every move on stage oozed cool and I loved her attitude. It turned out she was a serious Hare Krishna devotee, with a great love of God and an interest in all spiritual paths, including Islam. She often asked me about it, we went to some of the exhibitions by the Prince of Wales School of Traditional Arts together, and I also took her to a talk on Rumi, which happened to be given by Dr Nasr. He had made an impression on her, too, and for me he confirmed what I had long been thinking: in order to embrace my faith properly, I needed to integrate it more fully into my life. And that really meant I could no longer present entertainment shows. Too much of the material conflicted with my faith. God must have agreed, because in mid-1998, NBC pulled out of Europe. The powers-that-be had decided that the channel's mix of news and entertainment, drama, comedy and chat shows – a 'full programming channel'– just wasn't working there. The main problem was that most people wanted to watch TV in their own mother tongue, and English is a second language to Europeans. MTV Europe had adopted a localised approach for similar reasons. It was hoped that niche channels worked better; therefore NBC was planning to focus just on business and news. The timing from my point of view was perfect actually. I had just begun working on a new charity project, which I was really looking forward to getting off the ground. In the wake of the opening of the Pavarotti Music Centre, Mohammed Sacirbey, the UN ambassador to Bosnia, had asked me if I wanted to help organise a multicultural concert as part of a series of cultural and political events in Sarajevo scheduled to take place in September 1998. Called 'The Bridge', it was conceived as a way of promoting peaceful co-existence in Bosnia through political, cultural and religious dialogue. I accepted without hesitation.

On the agenda was a major music festival, and I was tasked with organising it. I used all my contacts to try and get the best artists on board. It had to be done at short notice, which was quite a challenge: I tried all the friends I had in the business but they were either booked out or not on the road and therefore didn't have a band in place. Then, flicking through the newspaper at work, I read a profile of the contemporary calligraphy artist and Islamic scholar Dr Ahmed Moustafa. His work was being exhibited at the Vatican museum by invitation of Pope John Paul II. The article also said that Moustafa would be giving a lecture at the Egyptian Cultural Centre in London and, since I loved Islamic art, I went along. Later that same afternoon I had an appointment with Mohammed Sacirbey and Yusuf Islam and was planning to persuade Yusuf Islam to headline 'The Bridge' festival in Sarajevo.

It was a very interesting lecture. Ahmed Moustafa began by quoting Plato – 'God is always doing geometry' – and went on to talk about the forms and proportions of Arabic letters, explaining how they were governed by strict geometric rules that give them a unique visual harmony. These were the same Pythagorean ratios that form the basis of musical concords and the Divine Section, he said. According to Pythagoras these mathematical laws not only govern the physical, but also the moral universe. Morality can be conceived of as harmony of the soul, a proper 'tuning' based on those same laws. 'Therefore, Arabic script, like music, has the power to have a moral and spiritual effect upon the viewer,' he stated.

I was fascinated by what I heard and had a look at Ahmed Moustafa's catalogue. Many of the pictures were done on canvas, others were embroidered tapestries. Ahmed's art was entirely inspired by the Quran and *hadith*, yet it had a contemporary feel, with the Arabic letters layered on top of one another in a feast of colours to create vibrant three-dimensional effects and shapes. Some of the work reminded me of video art and had a certain luminosity to it.

I approached his wife Catherine and she told me how successful his exhibition had been in Rome, that it seemed to have transcended cultural and religious boundaries and had deeply touched many of the cardinals. Pope John Paul II himself was most impressed, she said. I told her about 'The Bridge' project I was working on that aimed at mediation and dialogue between cultures and religions and we decided there and then that Ahmed's work needed to be exhibited in Sarajevo. She then introduced me to her husband, and he liked the idea too. Before long, we had agreed that the work could be transported directly from Rome to Sarajevo. Now all I had to do was convince Mohammed Sacirbey. Catherine gave me an exhibition catalogue to take along to my meeting with him and Yusuf Islam. I met them at the office of the new Brondesbury College for boys, one of the two successful independent faith schools which Yusuf Islam had created in the London borough of Brent and which became the benchmark for Islamic schools in Britain. Yusuf had become a serious philanthropist with an extraordinary portfolio of projects.

He gave me a very warm and respectful welcome. He no longer wore a white robe, and had returned to music, playing his first concert for seventeen years in 1997 in Sarajevo. They didn't take much persuading. Yusuf in particular loved the art, and it turned out that he knew Ahmed as well. He and Mohammed Sacirbey were keen to make it happen. I was fairly optimistic that he would also agree to perform at our festival, but when we discussed whether he would consider appearing on stage for a duet with Bono from U2, he refused, explaining that he would prefer not to appear together on stage with anyone who believed God had a mother. I knew it was the Muslim belief that God did not have children, nor was he born, as the 112th *surah* states and that Jesus was the son of Mary[2] – but despite their theological differences, I couldn't help thinking it would be amazing to see the two play together, also as a symbol of reconciliation. It was worth a try, but it wasn't to be.

The next few weeks were insanely busy. Finding bands was the first major task and then I had to book everyone's flights, find decent hotels and basically sort out all the logistics of the event. But transporting Ahmed's hugely valuable large-format art works to Sarajevo proved to be one of the most challenging jobs on my to-do list. Two weeks before the exhibition opened, as our excitement and impatience mounted, Ahmed, Catherine and I travelled to Bosnia. Catherine, a Scottish Muslim, became a close friend of mine and Ahmed, something of a mentor, was always happy to patiently answer my many questions on different aspects of Islam. On the ground in Sarajevo, we found ourselves plunged into complete chaos. Various bands cancelled and others had trouble with their visas. All sorts of unforeseen obstacles kept presenting themselves, not least because we were working with amateur event organisers rather than professionals. The biggest setback came when we were suddenly informed that the lorry carrying the art had gone missing. We went into collective shock. Various rumours started doing the rounds, the wildest being that the Mafia had waylaid the truck and stolen all of Ahmed's work. Mohammed Sacirbey immediately sent off a few men to track down the lorry. Ahmed and Catherine were on the brink of a nervous breakdown. But then, the afternoon before the official opening, the lorry came rattling down the street. Assisted by the helping hands of many volunteers, Ahmed managed to hang his work at the Umjetnička Galerija in record time. We worked day and night, and the end result was stunning. The exhibition's centrepiece was a huge Plexiglas cube, composed of 10 × 10 × 10 small cubes and opening in the middle onto exactly 99 cubes.[3] The artwork symbolised the Ka'ba, which is the Arabic word for cube, the house of God in Mecca. For Muslims, the number 99 has a special significance. God is said to have 99 beautiful names, each of which describes one of His attributes. These include Al-Ahad, The Unity, The Indivisible; Al-Ali, The Sublime;

Al-Aziz, The Almighty; Al-Haqq, The Truth, The Real; Al-Rahman, The Compassionate; Al-Hayy, The Living; Al-Alim, The All Knowing; Al-Karim, The Bountiful, The Generous; Al-Ghafur, The Forgiving; and Al-Wadud, The Loving. Ahmed explained to Catherine and me at dinner one evening how it is the aim of every Muslim to internalise some of these attributes and actually practise them. The spiritual teachers, the Shaykhs, sometimes even 'prescribe' certain names as spiritual medicine, as it were. Reciting selected names over and over again could help to assimilate these attributes into one's own self. The exhibition was opened by Alija Izetbegovic, then president of Bosnia and Herzegovina, to resounding applause. Politicians, religious experts, artists, musicians and a host of local dignitaries were in attendance, as well as the US ambassador. When the local Sufi choir came, they were so moved by the art that they broke out into an instant *dhikr*. The exhibition ran for another four weeks.

My favourite painting, 'Where the Two Oceans Meet', was a present from Ahmed to the Museum in Sarajevo. It was initially commissioned by Queen Elizabeth as a gift to the State of Pakistan on the fiftieth anniversary of partition. It is inspired by a verse from the Quran in *surah al-Rahman* which describes poetically how God created the world and set up a balance: *He released the two bodies of water. They meet, yet there is a barrier between them they do not cross* (55:19, 20).

A few years later I would witness this very phenomenon in Brazil, when I saw the *Encontro das Águas* – the meeting of waters – in Manaus. It is there that the Rio Negro and the Rio Grande meet, but without actually merging. Instead, their respectively black and sandy waters run side by side for several kilometres. I was blown away because the sight of it made me think of this verse in the Quran and also of Ahmed's lovely painting, which depicted in the most beautiful colours two entities that meet but are separated by an invisible barrier; a symbol for the harmonious co-existence of complementary opposites – Heaven and Earth, East and West, man and woman – and the creative tension between them.

The concert finally took place on 1 September 1998, in the Metalac Arena. Five minutes before the first act took to the stage, Mohammed Sacirbey gave me a bit of a shock asking me to host the entire event. It was unexpected and, even though I wasn't in the least bit prepared, I headed out onto the stage. The programme included Sarajevo's main religious choirs: Orthodox, Jewish and Sufi. The concert got underway with a performance by a young imam called Aziz Alili, who had come especially from Zagreb to sing 'Shahid' (God's witness). It was a song mourning and honouring the fallen in the war; it couldn't have been more appropriate. His angelic voice and the haunting melody of this special song sent shivers down my spine and moved many to tears. Aziz was not only a hugely talented singer; he was also a very good-looking young man and could probably have been a big star if he had wanted. But, being a *hafiz* of Quran, which means he knew the entire Book by heart, he had instead chosen to work as an imam in a mosque in Zagreb. The French Arabic fusion rocker band Djam & Fam, Eric Burdon and a few others put on a truly spectacular show, and finally, after midnight, the main act, Transglobal Underground, fronted by Natacha Atlas, took to the stage and grooved the house down. Natacha's steamy belly-dancing to African drums wasn't exactly Islamic, but for once it didn't matter. Everyone was so happy, dancing the night away and enjoying themselves; and even the Swiss cultural attaché joined the fray. At four a.m. I suddenly realised that I had lost my handbag, and with it my passport, plane ticket and wallet. I went back to the stadium to look for it and found the clean-up well underway. All the chairs were stacked in tall piles on the sides, and I soon located my bag on top of one of them. Some kind soul had obviously put it there. And to my surprise nothing was missing. Whereas in London only a few weeks later, I had coffee with Bob Geldof in his favourite

KRISTIANE BACKER

MTV VJ

Hamburg, 1984

With David Bowie at the launch of VH1 in Hamburg, 1995

Hosting an MTV show in Belgium

At the opening of Euro Disney in Paris, 1992

With the Rolling Stones and competition winners in Boston, 1995

Carrying the Olympic flame in Saragossa, 1992

Interviewing Lenny Kravitz

With Annie Lennox at the MTV Video Music Awards in LA, 1992

With friends Ruby, Dani, Chrissie, and Fa, December 2005

With Chrissie Hynde and
John McEnroe at Wimbledon

Interviewing Bob Geldof at the opening of Euro Disney, 1992

Imran and Moby in the
Himalayas, 1992

In Pakistan, 1992

In the Himalayas,
1994

Badshahi Mosque,
Lahore, 1992

With Dr Seyyed Hossein Nasr in Egypt, 2001

With Gai Eaton in Cairo's Khan-al-Khalili Market, 2001

With my father, 2006

With my mother and sister, 2005

With the former Bosnian President,
Ali Izetbegovic, Catherine and Ahmed
Moustafa, 1998 *(above)*

Tekkje in Blagaj near Mostar *(right)*

With the Sufi group at the Maqam of Ibn Ataillah in Cairo, 2003

Shaykh Abu Bakr Siraj ad-Din

At the Al-Azhar Mosque in Cairo, February 2010

The Ka'ba in Mecca during the Hajj, 2006

Climbing the Mountain of Light near Mecca, 2006

Mr Imam in front of the Prophet's Mosque in Medina

In front of the Haram Sharif in Mecca

Dr Amina with Mr
Imam and Aziz in
Arafat

Praying in Arafat

Jabal al-Rahmah,
Mount of Mercy,
at the end of the
Arafat Plain

Inspired by Muhammad media campaign, London, June 2010

At the Suleymaniye Mosque in London, May 2012

coffee shop that he called his 'office' on the Kings Road, and in full daylight my bag was stolen from underneath my seat.

The highlight of the trip to Bosnia was a visit to Mostar with Ahmed and Catherine. The Bosnian minister for culture had invited us and wanted to show us the centuries-old *tekkje* of the Naqshbandi order in nearby Blagaj, which his ancestor had helped establish. After a glorious drive through Bosnia's hills, we travelled alongside an idyllic river which eventually fed into a small lake surrounded by steep, rocky cliffs. Our destination was a quaint, white house with an almost wave-like roof and wooden window frames. It was built into the cliff side and overlooked the turquoise waters. It was a serene spot and, walking down the path along the river towards it, I could sense the atmosphere of spirituality. We went into the house, took off our shoes and found ourselves in a small room that was carpeted with red, handcrafted rugs and lined with cushions. This is where the sessions of communal *dikhr* took place. With the soothing sound of running water in the background, it was a peaceful place for prayer and contemplation. As a special treat, we were allowed to visit the *tekkje's* sanctuary, which housed the tombs of some big Sufi Shaykhs of the Naqshbandi order who had once resided here. Their coffins were kept on the first floor of the house, in a small room with a very low ceiling. Prayer beads lay on the green velvet draped over the coffins. At the head end were small pillars covered in fabric, with green turbans on top.

I entered the room cautiously, but withdrew quickly when I saw a young man praying at one of the coffins. He gestured to me that he was finished and that I was welcome to go in. As I passed him at the door, he suddenly mentioned my name with a question mark. 'Never in my life would I have expected to see an MTV presenter here!' he then exclaimed. I was equally surprised to be recognised in such a remote, spiritual place as this, especially since I was wearing a scarf to cover my hair.

While we were standing before the coffins, Ahmed

suggested we quietly recite the *Fatiha* for the Shaykhs. As I spoke the Arabic words, something happened to me that I had never experienced before. I suddenly felt an intense wave of energy coming at me from the direction of the coffins. I nearly fainted and a powerful feeling of love filled my chest. I had no idea what was happening to me. Even though I was dizzy, my heart was replete with this blissful feeling. It was as if something inside me had awakened that I never knew existed. This sensation lasted for the entire time we stood in front of the coffins, and only began to dissipate when we walked away.

When I told my friends what had happened, I learned that the friends of God, the *awliya,* are said to carry from their life of prayer and devotion a spiritual energy that never leaves them. It is called *baraka* or blessing. Traces of this *baraka* may emanate even from the tombs of these pious people. The young man who had been praying when we arrived was waiting for us outside. We had a brief conversation, and the exchange ended with him declaring that no doubt we would meet again one day.

On the way back, we visited the tombs of the Bogomils, an ancient Christian religious community that lived there for almost 500 years, from the tenth to the fifteenth century before the Orthodox Church eradicated them. The tombstones featured interesting designs, figures that appeared to be extending their oversized hands in gestures of peace, and other stones showed a crescent moon carved next to a cross – poignant proof, the minister pointed out, of the historical peaceful coexistence of Christianity and Islam.

Then it was time to say goodbye. The minister of culture had invited us for tea in the garden of his country home before we left. His ancestral villa had been completely destroyed in the war, so we arranged our chairs in the garden in front of the ruins. It was early evening, and as we sat there with the sun going down, we reminisced about recent events. I was still basking in the afterglow of what had happened at the *tekkje* that day, and was extremely happy that everything had gone so well with the concert and the exhibition. Catherine and Ahmed were also content – and grateful that his work had been so well received. I believe it was only there, in Sarajevo, that Ahmed fully realised the potential of his art to help bring cultures together and to awaken people spiritually.

To avoid any more problems like the ones we had experienced with the last transport operation, we had his work flown back to England on a Royal Air Force plane, officially organised at the highest level. Readjusting to my daily life back in London wasn't easy after those moving experiences, and added to that a heavy workload awaited me. I had fulfilled a long-standing dream of mine and bought a small, typically English two-storey house with two fireplaces and a balcony. There was just one catch: it needed to be completely renovated.

Chapter 10

My Spiritual Path

Never be without remembrance of Him,
for His remembrance gives wings and strength of flight
to the bird of the Spirit.

Rumi

My life had felt unsettled for years. I had always rented in London, moving every few years as young people in the capital tend to do, however I had come to realise that I needed a safe haven to call my own. After searching for nearly one year, my friend Dani told me she had seen a 'For sale' sign outside a little house near the Thames. It felt right immediately even though it obviously needed a lot of work. Fortunately, I had found a great architect to help me with the conversion. To begin with, I was told the renovations would take three months. That seemed reasonable enough, and I was somewhat irritated by people's reactions: 'Welcome to building hell!' some friends dryly remarked. Not me, I thought to myself. As it transpired they were being more realistic than I was and, before I knew it, twelve weeks had turned into twelve months. When I moved in on my birthday, only the guest room was ready. So for some time, I lived out of suitcases in the converted attic, while the workmen drilled and hammered away downstairs from dawn till dusk. It was indeed sheer building hell, but I didn't have a choice. I couldn't afford to pay rent on top of my mortgage forever. Progress was unbelievably slow. The first construction company went bust owing me quite a bit of money, and I fell out with the second – we constantly argued over everything from colours to the agreed number of coats of paint, installation of windows and heaters, sockets and switches. It was never-ending. One day during Ramadan, I felt so weak that I had to walk out in the middle of an argument with the workmen and lie down for ten minutes to gather my strength before I could get back in the ring. I was getting increasingly desperate until a friend of Dr Amina's saved the day by putting me in touch with two builders from Libya. Ahmed and Mustafa were brothers, and practising Muslims. They transformed the construction site into a lovely home. Mustafa was the older of the two and a model of friendliness and politeness. We soon got talking, and I found out that he and his brother came from a big Sufi family. Mustafa told me about his childhood in Libya, the regular *dhikrs* and *hadras* that took place at home, sacred sessions of praising God to the rhythmic beats of a drum. Growing up around Shaykhs and learning from them as they did, the brothers' lives revolved around spirituality. Mustafa could read people's hands and faces. He also gave me plenty of advice for my daily life, including the Muslim method of anger management, which came in particularly handy while I was living in a nerve-wracking building site called 'home'. The Prophet advised that when we felt anger or rage, we should sit down, and that if we were sitting already, we should lie down for a while. If that didn't help, then ritual washing, even just washing hands and face, was another way of quenching inner fire. Specific invocations, deep breathing and somehow disengaging from the situation could also help in an emergency. I tried to follow Mustafa's advice and found it very useful: consciously attempting to deal with negative feelings constructively instead of giving in to them inevitably had a calming effect. During our conversations, the brothers told me about an aunt of their friend Ahmed, who also knew Dr Amina and had recommended the building team in the first place. She happened to be visiting London that week. She had been a healer in a hospital in Libya and had worked with seriously ill patients to help alleviate their pain. Her healing powers were famous and, after moving to Dublin, she built up a loyal following of private patients. Ahmed asked me if I would like to be treated by her with prayer, to help me cope with the stress. The medicinal effects of the Quran might be just what I needed, I thought, so I agreed. One evening, Ahmed brought her round. As a traditional Arab woman she wore a long robe that brushed the floor and a headscarf. The three of us drank tea together, and then Ahmed left us alone. We sat down on the floor of the guest room upstairs, with a bowl of water between us. She laid her hands gently on my head, took a deep breath and began to pray in Arabic. We stayed like that for the next half an hour as she recited from the Quran. She never touched the bowl of water, but afterwards told me that the water had absorbed her prayers just as I had, and that I should drink it over the next few days. Prayers, she told me, were vibrations of energy that were absorbed by everything in the environment, not only by people. Healing through prayer and verses of the Quran is known as *ruqya*. It is a process of spiritual cleansing which helps banish negative energy and fortifies our spiritual beings, our souls. After my treatment, I did indeed feel more relaxed and happier and, over the next few days, I drank the water, sip by sip. Mustafa and Ahmed were brilliant at implementing all my ideas for the house and their very presence made for a pleasant atmosphere. They would silently invoke God, do *dhikr* while working, and play such lovely Arabic music that some of the neighbours would drop by just to get a taste of it. Mustafa understood Islamic art and interior design and had a sixth sense when it came to aesthetics. He mixed the perfect colours for the walls and decorated the kitchen with hand-glazed turquoise and dark blue tiles to give it an

Eastern feel, also turning wooden folding screens covered in arabesques and geometric patterns into window blinds. I had found the tiles and screens on my last trip to Pakistan with Ruby and had them shipped back to the UK. When my new house was finally finished it looked beautiful. Everyone who came to visit remarked on its positive energy, and for that I undoubtedly have Mustafa and Ahmed to thank. When all the work was done, I felt as though I had taken a major step forward – also in my faith. As soon as I moved in I was always able to find time for my five daily prayers, fast during Ramadan and enjoy the peace and quiet that a spiritual life requires.

Every move is a new beginning and a chance to take stock. My job at NBC had come to an end, and I was looking for new professional opportunities. While the building work was going on, I didn't have access to my papers and tapes to apply for jobs nor did I have a desk, a table or an office space, let alone peace to concentrate. So I decided to do something I had long dreamed of doing and enrolled at university.

I had been interested in medicine, psychology and nutrition ever since I was a child, and was particularly intrigued by the relationship between emotional problems and physical complaints. So I registered at the University of Westminster for a one-year course with Neal's Yard on herbal medicine and also signed up for Islamic Studies at Birkbeck College. But before term began, I was in for a pleasant surprise. It was Ramadan, and I went to a Turkish mosque with Dr Amina for *tarawiah* – the special prayers in Ramadan that follow the night prayers. One of the ladies there recommended reciting the 94th chapter after my prayers for blessings and ease during the most sacred night in Ramadan, *Laylat al Qadr*. *Qadr* means power or destiny. It was during this night that the Quran was first revealed to Prophet Muhammad. The only problem is no one knows exactly when this special night takes place: it could be on any of the uneven nights of the last ten days in Ramadan, most likely on the twenty-seventh night. But the whole ten-day period is a time of spiritual intensity for Muslims. Many even retreat to mosques for non-stop prayer. Visiting Mecca during this time, I heard, is an amazing experience.

That night, I read the 94th chapter as recommended, which took me nearly one hour. It was one of the first that I had memorised after becoming a Muslim, since it contained my name Yusra, meaning 'ease'. The line in that *surah* which is even repeated reads: *with hardship comes ease.*

The next morning, out of the blue, my friend Michael Radford called to ask if I'd like to use up some of his airmiles and visit him in California, where he was working with a colleague on a film script. I couldn't believe my luck and thanked God and Mike, in that order, for rescuing me from my building site and the London winter – at least for a couple of weeks. It felt indeed like God had heard my prayers and sent me a little bit of ease during my endless building works at home, which, however nice the builders now were, surely had to qualify as some kind of hardship. I was soon flying off to sunny California, where I met some very interesting ex-hippies, visionaries of sorts, who were following different spiritual paths from mine, but our hearts were in the same place, and our goal in life was the same: 'inner-tainment' instead of entertainment. Relaxed and inspired, I returned to London looking forward to beginning my studies.

∾

The course gave me an overview of various natural healing methods, such as homeopathy, Qigong, traditional Chinese medicine, herbal medicine, nutrition, flower remedies and aromatherapy. Meanwhile, at the London Muslim College, affiliated with Birkbeck University, I attended classes on the life of the Prophet, Islamic history and Islamic law. To my surprise,

I began to see parallels between the two fields – healing and religion. Homeopathy for example, a form of holistic healing, doesn't focus only on physical symptoms but takes all levels of the human being into account. It is about dissolving the layers that patients have acquired over time, much like peeling an onion, so that they return to their original healthy condition.

Religion is also a process of healing, I discovered – a healing of the soul. Even our language points to this relation. The words 'holy', 'wholesome' and 'healing' all have the same root. (In German, this is even more striking: *heilig*, *heil* and *heilen*.) Muslims believe that all humans are born in a state of purity, our *fitra*, and it is only in the course of our lives that we tarnish our soul through bad habits and wrong behaviour. Through spiritual practices such as prayer, recitation of Quran and *dhikr* we can cleanse these acquired 'black spots' in our soul and return towards our original primordial nature.[1] More so, *dhikr* is said to enliven the heart. The Prophet likened those who remember their Lord and those who don't to the living and the dead.[2] Through my studies I learned that as part of our evolvement as human beings we need to raise our creative energy upwards, towards the light, the Divine, and instead of getting stuck in the base chakra energy, to transform passion into compassion, learn to act from our hearts and our higher selves. Finding our purpose in life, that which God intended for us, is an important part of our development. Edward Bach, who invented the Bach Flowers, called it our 'soul journey'. It is a process that requires introspection, self-reflection and, most of all, absolute honesty with ourselves. Living a lie – pretending everything is fine when we are actually discontented – is hard work and, in the long run, even bad for our health. We pay a high price for compromising on this honesty – and neglecting ourselves. Finding our inner passion, our mission in life, and connecting with who we really are, our spiritual being or our higher self – this is the key to success and fulfilment. Our 'soul' purpose is our sole purpose in life.

I wanted to find my soul purpose, my reason for being on this earth. As an ex-MTV presenter, now a Muslim, what was to be my mission? I was an idealistic person, but nothing that could fulfil my idealism had presented itself to me. I prayed to God for guidance and asked Him: When will I be working for You? But I didn't receive an answer. For now I just had to be content with the notion that 'the journey is the destination' and enjoy the ride. Meanwhile my personal life continued to change and I felt that my new neighbourhood mirrored this inner development. I used to live near the fairy-tale, pastel-coloured Albert Bridge, which looked all glitzy and glamorous when it was lit up at night. My new home in contrast was near the more down-to-earth Battersea Bridge, which actually contained Islamic-looking arches in its railing. Now, when I wanted to see people, I often met up with Ahmed and Catherine Moustafa, Gai Eaton, Dr Amina or Ruby – friends of faith and mentors who had become like a small family to me.

I was delighted to discover though that some people from my former social circle and in the music business were also spiritually inclined. Teixeira for example was a radiant, slender and energetic woman, originally from Angola, who turned heads in her extravagant dresses but was also a passionate, hands-on, full-time mother. Together with her husband Tony Hambro, a banker and an extremely talented and prolific painter who also played the drums in a band, she used to throw fantastic dinner parties in their huge flat in Pimlico overlooking the Thames. Now she had minimised her social life to devote herself to her family and her spiritual path. Then there was Jacqueline from Austria, a former model, now a financial adviser and a practising Catholic who meditated regularly and taught yoga in her spare time. She used to be very sociable, but had become self-contained and now loved nothing more than reading different Holy Scriptures.

I would meet people like these at charity events, lectures and art exhibitions, or simply at home. I also had a friend called Cora, a witty lawyer from Ireland who stayed at my place for a while. She too was Catholic and we often had intense conversations about the values and practices of our respective religions. All these friends and I came to the same conclusion: faith doesn't divide people – it unites them. The common foundation is a worldview with a spiritual dimension, which includes God, a Creator, an Infinite Intelligence, or a Higher Power and the afterlife – for some reincarnation – and draws moral and ethical values from faith.

For me Ireland was the country in Europe that was closest to the Islamic way of life – except for the Guinness and the whiskey, of course. Faith mattered in Ireland in daily life a lot more than in the UK or Germany for example. I liked how the society was very family oriented. I got to know and love the Emerald Isle on several visits to my old school friend Nora. She lived on the south-west coast with a fisherman and their three children in a house that had a terrific view over the Atlantic and the Ring of Kerry from every window. It was in Ireland that she found her peace, her health and her faith. Every Sunday they all went to church. But she was open to other spiritual traditions as well. And like mother, like daughter: one day, eight-year-old Shauna wanted to watch me pray. She was curious and in awe about anything that had to do with God and said she also prayed. When we were out on a walk a fog suddenly descended and we found ourselves surrounded by clouds hanging heavy over the fields. 'When I see mist and fog, thunder and lightning, it makes me think that's God,' she told me. I was happy to see how as a child she had an innate sense of God; I think living in the countryside facilitated this, for being close to nature somehow connects people with creation and also the Creator.

On many long hikes across the hills and along the rugged coast, I learned Quranic verses in Arabic off by heart, and then I'd find a peaceful spot to take a rest, enjoy the scenery and read some of the works of the great spiritual master, Shaykh

Abd al-Qadir al-Gilani. One of his books even helped Nora make her decision to move from Hamburg to Ireland. Gilani's contribution to Islam was so immense that he became known as *Qutb al Aqtab*, the cardinal spiritual pole of his time. Born in the eleventh century in the Persian province of Gilan, he was well known for his honesty as a child. Legend has it that once, when he was attacked by thieves and they asked him if he had money, he replied that he did and showed them the gold coins sewn into the lining of his cloak. The thieves were ashamed and left him and his family alone. He moved to Baghdad to study law and later spent years wandering the deserts of Iraq. When he re-emerged he began preaching in public, and not only Muslims but also Jews and Christians would gather to listen and learn from him. Gilani was known to be a *wali Allah*, a friend of God, who was gifted with the ability to speak to people's souls and heal them spiritually. His book *Al Fath ar Rabbani* or *The Sublime Revelation* helped me to put things in perspective and focus on the essential. 'Purify your intentions, your inner being, your heart and be sincere in your actions,' he wrote. 'God looks into your heart, not at your outer form. He looks at what lies behind the clothes … He looks into your private sphere, not at your public show.' Reading these statements about what matters and what doesn't, I reflected on my former life, where I was now, and where I wanted to go – and also what kind of people I wanted to associate with. I knew I still had a long road ahead. But reading Gilani helped me find my direction and uplift me. 'The believer is secure in the knowledge that God will not make him experience something as a trial unless this will result in some benefit, either for this world or for the hereafter,' he says. To emphasise the point, he quotes the Prophet:

How wonderful is the situation of the believer, for all his affairs are good. If something good happens to him, he gives thanks for it and that is good for him; if something bad happens to him, he bears it with patience, and that is good for him. (*Sahih Muslim*)

Perceived in that way, our whole life is a win-win situation. Gilani helped me to look at the world with different eyes – God's eyes – and I felt happier and more content after reading even small passages of his books. Something else struck me about Gilani. Whenever I was troubled or in need of fresh input, I would open *Sublime Revelations* at random. I found that whichever page or passage my eyes fell on, Gilani seemed to be addressing my problem, and would unfailingly help me lift my particular burden. It was a mystery – but God obviously sends His messages in various ways, and Gilani's books were one of them.

~

However wonderful the teachings by classical Shaykhs, I realised that in order to progress on my spiritual path, I needed more than books, words of wisdom and friends. I felt a growing need for a teacher, a spiritual master who could lead me on my path to God. Gai Eaton had once told me the Sufi saying: 'Whoever has no Shaykh, his Shaykh is Satan.' And so I began to look. 'Seek and ye shall find, knock and the door will be opened,' says the Bible. It wasn't quite that straightforward, and my quest was a process of trial and error, with error usually prevailing. Once I found myself in a Sufi group around a Yemeni Shaykh. The women were only allowed to follow his words from a separate room on another floor in the house, watching him speak on a monitor that had been set up in a children's bedroom upstairs. After the Shaykh's speech, we laid out a tablecloth on the floor and crowded around it to eat together. I felt a lot of warmth from the women, but I knew this group wasn't for me. Trying to find my way home again, I asked a truck driver I passed on the road for directions. 'You're a long way from home,' he said, and that was how it felt. In another Sufi group based in my area, many of the members weren't actually Muslim. They drank alcohol and didn't follow an Islamic way of life. It might have worked for them, but I was following a more orthodox path. As so often, I visited Gai Eaton at his home in Purley to ask his advice. Gai suggested he introduce me to his teacher, with whom he had converted in Cairo all those years ago: Dr Martin Lings, also known as Shaykh Abu Bakr Siraj ad-Din. I had no idea that the scholar whose books I enjoyed reading so much was also a Sufi Shaykh and was curious to find out more about him. Gai told me that he had been born in England in 1909, had a Protestant upbringing and had studied English literature at Oxford. At that time he had developed an interest in world religions and was drawn to the works of René Guénon and Frithjof Schuon. He eventually became a student of Schuon and in 1938 joined his Sufi group in Basel, Switzerland, where he was initiated into the *Shadhiliya tariqa*, an order that is especially popular in North Africa. In the 1940s, he taught English at the University of Cairo, studied Arabic and Sufism and also worked as a personal secretary to René Guénon, who was known there as Shaykh Abdul Wahid. Gai met him in Egypt. 'During the anti-British uprisings in Egypt Lings esacaped with his wife back to England, continued his studies in Arabic,' Gai told me, 'and he wrote his PhD on the Algerian scholar and Sufi master Ahmed al-Alawi, who was also Schuon's Shaykh. It is published under the title *A Sufi Saint of the Twentieth Century* and is considered one of the most important works on Sufism in our times. Later Dr Lings worked at the British Museum as the Keeper of Oriental Manuscripts.' When I discovered that not only was Martin Lings a great scholar but also a spiritual teacher, I was thrilled by Gai's suggestion that I should meet him and see if he could perhaps become my own Shaykh. Gai arranged everything and I picked him up one morning in late April 1999. The drive to Kent was lovely, past rolling hills and valleys stretching into the horizon as far as the eye could see. The county's reputation as the Garden of England was definitely well deserved. When we arrived, the door was opened by an elderly gentleman dressed in a woollen Moroccan *jalabia*. He was slight in stature, had piercing blue eyes, a beard and a full head of grey hair. He welcomed us with a smile and invited us to enter; we followed him down the corridor of his little cottage into a garden ablaze with cardinal blue, red, yellow and white flowers, surrounded on all sides by open fields. He was a passionate gardener, he told me in his elegant Queen's English, and had a keen interest in the symbolism of colour. He sought out rare blooms all over the world and went out of his way to find exactly what he was looking for, such as a particular shade of blue that symbolised Divine perfection. 'Gardening is a sacred art and a balm for the soul,' he explained.

I knew instinctively I had found my Shaykh. He was not only wise and deeply spiritual, but also had a special aura about him – a *baraka* (blessing) that was the fruit of nearly seven decades of unfailing devotion to the remembrance of God. Lings was an orthodox Sunni Muslim who followed the Shariah and looked at everything from a spiritual perspective. He firmly upheld traditional values, while being realistic about living in the modern world. He had no television in his home, no computer or anything else that might distract him from the true purpose of life. But at the same time, he would be pragmatic about the need to be efficient in one's work, and if that meant using computers he would never dissuade his followers from doing so. What mattered in one's work was that it be done well, to the highest possible ethical and professional standards, and that one dedicated one's work to God and His creatures. In this manner, one could see work as a form of prayer, he explained.

The largest room in the house was the prayer room, the *zawiya*, which was flooded with light and exuded serenity. The room was sparsely furnished in traditional Moroccan style, a few striking calligraphies depicting the name 'Allah' and other sacred formulas adorned the walls, while a soft carpet, sheepskins, and a light Moroccan kelim lined the floor. At the far end of the room, a copy of the Quran lay on a stand. Dr Lings briefly introduced me to his wife Sayyida Rabia, who then chatted with Gai Eaton while I had my meeting with the Shaykh. I complimented Dr Lings on the lovely room and garden and he explained to me that the ambience at home needed to be conducive to the spiritual life, as it had a great effect on the soul. The decor should be beautiful, but simple, sober rather than garish. He suggested I create a prayer room in my own home, or at least reserve a corner of a room just for prayer and meditation. 'For "he who creates a space for God, God will create for him a space in Paradise,"' he said, quoting the Prophet.[3] Shaykh Abu Bakr wanted to know about my life and how I became a Muslim. I told him in brief and that I had read his books *What is Sufism?* and the biography on the Prophet, and how much I enjoyed reading the classical masters, but that I was looking for a spiritual teacher who could guide me practically. The Shaykh explained to me that *tariqa* essentially meant 'way': the way to God and by extension also Sufi order or brotherhood. Every authentic *tariqa* traced its spiritual lineage through the different Shaykhs back to the Prophet. Following this esoteric path involved hard work, discipline and spiritual effort. The fight against our rebellious lower self, the *nafs*, was part of this effort, as was cultivating virtuous behaviour, polite language and spiritual practice.

I was ready to give it my best shot, I told him, but was obviously far from perfect. He suggested I take time to see whether this path was for me. Beyond the rites that were binding for all Muslims, he explained that for those who wanted to go that extra mile on the path to God there were additional, voluntary rites such as the invocation of God's names or other formulas.

'And what is the aim of all these exercises?' I asked him.

'The objective of Sufism is sainthood,' he said. 'That we

become one of the *awliya*, the friends of God. Ultimately, the Sufi path is preparation for death, our meeting with God.'

He then outlined for me the essence of the spiritual path, the perpetual remembrance of God or *dhikr w*hich should continue to sing inwardly even in the midst of our daily activity. This was our connection with God and through the *dhikr* we would be able to experience paradisal joys already here and now. I for now should simply begin with reciting the first part of the *shahada, la ilaha illa' Llah*, out loud, quietly, or even just to myself for ten minutes or so, three times a day. That was a good start, he said. Before I left, he recommended some books, including his own biography of the Shaykh al-Alawi, and invited me to join the *majlis,* which took place every fortnight. I was overjoyed to have found a spiritual teacher whom I trusted and I was looking forward to the communal prayer meetings where I would meet like-minded Muslims.

The dress code at the *majlis* was traditional Islamic. This meant either saris with long-sleeved tops underneath or colourful *jalabias* for the ladies, with a loose scarf covering the head, and cream-coloured Moroccan *jalabias* and turbans for the men. So the first thing I did was buy a *jalabia* made by the British fashion designer Allegra Hicks. I had met her previously when I had consulted her on some of the designs for my home. She had since added kaftans to her collection, which were perfect for my purpose. When I tried one on at home and prayed in it, I found that it actually felt much more comfortable than praying in jeans. The loose fit of the kaftan suited the different prayer positions better, and it covered the body well. The *majlis* didn't take place in Kent but in a large house in South London. The group was mixed, comprising a couple from Sri Lanka, a few Pakistanis and Arabs, some Persians, a young American woman who had a Lebanese husband, a Brazilian lady and Sayyida Rabia, the Shaykh's wife. The women in the *tariqa* were addressed by the North African title *Sayyida*, which basically means 'lady', and the men as *Sidi*. The *zawiya* was quite a bit larger than the one in the Shaykh's house, but similarly sparsely decorated in a North African style with a few beautiful calligraphies adorning the walls and wicker matting all around the room.

We prayed together, the men in front, the women at the back, as was common practice in all the mosques I'd ever been to. The reason for this, I was told, was to prevent men from developing inappropriate thoughts as the different prayer positions involved bending and kneeling with one's head on the floor and one's backside in the air. After the ritual prayers, the men sat down together in a circle at the front of the room and the women remained at the back, sitting in rows. Then we recited the *wird*, a series of prayer formulas that begins with the *istighfar*, the plea for forgiveness. Holding our prayer beads – containing 99 beads corresponding to the 99 Names of Allah – we recited *astaghfirullah* ('I seek forgiveness from Allah') 99 times, and each time we pronounced the formula we moved one bead. After that we repeated several other formulas. The Shaykh addressed the *fuqara*, as the Sufis on the spiritual path are known. The word is plural for *faqir*, meaning spiritually poor – dependent on God. The Shaykh gave a speech pointing out the importance of concentrating on the Real, on God rather than the illusion, which is the world. We sang a few beautiful songs praising God and the Prophet, followed by the *hadra*, a sacred dance reserved only for the group's initiated members. I sat on the floor and watched. The Sufis stood up for the dance and performed a series of synchronised movements to the rhythms of a hand drum, reciting God's name throughout. It sounded like an intimate mantra, spoken with reverence and fervour. I didn't know if and when I would be allowed to take part in the *hadra*, but I was happy to be there and keen to come again. I wanted to be a good student, and in those first weeks and months, I practised *dhikr* several times a day. Initially I felt nothing. But taking regular time out did me good and had a calming effect. I told the Shaykh about my enthusiasm. He praised me but warned me presciently that it was important to practise the *dhikr* consistently even if I didn't feel like it. He added that moments of reluctance were not untypical and that I needed to resist them and carry on anyway. The best thing to do, he suggested, was to use every free moment for *dhikr* – for a true Sufi always had God in his heart and on his lips. The Shaykh turned out to be right, because my initial eagerness did eventually start to wane. Sometimes I was too tired, other times just lazy. Now and then, I was frustrated because nothing seemed to be happening – no signs from God, no enlightenment, nothing. But that wasn't the point, the Shaykh explained. What mattered was the inner connection with God, which builds slowly and only transforms us gradually. Another obstacle, however, was that I often found it hard to concentrate during the *dhikr*. I mentioned my problem to one of the ladies in the group, who suggested that whenever I noticed my thoughts drifting, I should invoke a little louder. I tried it at home and it helped, but only a little.

Nevertheless, I always loved the group meetings, the *majalis*. However stressed or anxious I was beforehand, I would return home feeling happy, relaxed and uplifted. These gatherings became something of a lifeline to me when things in other areas of my life got challenging. I was in the middle of a professional transition, which worried me – and my parents – and also I was still single and really wanted to meet someone.

But at least I had got to know people in Shaykh Abu Bakr's group who were kindred souls. They were pious and gracious and at the same time highly educated – many had PhDs and were Oxbridge graduates. Their approach to faith was spiritual and intellectual rather than dogmatic. And it wasn't a matter of mere theory either: faith permeated their entire lives. Many of them had even integrated their faith into their professions, writing books on spirituality, making documentaries about great masters in Islamic history, such as Imam al-Ghazali, or about the Hajj, Ramadan and other Islamic subjects; and others had translated metaphysical principles into architecture, interior and garden design. This was exactly what I would love to do, I thought – fuse my profession and my beliefs, if only I knew how. I was also impressed by the Sufis' attitude. They were all exceptionally polite, and quick to help others whenever they could. I never heard any one of them swear or curse. 'Islam is *adab*' – good manners – Gai Eaton often said, quoting the Prophet.

Sidi Hassan – Gai's Muslim name – was a perfect example of *adab*. Sometimes, when I drove down to Purley, he would make tea and bake a sponge cake; and I noticed how he always poured fresh milk from a bottle he had just opened for me, whereas he himself would first finish the old milk. And he made sure to feed his dog a few dog biscuits too, so she didn't feel left out.

I soon started meeting up with some of the other friends from the group and found out that even the Prince of Wales was an admirer of Shaykh Abu Bakr. Apparently they had private audiences every year. Glamorous Samiya was a trained lawyer who owned a jewellery store. She originally came from Sri Lanka and lived quite near me with her family in a big house in Holland Park. The interior was designed tastefully in a warm and welcoming East-West fusion style, while the centrepiece of the garden was a fountain decorated with Moroccan tiles. Samiya was married to one of the top surgeons in the country, and the couple combined traditional values and a spiritual life with contemporary zeitgeist. The best thing was that they always invited me and other new Muslims without families of their own to celebrate Eid at their home. At last I felt part of a warm and welcoming community on this special day of celebration. But not only that, she sometimes organised *iftar*, the breaking of the fast, for a few friends. And during the last ten days of Ramadan, Samyia and her husband usually held a small *majlis* on *Laylat al-Qadr*. On that occasion

Shaykh Abu Bakr made a rare exception and travelled from Kent to London to lead it.

We all sat on the floor in her living room around a tablecloth and broke our fast together with dates and milk, a soup and a simple meal. We then prayed *maghrib*, the evening prayer and did the rites together. Praying with others unfailingly gave me a sense of belonging and a spiritual connection. Even the Prophet had said that praying in congregation is twenty-seven times better than praying alone. I loved these gatherings for God. Inspired by my new friends in faith, I was doing my best to work more on myself. I did my *dhikr* regularly, sometimes also when standing in a queue or going for a walk. Idle time was the perfect opportunity to connect with God, I felt. I noticed that whenever I was out of sorts, the *dhikr* brought me back to my peaceful centre. In the Islamic bookstore near Regent's Park I bought a set of Quran CDs in Arabic – with an English translation for my car – so every long drive was now filled with the Divine message. And when I was stuck in traffic, I didn't get impatient and irritated any more, I just listened to the Quran. Empty moments were now filled with meaning and, instead of feeling lonely, I was in the best of company – with God. The combined effect of spiritual practice and learning, my interaction with the Sufi group and their good example slowly began to change me from within, the way I thought and felt about the world. I used to be free-spirited and didn't like being told what to do, and, especially as a teenager, I had often rebelled against rules. But now I found that I was happy to follow them – at least, to the best of my ability; after all, they came from above, from God, the supreme authority. Of course, this didn't mean I became a goodie-two-shoes and never slipped up – far from it. Old habits die hard, but at least I made an effort, and whenever I caught myself doing something or reacting in a way I shouldn't, I apologised to whomever I might have offended and, of course, to God. The Prophet says that we learn from our mistakes: 'A servant sins and makes mistakes in order to draw closer to God through prayer and remorse.' Mrs Khan, my first Islam teacher in Tooting, had given me similar advice. When I felt a bit down and depressed, she asked me to think back to what I had done in the last few days. My feeling was a sign of being far away from God and I needed to return by asking for forgiveness. I certainly felt that my faith was deepening and that I was learning essential knowledge that was benefiting me in my life, knowledge that was not commonly taught. One really had to look for it, sometimes in unusual places, but the effort was worth it. Every Sunday, Shaykh Abu Bakr and his wife Sayyida Rabia invited different *fuqara* to their home in Kent and, several times a year, I was amongst the lucky guests. These gatherings would always begin with afternoon tea. Despite his age, the Shaykh insisted on serving us himself. Then we would all go on a wonderful walk together, and each of us had an opportunity for a one-to-one chat with the Shaykh to discuss private matters or ask personal questions. On one such walk I was curious to find out how he saw the different religions working side by side – did they all lead to salvation or was one more valid than the other?

'Islam is the last of the revealed religions, the most complete and the most universal; it not only acknowledges all religions, it encompasses their truths as well,' the Shaykh explained. At the same time, '*Islam* means submission to God. And we can submit to God in different ways,' he said. 'All revealed religions were sent from Heaven to meet man's needs at different times.'[4] He compared the various forms of religions to points on the circumference of a circle, which all led to the centre, to God, like the spokes of a wheel. On the level of form they each differed but on the transcendental level they united. 'When we transcend the level of form we journey from multiplicity to unity, from the particular to the universal. Each authentic spiritual path followed with commitment leads to God. The Sacred, the nearness to God, the mystical experience, is at the heart of all authentic religions, and this is where they meet.'

I liked what he said. Shaykh Abu Bakr expressed what I had felt – both at the tomb of Santa Rita, and in Bosnia. He also told me how he had once been approached by somewhat zealous Muslims who wanted to know how best to convert everyone in the West to Islam. His reply to them was that 'it is far more important that people believe in God again. If everyone truly practised the religion of their culture, that would be a great achievement.' It was good to hear such a conciliatory worldview.

After the walk, it was the tradition that one of the ladies served an evening meal, which she had pre-cooked and brought along. It was an honour for us women to be able to cook for the Shaykh and the twelve or so friends present, although it was also a bit daunting because the pressure was on to get it right. I had a good reputation as a cook and had even been told I had *baraka* in my hands, which was flattering. But on one occasion, this 'blessing' deserted me. At home, I prepared a dish of couscous with chicken and vegetables and brought it in two large pots in my car to Kent. All I had to do was heat it up. Unfortunately, I didn't set the brand new oven to the correct temperature, so when the other women and I served dinner, the food was lukewarm. We had to take everyone's plates away again to reheat the food. I was mortified. When we said goodbye that evening after the *majlis*, I felt the Shaykh was just a little curt; he was obviously displeased. The worst of it, however, was that Gai Eaton called the next morning to tell me he had an upset stomach, and Shaykh Abu Bakr and a few of the others also got sick. Reheating must have awakened some dodgy bacteria. I expected never to be allowed to cook for the group again, but the opposite happened. The Shaykh invited me back only two weeks later – which was unusual – and, to my surprise, asked me to prepare the same meal again. I couldn't believe it and was very relieved. It was a wonderful example of the principle of spiritual generosity: forgiveness not punishment opens hearts.

And the heart, I discovered, had a special significance in Islam. The Quran talks about those who have hearts. But when speaking of the majority, it says: *It is not the eyes that are blind but the hearts* (22:46). Muslims even pray to God for *al-basira*, the clear vision of the heart, to be able to recognise the truth and make the best decisions. I have often heard Arabs use phrases such as 'ask your heart' or 'my heart tells me'.

Even in *The Little Prince*, Antoine de St. Exupéry writes that 'it is only with the heart that one can see; what is essential is invisible to the eye'. Perhaps because the heart is considered the seat of God within us. I longed to follow this way of the heart.

∽

In late 1999, I travelled with my Sufi group to Egypt for a big meeting in Cairo with Sufis and scholars from all over the world. It was a wonderful opportunity for the *fuqara* – especially for those who didn't live in London – to meet the Shaykh and to be in the company of fellow travellers on the path to God. For all of us, it was a chance to enjoy the atmosphere of a traditional Muslim country. I encountered an eclectic mix of people, who were all disciples of Shaykh Abu Bakr. They came from Jordan, Egypt, Malaysia, South Africa and Spain; there was also a young Turkish couple, the Hilalis and the Salazaars from London, the Persian Mustafa Majdub, who travelled with the Shaykh and sang beautifully in the *majlis*, and Sida Rida, a scholar of the Quran who lived with his wife Sayyidah Nureen near the Shaykh in Kent and was his close aide. Dr Seyyed Hossein Nasr, whose lecture I had attended in London, arrived later from the US with a group of his own students. I was amazed at the kind of converts I met in Cairo. Many of them were colourful characters, such as the charismatic Shems Friedlander, a graphic designer from New York who had once worked in the music industry and now made films about Rumi and taught at the American University. Then there was the journalist Abdallah

Schleifer, another American, who had been reporting from the Arab world for different media outlets for decades and was the long-time Bureau Chief for NBC News in Cairo. He later founded and directed the Adham Centre for Journalism at the American University of Cairo. I also met Gray Henry, a formidable lady from Louisville in the United States, whose ancestors had founded the city. She owned the spiritual publishing company Fons Vitae, and it was at her villa in the leafy district of Maadi that the Shaykh stayed when he was in town.

Cairo was a sprawling and vibrant metropolis. Amidst the hustle and bustle and general chaos we visited all the tourist sites, admiring the treasures of Tutankhamun and browsing through the Khan-el-Khalili market, the oldest in Cairo. We stocked up on exquisite handicrafts, including handmade prayer beads with silver inlay, blue and turquoise hand-blown glassware, and silver jewellery with Islamic designs and semi-precious stones. Some of the ladies took me to a bespoke tailor where we had special embroidered *jalabias* custom-made to wear at the *majalis*. We drank chai around the corner at the famous El-Fishawy cafe, smoked *shisha* and paid a visit to the nearby Bayt al-Suhaymi, a historic, beautifully restored mansion house in the old Islamic part of Cairo, an area that dates back to the tenth century. Every other morning, we rode out into the desert on handsome Arabian horses, galloping away in the morning sun with the pyramids in the distance. One time Sidi Rida and I raced back to the stables in a heart-stopping ride over rocks and crevices and up and down the desert dunes. Exhilarated as we were when we arrived, we were both relieved we had managed to stay on our horses.

However, we hadn't travelled all the way to this Islamic capital so steeped in spirituality just to have fun and see the sights; rather we were there to strengthen our souls. The *adhan* reverberated across the city from every single mosque calling the faithful to prayer five times a day and, although I loved to hear it, I felt fortunate not to be staying with some of the other friends at the Husayn Hotel right next to the major mosque in the old town. Sidi Hamid, an American convert who joined us from Washington, told me that he would almost fall out of bed every morning at four-thirty, jolted awake by what felt like the shouting of *Allahu akbar* … right into his ear.

As soon as these words resounded from one of the many minarets, most people seemed to stop work and head into the mosques in their droves to pray together. My friends and I also tried to join in wherever we were. There was a special feeling in those beautiful, ancient mosques, which would be completely full during lunchtime on Friday. It is the day of *jumah*, the communal prayer, which is an obligation for men. We decided to go to Friday prayer in the fourteenth-century, open-air Sultan Hassan Mosque, one of the largest buildings in the Muslim world. We took off our shoes and the men walked barefoot to the front while the women gathered towards the back in an elevated area from which we had the best view. In some mosques I had visited, the men got to bask in the splendour of the main prayer hall, while the women had to huddle together in small, separated rooms elsewhere, so I was glad to see it was different here. Huge as it was, the mosque was soon packed with thousands of people, most of whom wore long multi-coloured *jalabias*. In the middle of the courtyard at the huge fountain some worshippers were performing their ablution and children ran about playing. I imagined that the same scene could have taken place hundreds of years ago and I felt as though I had gone back in time. Egypt's Grand Mufti, Dr Ali Gum'a, gave a speech from the *minbar* high above the crowd. This was followed by the *jumah* prayers, where everyone filed in neat lines to pray two *rakat*. My shoulders touched the shoulders of the two women next to me and so did my knees. It really was a wonderful feeling to pray in this ancient mosque among all the other women while soaking up the atmosphere around us. Of course, we also visited Saydna Husayn – around the corner from the Khan-el-Khalili market – the mosque named after the

Prophet's grandson Husayn ibn Ali whose head is believed to be in the shrine. For Muslims this is the holiest place in Egypt. Many people from all over the world come here to pay their respects and pray for Husayn. But this wasn't the only famous shrine in Cairo I discovered. There were many tombs for eminent scholars or *awliyah*, the so-called friends of God. With Samiya, her husband Hilali and Safina, another friend from London, who was originally from Pakistan, we went on a *ziyara* (visit) to some of the tombs of the saints. I was pleased to discover that many of Cairo's saints were actually female. Without exception, all of the mausoleums were crowded with visitors. Sometimes I noticed a kind of energy emanating from the shrines, and although it wasn't as intense as what I had felt in Bosnia, it was a sweet reminder. Such visits to the tombs of saints are frowned upon by conservative schools of Islam such as Wahabism who fear that people are praying to saints – which in my experience they don't – instead of to God, and that, they argue, would be *shirk*, idolatry, the greatest sin of all. Live and let live, I thought. For me, the highlights of the trip were the *majalis* in the evenings. We were usually picked up in the early evening by a minibus from our hotel, and sometimes I got a lift with one of the friends from the group who lived in Cairo, an Austrian convert. He always drove Dr Nasr and two of his companions who were also staying in the Shepherd Hotel, right on the Nile and not far from Tahrir Square. As it was getting dark, we gathered outside the hotel, all dressed in our *jalabias*, and drove out to a mosque in the City of the Dead, a vast cemetery just outside Cairo, where not only thousands are buried but also many poor people live. The *majalis* took place in the mosque, which housed the *maqam* (dwelling) of the sage Ibn Ataillah al-Iskandari. The third Shaykh of the Shadhiliyya Sufi Order, he lived in the thirteenth century and wrote the first systematic treatise on *dhikr* called *The Key to Salvation* – a useful guide for the common problems in prayer and *dhikr* which I experienced only too often, such as wandering thoughts or not really feeling

God's presence. I resolved to order it when back in England to help me worship God like the Prophet recommended: 'as if we see Him, because if we don't see Him, He certainly sees us.'

There, at Ibn Ataillah's mosque, over 150 Sufis from all over the world prayed together and said the prayer formulas in unison, which felt quite powerful. Then Shaykh Abu Bakr addressed us, we sang songs and did the *hadra*, through which I sat down and watched as I wasn't initiated yet. The sheer sight was awesome.

I tried to soak up as much spiritual energy as possible here and at the other sacred places, and sometimes I would go off exploring by myself. One morning, I spent two hours in the Al-Azhar Mosque, an oasis of calm right at the centre of the ancient quarter called Islamic Cairo. I tried to do an extended, lone *dhikr*. After a while of sitting still and invoking God, I got up and wandered barefoot through the aisles, repeating my formulas, and then sat down again. Lost in contemplation, I suddenly noticed a cat padding towards me all the way from the other side of the mosque. It brushed against my legs and abruptly sprang into my lap, purring away contentedly while I stroked it. When I told some of my friends about my experience at dinner that night they weren't surprised. Their cats loved to join them when they were praying at home. Animals have an acute sense of the sacred, explained Dr Nasr. I was pleased because if even an animal had noticed my prayers, I felt I must have been doing something right. While in Cairo, I arranged to meet with Abdallah Schleifer for lunch at the Conrad Hotel directly opposite the Shepherd. He was an interesting personality and I thought I could learn from him. A tall, slim man in his early sixties, he was still working as a journalist, and running the media centre he had founded at the American University in Cairo. He had been a practising Muslim for over fifty years and was a member of various international Muslim and inter-religious organisations, as well as being a professor emeritus and a highly sought-after expert on the Middle East. Abdallah recalled his own journey to Islam. He was part of the Beat generation in the States, he told me, the literary scene that revolved around William S. Burroughs and inspired the hippie movement. 'Free love and experimental drugs were as much part of the bohemian counterculture as a rebellious attitude, poetry and prose,' he said. He soon ran away from the dark side of the Beat scene, however. 'Too many friends had died from drug overdoses, and promiscuity and indifference to family ties left me feeling intensely lonely,' he recalled. At the time, Abdallah was an 'existential agnostic' as he described it. 'I didn't deny the possibility of God, but simply couldn't comprehend Him,' he said. 'Most certainly not as an old man with a long white beard sitting magisterially on His throne above us in the sky.' I never really imagined God to be like that either, I agreed.

'What made you realise that, despite your wild lifestyle and all the drugs, you were actually deep down searching for spirituality?' I asked him.

'Perhaps it was my love of beauty,' Abdallah replied. 'Beauty, as the Platonists would put it, is the manifestation of The Good. Also, looking back in the context of the conservative society of the fifties and sixties, even our outrageous lifestyle was a kind of spiritual quest. But a dangerous one, because it centred around the idea that the truth could only be revealed by fearlessly experiencing everything. We even pursued our art by "disordering the senses" through drugs and sex, as the great nineteenth-century French poet Rimbaud, our inspiration, had suggested.' I could recognise some of what he told me from my own life and circle of friends. Sylvie's husband Caesar, for example, was aristocratic, handsome and an in-demand society jeweller. He was a member of the order of the Rosicrucians and studied medieval texts. Even his jewellery was inspired by these pursuits and we had many discussions about faith and philosophy. But one day he was found dead in a hotel room, his hands and throat slit after having consumed a cocktail of drugs. It was a deep shock to me because he had been a friend, and in fact I had seen him with his wife in Hamburg only two days before he died. At the funeral they played Lou Reed's 'Walk on the Wild Side', and the priest told me that he thought that Caesar's drug use was a misguided quest for spirituality. I felt he was probably right. Sadly he never saw the light before he died, far too young.

The serious danger posed by a romantic affinity to drugs and criminality was something that fortunately Abdallah had grown to understand in time, and he decided to head for Morocco. The old city of Tangier was a popular watering hole for the wandering Beat Generation. Alan Ginsberg regularly visited Tangier, and William S. Burroughs was still living there when Abdallah arrived. After spending a few months in North Africa, he grew to admire the beautiful artefacts, the architecture and the traditional patterns of urban 'design'– as well as the long Islamic dress for both men and women and their exquisite manners, such as the way they laid their right hands on their hearts in greeting to express heartfelt sincerity. 'It filled me with a strange blend of envy and despair,' he told me, 'because I realised that all of it – the aesthetics, even personal hygiene, the tolerance, respect and empathy for others – was based on the commands of God or of His Prophet. It was so obviously rooted in God, yet I could not comprehend God.'

Abdallah left Tangier in the throes of an existential crisis and on the verge of a nervous breakdown. 'On my first day back in America,' he remembered, 'in an act that cried out for faith, I took up my fairly incoherent English version of the Quran and, closing my eyes, opened it to a page at Will, not my will (my eyes were closed); and when I checked where my finger had stopped – it was a passage that affirmed that while God was beyond *our* comprehension, He comprehended all. "I can believe," I said at that moment, to myself and to God, in a God who tells me He is beyond human comprehension.'

In that life-changing moment in New York, he adopted

Islam. 'It was as if a veil was lifted,' he told me. I was fascinated by his story. God had shed light into his dark night of the soul, just when he needed it. And from then on Abdallah went on a spiritual path in pursuit of God's presence.

∾

Ramadan began on the last day of our trip. In Cairo, thousands had gathered at the Saydna Husayn Mosque in the city centre at sunset to look out for the crescent moon, to see if Ramadan would start that day or not. The city's various Sufi orders proceeded through the streets holding up banners and calling: 'Generous Ramadan, beautiful moon, where are you?' And when it was sighted in the night sky, they rejoiced and broke out into cheers. Tears welled in my eyes, so deeply was I moved by this jubilant welcoming of Ramadan, which was after all an arduous month of fasting and self-denial. The mood was joyful and festive – the cafes were full of people celebrating all night and looking forward to spending the next thirty days devoting themselves to God and denying their own bodily needs. I wished I could have spent the holy month in this special atmosphere but the next day we flew home. I fasted on the plane, even though it says in the Quran that there is no need to fast while travelling, but I was so inspired after my stay in Cairo that I didn't see why I shouldn't. After all, sitting in a plane for four hours is not exactly an arduous journey.

Chapter 11

Pledge of Allegiance

How should a bird fly except with its own kind?

Book II, *Mathnawi*

Christmas was coming, and I went to Hamburg to visit my family. I was still fasting and worried that my parents might be upset by the fact that I would only be eating after sunset. On Christmas Day, my whole family met for a traditional Christmas turkey at my cousin's, but we began with afternoon coffee and cake. My cousin's seven-year-old daughter suddenly piped up: 'We can't begin until Kristiane has broken her fast.' She insisted everyone wait, and so that's what my family did. Fortunately, that only meant a few more minutes – I am not sure they would have joined me if Ramadan had been over Easter, when dusk tends to fall rather later – but it was sweet of my family to show me solidarity. It hadn't been easy for my parents to understand my choice of faith, and this upset me as much as it did them, but I think they respected me for how conscientiously I lived my religion. Although they still didn't really understand me and weren't all that interested to hear about it in detail either. They let me pray in peace and never served me pork or alcohol, but of course they sometimes drank at dinnertime. On Christmas Eve I quoted some Bible verses to my dad that I had written down in an interfaith lecture in London and, despite his lack of interest in religion, he said he had heard them all before. I was surprised, but he told me that his mother had repeatedly quoted the exact same verses to him.

'You remind me of her a lot,' he told me. My aunt, my grandmother and even my great grandmother had all been devout Christians. 'But now we have to deal with more earthly matters,' he said. 'The Christmas tree needs to be decorated and perhaps someone could help prepare the dinner.' We were having fish, as usual on Christmas Eve, and so our conversation was cut short. It lingered in my mind, though. I had never taken much of an interest in my grandparents' faith as a child, but now I was curious to know more about it. I couldn't ask them, since they had passed away a long time ago, but I could remember how committed my great aunt had been to her parish community. It was like her second family. My Auntie Hertha had been the epitome of generosity, kindness and magnanimity. She never complained, even though she had lost her husband in the war and had no children, but was cheerful, considerate and unfailingly good to others. She was always knitting and crocheting stuffed animals and clothes for my sister, our cousins and me. When I cautiously broached the subject again with my dad the next morning, he suggested I attend the Christmas service on Boxing Day at the Elim Pentecostal Church, which my grandparents had belonged to and attended every week. They had witnessed mystical experiences, such as the distribution of the Holy Spirit and speaking in tongues, he said. He had never been terribly interested, so he couldn't give me any more details. After a bit of 'research', I found the location of the church and joined the service, eager to see what it would be like. The congregation sang fervently, everyone embraced one another warmly, there was a lot of passion and love and, for some reason or other, the vicar gave a sermon about fasting in solidarity. It all seemed very jolly and reminded me of the gospel churches I had visited in the States as a teenager. After the service I approached the vicar in the hope he might be able to tell me something about my grandparents. He was initially touched by my interest, but when I referred to his sermon and mentioned that I was in the middle of a fast myself because I was Muslim, his face clouded over. Rather than seeing the common ground between our respective religions, he said that anyone who heard Jesus' message but chose not to follow him as their Lord was damned. My initial joy was quickly dampened.

I had heard something very similar before from my first Islam teacher. Since Islam was the most recent monotheistic religion – God's latest update, as it were – she believed, like many Muslims today, that it rendered all previous religions null and void. And whoever continued to practise those 'obsolete' religions was condemned to Hell. I had contradicted her, vehemently pointing out that all religions had pious followers who prayed and did good deeds. I really couldn't imagine that those people, including my friends who were Catholics, were destined for Hell. From then on I never went back to her. I left the priest feeling disappointed and annoyed. Does it matter if people fast for the sake of God in Ramadan, Yom Kippur or Lent? Surely, the fact that fasting is considered an essential path to God in all religions is an indication of shared values. In an age when we all have the opportunity to travel and discover other cultures, and so much information is just a mouse click away, there is simply no excuse for that kind of blinkered thinking.[1]

I stayed in Hamburg until the Eid festival and marked the day with my first ever visit to the main mosque there, which happened to be Shiite. Located on the Alster Lake, this turquoise-blue mosque with its fountain at the front, artistic Persian tiles at the back, and two minarets towering just above the dome, has a beautiful Eastern feel to it. Walking along the lake in Hamburg in a headscarf – a first for me – felt very strange and I was almost paranoid that someone might recognise me. Once I was inside the mosque, I took off my shoes and relaxed. It was full, and after looking around for a while, I managed to find a little space next to a Kurdish lady. As always, I loved the

melodic Eid prayers. Afterwards the Kurdish lady invited me
to her Eid celebration at home. I had never met her before, but
perhaps she sensed that I was by myself and had no other plans.
Delighted by her invitation I accepted with pleasure. However,
first of all, I had another appointment. I was meeting Shaykha
Halima Krausen, a theologian from Hamburg who works at
the mosque, counselling women and couples about marriage
and family life in Islam. She is also involved in interfaith dialogue and often gives seminars in London, which is where I
had met her. During a lunch break at the An Nisa Society in
Wembley, where she lectured on 'Healing the Self', I discovered that she too was from Hamburg. Born into a Christian
family, she embraced Islam in her early teens, and went on
to marry a Pakistani. I liked her approach to faith, which was
refreshingly unconventional and down-to-earth. 'I didn't just
change denomination,' she told me. 'I discovered my path to
God.' Halima was nine when she read the Bible, and she felt
immediately drawn to the idea of Jesus and the resurrection.
But the concept that he had died for our sins and the idea of the
Trinity seemed strange to her. She started compiling a book of
favourite aphorisms drawn from religious texts she found in a
library. The majority of them were Islamic, and she soon made
up her mind. At the age of thirteen, she knew she was Muslim,
and she also knew it wouldn't be an easy ride. Sure enough, her
mother was shocked and asked the local priest as well as her
religious teacher to get her back on the straight and narrow.
'It was like going barefoot to hell and back,' recalled Halima.
She later travelled extensively in the Muslim world and took
courses in Islamic studies and theology. She was part of a team
that worked on a German Quran translation and other religious
texts, her special interest being women's issues and education.
After the Eid prayers at the mosque, I went to meet her at
a nearby cafe right on the lake, where many other Muslims
had gathered for an Eid coffee. Some of them recognised me
from TV. I took the opportunity to ask Halima one pressing

question that had been at the back of my mind for a long time: I wanted to know whether the Quran really legitimised men hitting their wives when they didn't obey them. Aghast, Halima pointed out that the Prophet strongly rebuked any husband who beat his wife. 'The Arabic word *daraba*, which is often translated as "beating", has many different meanings,' she explained, 'including to imprint, to explain with emphasis, to separate, to distance or to depart, basically a wake-up call.[2] And *this* should be the interpretation of this complex verb in the context of marriage,' she stressed.

Immediately a lively discussion ensued. 'Does a wife really have to obey her husband?' asked one of the other girls. 'According to the Quran, women and men are partners and therefore should resolve and discuss any issue in friendship,' Halima answered. 'In the context of the verse we were talking about (4:34), the word *nushuz* that is usually translated as 'disobedience' describes antisocial behaviour not just towards the husbands but towards *God* and *society* in general. And in the Quran it is not only applied to women, but also to men,' she concluded.

All of the girls had listened carefully to her brief explanation, grateful to hear her refreshing take on that difficult verse. We needed more enlightened scholars like her, we all agreed, and most importantly, to inspire the men, too! The girls asked me how I came to Islam in the first place and we had a lovely little celebration. It was an important experience for me: for the first time in my hometown of Hamburg I appeared in public as a Muslim and spent time with other Muslims. My day ended at a council house in Steilshoop, a neighbourhood of Hamburg cluttered with high rises. This was where the Kurdish lady who had invited me to celebrate the Eid festival lived with her family. As I walked in, I noticed immediately that they were Shias, unlike me. The walls were adorned with pictures of Prophet Muhammad and Ali, his cousin and son-in-law. Such images are actually controversial because depictions of living beings are usually seen as drawing the viewer into the earthly drama and away from contemplating God, which is the reason why conservative Sunnis disapprove of them. The only exceptions to the rule are stylised Persian or Indian miniatures. They are two-dimensional and try to capture the archetypal reality of the depicted figure rather than the earthly specificities. However, modern portraits of holy people, especially of Ali and his two sons, are popular amongst some Shia Muslims. Despite minor theological differences, I was happy to be invited, and felt that whether Shia or Sunni, new Muslim or born Muslim, we are all Muslims together.

After I had been introduced to everyone the lady gave me a ring as an Eid present and we all sat down on the floor with the children, the husband and various other relatives, and she served a delicious lamb dish. I loved the feeling of togetherness. Here I was in Hamburg, the city of my birth, participating for the first time in the Eid prayers and festivities with fellow Muslims. My family, the house I had grown up in and my old school were all just a few kilometres away. And even though I was celebrating Eid with people I barely knew, I felt close to them. I was a stranger here, but I was also at home. At last!

∾

Back in London Ruby and I toasted the New Year with sparkling elderflower water at a party we had been invited to by Michael Radford. As good Muslims, we wanted to see in the new millennium clean and serene. What's more, New Year's Eve fell right in the middle of Ramadan. As I watched the fireworks explode in the night sky over the Thames with my friends and my sister, who had flown in with her husband to be with me for this special New Year's Eve, my thoughts drifted back to Egypt and someone I had met there.

One day Dr Nasr had invited me to join him and Alfred, an Austrian friend of his who lived in Cairo and often drove him around. He knew the city well, particularly the holy places, and spoke fluent Arabic. Alfred had been divorced from his German-Egyptian wife for quite a while. He used to teach German literature at the Al-Azhar University and nowadays worked as a freelancer for a German TV station, organising shoots and interviews. He was a few years older than me, was exceptionally well-read and a free thinker with a passion for Sufism. I liked him, and we had spent a whole evening talking. It was odd to be speaking at length in German about faith – usually, everything to do with religion belonged to the English-language part of my life. It felt strangely intimate and familiar. I hadn't realised how much I missed talking about something so important to me in my own language. Perhaps Alfred felt the same. In any case, he promised to get in touch when he was next in Europe, and we had been writing to one another every day since.

A few months later Alfred was in southern Germany for work, and I was hosting an event in Würzburg, so we arranged to meet up and visit Dr Nasr, who was scheduled to speak at the World Economic Forum in Davos around the same time. Alfred picked me up at my conference and we drove south to Switzerland, stopping off at the birthplace of the great healer and alchemist Paracelsus. I had been reading a lot about this great healer during my natural medicine studies and after my one-year foundation course I decided to specialise in homeopathy. We also visited the Mecca of Switzerland, an imposing monastery in Einsiedeln, which is over 1,000 years old but still very active. It is an important station on the way of St James, the pilgrimage to Santiago de Compostela in Spain, and attracts hundreds of thousands of pilgrims each year, even from other faiths, such as Hinduism. The main reason is its Black Madonna: proof that the spirit transcends skin colour and race.

We sat in the Benedictine abbey and quietly prayed and contemplated for a while, taking in the atmosphere. But somehow, the ornate interior with its elaborate frescos in a feast of colours and a host of naked, golden angels didn't quite do it for me, impressive as it was.

'I much prefer the visual harmony of geometry and arabesques in Islamic architecture,' I told Alfred. He quite liked the flamboyance of the Baroque era, but he had grown up with this kind of style in Austria, whereas I came from the protestant northern Germany, where churches were more sober and linear in design.

We may have had different tastes in European architecture, but otherwise Alfred and I got along very well. He was courteous, amiable and highly intelligent. We were curious about each other's lives and one evening over dinner he told me how he had found his faith. He had begun studying religion intensively as a young man and had longed to read the Holy Scriptures in their original languages. For this reason, he had learned Sanskrit, Hebrew, Farsi, and eventually also Arabic so as to be able to read the Quran.

He said he was instantly captivated. 'My favourite passage is the story of Moses' initiation,' he told me. It is found in the 18th chapter called 'The Cave', which the Prophet recommended to be read every Friday. In it, 'Moses meets a mystic teacher named Al-Khidr (The Green Man), who prompts him to reflect upon the judgement of good and evil in the world, and tells him that he too often jumps to hasty conclusions, mistaking good for evil and vice versa,' said Alfred. 'In the course of the story, Moses comes to realise that nothing is ever as it seems.'

'I loved that story as well,' I replied. 'I was particularly surprised that even a Prophet could be told off for being impatient, and it certainly made me feel better about my own impatience.'

'Well, in the end Moses accepts that he should trust that all is good as it is,' Alfred pointed out. To him, the moral of the story was that *tawakkul* (complete trust in God) is the greatest wisdom and the best approach to life.

I was impressed by Alfred's vast knowledge of religions and ancient cultures. But I was even more delighted to meet a man who was following the same spiritual path as I was, who spoke my language and with whom I had a cultural affinity. We also shared a love of travelling and Eastern culture, and we worked in similar professions. Alfred was a profoundly spiritual person and would often speak enthusiastically of his 'power places' in Cairo and the desert where he would go 'to drink from the fountain of Divine grace', as he put it.

It wasn't long before we developed feelings for one another. Everything seemed to fit so well, but there wasn't much we could do about it because I insisted that we couldn't engage in a physical relationship if we weren't married. Alfred agreed. But should we get married so quickly? We began considering our options.

Eventually we reached Davos, where world leaders, economists and philosophers had gathered to discuss the future of the planet. The tiny winter-sport resort had been transformed into an international conference centre, packed with people, cars, guards and police, all terribly important. We weren't accredited, so we just enjoyed the atmosphere and the scenery. Whenever there was an opportunity we met up with Dr Nasr, who was happy to skip some of the official functions to spend time with friends. The three of us went up a ski lift to take in the view from the mountaintop, and he told us about the beautiful mountains of Persia. 'My country is regarded as the Switzerland of the East,' he said nostalgically. He had never been back after losing everything in the revolution.

Back in Davos we all had a hearty Swiss dinner in a cosy alpine restaurant. Since Dr Nasr had first introduced us, Alfred and I wanted to talk to him about the possibility of our marriage. I was thinking of giving up my studies in London and moving to Cairo, and Alfred was keen to take care of me. Dr Nasr talked to us about the meaning of love and marriage in Islam and our mutual responsibilities.

'Marriage is the natural state of being for man and woman,' he said, quoting from the Quran: *And We have made pairs of every thing, so that you would think* (51:49).

He reminded us that the Prophet Muhammad often spoke about the importance of marriage, even likening it to 'half of the religion'[3] and pronouncing that 'no structure is built in Islam more beloved to God than marriage.'[4] 'All love in the Islamic perspective should be in God and not separate from God,' explained Dr Nasr, elaborating on some of its spiritual dimensions. 'Love that excludes God and turns us away from Him, can lead to the ruin of the soul,' he observed. 'Whereas, when understood correctly, it can be a Divine gift and used as a ladder to reach real love, which is love for the *Source* of all love, which of course is God.'[5]

It all sounded rather beautiful, and my heart leapt with joy that I had finally found someone whom I could love for the sake of God and with whom I could hopefully enjoy the sort of relationship that had long been absent from my life. As Dr Nasr said, too much emphasis on external acts of worship alone can lead the soul to harden, and the closeness of a married couple who can relax and enjoy each other's company is a remedy to this kind of one-sided development. And that in turn inspires a desire for worship. But he also had words of warning. 'Marriage is prison,' he joked, 'a constant compromise. It requires us to negotiate all the time and curb our own selfish desires.' But ultimately it was a very good training of the ego, he said, and the best way to live.

'The Quran describes the intimate bond between husband and wife beautifully,' he reminded us, and cited the verse which states that spouses are *a garment for you, and you are a garment for them* (2:187), providing adornment, comfort and protection as well as covering our privacy and faults. 'You are both good people, and you love God, but you need to decide for yourselves whether you are compatible and can make the marriage work,' he said.

The time we had spent together might have been brief, but we were excited and optimistic. And in any case, even if Alfred and I had wanted to get to know one another better over a longer period of time, it would have been impossible due to the geographical distance. And as we both knew, Muslims rarely spend much time together before deciding to tie the knot. Couples fall in love *after* they've married. Marriages are mostly arranged by the parents and some only meet the prospective candidate once before making the decision, others a few times but always with a chaperone, or, in some instances, people meet up in safe public places over a period of time. One young British Pakistani chap had told me that he left it to his mother and sister to find him a wife because he was too busy with work and he trusted them. So much so that he didn't even feel the need to meet the bride they picked before marrying her. The couple turned out to be very happy in their arranged marriage and went on to have several children.

Alfred and I both came from a different culture so obviously we had our reservations. But even though taking such a significant step so quickly was a bit strange for me, it felt like an adventure and I looked forward to getting to know my future husband in the course of our marriage. When we were confident that we had evaluated the situation from all sides, we decided we would have an Islamic marriage in London. We picked a date when Dr Nasr would be in town and could act as one of our witnesses. I was optimistic my parents would be pleased that I had found a man with a background much like my own. If my husband had to be Muslim, I thought it might help that he could at least speak German with them. Excited about the prospect of getting married, I flew back to London and told my girlfriends the good news. They were all very happy for me and looking forward to meeting Alfred.

In the meantime, I read up on Islam and marriage. The Prophet famously loved women – a love that came from God and showed that 'the perfection of the human state is connected with love for other human beings, not simply with love for God', as Sachiko Murata writes in *The Tao of Islam*. And since all Muslim men are expected to emulate the Prophet, the love that Muhammad felt for women is by extension obligatory to all Muslim men. If only they were more aware of this important aspect of their religion, I thought, and underlined the passage. The Prophet said that even the smallest thing a man does for his wife, like putting a morsel of food into her mouth is rewarded by God.[6] I also read that sexuality in marriage is sacred in Islam and even pleasing to God. Apparently it is a blessing when a man takes the hand of his wife, an even greater blessing when he kisses her, and an even greater blessing when he sleeps with her.[7] Mystics see the act of lovemaking between man and wife as a reflection of the Divine act of Creation and, as Ibn al-Arabi put it, an occasion for experiencing 'God's greatest self-disclosure'. The pleasure it gives us comes from God and is a foretaste of Paradise. In contrast to the Catholic view, sexuality in a Muslim marriage is for pleasure and not for procreation, while children are an added bonus. The Quran moreover recommends that before intercourse the couple should first of all develop a spiritual relationship (2:223), while the Prophet explicitly instructed men 'never to fall upon a woman like an animal, but to first send an envoy'. 'What sort of an envoy?' asked his followers. 'Kisses and words,' he replied.[8]

I once told my Jewish girlfriend Rebecca that, in Islam, a man is expected to satisfy his wife physically. 'In that case, I'm converting,' she said.

It struck me that these teachings did indeed respect the nature of women – and men for that matter. And I liked the idea that sex takes place within marriage and is therefore linked not only to love but also to responsibility for women and children. Admittedly, I had often wondered how the ban on sex before marriage could really work, and I couldn't help feeling that getting married without testing the waters first was a bit rash. But I was learning that one could tell without physical intimacy whether there was chemistry or not. I liked Alfred, that was good enough for me and seemed in line with the Prophet's teachings.[9] Two months after our trip to Switzerland, Alfred came to London and we married before God in a *nikah* ceremony held in Shaykh Abu Bakr's *zawiya* in Kent. The word *nikah* means marriage as well as legal contract. In Islam, marriage is a civil contract that is revocable – a strong covenant but not a sacrament. Both bride and groom can define various terms and include any conditions of their liking in the contract, so I added a clause stating that if Alfred wanted to take a second wife, this would be a reason for divorce; and another ensuring some kind of security for me in case we had children and things went wrong. In Muslim societies, a state-appointed Muslim judge (*qadi*) usually conducts the *nikah* ceremony. But this can also be done in front of two witnesses by any trustworthy practising Muslim.

We were married by Shaykh Abu Bakr and our witnesses were Gai Eaton and Dr Nasr. My mother was there, but my father and his wife were away on a holiday that they had planned long before. Nonetheless, he had given us his blessing. It was a good opportunity for my mother to meet some of my Sufi friends she had heard so much about and also to see the *zawiya* where I prayed. We all wore traditional dress. Alfred had brought me a new *jalabia* from the tailor in Egypt and my mother wore a long skirt and jacket and even made the effort to put a scarf on her head, out of respect.

The ceremony was simple. Alfred and I sat before the Shaykh while Sidi Rida read from the Quran: *Among the signs of God is that He created spouses from yourselves for you to live with in tranquillity: He ordained love and kindness between you* (30:21). Then the Shaykh recited the marriage formula, asked us if we were willing to marry one another, and, after we had both answered *naam* (yes), we exchanged rings. Now, in the eyes of God, we were man and wife.

Then we all went to the home of Sidi Rida and his wife Sayy-idah Nureen to celebrate with a few friends from the *tariqa*. She had prepared some smoked salmon and other snacks to go with non-alcoholic champagne, and later we all went on to a dinner party at my favourite Lebanese restaurant where we were joined by more friends. It was a lovely evening and everyone liked Alfred – especially my mother who, I was glad to see, got on well with him. We spent a few very nice days together before she had to fly back to Hamburg.

I showed Alfred round London, we went on walks through the city, visiting exhibitions and meeting up with our Sufi friends. On Friday, Alfred didn't want to miss the *jumah* prayers at the London Central Mosque in Regent's Park. I showed him where I used to live all those years ago, we arranged a meeting point for after the prayers, and as I came out of the mosque with all the other women, there, for the first time, was my husband waiting for me amongst the hundreds of husbands waiting for their wives. It was a wonderful feeling.

Alfred had to leave after a week but, two months later, I flew to Egypt for our honeymoon. We went on a fabulous Nile cruise from Luxor to Aswan, where we stayed in the legendary Old Cataract Hotel, an idyllic place with an elegant Moorish interior design shaded by palm trees and with a view across the Nile. Over the next few days, Alfred introduced me to his world. We climbed into tombs in the Valley of the Kings and admired the spectacular Karnak Temple in Thebes, north of Luxor, while Alfred told me all about the amazing culture and history of the Pharaohs. The vast pillars of the Great Hypo-style Hall by Ramses II and the spectacular light show in the evening left me awestruck.

During the cruise, however, we had our first misunder-standing. Alfred was annoyed when our tour leader took us from one tourist shop to the next and spoke to me more than he thought was appropriate, so he was quite curt with him. We left the place in a huff and got back to the boat early. I didn't quite understand why he was making such a fuss, but told myself that perhaps this was the sort of thing Dr Nasr had meant when he had joked about marriage being a kind of a prison and an opportunity to practise the art of compromise.

Back in Cairo, Alfred took me to his weekend home in Abusir, a desert location not far from Cairo, which he said was closely associated with the Egyptian Osiris cult. On our walks in the desert we visited an ancient temple where incredible archaeological treasures such as huge original slabs of stone carved with hieroglyphs were just lying around. We stayed a few more days in Cairo, but not at his flat because he admitted that it was a bit uninhabitable. Alfred showed me his office, haggled on my behalf in the Khan-el-Khalili market and took me to some of his favourite shrines of especially pious people who were related to the Prophet.

After our honeymoon, I went back to London, where I had begun hosting an Internet show about environmental issues. Over two months passed before Alfred and I were able to see each other again. I flew back to Egypt and even though we were happy to be reunited after the long break, it felt like we were strangers and had to adjust to one another all over again. It was the height of summer. In the sweltering heat, we began apartment hunting in Zamalek, an international neighbour-hood located on the northern part of the Gezira Island and home to a number of embassies. Most of the apartment care-takers we met were friendly and helpful. They all wore long *jalabias* and I noticed that a lot of them had a round, brown mark on their foreheads. When I asked Alfred about it, he explained that it was the result of repeated praying but also told me that some Egyptians actually faked it.

It didn't take us too long to find a nice apartment, and we went to a bazaar with lots of dusty carpentry workshops to order some custom-made furniture. That night Alfred took me to a simple, brightly lit Koshari restaurant, the best in town, with a TV blaring away in the background. It served nothing but the delicious national dish made of noodles and spicy tomato sauce with chilli, lentils, rice and fried onions.

Another evening we went to witness a healing session of a different kind. Alfred was working on a book project about the *zar*, an ancient ceremony practised within what he called 'folk Islam', which has African and Pharaonic influences. According to some well-known anthropologists, such forms of healing, led by women, emerge wherever women are excluded from leading roles in the 'official' religious rituals, while conservatives frown upon these methods and declare them to be un-Islamic. But Alfred insisted that the *zar* didn't violate God's commands; in fact, the Shaykha we were about to visit was a very pious lady. I was curious to discover more about what Alfred described as a 'fascinating fringe phenomenon of Islamic culture'.

The session was held at the house of Shaykha Karima, a charismatic, warm personality. She was dressed in a blue *jalabia* and a black hijab, with kind, expressive eyes lined with black kohl and huge silver hoop earrings that showed beneath her turban. We took off our shoes and she led us into a small neon-lit room, painted ice-green, with a few simple benches lining the walls. A huge bunch of somewhat spooky claws hung on the wall near the entrance, while balloons and glitter dangled from the ceiling. We sat down underneath a verse from the Quran that adorned the wall opposite her patients. Most of the patients were women in their fifties. The Shaykha's healing abilities were famous particularly for psychological illnesses, possessions, and female and marital problems. Even certain health institutions sent patients her way because it was thought she could treat them better than classical psychiatry.

Then the ceremony began. An elderly man dressed in a long white robe with a crocheted prayer cap on his head lit an incense burner and started clearing the energy with the smoke. The Shaykha recited some verses from the Quran and various Arabic formulas to invoke the spirits for healing purposes. Eventually she and two female helpers began to drum, while a man made clicking sounds with a cymbal and another shook a rattle. They all began moving to the rhythm. Shaykha Karima invited the ladies to get up and dance with her while she sang her formulas and beat the drum in front of the patient being healed. The women slowly let loose, dancing without inhibition, swaying and whirling their arms up and down and around their bodies. When Shaykha Karima invited me to join in, I was a little hesitant at first but couldn't refuse her – and after all, I was the last person to turn down a bit of healing. As she beat her drums in my direction and the helpers clicked their cymbals around me, I began to move to the beat and went with the flow. It was a vibey, earthy healing session if ever there was one, and even though it was apparently only *zar*-lite – since the real McCoy involves the sacrifice of a chicken, goat or other animal, which then gets eaten for dinner as part of the healing ritual – it was good enough for me. Afterwards we all sipped tea together while the lady helpers shared a shisha pipe.

I enjoyed Cairo immensely. It was a fascinating world with a unique charm, rich culture and spirituality to spare, despite the chaos, pollution and heat. Alfred had to return to work and I went to visit a few people I knew, including a homeopath recommended by my teacher in London, to explore some work opportunities. However, as the days passed it became increasingly apparent that Alfred and I were actually very different people with different temperaments and contrasting backgrounds. I was lively and dynamic; he was more withdrawn and introspective. The lives we had led before we met were worlds apart. He had spent twenty years living in Cairo as a family man, adapting to the local culture, while I had been a young single woman at the heart of London's media world. Our ideas about what it meant to enjoy a comfortable existence didn't quite match. In short, planning a common future proved much harder than we had anticipated.

It also turned out that his ex-wife still played a far greater role in his life than I had expected. They still shared a car, so we had difficulties getting around, and she also refused to give him the key to his house in Abusir, where Alfred had said we were going to spend our weekends. Alfred was a gentleman and tried his best to make me feel happy, although there were times when I felt frustrated and even distraught. Eventually I began to feel ever more insecure about the entire set-up and, even though I had tried to find work myself, I couldn't see a professional future for me in Cairo either. I started to doubt that I could ever live comfortably and at peace with Alfred in this country.

After confiding in a few close friends back in London, I soon realised that giving up my whole life in Europe was too big a risk. 'What would you do if things didn't work out?' asked Bob, when I told him of my plans. I had a bad feeling about it all, and this eventually grew into outright panic. I ended up confessing my doubts to Alfred over the phone. He was upset but tried to be understanding and flew to London a couple of months later to start looking for a job there. But just as I had felt that the sort of life awaiting me in Egypt wasn't really for me, Alfred found it hard to imagine living in London long-term. With heavy hearts and after many long discussions we admitted to ourselves and to each other that our marriage, after all, wasn't meant to be. Our worlds, our personalities and our circumstances just weren't as compatible as we had hoped, and we realised we would both be happier simply being friends in faith. And that we vowed to remain, because we did have an inner connection.

We were both deeply saddened by the failure of our relationship, and its ending marked the start of a difficult time in my life. I blamed myself for not having paid proper attention to the practical aspects of the marriage, such as the problem of the geographical distance between us and the differences in our lifestyles. It was a classic case of 'love is blind', but at least I had lived and loved, and I was glad for the experience. And, I had done my best to keep to God's rules.

But, as the saying goes, a crisis is a terrible opportunity to waste, and I decided I wouldn't waste it.

I began to concentrate again on my homeopathy studies, and learned more about healing – especially about healing myself. Thanks to homeopathy, I was finally cured of the hay fever that had plagued me for decades. I began to understand the importance of banishing negativity, letting go of the past and looking ahead. I also learned about the law of attraction, which can be life-changing. It is based on the idea that everything is energy. Even thoughts and feelings are energy. And since like attracts like, energy attracts like energy: the energy we send out comes back to us. If we radiate positivity, we not only make others feel happy, we attract goodness into our life. Rumi explained it thus:

If you think of roses, you are a rose garden
If you think of thorns, you are fuel for the furnace

The law of attraction is even expressed in the Quran, I discovered, when Abraham's wife smiles with happiness and is *then* given glad tidings – the birth of her two sons Isaac and Jacob, although she is an old woman (11:71). If we want to change our outer circumstances, we first have to change our inner selves, our attitude and our behaviour. If we refine our own energy vibrations, for example by giving up alcohol or other drugs, taking homeopathic remedies, meditating or doing *dhikr*, we start to attract very different energies towards us. Inner change for the better has a positive effect on others and the outer world. Even this is stated in the Quran: *God does not change the condition of a people until they change their own condition* (13:11).

I wanted to improve myself, and this required that I examine my inner self – my life, my thoughts, my reactions and my dreams. I prayed, practised *dhikr* and studied, and of course I continued to attend the regular *majalis* of my Sufi group. The Shaykh was very sorry that the marriage he had officiated had failed, but he reminded me that everything that happens is God's will and that my task now was to focus on my journey to God. After a while, I was ready to be initiated into the group. At the ceremony, the Sufi pledges *bayah* (oath of allegiance) to the Shaykh of the *tariqa* – which is really a pledge to God. The ceremony recalls the first Muslims' pledge of allegiance:

> For those who pledge their loyalty to you (Prophet)
> are actually pledging their loyalty to God;
> the hand of God is over their hands.
> So if anyone reneges, he only reneges
> to his own detriment;
> And whoever fulfils what he has promised to God,
> God will give a great reward. (48:10)

It was all very serious, and I wondered if I was able to assume such a responsibility. Was I truly ready to promise God that I would obey all his commands? What would happen if I broke one of them, or lost my way on the path to Him?

I met up again with Gai Eaton to discuss the matter. This time he took me to The Chateau, an elegant and traditional English country house not far from his home in Purley. We had come here many times before, and for dessert we always ordered Eton Mess – a delicious concoction of meringue with strawberries and cream. Over dinner Gai assured me that many pious Muslims shared my concerns. I was a bit nervous, I confessed, and as usual, he knew exactly how to appease me. 'I felt the same, when I was about to be initiated in 1965,' he recalled. 'Before taking this step, I'd been plagued by doubts, which I eventually confessed to my Shaykh. I'd always been a rebel at heart,' he reminded me. 'I feared I might one day flout some command or other simply because I found it so hard to obey rules.'

Gai sat up a bit straighter and lowered his voice authoritatively as he told me what his Shaykh had advised him. 'We don't give orders, and we won't throw you in jail if you disobey Islamic principles and rules,' he said. 'That is between you and God. All we ask of you is the *dhikr*. Nothing else.'

It was a convincing performance and I felt relieved by Gai's anecdote, not least because we seemed to have a somewhat similar nature. But I knew that I wanted to practise the *dhikr* and do my very best with everything else, too.

My initiation took place a few weeks later in the same large *zawiya* in which the *majalis* were held. The men, including the Shaykh, formed a circle, while the women gathered in rows on the other side of the room. As always when a *faqir* or *faqira* was initiated into the group, we melodically recited Arabic verses from the Quran, including the lines: *It is God who sent tranquillity down into the hearts of the believers, that they may add faith to their faith* (48:4).

When Shaykh Abu Bakr called me by my Muslim name, Yusra, I stood up and slowly approached the circle of men. I entered it, and sat down before the Shaykh. It was a special moment and I felt the attention of the whole group upon me. The Shaykh prayed and after a while took my hand, which he then held with both his hands while quietly praying. He let my hand go and said '*al Fatiha*', so everyone raised their hands and recited the opening prayer of the Quran followed by silent prayers for me. I looked down, feeling grateful for everyone's *duas* and good wishes. Finally I got up, put my hand on my heart as a greeting, whispering *assalamu alaikum*, and without showing my back to the Shaykkh, returned to my place. I was now formally initiated.

From now on, I was officially a member of the *tariqa*, and that meant I was allowed to participate in the *hadra*. It felt great although I soon realised I had to practise breathing in sync with the drum. When I sat back down again, I could feel the effects of the *dhikr* coursing through me. After the *majlis* the others offered their congratulations, wishing me *mabruk*, and then the Shaykh spoke to me for a while in private. He gave me a new formula for my *dhikr* and reminded me that God truly *is* present when I call Him. The name Allah is like a sacrament, and a distillation of all His other names. Then the Shaykh entrusted me with my first major spiritual task, the *khalwa*. This is a spiritual retreat, a time-out with God. I was to spend six hours – ideally, that same night – concentrating non-stop on the *dhikr* and, while doing so, not speaking to anyone, in order to prepare my soul for the presence of the Sacred.

As soon as I got home, I dimmed the lights, sat on the floor and began my *khalwa*. I found it hard to concentrate for so long, so I kept changing positions. After sitting for quite a while on the floor with crossed legs, invoking God, I got up and remembered God while standing, then walking around the room and sitting down again. As I got more tired I lay down on my side, before sitting up again – but I never stopped repeating my formula, either silently or in a low voice. The *dhikr* would grow inside me and felt like a wave pulsating through my heart chakra until I would lose my concentration and feel nothing – just impatience because time was passing so slowly. Eventually I sensed a deep tranquillity and then tiredness. I ran a gamut of emotions, and the exercise was also a test of endurance. After what seemed like an eternity, dawn broke and my six hours were up. I went to bed, sleepy but spiritually invigorated and happy.

Chapter 12

A New Beginning

Umrah is an expiation for the sins committed between it
and the previous *umrah*

Prophet Muhammad[1]

I was gradually advancing on my spiritual path, and after four
years of studying, I was now a qualified homeopath. My practice
was up and running, but I still couldn't live off my new-found
vocation. I had hired a small room in the neighbourhood, but
patients were turning up late, didn't show up at all, or took
far more time than allocated. My online TV job, which I had
enjoyed a lot, had come to an end because the Internet portal
had shut down – it was too much ahead of its time. I continued
hosting galas and conferences in Europe, but it was an uncertain existence and I had a mortgage to pay. None of my efforts
to land a job on German TV, which was still my biggest potential market, came to fruition. Agents there strongly advised me
not to mention anything about my religion because it would
only serve to further hinder my career. When I was approached
to write a book about my experiences, their unanimous reply
was: 'If any corporate company or TV channel knew you are
a Muslim, no one would hire you. It's a negative image.' As I
couldn't afford to not work, I continued to bite my tongue and
keep quiet about my faith in Germany, even though I itched
to speak out every time I saw poisonous media coverage that
depicted Islam in a way I didn't recognise. It was frustrating
and reinforced my decision to continue living in London.

Meanwhile the regular *majalis* as well as conversations with my Muslim friends helped me see these trials from a spiritual perspective, to be patient and trust in God instead of feeling worried and upset. I got used to the fact that there was no security or stability in my life and came to see that feeling safe was a state of mind and being. When everything looked bleak despite my attempts to make things work, I prayed in despair and gained the strength and patience to carry on. 'Sometimes I close all the doors to my servants so they don't have any doors to knock on but My door,' God said on the tongue of the Prophet, Dr Amina told me. And as praying more meant getting closer to God, that was a benefit in itself. I often thought that if it wasn't for my faith, I wouldn't have known how to cope with the pressure.

I tried to be steadfast with the spiritual practice and eventually I noticed that whenever I did *dhikr*, my consciousness and my inner self would respond to the formulas I recited and sweep me away from my external tribulations to a serene place inside myself. Sometimes I experienced a beautiful feeling; it was as if a warm wave of delight welled up from inside of me. On good days, I would feel the rhythm of *dhikr* echoing in my body, wherever I was and whatever I was doing – whether I was going for a walk in the park, sitting at my computer or kneeling on my prayer mat. They say *dhikr* gives a different flavour to life, the flavour of Paradise.

In time, I was able to worry less and trust more. I also became more patient and better able to contain myself when someone irritated me; at least most of the time. At one point, my mother complimented me for having become more polite and considerate. I must have been quite a nightmare at times before. Best of all, it didn't always feel like an effort, but something I wanted to do. Of course, there were still times when I would lose my new-found serenity – and this affected me far more than it used to: it felt like a step back.

The spiritual practice in my own home was all well and good, but having been a Muslim for nearly six years now I felt an increasing longing to visit the centre of Islam, the House of God in Mecca and the tomb of the Prophet in Medina. I also felt that it would be a necessary spiritual purification for me, since although my past sins were hopefully already forgiven at the time I became Muslim, I had probably accumulated new ones. Our Shaykh travelled to those two most sacred places in Islam every year and performed Umrah with some of the friends in the Sufi group and, in January 2001, I vowed to join them and go on my first pilgrimage to Mecca.

Unlike the Hajj, which can only be performed during a certain month in the Islamic moon calendar, one can go on Umrah, the 'lesser pilgrimage', at any time of year. We first flew to Cairo to participate in the annual Sufi gatherings where I had met Alfred the year before. The drive from the airport into town past the many ancient monuments and mosques with lavishly decorated domes and minarets was still familiar, and memories came rushing back to me. During my stay in Cairo I frequently met up with Alfred, which was painful at times but also cathartic. Discussing face-to-face what had gone wrong in our marriage brought peace to us both. Because there was still a remnant of sadness left, I decided to go for a healing session with Alfred at the *zar*; this time not as a spectator but as a patient. Dr Nasr was also curious, as was Sayyidah Bahia, one of our friends from the US, who was also in need of a treatment since her marriage of twenty-five years had just broken down. Together we drove to Shaykha Karima's house. She was happy to see us and welcomed us in. The ceremony was exactly the same as before: Sayyidah Bahia and I joined in the dancing, there was a lot of drumming and cymbal-clicking, and I felt a little lighter afterwards. As I had come for healing this time, the Shaykha asked me to leave a personal item with her, so I decided to give her my tights before I left. She sat with me for a little while, tuning into my problem, and said she would continue to pray for me. She also prescribed me a medicine: the next day I was to feed three cats with milk and bread. That was easy enough – there were zillions of them prowling around Cairo's Old Town. I can't say whether it helped or not, but at least those cats had a good meal that day.

After that I was busy accompanying Gai Eaton around town. I had managed to persuade him to join us all and celebrate his eightieth birthday in Cairo. It had been quite some time since Gai had last been in the Arab world, which had influenced him so significantly in his younger years. It was a wonderful experience for him to participate in the *majalis* in Cairo – and of course to be back in a Muslim country again. He was shocked, however, to see how much Cairo had changed in the past fifty years. He barely recognised the city he had once known so well. The population of Cairo now exceeded the entire population of Egypt when Gai was a boy, and its sprawling suburbs reached almost to the Pyramids, which he remembered as being surrounded by desert. Much to his horror, a Kentucky Fried Chicken had opened directly opposite the famous Sphinx. But despite these developments, he was delighted to be back.

For his birthday, I arranged a dinner with some of our Sufi friends from London, Cairo and the US in an atmospheric Indian restaurant at the elegant Mena House Hotel near the Pyramids. I wanted to thank him for his support over the years. Gai entertained us with his customary wit and charm, and after a sumptuous meal we listened to classical Indian music. I was thrilled to see him enjoying himself so much.

Soon it was time to start preparing for our impending pilgrimage. Together with Safina, who was also going on Umrah, I went back to the Khan-el-Khalili market to look for fabric, and chose an off-white material with shiny stripes. I had it made into an embroidered *jalabia*, which would be my *ihram* (the customary white robe a pilgrim wears to signify the state of consecration). During the pilgrimage, a woman has to cover herself completely, apart from her face and hands; not a single hair is allowed to show from beneath her headscarf. We also bought a few thin cotton head coverings in off-white and black to wear underneath our headscarves. The *ihram* for men consists of two unhemmed pieces of cloth tied together and secured with a belt, or nowadays some pins. Both men and women wear white. Shaykh Abu Bakr spoke to those of us going on Umrah with him and explained that the simple white dress also symbolised brotherhood and equality before God.

When the Umrah was accepted, God wiped out all our sins and we were returned to the pure state we were born in, said the Shaykh. Since the pilgrimage signified a new beginning, it seemed to me like an opportunity to choose a new name for myself. The Shaykh didn't recommend it but left it to me to decide. I had only ever used the name Yusra when I was with my Muslim friends, but I never really liked it that much, and I associated it with the negative experiences of my old Sufi group.

Moreover, the name stood for 'ease', and what with the professional and private obstacles I had faced since becoming a Muslim, this was something my life most definitely seemed to lack. Maybe my feelings proved that I still had some way to go in overcoming my natural impatience and the name actually did provide some ease for me in those difficult times, though I didn't recognise it. I sympathised with the protagonist in the poem 'Footprints in the Sand', who sometimes felt deserted by God. I happened to stumble across it when visiting the Marian Shrine in Knock, while holidaying in Ireland with my friend Dani a few years previously. We had flown to Knock with Ryanair and spontaneously decided to visit the Roman Catholic pilgrimage site. We had no idea that by chance we had picked the anniversary of the apparition of the Virgin Mary for our visit, and we found ourselves amid thousands of pilgrims who had gathered at this holy site in search of healing and blessing.

'Footprints in the Sand' by Mary Stevenson moved me every time I read it:

One night I dreamed I was walking along the beach with the Lord.
Many scenes from my life flashed across the sky.
In each scene I noticed footprints in the sand.
Sometimes there were two sets of footprints,
other times there was one only.
This bothered me because I noticed that during the low periods of my life, when I was suffering from anguish, sorrow or defeat, I could see only one set of footprints, so I said to the Lord,
'You promised me Lord,
that if I followed you,
you would walk with me always.
But I have noticed that during the most trying periods of my life there has only been one set of footprints in the sand.
Why, when I needed you most, have you not been there for me?'
The Lord replied,
'My precious child, I love you and would never leave you during your times of trial and suffering
When you saw only one set of footprints,
it was then that I carried you.'

In Cairo, before we set off on our Umrah, I also spoke to Dr Nasr, who was very sorry my marriage hadn't worked out and recommended I pray for forgiveness during my pilgrimage to the house of God, the Ka'ba in Mecca.

To mark my new beginning, I chose the name 'Zahra', which means both 'flower' and 'radiance'. Dr Nasr liked my choice. 'The Prophet's daughter, Fatima al-Zahra, is a role model for all Muslim women,' he told me, adding that she was very close to her father, deeply spiritual and used to stand up for the rights of the poor, the underprivileged and the suffering.

I loved the meaning of Zahra and felt she was the perfect role model for me to follow. Henceforth, I not only had two Christian names, but also two Islamic ones.

The matter settled, I flew with Sayyidah Safina and another girlfriend from the group to Jeddah in Saudi Arabia, reading up on the plane about the origins of Mecca and the significance of the Umrah rites. Arriving in the heartland of Islam was fraught with difficulty – unmarried women without family couldn't just enter the country; they needed a *mahram*, a male companion to whom marriage is prohibited, usually a family member, which I of course didn't have. Alternatively one could go as part of an official Umrah group which would arrange everything and also provide the obligatory *mahram*. An invitation from a Saudi citizen, who would vouch for one, combined with a business visa could be another option. As I was already going with my own individual group, and my Shaykh would be my *mahram*, I had opted to secure myself an invitation. Back in London, a Saudi acquaintance of Dr Amina's had offered to write a formal letter to the authorities. This was supposed to have been sent but, as I found out when I arrived, the officials hadn't received the letter. I wasn't allowed in, and although I tried desperately to explain my situation, my efforts were in vain. To make matters worse, the driver who was supposed to be picking me up wasn't there. I tried to get in touch with him, promising the authorities that he could vouch for me, but he was unreachable. By this point, my two fellow travellers had melted away, none too keen on spending the whole night at the airport, and they had their own accommodation to sort out. So I was left alone at Jeddah airport and felt pretty lost. I didn't know what to do.

Suddenly I saw an official with a long beard pick up my suitcase and disappear towards Departures. I leapt up from my seat, ran after him and demanded that he return my luggage, telling him I was here to go on Umrah. We had a heated discussion – he was as insistent as I was – and it was all very tiring. Eventually, my impassioned protests seemed to work, and the immigration officials finally managed to reach my driver, who had been on his way home. There had been a mix-up with my name and he thought I wasn't on the plane. He arranged to have the letter from Dr Amina's friend in Riyadh faxed to a restaurant in Jeddah, and eventually showed up looking harried but with the letter in his hand. I was finally allowed into Saudi Arabia. I got to my hotel an hour later and fell asleep the minute my head touched the pillow.

The next day, the first thing I did was ask the driver to show me around and take me shopping for an *abaya*, the national dress for women in the Kingdom and some other Gulf States, so that I wouldn't stand out. There were many different styles of *abaya*, all black, long-sleeved and floor-length. I bought a light one that closed at the front and an elegant black scarf to cover my hair. Safina had told me beforehand that one could get particularly fine black scarves in Saudi Arabia, so my purchases seemed like a good investment. In my new, modest attire, I set off on a tour of the city. The driver pointed out some traditional family residences decorated with ornate woodcuts, a museum about the history of Mecca, Medina and Jeddah, and then he showed me a large, empty parking lot. 'This is where executions are held,' he said. My blood ran cold. I asked him to drive on.

Disturbed by what I had seen, I later researched the death penalty and found out from Amnesty International that it is practised in fifty-eight countries around the world, including China, India, Indonesia and the US, but only Saudi Arabia and Iran allow public executions. Many scholars today, such as Tariq Ramadan, propose seriously rethinking interpretations of the Shariah and are meanwhile calling for a moratorium on corporal punishment, stoning and the death penalty. After all, the Prophet Muhammad requested 1,400 years ago that judges first take into account all options of forgiveness and reconciliation before handing down their rulings and that they lean towards mercy rather than punishment. Islamic jurisprudence should reflect Muhammad's nature, which the Quran describes as gentle, compassionate and kind (9:128).

I put these thoughts out of my mind as I set off for my next stop. For a long time I had been harbouring a plan to develop a range of cosmetics made from natural ingredients. Some of the best perfume oils in the world are said to come from Saudi Arabia, and historically, perfume has always played an important role in Arabian society, around the home, on clothes, and on the body. Ever since my first trip to Pakistan I had loved these natural perfume oils and also the healing remedies I had discovered, and I liked the idea of a business scheme that was a fusion of East and West.

I managed to arrange meetings with two well-known *parfumiers* in Jeddah. The first one I visited had a luxurious shop in a side street, full of bottles and vials of perfume made from natural oils. Arab princes and princesses came here for their bespoke perfumes and to have their own personal scent created. Fascinated, I watched the parfumier pour a precious oil from a large bottle he held up high into a tiny one without spilling a drop. I sampled some exotic scents I had never encountered before. Some particularly heady fragrances such as real musk or ambergris are prohibited in the West because of animal rights issues, and the very popular Arabian scent *oud* is hard to find. The parfumier showed me a piece of *oud* which was about fifty centimetres long and cost $10,000. Rich and earthy, it is often used as incense for special occasions. Before the *majlis* at his home our Shaykh often burned chips of *oud* in a special burner, suffusing the *zawiya* (prayer room) with its fragrance.

I bought a small portion of those valuable chips and the store owner gave me a few samples as a gift, including *ward Taifi,* a rose scent known as the queen of roses. It comes from the mountain town of Taif, south of Mecca, where the air is said to be exceptionally pure. This is what gives *ward Taifi* its exquisite fragrance. Taif also has a special significance for Muslims: the town played a key role in the life of the Prophet – it was here that he sought refuge when he was forced to flee Mecca. But its people insulted and attacked him with rocks and stones, and when he was left with bleeding feet and wounds all over his body, he prayed to God:

> To You, my Lord,
> I complain of my weakness,
> lack of support and the humiliation I am made to receive.
> Most Compassionate and most Merciful!
> You are the Lord of the weak,
> and You are my Lord.
> To whom do You leave me?
> To a distant person who receives me with hostility?
> Or to an enemy You have given power over me?
> As long as you are not displeased with me,
> I do not care what I face …
> To You I submit,
> until I earn Your pleasure …[2]

Full of sorrow, the Prophet set off back to Mecca and prayed that those who attacked him and their children would find God and worship Him. His prayer in the face of hatred and violence teaches us that when we are faced with the same, we must not react with blind rage or revenge, but with patience, hope and forgiveness as well as praying for our enemies and their descendants to become righteous. This is my association with *ward Taifi*: its fragrance reminds me of the Prophet's grace.

I thanked the parfumier for his help and left the store with my treasures. At the second shop I visited, I encountered a salesman – not an Arab, incidentally – who greeted me with a curt gesture instructing me to cover my face. I felt indignant, since I had made every effort to comply with the country's customs. I was wearing my new *abaya* and my double hijab so I knew that not one hair was showing. 'The Quran doesn't order women to wear a face veil,' I countered. 'Why don't you pay attention to God rather than my outfit?' He promptly left the room and returned with his boss, who thankfully adhered to that fundamental belief, shared by the religious and non-religious alike, that the customer is king, or, in my case, queen. He proceeded to ignore his salesman and went out of his way to be helpful and obliging, and he added many more samples to my heap of treasures.

In the evening, the Shaykh called us together to prepare us for the imminent trip to Mecca. We sat around him on cushions at the home of Bodo Rasch, a German architect who worked in Saudi Arabia and had a flat in Jeddah and a house in Medina. I was looking forward to hearing what the Shaykh had to say. He started off by telling us about the house of God that we were about to visit. 'The cube-shaped sanctuary Ka'ba in Mecca is the oldest temple and the oldest site of pilgrimage in the world,' he said. 'About 4,000 years ago, Abraham, the patriarch of monotheism, rebuilt the original sanctuary of Adam together with his son Ishmael. The pilgrimage they proclaimed on God's order has continued to be performed to this very day.'

The Shaykh himself went on Umrah every year as part of an extensive journey that took him from Egypt, Mecca and Medina to Pakistan and Malaysia. We admired his energy and willingness to travel so far and wide, despite his advancing years, in order to visit his disciples around the world. We laid out a tablecloth and shared a lovely meal that one of the Saudi friends had brought, chatting until late into the night. But before eating, Shaykh Abu Bakr took his *sibha*, his prayer beads, in his hand. We did the same and he began to lead the small *majlis*. During the *dhikr*, I suddenly noticed that same feeling of love emerging in my chest that I had felt before at holy sites. It became increasingly intense and so beautiful that

I didn't want the *dhikr* to end and I continued for a bit when the others had finished. The feeling was more powerful than it had ever been before and I wondered if it was the sacred energy emanating from the centres of Islam in Mecca and Medina, the perfume of proximity that was somehow reaching me.

The next day we set off at sunset. Mecca was an hour's drive away; it was refreshingly cool outside, and we had decided to travel at night to avoid the heat. Before we left, we had all completed our big ablution known as *ghusl*. This involves taking a shower to wash every part of the body, rinsing the mouth and nose three times, then washing the face three times, as well as the arms, ears and neck. The hair must be rinsed right down to the roots, and then the feet. *Wudhu* is a less extensive version of this ritual washing and is done before each of the five daily prayers. Both serve as purification and spiritual protection, but during *wudhu*, only the face, mouth, nose, lower arms, ears, neck and feet are washed, and one's hair just gets a wipe with wet hands. After completing the washing, I dressed in my *ihram*, prayed two *rakat* (sets of prayer) and declared my intention to God to go on Umrah. I then went down to the hotel lobby to meet my two *tariqa* friends. We felt we looked very pious in our pilgrims' outfits without make-up – like three nuns. We took some photos to capture the feeling and resolved to spend the next few days living up to our respectable appearance.

A person in *ihram* (a state of consecration) is subject to certain rules that apply to all pilgrims. They are not allowed to have sexual intercourse, kill animals, wear make-up, or remove bodily hair – which means that men cannot shave. They are also expected to put aside negative feelings such as pride, anger or grudges and to behave in a modest way that will please God.

On the journey, we recited the pilgrim's prayer *labbaika Allahumma labbaik* ... which, roughly translated, means, 'O my Lord, here I am at Your service, here I am.' After driving for about forty-five minutes, we reached the outskirts of Mecca and were met by the sight of a vast, surreal-looking monument: a green neon Quran stand complete with a mock-up of an open book marked the spot beyond which non-Muslims were not allowed to go. The sacred territory, the *Haram*, begins exactly twenty-two kilometres from the Ka'ba, the most sacred site in Islam. This encompasses the city around the Sacred Mosque and the whole territory surrounding it up to several kilometres in every direction. Its sacred status ensures safety and protection for everyone and everything inside its boundaries, including animals and plants. It is a place of peace, where violence and aggression are banned.

We drove on past countless ultra-modern, less than holy-looking high rises and hotels, and eventually stopped outside a white marbled courtyard that led to a huge building made of shiny grey marble with several tall, thin minarets pointing towards the sky. In front of us was the *Masjid al-Haram*, the Sacred Mosque, with the Ka'ba at its centre. The Grand Mosque is monumental in scale, covering over 356,000 square metres and containing three storeys linked by escalators. At busy times, such as during the Hajj and Ramadan, over two million pilgrims pray here at the same time. The courtyard around the mosque, paved with white marble and cleaned several times a day, provides space for a further million pilgrims. Everywhere I looked there were pilgrims, most of them dressed in white. They came from all over the world – and were here for the same reason as I was. We took off our shoes and entered the vast mosque barefoot. We passed numerous pillars and pilgrims in white on our way towards the inner courtyard. When I saw the Ka'ba for the very first time, I was stunned. For a while I just stood still and said a prayer while gazing in reverence at this big black cube standing on polished white marble and surrounded by white-robed pilgrims circling around it in prayer.

The Ka'ba is considered the oldest house of worship in the history of mankind. It is believed that the first man, Adam, built the original temple as a reflection of the Divine throne. Noah's Ark sailed around it seven times, and later Abraham and his son Ishmael rebuilt the Ka'ba on the old foundations. We joined the stream of praying pilgrims proceeding slowly counter-clockwise around the Ka'ba. This ritual circumambulation is called the *tawaf*. Since we were there between Ramadan and the Hajj, the Grand Mosque was relatively empty and when we walked around the Ka'ba we were able to get close enough to touch it. The granite walls were covered with the *kiswah*, a black brocade cloth decorated with gold-embroidered calligraphies from the Quran, which is replaced every year. The four corners of the Ka'ba cube point roughly towards the four cardinal directions of the compass and located in the eastern corner, near the door of the Ka'ba, is the famous Black Stone (*al-hajar al-aswad*). Our Shaykh told us that it is a celestial meteorite originating not from space but from Paradise, given to Abraham by the Archangel Gabriel. According to the Prophet Muhammad, 'It descended from Paradise whiter than milk, but the sins of the sons of Adam turned it black'. The Prophet is said to have kissed the black stone on his pilgrimages and therefore pilgrims today do the same. 'It symbolises in a sense the renewal of the pre-eternal covenant with God,' said our Shaykh. Those who cannot reach it extend their right hand in its direction every time they pass it when walking around the Ka'ba. I was lucky, because I was able to get right up to the stone several times. It seemed to glow from within. I touched my lips to it and afterwards felt as though I had been kissed, too. As I continued around I observed big, strong men leaning their hands on the door of Ka'ba, weeping like children. I also noticed an intense, sweet musk fragrance, which is said to have been the Prophet's favourite scent. It came from the walls of the Ka'ba, which are perfumed with scented oil. The walls inside are also perfumed and engraved with various verses from the Quran. Otherwise, the interior is empty. In the time of Muhammad, it is said to have contained many idols and statues worshipped by the Meccan polytheists in pre-Islamic times. The Prophet cleared these from the house of God and later, on God's orders, changed the direction of prayer from Jerusalem to Mecca. The Ka'ba has served as the spiritual centre, the heart of Islam, ever since, and today some 1.5 billion Muslims around the world pray in its direction five times every day. In the same way as the Prophet cleansed the Ka'ba of false gods, we too are asked to purify our heart of all illusions and idols so that God may inhabit it.

I placed both my hands on the Ka'ba, and prayed with all my might for my family, my friends and myself, for relief of suffering and peace in the world. It was a deep conversation with God. Eventually, having said everything I could think of in that moment, I took my hands off the stone wall again, and the flow of pilgrims carried me forward. I felt happy and alert, concentrating on my prayers. Walking around the Ka'ba, I realised that God truly was the centre of the universe. After going round it seven times, we prayed two *rakat* at what is known as the Station of Abraham, where his footprint is displayed in a gold cabinet. According to the Quran, Abraham stood here during the construction of the upper parts of the Ka'ba, with Ishmael sitting on his shoulders. Abraham prayed to God to make this site a place of peace and safety.

On the edge of the inner courtyard of the *Haram* we found the Zamzam well, the sacred spring that has gushed water since the times of Abraham. According to Islam, Abraham did not send his second wife Hagar, the mother of Ishmael, into the desert alone, as the Old Testament says, but accompanied her. Later, at God's command, he left his wife and infant son with some water and dates in a barren valley. Eventually they grew thirsty, and the baby began to cry. Hagar ran back and forth between the two hills of Safa and Marwah in the scorching heat, desperately looking for water or signs of help, and praying. Eventually, an angel appeared to her, striking the ground with his wing. Suddenly, at that very spot, water sprang out – said to have come straight from Paradise. When Abraham returned, he built the house of God on the site of this miraculous well. This, it is said, was the origin of Mecca.

As pilgrims we effectively slip into the role of our spiritual ancestress and run back and forth between the hills seven times. This symbolises our own quest in this world for whatever we are seeking and God's Mercy which fulfils our quest even beyond our expectiations. The Zamzam spring today supplies millions of pilgrims with water. This journey is known as *sa'y*, and each leg of it covers 400 metres. Even though he was ninety years old, Shaykh Abu Bakr performed *sa'y* with remarkable vigour walking the distance of 400 metres between the hills the prescribed seven times together with us as a group. At the end of the Umrah, one of our friends cut off a small strand of my hair – in keeping with pilgrim tradition. She had brought along a tiny pair of scissors specifically for this very purpose. Many men shave their heads to mark a new beginning.

We had completed our Umrah, but our visit wasn't over yet. The next day we flew on to Medina, where the Prophet had emigrated in the year 622, after leaving Mecca. He lived here until his death ten years later. Muhammad and his followers had been persecuted by Mecca's leading tribe, the Quraysh, who were hostile to his monotheistic teachings and determined to assassinate him. In contrast, the people of Medina welcomed the Prophet and his followers with great hospitality and it was here that he was able to unite various feuding tribes and build the first Muslim community. Eight years later, he returned to Mecca and purified the Ka'ba from all the idols, but he refrained from punishing his erstwhile persecutors. As a result of his mercy, the majority of Meccans converted to Islam.

Arabs call the Prophet's city Medina *al munawarrah*, 'the

radiant city' – radiant, because it is here that the Prophet is buried, and his *baraka* is all pervading. I noticed a sweetness to Medina in both the atmosphere and the people.

As soon as we arrived, we went for an early lunch at the home of Bodo Rasch, who is widely known as 'Allah's architect' because of the work he has done on some of the holy sites in Saudi Arabia. Among his clients was the influential Bin Laden family, represented by the Saudi Binladin Group, a global construction and equity management conglomerate. The family had commissioned him to build vast parasols in the front courtyard of the Prophet's Mosque in Medina in order to shade pilgrims from the beating sun. He also designed a gigantic camp of fireproof tents for pilgrims in the Mina Valley. Unfortunately, Bodo Rasch had to leave before we arrived – however I met him not long after in London.

The lunch was splendid, and it felt wonderful to sit together with friends in faith and our Shaykh, who spoke with great love about Muhammad. He was, after all, an authority on the Prophet, having written his biography based on the earliest sources available. We all wore our best *jalabias*, for we were about to visit Prophet Muhammad. Straight after lunch, a driver was waiting to take the women to the Prophet's Mosque, because visiting hours for women at the Prophet's tomb are short – between one and three p.m. only. Even from a distance one can see the famous green dome on the white mosque structure, indicating the location of Muhammad's grave. It is situated in the house he used to share with his wife Aisha. He is buried between the First Caliph, Abu Bakr, who led the *ummah* (community of believers) after Muhammad's death, and the Second Caliph, Umar. The actual tombs are inaccessible because they are cordoned off with black cloth behind gold metal doors decorated with Quranic calligraphy. The place right next to Muhammad, however, is kept empty; it is reserved for Jesus, who is revered as a Prophet in Islam and who, it is believed, will one day return as the

Messiah. We stood behind a balustrade, looking at those metal doors, raised our hands and silently recited the *Fatiha* and other prayers for Muhammad and the two Caliphs. I felt the familiar stirrings of warm, gentle, all-encompassing love in my chest. I didn't want to leave, but in due course a lady in a black *abaya* asked us to move on. We said our afternoon prayers in silence and then joined the rest of the group for a sightseeing tour in the footsteps of Muhammad. Walking across the grounds where Prophet Muhammad and his followers had once lived and prayed filled me with joy and awe. We visited a number of landmarks in Islamic history, including Mount Uhud, where in 625 Muhammad suffered a bitter defeat against his enemies from Mecca and only just escaped with his life. It was a period full of trials and tribulations. We also visited the Qiblatain Mosque, the name of which derives from a word meaning two directions of prayer. It occupies the site where God commanded Muhammad to change the direction of prayer from Jerusalem to Mecca. This shining white building once even contained two *mihrabs* (prayer niches), but sadly, during recent renovations, the old prayer niche facing Jerusalem was removed, so that only the one facing Mecca remains.

For the evening prayers, *maghrib*, we returned to the Prophet's Mosque. I loved hearing the *adhan*. And then the Imam recited the verses with such emotion and nuance, alternating between gentle whispers and rousing intonation, that I felt shivers run down my spine and was moved to tears. It was the most beautiful prayer I had ever heard.

As the trip drew to an end, a few of us made a second brief visit to Mecca to perform another Umrah. Since we were in the land of the Prophet, we were keen to absorb as much sacred energy as we could. This time we stayed at one of the five-star high-rise hotels that had been built in recent years right opposite the Sacred Mosque. Shaykh Abu Bakr told us of the time when the mosque was the tallest building far and wide, and stood pretty much alone. Those days were long gone. Nevertheless, it was wonderful to be able to visit the Ka'ba so easily and to watch the flood of pilgrims around the black cube even from our hotel rooms.

This time, we performed our *tawaf* deep into the night. The mosque was more or less empty and very quiet, and the magic of the night intensified the holy atmosphere. We stayed doing *dhikr* until the call for prayer echoed in the cool, clear morning air. Together we recited the Morning Prayer, *fajr*, and welcomed the new dawn.

A new beginning. That is what I hoped awaited me as we set off back to London.

Chapter 13

Islam of the Heart

It is not people's eyes that are blind, but their hearts.
Quran 22:46

A few months later, in spring 2001, I received a call from Bodo Rasch, asking if I was still single. I was a bit taken aback by his question, but he told me he had an acquaintance with whom I might get along well. In Muslim circles introductions like this are common, and Ruby and Fa both told me that mothers and aunties spend a lot of time trying to matchmake on behalf of their children as soon as they turn fifteen or so, and I have actually seen Ruby make enquiries herself about young boys who might be suitable husbands for her nieces. So far, I had only ever had one introduction, which hadn't worked out. So I was surprised but grateful that Bodo had thought of me and taken the trouble to call. The name of his acquaintance was Bakr Bin Laden, which meant nothing to me, but Bodo told me that he came from a Saudi family that owned a large construction firm and was also one of Bodo's best clients. I gave him permission to pass on my phone number and, before too long, Bakr got in touch.

His English was very good and he had a sense of humour. We chatted for a while on the phone, and at one point he played a game with me: 'Guess how many brothers and sisters I have,' he asked me. 'You can have plus or minus ten, and if you get it right you'll win a trip around the world.' Bakr seemed pretty confident I wouldn't succeed and gave me three guesses. Fifteen, I said. Twenty-eight? Forty? Wrong, wrong, and wrong again. 'The right answer is fifty-four! And they all have the same father,' he added proudly. Well, what a start, I thought to myself.

We talked on the phone a few more times, and arranged to meet for dinner the next time Bakr was in London. He turned out to be kind and charming. Over dinner he described himself as moderately religious. He had studied in the West and was obviously a man of the world – and a rather privileged one at that. He told me he travelled in a private jet and regularly spent time on the Côte d'Azur and Marbella. Only in passing did he mention a shadowy half-brother, who had been cast out by the family.

Bakr was likeable and entertaining, but I think we both realised that we weren't made for each other. I didn't hear from him again until a few months later, when he called me with an idea for a TV show he wanted us to develop together. It was to be an international travel guide to cities and their culture. It sounded great, and I was keen on the idea of co-producing and presenting it. He asked me to help him find a network and a production company, which I did. I managed to get a former BBC producer on board and negotiated with a production company that already made programmes for *Discovery Channel*. I met the boss, pitched the idea and mentioned that I had financial backing. He seemed enthusiastic and was confident we could get it on the air.

That same day in early September 2001, I flew off to Los Angeles to visit my old friend Steve Fargnoli. He had been diagnosed with cancer two years earlier, when he was just fifty, and it looked like he was losing his battle with the disease and might die at any time. Prince, the most successful rock star he had represented, his big discovery and an artist he had loved, had fired him at the height of his success. I often thought that Steve had never really got over this disappointment.

Like many of his friends, I wanted to see Steve to say

goodbye. Mark Booth, who had hired me at MTV, the composer Joseph Vitarelli, Sinead O'Connor, Janet Street Porter, a few of Steve's ex-girlfriends and his New York partner Arma Andon were among the crowd going in and out of his suite on the top floor of the stylish W Hotel. We all did our best to make his last days as comfortable and happy as possible, despite his failing health. Sinead had recently been ordained a priestess and had some lengthy private chats with Steve about his journey ahead. I was so sad to see him like this and managed to spend a little time with him too, although I wasn't able to say goodbye as I would have wanted to because, for reasons I didn't understand, his ex-girlfriends made it quite difficult for me to visit him. I admired Steve for his gracious and courageous attitude and he even managed to joke and laugh in those last days of his life. Shortly before he died, we celebrated his birthday with a big cake.

One day when I was in his suite, the entire room suddenly started shaking and trembling and the chandelier swung dramatically from one side to the other. I had never experienced an earthquake before and was frightened at first but then just went with it, comforted by the knowledge that the hotel, like all the skyscrapers in LA, was built in such a way that it could sway with the tremors. The news later said the earthquake measured about 4.5 on the Richter scale and the epicentre was less than a mile away.

In between my difficult visits to Steve's sickbed, I went with my friend Michael Radford – who was kindly letting me stay at his house – for walks in the Santa Monica Mountains and browsed through the famous spiritual bookstore, Bodhi Tree on Melrose Avenue. It stocked a vast array of Rumi literature, DVDs and CDs. I bought *A Gift of Love: Music Inspired by the Love Poems of Rumi,* presented by Deepak Chopra and friends, including Goldie Hawn, Madonna, Martin Sheen and Demi Moore, as well as five copies of a very lavish edition of *The Illuminated Rumi,* with magical illustrations by the US artist and visionary Michael Green. These were going to be gifts to my friends Fa, Ruby, Jim and Mike, and one was for myself. Sufism – and particularly the Persian philosopher and mystical poet Jalaluddin Rumi – had become fashionable in the States. Donna Karan had used Rumi recitations as a soundtrack to one of her catwalk shows, Oliver Stone had revealed that he wanted to make a film about Rumi's life, and Rumi poetry had become a bestseller. Sufism's popularity was surpassed only by the Kabbalah movement. At the Bodhi Tree bookshop I picked up a spiritual paper on my way out and, when browsing through it, I discovered with delight that in essence the mystical dimension of Judaism is very similar to Sufism in its loving worship of the One, in its belief in the way of the heart and in various other metaphysical and ontological teachings. Even some of the expressions were similar, such as shalom or salam for peace and *nefesh* or *nafs* for the ego which needs to be overcome. Both teachings go back to the wisdom of Abraham although, of course, the Kabbalah came through Judaism and Sufism from Islam but both mystical traditions originate in the same Divine source.

The Kabbalah was certainly all the rage in Hollywood when I was there. At one film industry party Mike invited me to, all the guests were talking about it, apart from movies of course – including Goldie Hawn and Ben Stiller. I was happy the showbiz set seemed to be embracing spirituality and hoped that it was more than just the latest fad or lifestyle accessory.

On the evening of 10 September, Mike and I were invited to dinner along with some other friends, including the producer Julia Verdin who had worked on a film with Mike and her friend Elizabeth Hurley. I hadn't seen her for a long time. When we met, shortly after I arrived in London, she was an actress who had just got her first break with a part in a UK TV series and was friends with my flatmate Caroline and with Tony James from Sigue Sigue Sputnik. We occasionally went out together while Hugh, her more seriously inclined boyfriend, stayed home studying acting roles. I liked her. She was witty, clever and down-to-earth. I stayed with her for a week after the MTV Video Music Awards in LA in 1992 and had happy memories of taking her dog for walks in the hills of Santa Monica and going out at night. She loved inviting friends round for dinner and traditional English Sunday lunch – roast chicken and mash with generous lashings of butter, because 'everything just tastes so much better with a lot of butter in it,' she said. 'Hugh is a huge cricket fan and would love to meet Imran,' she had told me. I introduced them in 1993, when she brought Hugh along to my birthday party organised by Steve. Only months later, Hugh Grant shot to fame with his movie *Four Weddings and a Funeral*. But when Liz showed up at the London premiere in 'that dress', she stole the show. It was by Versace – tight, black and held together with nothing but a few large safety pins. Her 'less is more' strategy worked, propelling Liz into the forefront of international celebrity. Coupled with good looks and personality, marketing skills can go a long way. We had lost touch over the last seven years, when she had been circling in another orbit, and now were delighted to have an opportunity to catch up. She was just giving up smoking, she said, and was feeling rather edgy. Elizabeth asked me how long I was staying. 'My flight's tomorrow, but I'm not sure if I'll go,' I heard myself say, even though the ticket was non-changeable and non-refundable.

The next morning, I was woken by someone shouting: 'Our country is at war!' It was much too early for me and I simply turned over and went back to sleep. Later, over breakfast, I asked Mike to switch on the TV. Speechless with horror, we watched the plumes of smoke rising above New York in the aftermath of the terrorist attacks on the World Trade Center. We couldn't believe what we were seeing and spent the next few hours glued to the screen. I soon realised I could forget about flying home: LAX airport was closed and no planes would be taking off for the next week or so.

Deeply upset, we went on a long hike in the mountains, talking about this horrific event and asking ourselves how Muslims could have perpetrated such an atrocity. I tried to explain that the attacks were completely un-Islamic, and even though I knew Mike understood what I was saying, he still had to vent his anger. I felt terrible too, but being a Muslim made the situation instantly more complicated. A lot of people became hostile towards me. When I went to visit Steve that day, everyone was watching the footage of the attacks on TV. 'If I hear the word Allah one more time, you're out of here!' snapped one of Steve's American ex-girlfriends suddenly. I hadn't said anything. Another of Steve's American friends suggested: 'We should bomb the entire Middle East and get rid of all the terrorists in one go.' A few of the others agreed. It felt as if some of the anger and aggression was directed at me personally.

It was all utterly unreal and I'm not sure Steve understood what had happened: he was on heavy doses of morphine at that point and at times thought he was directing a video clip. Arma kept shaking his head and repeating: 'I was supposed to be on that flight. I can't believe it. Steve dying saved my life.'

'What do you mean?' I asked him.

'I was booked to go to LA from Boston on the exact same flight that was hijacked and hit the twin towers!' he exclaimed in utter disbelief. 'If I hadn't received a call from Joe Vitarelli, who said if you want to see Steve alive you better come here Monday and not Tuesday 'cause he may not be there any more, I would have been dead right now.' Arma was in a state of shock, but so were we all.

He tried to ease the tension in Steve's suite and took me for lunch. He was quite upset on my behalf he told me. 'It's unacceptable the way they're treating you. I called them all out and told them off,' he said. 'They must be jealous!' Jealous of what, I wondered, but I shrugged it off. I had encountered female jealousy all my life.

The day Steve died, Arma and I were sitting on the terrace of a restaurant overlooking the ocean, when a huge seagull landed on the railing a few metres away. It stared at us and then meandered over.

'Look, this must be Steve,' said Arma. 'He's here with us.' It was a nice thought.

'But I don't believe in reincarnation,' I told him. 'Everyone's soul is unique and when we die, the soul goes to another realm, to God.' Still, the presence of the seagull was a bit eerie, and he kept us company throughout lunch.

A few days later over brunch with Mike in Santa Barbara, we were talking about work when I mentioned the TV show I had been asked to develop by Bakr Bin Laden. Suddenly I felt as if the whole restaurant had gone silent and was looking at me. Mike noticed it too. I could understand the extent of America's rage and sorrow. It was justifiable and only human. But I found it chilling how some Americans were aiming their anger at Muslims in general. We had to put up with insults, discrimination and outright aggression every day, especially those who looked like Muslims – girls who wore hijab or men with a darker skin colour and beards. Many Muslims were detained without charge and questioned by the authorities. In Texas, armed Americans attacked a mosque and random murders were reported around the country. In LA, an Egyptian store owner who was actually Christian was shot, while in Arizona the owner of a petrol garage was murdered – he was a Sikh and wore a white turban, which symbolises peace and understanding.

I felt quite uncomfortable and was apprehensive when Mike asked me to join him for dinner that week with his agent Rose and her husband, who lived in a secluded villa in the exclusive suburb of Bel Air. They were Jewish, so, being not only German but Muslim to boot, I was worried that I might have a less than warm reception given recent events. But my hosts confounded my expectations and turned out to be welcoming, well-informed and open-minded. They had Muslim friends themselves, they assured me, and were well aware that many Muslims had also died in the World Trade Center. They wouldn't have dreamt of showing me any hostility or pronouncing all Muslims guilty by association. Their grief was genuine but devoid of any aggression. Once again, I realised that when faith went hand-in-hand with learning and a desire to look beyond one's own horizons it was the perfect antidote to violence and extremism. Mike was very taken by something he had heard an Afro-American pastor say during an interview on US TV just after the events, and quoted him often, including that evening: 'I am shocked as an American, devastated as a New Yorker, and, as a black man, I ask myself what we did to deserve this.' Of course, none of those people, of whatever colour or religion, deserved to be killed by terrorists, but I agreed that some self-reflection on the grievances of other peoples due to Western foreign policy was necessary so that they too could live in dignity, with peace and justice.

On the flight back to London, I read a long article about the Bin Laden family and their business interests in the US. They owned a string of shopping malls, apartment buildings, luxury estates and even an airport. They also financed a Visiting Scholars Fund at Harvard and a fellowship programme at the Oxford Centre for Islamic Studies. As a prominent businessman, the 'true ruler of Jeddah', Bakr, in particular, enjoyed an international reputation and was obviously a man of influence. Only weeks later he was a guest at a dinner hosted by Prince Charles at Highgrove to support the Oxford Centre for Islamic Studies. I never heard from him again. I assume after 9/11 he had more pressing concerns than making TV programmes.

I was really glad to be back home, to speak to my family and friends about everything and to take stock of the situation. The mood in England was also tense, with everyone discussing the attacks and their repercussions. On the wall of a mosque, someone had sprayed the message, 'Avenge the USA, kill a Muslim.' With his initial inflammatory rhetoric and calls for a 'crusade' on terrorism, George W. Bush had sparked talk of a 'clash of civilisations' between Christians and Muslims, and sowed seeds of hatred and mistrust against Islam.

But over time, normality was restored and people learned to distinguish between Muslims and terrorists. Still, I felt compelled to do some research on the subject. I read about the sacred principle of *jihad* and the generosity and mercy shown to his enemies during the crusades by Saladin, who even compensated the widows of enemy soldiers out of his own treasury. His magnanimity won the respect of Europeans and he became a celebrated example of the principle of chivalry. I also discussed the topic with various scholars I knew, including Gai Eaton, Halima Krausen and Reza Shah Kazemi. They all said the same: life is sacred in Islam, suicide is considered a sin, and peace is at the very heart of the religion. There is no justification for violence or terrorism in the Quran or in Islamic ethics.[1] The Quran states that *if anyone kills a person ... it is as if he kills all mankind* (5:32). And it describes Muslims as a *community of the middle way* (2:143), which means there is no room for extremism in Islam. When violent extremists commit murder in the name of Allah, it is a dangerous distortion of its teachings, and they do so to the detriment of the vast majority of peaceful and law-abiding Muslims, who then become objects of public hatred.

I went to visit Gai Eaton at his home and after a passionate greeting from Twink, his little Highland terrier, Gai and I sat down in the living room, he at his antique desk in a big, comfortable office chair, and I on the sofa next to Twink who was busy chewing her toy bone. Gai lit a cigarette and told me a story: 'In the battle of Badr in 624, the people of Mecca wanted to destroy Medina's young Islamic community. But the battle was won by the Prophet and his troops. On their way home, the Prophet said to his companions: "You have returned from the lesser *jihad* to the greater *jihad* (*jihad al-akbar*)." His followers asked him what that greater *jihad* was. "The struggle against your passionate soul,"[2] he replied.

'So what does this greater *jihad* entail?' I asked him.

'It is the effort to practise our faith,' Gai replied. 'To pray five times every day is an effort, to veil one's selfish desires and conduct life in accordance with Islamic ethics and laws. The greatest "spiritual warriors" are the saints armed not with weapons but with prayer and prayer beads.' While it all made sense I wanted to know more about the idea that we needed to go out and fight *jihad*.

'What the Prophet called the lesser *jihad*, the outward struggle, is legitimate only as defence against outside aggression or resistance to an oppressive, unjust regime, when all diplomatic options have been exhausted. But there are strict ethical principles to observe,' Gai explained. 'The inviolability of non-combatants such as the elderly and monks in their monasteries, women and children must be protected, and even animals and trees must remain unharmed,'[3] he said. 'Another important point is that only a legitimate head of an Islamic state and the authoritative scholars, the *ulema*, can authorise and call for *jihad* as an act of defence in their respective country. But no fanatic has the right to proclaim a *jihad* in another country and perpetrate acts of terrorism in the name of *jihad*.'

'So basically Osama Bin Laden declaring *jihad* in the US was against the Shariah?' I asked, to clarify the point. 'Most certainly!' he responded. 'And even when carrying out a legitimate *jihad*, the Quran calls us to be moderate and not to get carried away by anger or desire for revenge.'

Gai asked me to get the Quran from the bookshelf and find his reading glasses. He leafed through the book while I emptied his ashtray and played with Twink until he found what he was looking for: *Fight in God's cause against those who fight you, but do not exceed the limits: God does not love those who exceed the limits* (2:190).

'Terrorism,' he said with disdain, 'is rooted in hatred and revenge, and the Quran warns us: *do not let hatred of others lead you away from justice* (5:8).'

I made a note of those verses, and asked about suicide attacks in the name of God. 'The idea that a suicide attack is a ticket to Paradise is wholly un-Islamic,' Gai stressed. 'Suicide is forbidden in Islam. And there are far more commendable ways of fighting for justice, which *is* an Islamic principle.' To illustrate his point, he quoted Muhammad, who is famously believed to have said: 'The ink of a scholar is worth infinitely more than the blood of a martyr,'[4] adding that the scholars were the heirs of the Prophets,[5] as Muhammad had also stated.

I thought about it for a moment. 'In our day and age, the ink of a scholar would be a camera, a microphone, a mobile or a computer. Islam needs media work, not bombs,' I replied. Being well versed in media matters himself, Gai laughed and agreed. And then it was time to prepare dinner for Twink and order our own.

∽

Life went on and, for the first time in nearly a decade, I was back on German TV, with a five-minute slot once a week. Every month I flew to Cologne to present a short programme giving natural health tips on RTL. One day when I was at the airport waiting to board the plane, I noticed a group of women in black *abayas* and headscarves. For some reason, I was moved to speak to them. Not something I would normally do, but I had recently been toying with the idea of moving back to Germany. I asked them how they felt in Germany as Muslims. 'Very happy,' one of the women said. 'Germans are very nice people.' I was glad to hear it and we continued chatting for a while. As we were walking towards the plane, she told me she came from Yemen but lived in Saudi Arabia. I thought to myself that she probably didn't have much affinity with Sufism in that case, since by and large Saudi Arabia rejects Sufism. Later, in the plane, I saw how she took out her prayer beads and started doing *dhikr*. I looked for my own and when I turned back to her, we smiled at each other, holding our beads in the air. When we landed she gave me the phone number of a friend of hers in London and suggested I call her. I gave her my number too but, once I got back home, I forgot about our meeting.

A few weeks later, the friend she had wanted me to get in touch with rang and invited me for lunch. Fadwa also came from Yemen and lived not far from me in South Kensington. The day I went to meet her, she was wearing a long, floral robe and a headscarf tied into a turban. We sat together on her sofa and chatted, while a maid served us a meal. It turned out the lady I had met at the airport was the mother of a famous Sufi Shaykh from Yemen called Habib Ali al-Jifri. Fadwa was curious to hear why I had become a Muslim and what my experiences had been since my conversion. She also asked if I was married. I told her everything and explained how I sometimes felt I was caught between two cultures and didn't really fit in anywhere. 'Of course I'd like to marry a practising Muslim, someone I can share my life and also my religion with, but I just haven't met the right man yet,' I told her. Fadwa was sympathetic and understood my dilemma. 'Concentrate on your relationship with God; purify yourself, your life and your intentions. Better your religion!' she recommended. 'If you are patient and steadfast, then you will be rewarded, *insha' Allah.*'

We talked about other topics and I asked her about the 'evil eye' that I had heard about. 'Does it actually exist?' I wondered. 'Oh yes, it does,' she replied. 'A lot of it comes from jealousy. The evil eye is said to be the jealous eye.' 'So what can we do to protect ourselves from other people's jealousy?' I asked her, thinking that I had encountered it a lot. 'Pray *surah al-Falaq*, the second to last chapter in the Quran which specifically says *I seek refuge from the envier who envies,* suggested Fadwa. 'Best is to say the short last three chapters every morning and every evening for general protection. And also, when you admire something beautiful, say: *masha' Allah,* as God has willed, so you recognise that everything good comes from God.' She was a fountain of faith and good advice and I happily agreed when she asked me to stay in touch and to come over again soon.

From the first day of our meeting, I saw Fadwa as a strong, well-educated and pious woman with a mind of her own. Shortly after we got to know one another, she came to me for homeopathic treatment, showing up on my doorstep swathed in black from head to toe. I was a little taken aback. 'Gosh, your husband must be very strict!' I exclaimed and invited her inside.

She laughed. 'On the contrary, he's Turkish and doesn't want me to wear *niqab*! It is my choice,' she stressed. She wore a full face veil because that is what the Prophet's wives had done, and she felt more comfortable that way. She only took off her veil in front of women, but would never dream of judging another woman for not doing the same. I was astonished and revised my opinion that women wearing *niqab* were invariably oppressed by their husbands, and were a bit narrow-minded and dogmatic. Fadwa was none of these. She was incredibly warm and generous and embraced the path of *tasawwuf* – the Arabic term for Sufism – with all her heart. Her love for God and the Prophet, of whom she is a descendent, was infectious. She radiated an extraordinarily pure aura and spending time with her filled me with a great sense of inner peace. Everything in her family and her household was also clean and serene and of course halal (ethically and ritually pure the way she understood it). This included the segregation of the sexes: Fadwa didn't mix with men except to seek Islamic knowledge or to greet family and she told me she felt more relaxed in the company of women. Before long I introduced her to Dr Amina, who soon became part of the 'gang' with Fadwa too.

To celebrate the birthday of Prophet Muhammad, we were both invited to a big party at Fadwa's home, a *mawlid*. More than fifty women and children from different backgrounds – Arab, European, Turkish and Pakistani attended. Everyone was dressed in beautiful long robes, and some of us wore green scarves, because green was the Prophet's favourite colour and it is also the colour of Paradise as mentioned in the Quran. A group of Syrian singers first led a *dhikr* and then sang beautiful *nashids*, Islamic songs accompanied by a hand drum, and we all joined in. Another lady spoke about the mercy of the Prophet, how much even the animals and the trees loved him. One of Fadwa's friends, Zain, gave me prayers to read in different situations. We all shared a delicious Arabic meal, topped by Fadwa's famous date cake, served warm with cream, and talked and laughed until late in the night. It was a lovely evening full of warmth and inspiration.

Fadwa became my closest friend in faith, a sister and a Shaykha to me. I wasn't the only one who appreciated her so much. She went out of her way to be there particularly for new Muslims and any women who needed support. She often welcomed Shaykhs from abroad to speak at her home, such as Hamza Yusuf from the US or Habib Ali al Jifri from Abu Dhabi, which is where the Yemeni Shaykh lived. She and her husband counted Yusuf Islam, formerly Cat Stevens, and his family among their friends – her children attended the Islamia school which he founded.

I had always had the greatest respect for the path Yusuf Islam has chosen, and was of course a huge fan of his music. I bumped into him at several Muslim arts events and we usually had a little chat. He was busy with his production company Mountain of Light and I was delighted that he was writing music again. When I received an invitation that year to a charity event at which he would be speaking as guest of honour, I was thrilled. It wasn't a Muslim event. The evening was attended by a broad mix of people from socialites and aristocrats to movers and shakers I knew from the music industry, including Rob Dickens, the former Chairman of Warner Music UK, and any number of fans, who had all paid fifty pounds to listen to the story of why Cat Stevens became Yusuf Islam. He had sold over sixty million records and was an international star with a string of hits to his name when he decided to turn his back on music in the late seventies.

Yusuf Islam took to the stage sporting a well-trimmed beard and a beige suit. He came across as poised, humorous and confident – just like the superstar he was. The audience was spellbound, carefully listening to his every word. His spiritual awakening had been sparked, he said, by a near-death experience he'd had while swimming one day off Malibu beach. The current pulled him out to sea and he was convinced he was going to die. 'At that moment, I prayed to God and promised that I would devote myself to Him if only He saved my life.' He kept his promise and embarked on a spiritual quest that eventually led him to Islam.

It was the timeless nature of the message that convinced him. 'The words of the Quran all seemed strangely familiar yet so unlike anything I had ever read before,' he told us. He embraced Islam in 1977, and changed his name to Yusuf, the Arabic for Joseph. 'I identified with the story of Joseph in the Quran,' he said. 'His brothers sold him like goods in the market place.' Yusuf felt the music business had treated him not like an artist but as a commodity.

Extraordinary, I thought. Even then commerce controlled the music industry. With Prince and George Michael complaining bitterly of similar treatment years later, it seemed like nothing had changed – at least not for the better. In 1979 Yusuf cut himself off from that world in order to find God and serve Him. I was glad to see so many people listening to his story that night and asking questions. 'Why did you stop singing when you became a Muslim?' asked someone. This was the question on everyone's mind. Muslim or non-Muslim, all his fans around the world had thought it tragic that he had neglected his talent, which, after all, was a gift from God.

'What had seemed to the outer world like a 180-degree turn was in fact a gradual shift. I'd always been on a spiritual quest,' he explained. 'My music reflected that. My near-death experience simply served as a reminder that I needed to follow this path with greater determination.' He also said he had needed time out, because he had reached a point where he could only withstand the pressures of showbiz with hard drink and drugs.

His transformation must have required enormous strength, which goes to show how faith can move mountains, I thought to myself. I was also fascinated to hear Yusuf explain that in the early days of his life as a Muslim he had been influenced by Wahabism, an austere branch within Sunni Islam, which advocates a rigid, literalist interpretation and rejects any form of music. He even admitted: 'If I could do it again, I'd do it differently now.'

That same year, I saw Yusuf play at the Royal Albert Hall in London at the anniversary celebration of Islamia, the school he had founded. For the first time in twenty-five years he sang 'Peace Train'. It was a historic event.

∾

I came a little bit closer to finding my own inner peace shortly afterwards in Ireland when visiting my friend Nora. She picked me up from Cork airport and we drove down to the south-west coast. We stopped at a small pub restaurant for lunch and sat outside enjoying the view over the lush green countryside and catching up. Just as my fresh crab sandwich arrived, my phone rang.

'Hi baby, how are you?' a deep and strangely familiar-sounding voice asked me. 'It's Imran!'

'Gosh, what a surprise,' I exclaimed, leaving the table so I could speak to him in private. '*Assalamu alaikum!*' I said to him for the first time. '*Wa alaikum as salam,*' he replied.

He told me he was separated and was calling to apologise for the pain he had caused me all those years ago. 'I forgave you a long time ago, and from my heart,' I replied, still baffled by this unexpected call. He and his wife were divorcing, he told me, and said that he felt he had been paying for having made me suffer. I was sorry to hear it. 'I've been praying a lot for you,' he said.

I thanked him. 'I also prayed for you two on your wedding day,' I added.

'Well, it didn't help,' he responded drily.

We caught up with each other's news and, even though nine years had passed, I really was glad he had called. Better late than never. I had long forgotten about the heartbreak of our split and really had forgiven him, but even so, his apology healed a faraway corner of my heart that had been left scarred. He was happy to hear that I was a practising Muslim.

∽

To deepen my knowledge of Islam I went on a number of courses, sometimes together with Dr Amina. We studied different *surahs* in depth at Utrujj, a private school run by Shaykh Haytham Tamim from Lebanon who has studied Quran, *hadith* and *fiqh* (Islamic jurisprudence) with scholars in Syria and Medina, and on Sundays I joined a Quran study group for one year at the family home of a friend's aunt, who was a doctor. The teacher was from Kashmir and the students mixed – Pakistani, Arab and British, young and old. We studied the 'Noble Quran' verse by verse, comparing different translations and commentaries, and cross-referencing with other Holy Scriptures such as the Old and New Testament. The teacher patiently answered everyone's questions and we always finished the class with a cup of tea and a chat. I invariably returned home feeling inspired. When people meet for the love of God, they say that angels are also present.

I soon realised, however, that in order to understand the

Quran at a deeper level, I needed to learn the language it was revealed in – Arabic. A translation can only ever be a subjective interpretation of the original meaning and, however skilled it is, no translation can do justice to the beauty and poetry of the original, nor can it adequately convey the different meanings of almost every word. I have seen enormous differences in Quran translations and interpretations of many key issues, including those related to women.

Motivated by my quest to understand the Quran more profoundly, I signed up for a university course at the Muslim College, but learning Arabic was no easy undertaking. All the other students in the beginner's class already knew the alphabet and could read and write in Arabic. I had to spend hours every day at home trying to catch up and I soon gave up. I had too much else going on. I decided that my best bet was to do an intensive course in an Arab country first and then to rejoin the class. It wasn't long before an opportunity presented itself.

In the autumn of 2004, a few friends from my *tariqa* were going to attend a Sufi conference in Morocco, to which Gai Eaton had also been invited. He wasn't feeling well, and asked me to go in his place. I was thrilled. The event was to be held in Marrakech, where Sufism had long been flourishing. It was an extraordinary gathering. Hundreds of Sufis – scholars, writers, artists, lawyers and anthropologists from all over the world – had been invited to the city by the Moroccan Ministry of Religious Endowments and Islamic Affairs under the auspices of the King of Morocco, Muhammad VI. He was a firm supporter of Sufism, which traditionally shaped Morocco's spiritual, cultural and social identity.

The conference was conceived as a response to the terrorist attacks in Casablanca the previous year, and the aim was to promote Sufism as an antidote to violent extremism, a notion that was received critically by some, who said that Sufism was a path to God and could not become a political tool. There were many familiar faces there, including the two girlfriends

I had been on Umrah with and the Salazars from London, Dr Nasr, who gave the keynote address, Gray Henry from the United States, and Sidi Faisal, a Moroccan friend I had met before in Egypt. He invited everyone to his estate just outside Marrakech for a very generous lunch.

As part of the programme we all went to visit the seven patron saints, the spiritual guardians and protectors of Marrakech, in the *medina*. As in Cairo, the tombs of these saints were thronging with pious visitors. Home to a great number of Sufi orders and even more *zawiyas*, where followers have been doing *dhikr* since time immemorial, the Old Town had a warm and welcoming feel to it, not least because most of the houses were painted a deep terracotta pink.

The heart of the trip was a visit to the Shrine of the eight-century Berber Sufi Shaykh and scholar Sidi Shikr, whose residence a few hours away from Marrakech had always been a spiritual refuge and a centre of learning. We boarded two buses that took us out of town and into the desert. For *zuhr* we stopped on the way, and a few hundred of us prayed in lines on huge mats that were laid out on the desert sand. It was an extraordinary site and a wonderful feeling to pray together under the sun. When we arrived at our destination, we took a tour of Sidi Shikr's shrine and attached school, where the Shaykh used to teach the principles of Islam to the Berbers. After a leisurely lunch of tagine and couscous in a large Moroccan-style marquee, we headed back to Marrakech. Every evening after dinner we were treated to a live performance of Arabo-Andalusian music at an atmospheric *riad*. I had never seen such all-pervading architectural beauty. Every site we visited was an architectural treasure, similar in style to the Alhambra Palace in Granada. I loved every minute of the trip. On the last night, the organisers invited us to a lavish candlelit dinner in the Bahia Palace. It was a balmy evening and a most romantic setting, with Sufi music playing softly in the background until late into the night. I swiftly found myself falling in love with this atmospheric city. When one of the conference organisers recommended a private teacher who specialised in classical rather than Moroccan Arabic, I resolved to come back as soon as possible to study.

On my second visit to Marrakech, I stayed for three weeks. My friends Michael Radford, his pregnant wife Emma, Said Aburish, a writer friend from London, and his girlfriend Nancy joined me for the first week. We spent New Year's Eve together listening to *oud* players and enjoying a delicious homemade couscous. Once again, Marrakech worked its magic on me. We explored some of the enchanting gardens tucked away inside the city that are designed to symbolise Paradise. I particularly loved the Menara Garden – an oasis of tranquillity centred around a still lake that on a good day reflected the scenery like a mirror.

Mike's friend, a scriptwriter who lived in Marrakech, took us shopping in the *medina*. With Nancy and Said I had coffee in the famous Jama Effna square, where we admired the snake charmers, jugglers and the street artists. Every evening we had dinner in one of the fabulously beautiful traditional res-taurants in the nearby *medina*, although we were told that in Morocco the best food is eaten at home.

I noticed on this visit how much of the *medina* had been bought up by wealthy Europeans. There were Western art gal-leries, luxury hotels, expensive restaurants and discos galore. Celebrities from Madonna, Kate Moss and Gérard Depardieu to Richard Branson's sister had all bought property in this former royal city. It felt a bit like a hedonistic enclave in the middle of North Africa, not in keeping with the indigenous Islamic culture. I sincerely hoped that Marrakech wouldn't become the new Marbella.

Once my friends left, I began my Arabic lessons. I moved into a traditional Moroccan townhouse, a *riad*, in the middle of the *medina*. The landlord went out of his way to look after his tenants and proved to me once again that Arab hospitality is unsurpassable. His housekeeper spoiled me, dishing up pancakes and peppermint tea for breakfast and making mouth-watering tajines and couscous for dinner. My tutor visited me every day, acquainting me with Arabic lettering, pronunciation, grammar and vocabulary. While in Marrakech, I loved praying in the Koutoubia Mosque, which only Muslims may enter. It dates back to the twelfth century, and its seventy-metre-high minaret is the city's main landmark. The name derives from the Arabic *al-Koutoubiyin,* meaning bookseller, as the mosque used to be surrounded by booksellers. The Koutoubia is the largest mosque in the city and can accommodate about 25,000 worshippers. It wasn't that busy most days when I was there, but for *jumah* prayers on Fridays it always became crowded. The interior was painted an immaculate white and the many Moorish-style arches provided a striking image of visual harmony, flawless perfection and purity. Apart from praying, I just enjoyed sitting there, doing my *dhikr* and taking in the tranquil atmosphere of this ancient, beautiful mosque.

One morning Jaafar, the friend who had arranged everything for me in Marrakech, called me with the devastating news that Shaykh Abu Bakr had passed away. It was so unexpected and I was deeply saddened. I immediately called Gai in London who hadn't even heard. I went to a local *zawiya* right near my *riad* and overcome by grief prayed for him intensely until I cried and couldn't stop my tears. When one of the women who was sitting there contemplating came over to try and comfort me, I told her I was alright but that someone very dear to me had just died. 'Dont't be sad', she said, 'your friend is in a great place, with God!' Then she quoted the Quranic verse: *Innalillahi wa inna ilayhi wa rajeun.* 'From God we come and to Him we return'.

I needed to be on my own to try and deal with this loss. The Shaykh, his teachings and my spiritual group were everything to me, my whole reason for living in London despite not really finding work there. Now I felt as though my heart had lost its anchor. When I called Gai again, he told me that the Shaykh had actually been well and even had been on his daily walks just days before his passing away. I wished I wasn't so far away, because it meant I couldn't fly back for the funeral, which was to take place within forty-eight hours in keeping with Muslim custom. But I continued to pray in Marrakech for my Shaykh. And Jaafar, who was working for the religious ministry, ensured that in all the mosques of Marrakech imams would pray with their congregation for Shaykh Abu Bakr who was deeply respected in Morocco.

On Friday morning, the Islamic weekly holiday, I participated in a communal *dhikr* at the tomb of the city's first patron saint, Sidi Abbas Sebti. He lived in the seventh century and was famous for his work with the poor and needy, and particularly the blind. On entering the mosque complex, I passed a row of blind men, deep in prayer. 'The blind are the true seers – *les voyeurs* – for they see with their hearts,' a Moroccan mystic told me. The interior of the mausoleum is breathtaking. The ground and parts of the walls are decorated with tiled geometric mosaics, magnificently set off by the white background. I just loved the Moroccan aesthetics.

Around twenty men in traditional *jalabias* sat in a circle on the ground next to the tomb of the saint, singing love songs for God and the Prophet in deep, resonant voices. I joined a group of women sitting to the left of the entrance. They also wore *jalabias* and headscarves, as I did, and we quietly did our *dhikr*. At one point, a guard passed by and poured warm rose water into our palms from an antique jug, and eventually he treated us all to a glass of peppermint tea. It was enchanting.

I experienced Morocco as a country that was both traditional and modern, religious and open-minded, and where Sufism was an inherent part of the culture. Many women worked, and society on the whole wasn't segregated. Due to the geographic proximity to Europe and the historic links with

France and Spain, as well as the thriving Moroccan tourist and film industries, the country is altogether very open to the West. My greatest joy however was witnessing and experiencing traditional Sufism in such exceptional ways. In other parts of the world, the spiritual dimension is either frowned upon or exists only on the fringes of society or underground, and is often criticised as an illegitimate innovation, *bi'da*. Not so in Morocco. There it was accepted that orthodox Sufis were the ones who best understood the innermost soul and the spirit of the Prophet, and internalised his qualities, such as sincerity, magnanimity and impeccable manners. Crucially, the great Islamic theologian Imam al-Ghazali made a vital contribution to Islam when he definitively justified all authentic Sufi practices as part of the Shariah of Islam.

∾

Six months later, I found out first hand just how difficult it could be for Sufis to practise their faith in some Muslim-majority countries, when I accompanied Dr Nasr and a few of his students on a lecture tour of Turkey. Our itinerary included Istanbul and Konya, home to the famous Rumi Mausoleum.

In contrast to Morocco, Sufi practices have been officially banned in Turkey since Kemal Atatürk secularised the country in the 1920s. Anyone caught taking part in a Sufi ritual, in a *tekke* or a *zawiya,* could be taken to a police station and cross-examined, and in the 1930s members of Sufi orders were even imprisoned. For years, those who were seen to practise Islam openly, going to the mosque on Fridays, for example, might have found this to be an obstacle to their career, especially within the education system and the army. Moreover, women were not allowed to wear a headscarf in universities and other public institutions.

However, Islam is firmly anchored in Turkey's historical and cultural consciousness, and, although the ban on Sufism remained, restrictions later relaxed under a government more lenient towards all religions. The situation vis-à-vis Sufi orders then became one of 'don't ask – don't tell'. Despite militant secularists describing Sufis as 'bogeymen' and 'anti-republic', a number of prominent political figures later emerged from Sufi circles. The Sufi orders have adjusted themselves to the situation by operating under the banner of cultural centres, artistic, folkloric and historical associations.

At a former Sufi *tekke* in Istanbul's Galata district, which has been transformed into a museum, I saw an ancient tree growing out of the marble gravestone of a saint. It was as though it drew its nourishment from the *baraka* emanating from the heart of the saint, and, to me, it symbolised Turkey's roots in Sufism.

Rumi, who loved all religions and whose own religion, as he himself said, was love, spent many years in Turkey. It was there, in the thirteenth century, that his followers founded the Mevlevi Order, whose members today are also known as the Whirling Dervishes, and it is in Konya, the heart of Anatolia, that he lies buried. His mausoleum, which used to be the lodge of the order, is today a museum and the second most visited tourist attraction after Topkapi Palace in Istanbul. Amongst Persians it is known as the second Ka'ba.

Rumi's poetic insights had always inspired me even before I became Muslim and I was excited to visit Maulana's tomb. To refresh my memory and feel his spirit, so to speak, I read on the flight to Konya *Sufi Path of Love* by William Chittick, a wonderful compilation of Rumi's spiritual teachings. The great master's resting place is situated under a turquoise-tiled dome of a traditional Seljuk house, which lies behind a courtyard with a fountain and a souvenir shop. The interior of the mausoleum is simple: the walls are decorated with just a few striking Quranic calligraphies and some sweeping arabesques. Several great masters and some of Rumi's family members are also buried here. The coffins are all wrapped in cloth, and a turban had been positioned at the head of each of them. Jalaluddin Rumi's tomb is situated right at the back of the mausoleum. It is covered with brocade fabric, embroidered with verses from the Quran, and the wall behind it is adorned with gold-coloured calligraphies of yet more verses. We stayed a while in front of it, praying for his soul and blessings. Opposite the tomb was an exhibition with a collection of relics from Rumi's life, including prayer beads, coats, the famous *ney* (bamboo flute), *dafs* (hand drums), and *ouds*, as well as some of his best-known poetry collections in various languages. On the way out I couldn't resist popping into the souvenir shop and buying two Rumi cups – one for Ruby and one for myself – as a symbol of the cup of the heart that we needed to empty.

Back in Istanbul we visited some of the fabulous mosques, such as the imposing multi-domed Sultan Ahmed, otherwise known as the Blue Mosque, with its six tall, thin minarets, where we joined the *jumah* prayers on the Friday. Inside, the various domes were painted with countless flower motifs and decorated with magnificent blue tiles. Huge circular candle stands hung from the ceiling; soft red carpet lined the floor. We took off our shoes and I joined the women on the balcony where we had the best view over the entire space. This is another rare mosque where women can fully enjoy the splendour and glory of the ancient architecture and pray either in specially designated areas at the back or in the gallery. It was wonderful to be here, to absorb the *baraka* and join the Friday prayers with a few thousand other worshippers. I returned as often as I could.

We also browsed the Grand Bazaar and went to one of the ancient hammams for a relaxing scrub. When we took a boat trip down the Bosporus, the most magnificent sunset I had ever seen awaited us, bathing the entire sea in a deep red-orange. But the highlight of our journey was a visit to the Jerrahi order where we witnessed the *sema* (worship ceremony), which culminated in the sacred dance of the legendary Whirling

Dervishes. It took place in secret in a *tekke* that looked completely unassuming from the outside. No one would ever have imagined that, inside, spiritual ceremonies were held regularly. Our group had been invited to join the *dhikr* there on a Thursday evening, the eve of the Islamic holy day, which is the traditional time for *dhikr* anywhere in the world. We took off our shoes at the door to the *tekke,* went inside and sat down on the floor to eat with the others. Men and women sat and ate separately. The building was relatively big, with high ceilings, a gallery for the women, calligraphies on the walls and a prayer niche colourfully decorated with floral tiles. After our meal, we prayed *maghrib*, the evening prayer, and then the *sema* began. Led by a Shaykh, the men repeated various formulas of praise and names of God, first sitting down, then standing in tight rows, holding each other, and moving in an orderly way to the beat of the *daf* – at times choreographed by the Shaykh, who ticked off those who fell out of line. All the while, they swayed rhythmically to and fro, and, gradually their movements and exclamations became increasingly fervent. The ceremony went on for over an hour, with the women joining in from the gallery and moving with the rhythm. Some of them were in visible raptures, tears coursing down their cheeks.

The crowning glory unfolded as a few of the dervishes slowly and deliberately approached the middle of the room. They all wore tall, felt hats and long black cloaks, which they then proceeded to take off with a gentle bow. The cloak is a symbol of the wearer's own grave; when the dervish sheds his self, he is spiritually reborn. A *ney* flute started playing haunting tunes of love and longing that stirred my soul. The dervishes began turning slowly on their axes, getting faster and faster until their long white skirts were lifted by the movement and whirled around them like swirling water. They looked like spinning tops and seemed to hover above the ground. I was hypnotised by the elegance and perfect harmony of this sacred dance.

It is intended to plunge the dervish into a state of concentration on Allah, said Shaykh Abu Bakr, who described its symbolism thus:

> The motionless unseen centre is the Divine presence and everything is concentrated on that. As to what we see, there are circles within circles. The circle itself represents Heaven on Earth. The central circle is man's body which rotates around the unseen centre. Beyond that an outer circle is traced by the arms held out and also by the lower garments which through the whirling flow outwards and form a circle around the body of man.
>
> The arms bear witness to a feature of man as he was created in his function of mediator between Heaven and Earth. The right palm of the dervish faces upwards to receive graces from Heaven and the left palm faces downwards to transmit these graces to Earth. This dance is the most eloquent image of what man was and what he must again become. (*Rumi, The Wings of Love* by Shems Friedlander)

When we left, I happened to notice that not one of the dervishes so much as even looked at the women, a sign of their piety.

The Turkish tourist board is well aware of the fascination exerted by the Whirling Dervishes, and they have become a major element of their campaigns. There are plenty of public shows all over the country and even abroad, where dervishes perform for entertainment. Some criticise these events for being wholly commercial, and maintain that the deeper meaning of the sacred dance has been lost. On the other hand, at least it allows people a glimpse of the intoxicating beauty of this Sufi meditation of love and, who knows, a spiritual spark might just be ignited. As Rumi said: 'All loves are a bridge to Divine love. Yet, those who have not had a taste of it do not know!'

Ironically, Rumi, known as the Sufi mystic and poet of love, who expressed the heart of Islam like no other, is almost as popular in the United States and Europe as he is in Turkey and Iran. So it could be argued that Sufism represents a spiritual and cultural bridge between East and West. And this spiritual dimension within Islam could perhaps even provide an antidote to extremism. Although Sufism must remain above any political calculations, one thing is for sure: there's no such thing as a Sufi terrorist.

Chapter 14

Journey to the Heart: The Hajj

We all became brothers.

Malcolm X

A decade had passed since I had embraced Islam and a lot had changed in those years. I lived according to Islamic principles and had left much of my old life behind. I prayed regularly, fasted during Ramadan, celebrated Islamic festivals, and had a circle of friends who shared and supported me in my spiritual beliefs.

But I had yet to take one of the most important steps on my journey to God: the Hajj. All practising Muslims aim to embark on this journey at least once in their lives. I'd had a foretaste of the experience on the Umrah. The two pilgrimages are quite similar but Umrah is smaller and voluntary, while the Hajj is the largest annual pilgrimage in the world and the fifth pillar of Islam. It is the duty of every able-bodied Muslim who can afford it to perform Hajj once in a lifetime. And while the Umrah can be undertaken at any time, the Hajj can only be done at a fixed time in the year: from the eighth to the twelfth day of *Dhul al-Hijjah,* the twelfth and last month of the Islamic calendar. During this period, Mecca is teeming with some three million pilgrims – which makes the Hajj the biggest event in the world and a logistical feat. Over time, the Holy Mosque has been extended: it now encompasses three storeys and continues to expand. The pilgrimage also takes in Mina and its tent city, which provides temporary accommodation for pilgrims about five kilometres to the east of Mecca during the ritual of the symbolic stoning of the devil. It is here that Abraham is said to have stoned the devil that came between him and the command that Allah had sent him.

Many pilgrims who go on Hajj contemplate the possibility they may not return home. In the old days, before the advent of planes, trains and cars, the journey to Mecca was long, arduous and often dangerous. Even today many write their will before setting off, say their farewells to their relatives and try to make peace with adversaries. Nowadays it can still be strenuous, and it is not uncommon for old people to die a natural death in Mecca brought about by the stresses and strains of the journey. The bodies of the deceased are laid to rest close to the Ka'ba, and after the ritual prayers the pilgrims say the special funeral prayers together.

In August 2005 I went on holiday with my dad and his wife to the same resort on Germany's North Sea coast where we used to go when I was a child. I prayed *fajr* and then repeatedly read a verse from the Quran that Zain had recommended to me from *surah al-Hajj*: *Proclaim the Pilgrimage to all people. They will come to you on foot and on every kind of lean camel, emerging from every deep mountain pass to attain benefits.*

I went back to bed and then suddenly dreamt that I heard an unusually deep and mighty voice that sounded as though it was emanating from the cosmos rather than from a human being. 'You want to go on Hajj?' this sonorous voice asked me. Next I dreamt about my architect from years ago, which reminded me that I still hadn't paid an outstanding bill. To me the meaning was obvious: God was inviting me to go on Hajj, but before that I needed to settle my debts. Muslims may only embark on their pilgrimage if they are debt-free or at least have made an arrangement for repayment. Debts are considered to be very serious in Islam. The Prophet is believed to have said that after the major sins, the greatest sin is when someone dies with debts and leaves behind no assets to pay them off. He refused to say the funeral prayers for someone who had died with debts until they had been settled by family or friends.

They say whenever an opportunity to go on Hajj presents itself, one should seize it because it may never come again. In 2005, the Hajj season fell in the Christmas period and also happened to coincide with my fortieth birthday. There was nothing stopping me, and in fact a few friends of mine were also thinking about going. It was a perfect opportunity – even though I had always harboured hopes that one day I would go on Hajj with my husband. But since there wasn't any sign of him, there was no point in further delaying my religious duty. Paying off my debts turned out to be the least of my worries. But then, in the autumn, I suddenly suffered a slipped disc and an MRI scan indicated that I needed surgery. There were some days I couldn't even stand upright or walk straight without having to squat intermittently to relax my back, but I was determined to avoid an operation. Dr Amina prescribed regular physiotherapy as well as anti-inflammatories and heavy painkillers, which I could only take early in the mornings and in the evenings since it was Ramadan. They were so strong that I often felt quite high. Fadwa and her friend Zain were the first to visit and they did their best to boost my morale, reminding me what al-Gilani said:

A sick person is Allah's guest for as long as he is ill. Every
day he is sick, God gives him countless rewards, as long as
he says 'al hamdulillah', praise be to God, and does not fight
it and complain. When God returns to him his health, he
expiates his sins and gives him the status of the newly-born
(completely pure and free of any sin). Illness is a mercy and a
blessing.

Those words comforted me and eventually the pain began to ease, but the physiotherapist I was seeing three times a week explicitly advised me against going on Hajj. The pilgrimage was an extreme physical challenge and the long bus journey would be poison for my back. I accepted his advice. After a few weeks, however, I was feeling better – well enough to start strengthening my core muscles with Pilates exercises that would support my spine like an inner corset. After our annual *majlis* for Laylat al-Qadr at the house of my friend Samiya, I took the opportunity to show my X-rays to her husband Hilali, one of the top back surgeons in the UK. He attested that it was a serious disc prolapse but recognised that I had obviously made an extraordinary recovery by the grace of God and that if I was now pain-free, there really was no reason why I shouldn't go on Hajj. It was my Ramadan miracle.

I really got excited when I found out that Dr Amina, who had been to Mecca several times, was thinking of going again. Hajj travel agents offer a range of options that vary from basic to luxurious. Dr Amina suggested we go for the simplest category. She had enjoyed a previous Hajj organised by a tour operator near the Regent's Park Mosque which, in my experience, involved better organisation and was more personal than other, more expensive ones. I decided to go there to pick up some information. Hamdi, the director, went out of his way to explain the different stages of the journey and made no bones about the modest standard of the accommodation. He gave me a video to watch at home to make sure I knew what I was letting myself in for. The film didn't try to disguise the fact that this particular 'package' was a true hardship Hajj and very strenuous – but it was definitely a Hajj with heart. I now knew what to expect and decided to go ahead and book. A real pilgrimage shouldn't be confused with a luxury holiday, I told myself.

They say that no one can perform Hajj without an invitation from God, and until one is actually sitting on the plane to Mecca a lot can happen and a lot can go wrong. No sooner had I booked my trip than the first obstacle presented itself: a precondition for a Hajj visa is a passport that will remain valid for at least six months after the pilgrim has entered Saudi Arabia. Mine was about to run out. But once again I was lucky. On the advice of my mother during my last visit to Hamburg I had already applied for a new passport. So I called the German authorities, negotiated with them and persuaded them to make an exception and let my mother pick up the passport on my behalf. Although she was actually quite worried about me going on Hajj and wished I wouldn't, she sent the passport by overnight courier to London and it arrived just in time for me to apply for a visa. 'You never know who Allah's soldiers are,' said a friend at the time.

Dr Amina and I were to join a group of fifty British pilgrims, and a further fifty Egyptians would meet us in Cairo. The travel agency arranged everything from the visa to accommodation and transport from one ritual site to another. For the single women the leader of our Hajj group acted as our *mahram*, or male companion. An Al Azhar-educated imam who sometimes preached at the Regent's Park Mosque was to accompany our group, explaining the various rituals we undertook and answering the many questions that would arise during the trip. We were all given an ID on a string in both Arabic and English, complete with photo, phone numbers, name of local contact person and addresses of the places where we were staying in Mecca and Medina. We were told to wear our IDs around our necks at all times in case we got lost.

By December, my preparations for the trip were in full swing. We would be sleeping in tents and even outdoors under the stars, so I bought a sleeping bag, a travel pillow, mattress and an easy-dry towel. It can get bitterly cold in the desert at night and I intended to be well prepared. I packed several *ihram* robes and comfortable shoes, since we would be doing a lot of walking, a special roll to wrap around my waist as support for my back on those long drives, and a homeopathic first-aid kit that included remedies against colds – every Hajj pilgrim apparently goes down with flu. I also had a flat shoulder bag made for my Quran and other essential items by my tailor and mender Nina, who came from India, was very spiritual and had become a dear friend and consultant on all areas in life, like she was to most of her clients. For over a decade I had brought all my clothes to her to take in, let out or mend.

Just before we were due to leave, Islam Channel asked me if I would be interested in reporting for them from the Hajj. I considered it but decided that I would like my first Hajj to be for God, and God alone. I wanted to be able to concentrate fully on the experience, so I politely declined.

Friends gave me advice and many useful presents such as a small booklet to wear around my neck containing essential information on all the Hajj rituals and prayers. I promised everyone I would pray for them in the Holy Mosque.

Finally, the big day arrived. First, we flew to Cairo, and during a five-hour layover, I got talking to some of my fellow pilgrims: a Finnish woman who was on her second Hajj, Fatima, a Caribbean lady in a wheelchair, Mr Imam, a Sufi from Bangladesh in his eighties and a friend of Dr Amina's, and also a young man called Aziz accompanying Mr Imam. They both belonged to Sheikh Nazim's Sufi group and became my Hajj brothers. In the middle of the night we flew on from Cairo to Jeddah. The plane was packed with pilgrims, most of them clad in white *ihram* robes like Abraham used to wear. In fact they say that making the pilgrimage is going back to the time of Abraham. So many of the rituals are associated with the patriarch of monotheism.

When we landed in Jeddah we went straight to the airport's special pilgrimage terminal, where we waited several hours for the bus to Medina, our first destination. It was the middle of the night, but the airport was teeming with pilgrims waiting for their transfers under the vast white canopies designed by Bodo Rasch. At the airport bazaar, pilgrims could buy everything they needed for the Hajj, from folding plastic mats to sleep on in the desert, to *ihram* robes and prayer beads.

Many people had set up camp on the floor and gone to sleep. I wandered around the airport for a while and found a prayer corner especially for women where I prayed *fajr* (the morning prayers). It began to get warmer after sunrise, and I felt as though I had been transported to a different world.

The journey to Medina was strenuous. The bus was tiny, uncomfortable and crammed full of pilgrims wedged next to one another like sardines. I tried to get some sleep, but woke up whenever my head fell onto the shoulder of the imam's wife, who was next to me. I began to realise that going on Hajj was a physical challenge not to be underestimated. But I comforted myself with the thought that the reward for every discomfort I suffered for God was a spiritual blessing. At some point we made a pit stop and had a cup of tea. A woman told me off for a few strands of hair that had escaped from my headscarf, even though I was wearing a particularly wide headband underneath. 'You should wrap the headscarf round your head twice like the rest of us and then secure it with pins,' she suggested. 'Only then will it stay in place.' Fortunately, I had followed Dr Amina's advice and packed a supply of safety pins.

Once in Medina, Dr Amina and I moved into the room we were to share with five others. One of them was Fatima. Her wheelchair was usually pushed by Dr Amina who was in her late sixties by now, but the men clearly had other priorities. As my doctor, she had forbidden me from helping out because I was still recovering from the slipped disc. So Fatima was fortunate enough to receive Harley Street private medical care from Dr Amina. It was her fifth Hajj and she was no doubt rewarded for her dedication with many spiritual blessings. Sadly, Fatima died not long after returning from Hajj.

The apartment we were staying in had no comforts whatsoever – initially, not even running water. After the long journey, there was nothing I wanted more than a shower. But we had chosen the hardship Hajj, and we had no choice but to get on with it. As an experienced pilgrim, Dr Amina had brought with her some spray bottles, which she handed out to her room mates so we all managed to at least refresh our faces before getting ready to catch the bus to the Prophet's Mosque.

We got off as near to the main entrance as the bus would take us and everyone we passed was heading in one direction – to the mosque. They all wore long, traditional robes of varying colours. We walked along the pedestrian area past carpet dealers, sandal sellers and jewellery stores until we saw the imposing mosque laid out before us in all its glory. The sun was setting, and the dusky pink heavens perfectly set off the building's sublime architecture and ten minarets soaring into the sky. The call to prayer rang out loud and clear from one of them, and the pilgrims shifted up a gear as they streamed towards the mosque. At the entrance to the courtyard, my companions and I separated from the men and went to the women's area.

I was thrilled to be back at the Prophet's Mosque and so awestruck by the beauty of the domes and minarets framed against the evening sky that I spontaneously got out my camera and took a few pictures. When I photographed some of the women who had gathered here to pray, a mosque attendant swaddled in black instantly called me over, demanded to know my name and tried to confiscate my camera. In Saudi Arabia, women who veil their faces don't want to be photographed, she told me. Fortunately, I managed to persuade her to let me keep my camera and promised her I wouldn't take any more pictures. On my best behaviour, I sat down next to the other women, although I wasn't able to take part in the ritual prayer. Women who are menstruating can only do personal prayers but not the five daily ritual prayers. Some say they shouldn't even enter the sacred mosques in Mecca or Medina, but there are *hadith*s that report the Prophet himself asked his wife Aisha to fetch him a prayer mat from the mosque even though she was menstruating at the time. Either way, I decided to stay in the courtyard.

It was a shame, because of course I wanted to join the prayers, but I was glad my period would be finished by the time I got to Mecca because otherwise I wouldn't be allowed to perform the circumambulations of the Ka'ba and would have to make up for it later. To avoid this situation, some women take hormone tablets to delay their periods before they go on Hajj. For me it was wonderful enough just to be there, do *dhikr*, listen to the imam and watch the other women bowing in prayer, straightening up and kneeling in perfect unison.

When we returned to our flat, we were relieved to find that the taps were fixed and we had water. After a well-deserved shower and a portion of dahl with roti bread, I went to bed exhausted. The mattress was hard and uncomfortable but I fell asleep within minutes – only to be woken at three a.m. by glaring neon light. Some of the other women were already up and getting ready for the *fajr* morning prayer in the Prophet's Mosque. Unless we caught the bus at five a.m., we knew we wouldn't have a chance of securing a place in the mosque. And we certainly didn't want to miss it, because one prayer there counted as much as one thousand prayers in all the other mosques of the world, apart from in Mecca.

In the evening we had a group meeting with the organisers and the imam to prepare us for the coming few days. 'The way we experience the pilgrimage is a reflection of our inner state,' the imam said. 'To some of us it will be a strenuous trial, whereas to others every step of the way is a joy, despite the privations and discomfort.' And then we each went back to our respective wings – women and men separated – and got to know each other a little better over a simple dinner.

It was 25 December, but there in Medina, Christmas felt very far away. Nevertheless, in the course of the day I did receive a few text messages from family and friends in Germany and England wishing me a Happy Christmas. They felt like messages from another universe.

A few days later I was allowed to join in with the ritual

prayers. It was a cool morning and still dark when I arrived at the mosque only to be frisked by two heavily veiled security guards. They rifled through my bag and this time they confiscated my camera although I hadn't even used it. They stored it in a locker and told me I could pick it up after the prayers. In time, I learned the trick of hiding my camera and mobile phone in my robes so that no one could find them.

We didn't usually all go out together, but split up into smaller groups. I helped Aziz look after Mr Imam, who gave me precious prayer tips and wise advice. Sometimes I was happy to be by myself. I enjoyed watching all the comings and goings at the mosque and the many diverse people I saw. They came from all over the world and I never tired of the variety of faces, colours and outfits. There were women from Mali looking regal and elegant in gorgeous lilac, orange, and green robes, wearing matching turbans with a strip of fabric hanging down the side. Indonesian women all had white gloves and white headscarves that hung to their breast and were embroidered with lace. The Persian women usually wore long black or blue robes with grey chadors that came down below their hips while Moroccans could be recognised by the hoods on their *jalabias*. Another group of women sported bright yellow veils with blue labels sewn onto them, which indicated that they came from Kerala in India. I also heard German, French, English and American voices. On my wanderings, I came across men from Tajikistan wearing black quilted satin and velvet coats, and matching black gold-framed caps. There were other men with Palestinian scarves wrapped around their heads, shiny silver-black turbans, traditional Arab headdress, or just small white caps. Many Pakistanis had long, henna-dyed beards. I saw rich people and poor, elderly, children and babies. Medina felt like a microcosm of the whole world.

Women were still only allowed to visit the Prophet's tomb early in the morning and at midday. When I went at noon, the experience was anything but edifying. First I had to spend an hour in the anteroom, which was soon overcrowded with women. Male guards tried to manage the crowd by forming a chain, holding hands. When the door to the tomb was finally opened, the mass of women pushed and jostled so much that the row of guards scattered and I found myself crushed so hard against a pillar that I could hardly breathe and ended up with bruises. I reached the actual tomb only to find it was draped in a white sheet, and within seconds I was being herded away by a number of veiled guards in black barking *yalla, haja, yalla!* – 'come on, pilgrim, come on' – at me. The next time I tried, I decided that praying near the Prophet's tomb was just as good as doing it right in front of the tomb; so I prayed in the court-yard in the middle of the men's area, which happened to be relatively empty, until I was chased away by a guard.

Together with Mr Imam and Aziz I explored the vicinity of the mosque and browsed through the shops. We found lovely handmade wooden prayer beads, along with perfume oils, robes, shawls and jewellery – and some useful items for *hajjis* such as face masks, tissues and vitamin C tablets, which I wasted no time scooping up. For days, I had been fighting off a cold with Echinacea and Oscilococcinum, a homeopathic miracle treatment for colds and flu, but even that had begun to fail. With millions of people constantly coughing and sneez-ing around us, it was impossible to avoid catching the Hajj flu.

After six days of getting up at three a.m. in order to make it to the *fajr* prayers in the mosque on time, I decided that I deserved a lie-in. When I finally woke up again everyone was gone, so I had a leisurely shower and prayed alone in my room. I felt like a zombie. I had a burning sore throat, which my homeopathic globules could only banish momentarily. The combination of constant chatter from the women in the room, often as early as three a.m., harsh neon lighting, a rock-hard mattress and long queues outside the bathroom every night to get ready for *fajr* – there were three bathrooms for fifty people – was all beginning to get to me. How much I would have given for just one night in a nice hotel. But what could I do? I had chosen to go on a hardship Hajj, and I had got one.

Dr Amina told me that single women usually received marriage proposals while on Hajj. 'If they don't, there must be something wrong with them,' she said earnestly. I wasn't sure if she really meant it and was wondering where I stood. The actual offer had to be made either shortly before or after the Hajj, because talking about marriage to a prospective candidate during Hajj is *haram*, forbidden. As it happened, Dr Amina had an acquaintance who had invited us to a fabulous dinner in Medina. Her brother was also there, and, shortly afterwards, he let it be known that he was interested in me. He was nice, but not really my type, and, moreover, he was a convert to Christianity. What I wanted more than anything was a husband I could share my faith with. But it wasn't long before I had another suitor. Lubna, one of the women in my travel group, was keen to set me up with her brother, who lived in Cairo. He was in Medina as well, and we met for tea in a hotel lobby, with Lubna acting as chaperone. She also had to double as interpreter, since her brother didn't speak a word of English and my Arabic still wasn't up to much. Although not unattractive, the instant I set eyes on him, I was put off by his long beard. It wasn't so much a question of looks, although I'm not that keen on long beards, particularly when combined with very short hair, but what the beard stood for: a particular mindset that I knew I could never share. It might be an unfair assumption and I know there are exceptions, but in his case, I had a point. He told me in no uncertain terms that he expected his third wife-to-be to wear a full veil that also covered her face and only ever *abayas* or other long robes of subdued colours. For the sake of politeness, I told him I would think about it, but later I thanked Lubna for her friendly gesture and told her I wasn't interested. At least there was nothing wrong with me, I thought to myself, relieved.

On 30 December, we left for Mecca. We were all excited and a bit nervous because now it was getting serious: our meeting with God was imminent. And so was the return to our own inner heart, which needed to be cleansed of all impurities. The mysterious, black-shrouded, empty Ka'ba being the outward symbol for it. While we were packing and preparing ourselves, one of the women I shared the room with came up to me. 'If there's anything I have done to annoy you, please forgive me!' she said.

'I would be glad to forgive you if I knew what for,' I answered, taken aback. She explained that she might have unintentionally offended or irritated me. To be on the safe side, I apologised to her as well. Then all the women in the room exchanged apologies with one another. Yes, we had all got on each other's nerves but, under the circumstances, I felt it was entirely understandable and only to be expected. Even so, we were pilgrims, and it was important to forgive and be forgiven.

At two o'clock in the afternoon, after we had performed our *ghusl*, to symbolically wash away our impurities, and dressed in our *ihram*, we gathered outside our flat to catch the bus to Mecca. Now without even a hint of mascara or eye pencil, which I usually wore, I felt almost naked and a bit embarrassed at facing the world without it. In the state of *ihram* all negative emotions such as anger and irritation must be avoided. The magic word on Hajj is *sabr*, patience.

It was the middle of the night when we reached the checkpoint that marks the start of the *Haram*, the sacred area that only Muslims are allowed to enter. After we passed another bazaar selling everything a pilgrim could possibly need on Hajj, we reached the mosque which stood amid atmospherically lit gardens of palm trees. A tide of pilgrims dressed in white came towards us, while another group was heading towards the mosque. We followed in their wake. Before entering the sacred area to perform Hajj, the pilgrim must declare his intention to do so to God with two *rakat*. The prayer room was heaving with pilgrims jostling for space. In their rush to snag the last spots, a few women walked right across my prayer mat while I was praying, which is considered bad manners as it interrupts the communion with God. But what with all the commotion, it couldn't always be avoided and I had done it as well to others. As soon as I had finished my prayers a beautiful young African woman came up to me and with a radiant smile apologised for having walked across my prayer mat. I was so touched by her gesture that I found myself close to tears.

On Hajj people's hearts soften, they say. 'Dear God, forgive us our mistakes and our selfishness and lack of consideration,' I prayed quietly to myself. Then the Hajj began.

∾

We eventually arrived in Mecca, where it was a lot hotter than it had been in Medina. The apartment we were staying in was a forty-minute walk from the *Haram Sharif*, the Holy Mosque, so we jumped on one of the minibuses that ran through the city day and night. Mecca itself was pretty run-down, except for the area surrounding the *Haram*, which was scattered with cranes and half-finished high rises soaring into the sky. There had been a construction boom since my last visit and the sleek glass and steel facades of the many new five-star hotels and upmarket stores glittered in the sun. The skyscrapers all dwarfed the mosque and seemed to me like a symbol of human hubris. But fair enough. The hotels are needed to accommodate the millions of pilgrims in peak season. Our imam suggested that to avoid getting lost in the sea of people, we should all perform *tawaf* as a group, with the men on the outside and the women on the inside. I put my sandals into my flat bag and entered the mosque barefoot reciting the prayer *labbaika Allahumma labbaik* (Here I am at your service, my God, here I am), as did the others. We passed a number of pilgrims reciting the same verse before finally sighting the majestic Ka'ba, the heart of Islam and the House of God.

In contrast to when I was here the first time to perform the Umrah, the courtyard was completely full with people mostly dressed in white walking around it, deeply immersed in prayer. I took Mr Imam by the hand and we joined the stream of praying pilgrims. The crowd was pushing and shoving and we could only move ahead slowly. Sometimes there would be gridlock, but then the crowd would open again and we would walk forward. Pilgrims recite different prayers depending on which side of the Ka'ba they are passing, and it is said that personal prayers are best offered between the Yemeni corner that points towards Yemen and the Black Stone. There, pilgrims say a prayer in Arabic from the Quran as the Prophet once did: '*Our God, give us good in this world and in our future life and deliver us from the punishment of fire,*[1] *and bring us to Paradise with righteous people.*'[2] I could hear other pilgrims recite the prayer loudly and fervently together and I joined in. It was an incredible feeling, completely suspended from time and space – being at one with everyone and at the same time immersed in the Divine – like everyone else around me, our hearts wholly connected with God.

All in all we spent almost two hours doing *tawaf*, and the elderly gentleman by my side was visibly exhausted by the end. We drank some Zamzam water and took a short rest. According to the Prophet, this special water heals body and soul; it serves whatever purpose one intends it to serve: 'If you drink it in order to be healed, you will be healed by God's grace … If you drink it to quench your thirst, then you will be refreshed.'[3] Every Muslim loves Zamzam water; it tastes slightly sweet and its consistency is thicker than normal water. When I drank it I said a little prayer. Reenergised, we performed *say* in the midst of the crowd (walking rapidly between two hills seven times as Hagar, Abraham's wife had done when searching for water for her baby boy). On two floors there are several lanes, one in each direction and two in the middle for wheelchairs only. I took Mr Imam by the hand and we joined the walking crowd on the ground floor. Every time we got up one of the hills we said a special prayer. To my surprise, Mr Imam and I were the fastest in our group. I hope I'll be as fit as him when I'm ninety!

After completing the first part of our Hajj we could take off our *ihram*s and relax. But none of us felt like it – we all wanted to spend as much time as possible in the Sacred Mosque close to the Ka'ba. Here every prayer is worth as much as 100,000 prayers in any ordinary mosque.

The first day of the New Year had been earmarked for a trip to the famous Hira cave, some three miles north-east of Mecca on the Jabal al-Noor, the Mountain of Light. The Prophet often came here to meditate and it was there that he is said to have received his first revelation from Allah. Muslims follow his example and from time to time try to retreat from the world to commune with God – although admittedly few manage to do so on a regular basis. Climbing the mountain was hard work. Mr Imam only got a third of the way up before he opted to sit down by the side of the path with some of the other pilgrims in our group and wait for the rest of us to return.

With no handrail, the path, which was steep and very slippery, wasn't exactly secure. Also, there were so many people at the top that we realised we wouldn't actually be able to enter the cave. Above the entrance was an inscription of the first verse in the Quran to be revealed to Muhammad:

Read! In the name of your Sustainer, who created: created man of clotted blood. Read, for your Lord is most generous, the one who taught the use of the pen, taught man what he did not know. (96:1–5)

On our way back down the mountain, we passed throngs of poor, often disabled people sitting by the wayside pleading for alms. It was impossible to walk past without giving them something, even though we were well aware that some of them might have been hustlers looking to exploit charitable *hajjis*. The Hajj season was a busy time for them. We were approached ourselves by a well-dressed family telling us they were pilgrims who had been robbed and that they needed 1,000 rials to get by. We had been warned about such people and pointed them towards the Hajj office which deals with stranded or robbed pilgrims.

When Mr Imam and I took a taxi to our accommodation, the driver made all sorts of random detours in order to increase the price of the journey. To add insult to injury, he told me I should cover my face with a veil. I retorted in broken Arabic that nothing in the Quran required women to cover their faces, adding that it was actually forbidden to wear a veil in the Holy Mosque. I also told him his car was a wreck. 'Don't worry, I'll get you to your destination in one piece,' he said. Feeling slightly nervous, I pointed to the miniature Quran that hung from his rear-view mirror. 'I can see the Quran there, so I'm not worried,' I replied.

We related the anecdote to Dr Amina when we met up later. 'That's nothing compared to what I experienced,' she replied. 'Before I could do my *tawaf* around the Ka'ba, I had to do *tawaf* around Mecca. At eleven in the evening I jumped into a taxi to the mosque, but instead of taking me to the *Haram*, the driver went on the motorway to Jeddah and raced off. He didn't respond to my protests, so I opened the door as he was travelling at 70mph and screamed, forcing him to stop.'

'My God, you could have died!' I exclaimed.

But Dr Amina assured me she was alright. 'I had to walk back along the motorway against the oncoming traffic and forty minutes later I finally arrived at the *Haram*,' she told us.

'Thank God you're still in one piece!' I said, giving her a hug.

In the afternoon we went back to the mosque for *maghrib* and *isha* prayers. I took Mr Imam up to the third floor, found a good spot for him to sit and deposited my newly purchased green chequered prayer mat next to him, then went back down to do *tawaf*. I dived into the sea of pilgrims. Now that I was on my own I was free to move about within the crowd at my own pace and I resolved to try and touch the Ka'ba. As I circled God's House I gradually got closer, even though it wasn't easy with the many groups of pilgrims holding hands and blocking the way. There were men carrying children on their shoulders and I saw one woman holding a baby in a sling. I was touched to see couples performing the *tawaf* together, the man walking behind his wife with his arms protectively round her. *In sha' Allah*, I too will be able to do Hajj one day as a wife, so lovingly protected by my husband, I prayed spontaneously to God. The closer I got to the Ka'ba, the denser the crowd became. When I passed the Yemeni corner, I saw two guards undoing the plastic ropes that had been put up so that the area could be cleaned. It's now or never, I thought, and dashed ahead along with many others to try and touch the Ka'ba. And there I was, right in front of it. I laid my hands on it and prayed from the bottom of my heart for my family and my friends that all their dreams – I had a long list of their wishes – and mine might come true. I really emptied my heart before God until the crowd carried me away and I melted again in the stream of pilgrims. 'Surrendering ourselves' and 'going with the flow' is part of the experience of the *tawaf*, it shows how insignificant we are within the universe and our ultimate powerlessness. At the same time I felt exceptionally alert, calm and filled with God. I returned to Mr Imam feeling elated and satisfied. He was happy to smell the scent of musk that lingered on my hands for the rest of the evening. It was a perfect start to the year.

More and more people arrived in Mecca each day, and at one point the city was closed and no one else allowed in. Nearly three million pilgrims had gathered there and every inch of the city was packed with people. The crowds reminded me of a mega rock concert or football match but one that lasted all day every day for weeks on end – although the people of course had a very different aura. Sometimes I daydreamed about escaping the throngs of pilgrims and being by myself somewhere far away in lush green nature – or by the sea.

We spent most of our time at the mosque, and often visited in the evening to do *tawaf*, sit near the Ka'ba or on one of the upper floors, and pray until dawn. It wasn't quite so busy at night and it was calmest between one and three in the morning, after which it would start to quickly fill up again. Some of the pilgrims came from faraway villages and had no idea how to use the escalator, so often I would take an elderly woman by the hand and help her. When I was doing *tawaf* on the ground floor I sometimes felt a shove from behind or an elbow in my ribs. When I turned around it was usually an impatient, long-bearded man. Others I noticed jumping and pushing wildly in an effort to fight their way through the crowd to the Black Stone. I didn't dare to even try to get near, it looked too dangerous. I was amazed by how people can't help but be who they are, even in the Holy Mosque, complete with their bad manners and habits. By far the most polite were the Indonesians and Malaysians, who kept their elbows to themselves and were always gentle and friendly. Soon I developed strategies to deal with the constant jostling and kept my arms close to my body, with my palms facing forwards to protect my chest and create a tiny bit of space in front of me. To my great surprise, my back wasn't suffering from all the jostling and walking barefoot on the marble ground every day. In fact, it probably did it good and I was feeling better all the time.

In the run-up to the climax of the Hajj, prices in Mecca were soaring by the day, the principles of mercy and spirituality went out of the window and were replaced by the rules of supply and demand. A taxi from our apartment to the *Haram* had gone up from 20 or 40 to 100 Saudi rial. The city was bursting at its seams, with taxis and buses so full that we had to wait at least two hours after prayers before we could find a space in a minibus or taxi. Most of the time we opted instead to remain in the mosque or to find some place nearby where we could get a bite to eat. But the cafes and restaurants close to the Ka'ba were also full, and the streets were increasingly strewn with rubbish. If the prices seemed high to me, they were prohibitive to many of the other pilgrims who had travelled to Mecca. Many *hajjis* come from humble backgrounds, and going on the journey of a lifetime can be a very costly undertaking. In Bangladesh, for example, it would cost approximately 1,500 euros per person – a huge sum to the average Bangladeshi, Mr Imam explained to us. Family members often clubbed together so that one of them would be able to go on the pilgrimage.

The culmination of the Hajj began on the 8th of January. The imam explained the significance of the pilgrimage: it stands for death and rebirth, spiritual renewal and affirmation of our original covenant with God. On Hajj we visit God's house and we meet Him there. In Mecca, we are not only at the heart of Islam but have also returned to our source. But really, 'the essence of the Hajj is Arafat. On the ninth day of the Hajj month all pilgrims gather on the great Plain of Arafat to offer their deepest heartfelt prayers. It's a reminder of Resurrection, when everyone will stand "naked" before God on Judgement Day and nothing counts but our actions and their effects upon our soul'.

After listening to these words, we once again donned our simple white robes. The colour signifies purity and also spiritual death – pilgrims in the state of *ihram* forget about all wordly attachments and just focus on their relationship with God. I loved the fact that whether king or beggar, everyone wears the same, for in the sight of God *the noblest of you … is the best in conduct* (49:13). Then we set off for Mina. Nearly three million pilgrims were all heading in the same direction, so the bus ride took over eight hours even though the tent city is only five kilometres from Mecca. It's a logistical feat that the Saudis manage to rise to with efficiency, patience and God on their side. We reached our destination in the middle of the desert at two-thirty a.m. and made our way through a labyrinth of tents to the section where four tents had been reserved for our group – two for the men and two for the women. Unexpectedly, they were amazingly comfortable, lined with carpets and even boasting air conditioning and fresh, cool drinking water. I unpacked my sleeping bag, settled down in a corner of our tent and tried to get some sleep. But my cold had got worse, and I tossed and turned for hours feeling dreadful. When someone switched on the glaring neon light at four a.m. to get ready for the morning prayer I asked them to please switch it off again, since the lanterns outside cast more than enough light. It felt like the prayers lasted forever, and after a torrent of Arabic I was finally able to get a few hours sleep.

The next morning it was baking hot outside so I spent most of the day inside the tent, reading the Quran and doing *dhikr*. Trying to wash or use the bathroom was a minor adventure every time. There were special areas for washing, with open-air sinks on either side. The ones in the blistering sunshine were for women and the ones in the shade on the other side were for men. 'Ladies first' obviously wasn't the policy here. The showers were inside the toilet cubicles. The queues were long, but we soon found out that the further we went away from our tent, the fewer the people and the cleaner the facilities.

After evening prayers I went on a walk with a few of my Hajj sisters. We wandered a little way up a hill to get a bird's eye view of the vast tent city stretching towards the horizon before strolling to the market to stock up on yoghurt, bread, cheese, olives and water. I bought a light gold prayer mat with a black Ka'ba in the middle, which I thought would be good for travelling. Later that evening I ventured off to have a shower, did my ritual washing, the *ghusl,* and put on a fresh *ihram* robe in preparation for our trip to Arafat. The imam reiterated to us the significance of the Arafat ritual, the very essence of the Hajj. Pilgrims spend the day on the Plain of Arafat, commune with God and ask for forgiveness. On this day, God is said to forgive everyone present and also those who are not there but are conscious of this special day.

On his own Hajj, Prophet Muhammad climbed Jabal al-Rahmah, the Mount of Mercy on the Plain of Arafat, where the last verses of the Noble Quran were revealed to him and he gave his famous farewell sermon. Apart from the idea of forgiveness, the day of Arafat is also about sacrifice and obedience. Pilgrims are asked to check and strengthen their God-consciousness. It was here that Abraham passed the hardest test of all when God asked him to sacrifice his first-born son, Ismael. *Eid al-Adha*, the Festival of Sacrifice, traditionally starts on the tenth day of the month of Hajj, after pilgrims descend from Arafat. All Muslims around the world who can afford it are expected to kill an animal of sacrifice (*qurbani*) or to donate an equivalent amount to charity in memory of Abraham's willingness to sacrifice his son as an act of obedience to God. Those who cannot afford it fast for several days instead. The meat of the slaughtered sheep on the Hajj is distributed to Muslims throughout the world. And those who do it at home share it between family, friends and neighbours, as well as giving some to the poor and needy. The Arafat ritual therefore combines four main elements of Islam: forgiveness, obedience to God, trust in God, and charity.

The imam advised us not to eat or drink too much in Arafat, because the toilets there were far more basic than in Mina and there would be even fewer at the destination after that. We were scheduled to leave Mina for Arafat sometime between midnight and dawn, spend the day on the Plain of Arafat, and then move on to Muzdalifah, where we would sleep under the stars. We set off at four a.m. and an hour later reached the Plain of Arafat, fourteen kilometres away. The sun was rising over the arid desert landscape, and another tent city nestled in the hills around us. After we had found our quarters I decided to venture out and walk to the Mount of Mercy. There, on his final pilgrimage towards the end of his life, Muhammad delivered his Farewell Sermon to over 100,000 of his companions and warned the men to say their prayers and to take care of their wives.

Before I left I tried to get my bearings and, on Dr Amina's advice, remember the mountain scenery in the distance in relation to our tent so that I would be able to recognise it amid the sea of identical tents on my way back. If all else failed, I still had my identity card and some mobile phone numbers around my neck. It was a bit of a risk but I couldn't resist. So I began to make my way towards the sacred Mount. I passed through bushes and then along a sandy path until I reached a street and saw a number of huge yellow signposts demarcating the Plain of Arafat. I carried on in the direction of where I imagined Jabal al-Rahmah to be, although I couldn't see it yet because it was hidden behind trees. Eventually the sacred Mount peaked through the vegetation; it was dotted with pilgrims in white. As I reached its foot I joined the crowds climbing the sixty-metre hill until I was stopped in my tracks by a two-metre-high rock that I knew I couldn't possibly scale. As I stood there wondering what to do, a hand suddenly extended from above and a fellow pilgrim pulled me up. It was lovely to feel how during Hajj people looked out for each other. I thanked him and marvelled to myself at the inner connection I sensed between the pilgrims, despite the fact that we all came from different corners of the earth, didn't know one other and would never see each other again. When I finally reached the top I asked someone to take a photograph, but he didn't know how to operate an automatic camera. The next person I asked managed to press the button just fine. I found myself a great spot between all the other pilgrims with a view across the entire Plain of Arafat in the direction of the Ka'ba, as several signs indicated. I stood there gazing across the masses of pilgrims gathered among the shrubs, trees and tents to the mountain range towering on the horizon. Although it was only about eight o'clock in the morning it was already getting hot, and I was glad I had brought along the sunshade we had been given on arrival. I sat beneath it and started praying. After about forty-five minutes, I slowly climbed down the hill, which by now was heaving with pilgrims, and then followed the road back to our camp. Rubbish was piled up here and there, and several makeshift stalls were selling snacks. I was longing for a cup of tea and managed to get one with milk and sugar, which I savoured together with two eggs sprinkled with salt. Ever more busloads of pilgrims were arriving all the time, with some buses so crowded that even the roofs were packed with pilgrims. It was getting hot, and fortunately, with God's help and female intuition worthy of a girl scout, I miraculously managed to find my way back to our tent.

Hajj is Arafat, they say, and the time between afternoon prayers and sunset on the Day of Forgiveness is the most blessed time, when all prayers are heard. So many angels are said to be in Arafat that, if you threw a needle into the air, you would pierce one.

For the rest of the day I relaxed and napped in our big tent, as did most of the others so that we would feel fit again when it was most important. After the *asr* prayers I stepped outside and joined the other pilgrims. Hundreds of thousands or rather millions stood there in contemplative vigil, with raised hands so as to receive God's blessing. The occasion is supposed to remind us of Judgement Day, when no worldly riches count, just the purity of our hearts and our actions. I lifted my hands and mustered all my concentration and energy to pray fervently for my family and friends and everyone who had ever helped me, for the needy, for world peace and for *khayr* (goodness) in the future. I also prayed for forgiveness from everyone I had ever hurt and for those who had hurt me. We stood there praying until sunset.

Then it was time to head to Muzdalifah. We arrived to find people lying in the darkish sand on plastic mats, in sleeping bags or under blankets as far as the eye could see. We threaded our way through them and found a space to set up camp for the night. Each of us collected forty-nine pebbles no bigger than one or two centimetres, and then we were ready to spend the night under the stars. As the temperature dropped, I crawled into my sleeping bag and gazed up at the sky. I had barely shut my eyes when I was jolted back to consciousness by someone calling my name. When I looked up, everyone was gone, except for one of our guides who was also just setting off. It turned out that my group had decided to get a headstart on the crowds leaving for Mina the next day and had already left. If I wanted to join them I would have to leave that instant. The bus could come any minute. As it turned out, none of the buses that arrived was ours, and we waited for over an hour by the roadside at the bottom of the field.

As soon as we got back to Mina we set off on foot for the Jamarat. In the late eighties, the Australian rock band INXS had a hit single called 'Devil Inside' containing the line 'every single one of us the devil inside'. And that is exactly what the stoning ritual is all about: chasing away all one's base desires and destructive impulses such as impatience, pride, anger, greed and envy – in short, all the temptations that make us behave badly and lure us off the right path.

It was the middle of the night and I was so tired I could hardly keep my eyes open. There was just enough time to buy a quick cup of tea for Dr Amina, Fatima and myself at one of the twenty-four-hour stands on the sand road near our tent. The route to the Jamarat from our tent was about four kilometres long, a bit of a trek at that early hour. We followed huge, illuminated signposts showing the way to the Devil. Morning had broken by the time we arrived. The Jamarat nowadays consists of three huge concave walls, with a basin below to collect the pebbles. A footbridge called the Jamarat Bridge has been built alongside them so pilgrims can throw their stones from the ground level or the bridge. We chose the bridge.

Over the years, the event has claimed many lives. Muhammad is said to have stoned the Devil immediately after midday prayers and, since many Muslims like to follow the Prophet's example down to the last detail, it is during the apocalyptic pebble storms at around midday that most of the accidents happen. Fortunately our organisers chose not to stick to this literalist interpretation of the schedule and we continued to stone for the next two days at dawn, bearing in mind that the relevant authorities had deemed the stoning to be valid during a twenty-four-hour time span. This wise decision may well have saved our lives. Around noon one day, we heard there had been a stampede on the eastern access ramp of the bridge and at least 346 people had died, with a few hundred more injured. After this fatal incident a new multi-level bridge was later built by the Bin Laden group to contain the crowds more easily.

In the twilight of the rising dawn, I hurled my pebbles with all my might at the wall, determined to banish the *shaytan*, as the force of evil is called in Arabic. I walked back to Mina with Dr Amina and we finally found time to catch up. We both agreed that we had enjoyed this active dimension to our religious practice because it allowed us to experience faith not just in the mind but also with body and soul. The Hajj is a true trial on all levels: physically, emotionally and spiritually.

Back in my tent, I had a little breakfast, took a shower and exchanged my *ihram* dress for a long, colourful robe I had bought in Medina. Today was Eid. Traditionally families come together; children receive presents; and members of the family who have been on the Hajj share their experiences. To celebrate the pilgrimage, and also as a symbol of a new beginning, many of the men in my group shaved one another's heads, while the women just cut off small strands of hair, as we had done after the Umrah. My tent mates removed each other's facial hair using the Indian threading method, skilfully running a thread over the face to pull out any unwanted hair. We were served a delicious curry by a neighbouring group who felt like being charitable on this Feast of Sacrifice. I spent the rest of the day with the other women in the tent.

The Prophet is believed to have remained in Mina for three days on his own Hajj, so we also spent a further three days in the tent city, which was physically and mentally exhausting. It was boiling hot during the day. Dr Amina even suffered from mild sunstroke because she made the mistake of briefly going out during the midday heat. We slept in our sleeping bags on the hard ground, and the food we ate was very simple. I was by far the tallest woman in our group, so my tent mates were constantly asking me to plug and unplug their mobile phone chargers from the socket safely positioned two metres up the wall. In return they offered to pray for me – the best reward. A more mundane recompense however was the gift of a plastic plate, which came in most handy.

I got on very well with all of them, though not everything in our tent was always rosy. Two of the women wanted to make sure there wasn't even the tiniest gap in the walls of the tent, which men could theoretically look through. But this also meant that no fresh air whatsoever could get in, and it got unbearably stuffy. One of the pilgrims argued that men and women slept next to one another in Muzdalifah and even in the Holy Mosque, so how could a small gap in our women's tent to let in air be a problem? But she couldn't convince the conservatives. The tent remained hermetically sealed and we all sweated.

After three days in the tent city of Mina it was finally time to return to Mecca and civilisation. My bed in the apartment felt comfortable beyond belief. All we had to do now to complete our Hajj was a farewell *tawaf*. To honour the occasion and because I was absolutely fed up with doing my ritual washing in packed and wet public washrooms, I decided to perform my *wudhu* in style at the Intercontinental Hotel right opposite the Ka'ba. The concierge was kind enough to let me in, even though the bathrooms were reserved for hotel guests only.

The pristine toilets, marbled washroom with shiny silver fittings and huge wall-to-wall mirror were a real treat. Without make-up and in my dusty Moroccan *jalabia*, I felt I looked like a tramp next to the women from Riyadh, all dressed in elegant black *abayas* and dripping with diamonds. But pilgrims can't be vain. We had a little chat while letting our hair down and getting ready; they even complimented me on my hair before we tucked it all away again and they put their black face veils back on. When I asked them if they minded wearing them, they replied not at all, they had worn them since they were teenagers, so didn't know any different.

Aziz, Mr Imam and I completed our final *tawaf* and then congratulated one another with the traditional pilgrims' exclamation *Hajj mabrur*, accepted Hajj. But no sooner was the Hajj over than the *shaytan* was back again. After walking nearly all the way from the apartment to the mosque due to lack of transport, and then doing the farewell *tawaf*, we were pretty exhausted, especially poor Mr Imam. I tried to hail a taxi to take us back to the apartment but none would stop – they were all too busy going to Jeddah. I pointed to our ninety-year-old friend who urgently needed a rest, but nobody seemed to care and I finally lost my temper with one of the drivers. On reflection I was disappointed with myself, for despite all my efforts over the last three days to banish that *shaytan*, they obviously hadn't been quite enough. Among the lessons I learned on Hajj was that I needed to be mindful and keep the inner connection with God at all times and that self-improvement is definitely a never-ending struggle. We had to walk all the way back to the other end of the vast mosque complex to catch a bus, but before we set off we lay down for a while to rest and gather our energies again.

On our last day in Mecca I went to buy a few souvenirs and a large container of Zamzam water to share with my friends back home, and then the journey to the heart came to an end. It had lasted three and a half weeks and taken everything out of me and my companions. We had dealt with all sorts of challenges, learned patience – *sabr* – how to sleep sitting and standing up; we had performed every Hajj ritual; begged God for forgiveness, and opened our hearts. We felt a deep bond between us and one step closer to God.

> I had come to the Centre of the Universe, where the physical and metaphysical worlds meet. I was floating in that wonderful sea of humanity, turning like stars in a galaxy, around the house of God ...
> I had at last found that dimension where human existence ceases to be held by the gravitation of sensual and worldly desires, where the soul is freed in an atmosphere of obedience and peaceful submission to the Divine Presence.

These moving words written by Yusuf Islam after his own Hajj in 1980 so eloquently express the profound experience of this eternal ritual of Islam.

∽

Back in London, I slept for more than twelve hours – in a proper bed at last. When I woke up, I felt like I was awaking from an amazing dream. My heart and mind were still in Mecca and Medina and I was filled with a deep sense of tranquility. It was as though I was wrapped in a heavenly cloud. The feeling stayed with me for weeks and I didn't want it to go away. It was a while before I felt like seeing anyone again, and the only people I talked to were my parents and a few of my closest Muslim friends. I needed to process my experiences and was reluctant to come down from the cloud I was floating on. And I also needed time to get rid of my Hajj flu. Although, 'one never really quite recovers from the Hajj – in a good sense,' as Shaykh Abu Bakr once said, meaning one doesn't just go back to one's old life but concentrates more sincerely on one's relationship with God. The challenge for me now was one faced by all who return from Hajj: to keep the state of purity.

The American scholar, Shaykh Hamza Yusuf, told me a story just a few weeks after my Hajj, at an event in the Shakespeare Globe Theatre to honour the late Shaykh Abu Bakr Siraj ad-Din.

In the Middle Ages, the great spiritual master Muhyiddin Ibn Arabi travelled with a group of learned men, who were his followers, from Andalusia to Egypt to meet up with some friends in faith. At the end of a banquet held in their honour, their host produced a bowl of mouth-watering fruit. The travellers thanked him and helped themselves. Eventually, there was nothing left. Just as everyone stood up to leave, the bowl broke. Ibn Arabi asked his learned friends if they knew why. They told him they did not, and he explained that the bowl was new and was actually a urinal. There were so many guests at the banquet that it had been used instead as a fruit bowl. 'After you eminent friends of God had touched it, it was not only purified but also enobled,' he said. 'In order to avoid reverting to its original purpose, the bowl broke. Do you understand the deeper meaning of the story?' Ibn Arabi asked his followers. They said they did not. 'The bowl symbolises the human heart,' he explained. 'Whoever purifies his heart with spiritual exercises, such as the pilgrimage to Mecca, but then makes the mistake of tarnishing it again, his heart will break.'

I was determined that nothing, from now on, would break my heart.

Chapter 15

Marriage

You know what love is?
It is all kindness, generosity.

Jalaluddin Rumi

It had always been my dream to marry a practising Muslim who could bridge the worlds I lived in and was at home in the East as well as the West. Shortly after my Hajj it seemed as if my prayers had been answered. Ruby and I heard about an exclusive matrimonial website from a Muslim friend who worked for the United Nations in New York. Initially, I had some reservations about whether I was going to find 'Mr Right' on the Internet, but she pointed out that Muslims worldwide were now using the Internet to find marriage partners. Back in Medina, Aziz had also told me that this was how he had met his Algerian fiancée. Nothing ventured, nothing gained, Ruby and I decided. But I wasn't going to get my hopes up.

As it happened, it wasn't long before I did find a man I liked. Rachid was a Moroccan TV journalist who had spent years working in the US. According to the website, we were a perfect match. He was handsome and smart, and looked very attractive in his picture. We seemed well suited, apart from the fact that he lived far away – ironically and much to my amusement in a place called Germantown, near Washington DC. Soon we were in touch regularly by email and phone, establishing that there had been several occasions when our paths could easily have crossed. He had reported from the 1992 Olympics in

335

Barcelona, for example. We discovered other parallels in our lives. Rachid told me he was a practising Muslim who prayed and fasted, which I liked. Yet he also enjoyed cultural pursuits, sport and reading – just like me. He interviewed politicians and sportsmen and used to socialise quite a bit before he became more focused on the faith. That too sounded similar to my own experience. We discussed our religion and how to incorporate Islamic principles into daily life. He told me that he was not interested in a narrow, literalist approach, adding that his grandfather was a Shaykh and that his family was rooted in the Sufi tradition. Everything he said resonated with me as it mirrored my own principles. Rachid told me he had financed his studies at various Ivy League universities by working as a journalist and had always sent money home to support his family in Morocco. He was clearly talented and seemed to be a responsible person. When he sent me an e-rose on Valentine's Day, my heart skipped a beat, and later that evening my girl-friends took one look at me and asked if there was a new man in my life. Something was happening that I had never thought possible – after all, so far we hadn't even met.

I was thrilled when Rachid sent an email proposing *nikah* (Islamic marriage) and while this would be unthinkable in Western culture, it proved his sincerity and faith to me – any future relationship between us could only be halal, within marriage. Rachid suggested he quit his work in DC and move to London to look for a new job here so that I wouldn't have to be uprooted, and, if that didn't work out, we could move somewhere else together, which sounded perfect. However, as he would be settling in London, this meant that I would need to support him for the first six months, but he promised he would then take care of me for the rest of my life. Having just returned from the Hajj, my heart was wide open and everything looked bright and hopeful to me. We were emailing each other almost every day except for one weekend when he had a conference in Canada and temporarily disappeared.

I went to consult Shaykh Haytham Tamim of the Utrujj Foundation, whose Islamic courses I had been attending on and off for years, and, much to my surprise, he advised me against the marriage for several reasons including our very different temperaments. He also advised that 'in Islam it is the husband's obligation to pay for the upkeep of his wife'. My friend Dr Amina agreed. I decided not to listen, because Rachid and I seemed so well suited and I had actually fallen in love with him. Moreover, I had been single for far too long – and that isn't how it's meant to be in Islam either. I didn't want those mundane issues to stand in the way of our happiness, and I knew plenty of women who had supported their husbands initially and were very happy in the long run. I accepted Rachid's proposal on condition that we got along well when we actually met, and I sent packing the other admirers who had turned up after the Hajj.

Rachid arrived in London over Easter and in great anticipation I picked him up at the airport. I was quite nervous and read a paper while I waited at the gate. 'Ms Kristiane?' I heard someone say. It was him. He looked nice with his big brown eyes and a darkish complexion, though a bit older than on the website photo. On the way in to London, he asked me what I thought of him so far, and I told him that I liked him. His first impression was positive too, he said. In fact he later admitted that the minute he saw me at the airport in my long, light beige Moroccan coat, he thought to himself: this is my wife. Back home I prepared dinner and over the next couple of days we found we could relate to one another on many different levels and began to establish a deeper connection. Jennifer, my housemate at the time, had a friend staying that weekend and, in a quiet moment, they both told me they liked him. We decided to go ahead with the *nikah*, which Fadwa had offered to host at her home, with just a few friends present.

It was a Friday, so Rachid and I first went to Regent's Park Mosque for *jumah* prayer, where we met Mr Imam from my Hajj, who was to be my *wakil*, the man who would give me away. We took photos in front of the famous gate in the park near the mosque where I had seen so many couples take wedding photographs before, and then we drove to Fadwa's.

My girlfriends, the imam and the two witnesses – Fadwa's son and his friend – were waiting for us. The imam spoke a few words about our respective obligations in marriage, that both husband and wife must keep each other's trust and always treat one another with respect and kindness, and that part of the groom's duty is to take care of all the financial needs of his wife. After we exchanged rings Fa took photographs and we all sat down for lunch, albeit segregated; Rachid was with Mr Imam and the other men and I with my girlfriends. Soon though I went over to sit with my husband and Mr Imam. Ruby also joined us and we came up with an idea to fly to Washington together so that I could visit Rachid and she could meet a friend of hers.

Rachid and I spent a happy week together getting to know each other despite a few minor misunderstandings. Friends had advised me that the first year was always the most difficult in a Muslim marriage because the spouses were still getting to know one another. I showed him my favourite places in London and one day we went for a walk in Hyde Park. 'Now that you are my wife, there is no more need for your social contacts with other men,' Rachid explained to me. 'You have a husband now.' I basically agreed. I knew other Muslim men had the same idea and I was perfectly happy to focus on our marriage.

On leaving, Rachid was sad he had to fly back to the States without his bride, and so was I. Luckily, only a couple of weeks later I was able to visit him in DC. Ruby was with me on the flight, and together we decided which of my male contacts to delete from my phone, as Rachid had asked. There and then, I got rid of all the numbers I no longer needed.

Rachid was waiting for me at the airport with a bouquet

of red roses, and over the next few days he took me to see the sights in Washington, including Capitol Hill, the White House, and the National Air and Space museum. We went for dinner in the atmospheric Dupont Circle and hung out at Kramerbooks & Afterwords, the coolest bookstore I had ever been to, which even had live music at night. One evening we met up with Ruby and her friend in a Moroccan restaurant to celebrate our wedding. In the evenings I really enjoyed praying together. Rachid's Arabic recitation was very beautiful, and sometimes after the prayers he would put his hands on my head and say some extra prayers in Arabic for me. Another day Rachid showed me his alma mater. As we were walking around the campus, I asked him if he still had some old pictures to show me, but he explained that he had destroyed every photograph he owned that had a woman in it. What a shame, I thought, especially as he had told me that some of them were well-known Hollywood actresses. But then suddenly Rachid said he expected me to do the same.

'What?' I exclaimed.

'Yes, you need to destroy all photographs that have men in them from your past life,' he insisted. I protested and explained that some of my photos were important professional pictures. He agreed I could keep a minimum but all the rest – and particularly those with ex-boyfriends in them – were to be destroyed. 'There is no need for them,' he said. 'Why should we have other men in the house?' In his attempt to 'purify my life', he asked me to throw out all gifts from men as well. It seemed excessive to me, but I didn't want to appear to be clinging to the past or to material possessions. I never really looked at the photographs anyway, I reasoned to myself and, as it meant so much to him, I agreed to do some clearing out.

We continued touring the beautiful old university and then had lunch in a cosy cafe nearby where he used to go as a student. From there we called my dad. Rachid officially asked him for my hand in marriage, and we began to cement our plans

– when exactly he would come to London and move in with me, how to organise everything and so on. But then it suddenly turned out that Rachid was paying off a loan and was thinking of taking up a well-paid job in a high-risk area for six months or so where spouses wouldn't be allowed to visit. The only way for us to actually live together, as planned, was if I would also take care of the loan and he would refund me as soon as he could. The last thing I wanted as a newlywed was to live apart from my husband for an indefinite period of time. I was in love with him and longed to live together. Surely an extended separation so early on couldn't be good for our marriage or for our plans to start a family, so I agreed without hesitation.

Rachid suggested we conduct a civil marriage in the US. So far we had only done the *nikah,* which is a marriage before God alone. In Muslim-majority countries it is automatically registered officially, while in the West that has to be done separately. Before marrying in a civil ceremony I wanted us to find out about its legal implications, which we hadn't yet done. I also wanted to have my parents present, so we left it for the time being and instead went on a belated honeymoon to the Poconos, a popular romantic getaway. Predictably the room contained a heart-shaped jacuzzi and a four-poster bed with a lace ceiling – a kitschy contrast to the unspoiled countryside outside. On long walks through the woods we hatched a plan to celebrate our wedding a month later in traditional style in Morocco, where I would be going to speak at the Fez Festival of Sacred Music. Rachid would join me there straight from the US.

Those days with Rachid in the States were lovely; we had such fun together, sharing the same sense of humour. He just mentioned again that I needed to break off all contact with male friends and acquaintances. I assured him that I had already deleted all the numbers of male friends from my mobile and wasn't intending to contact anyone. 'But what if someone calls me?' I asked. He suggested I tell everyone that

I was married now and that they were not to contact me any more. This was obviously a matter of great importance to Rachid that was going to take some getting used to for me. I could understand that admirers and exes – mine and his – had no place in our life together, but I had a few platonic friends I had known over the years who meant a lot to me.

Back home I gave up my friendships as he had repeatedly requested and encountered approval from a Syrian acquaintance, but otherwise astonishment, genuine concern and upset from my few male friends. Alfred was actually the only Western friend who understood what was happening because he knew the mentality. He wished me well. 'I just hope you will be respected for who you are and you will be able to retain your freedom to think,' he said.

And to show Rachid my sincere intentions, I also deleted all male contacts from my filofax and computer, gave away some stuff to charity and tore up old photographs depicting men. But I rescued a few and took them to Germany to store in my dad's attic. Needless to say, my father and his wife were surprised. 'These experiences are part of your life and made you who you are today,' they argued. I agreed but felt that at least this way the most precious photographs could be saved. I visited my old school friend Claudia to tell her all about my marriage and to invite her to the wedding party in Morocco. When I spoke to Rachid on the phone later, he wanted to know how the visit went and I told him that we had a lovely family lunch with the children and Claudia's husband. To my surprise he got seriously angry because I had sat with another man. As a newly married wife, I began to feel torn between my husband's expectations and my normal life with friends and family. I tried to be understanding and patient but often felt tense.

Rachid and I organised our Moroccan wedding party on the phone, together with his sister who lived in Morocco. This wasn't easy due to time differences, logistics and misunderstandings, and there were a number of times when Rachid threatened to call the whole thing off (never mind that some of the guests had already booked their flights). At one point, I received a call from my seventy-year-old friend Said Aburish, congratulating me on my marriage and inviting me, together with our mutual friend Agenta, for lunch. I explained that this might not be possible and that I needed to ask my husband's permission first. Astonished, Said protested that he was like an older brother to me, and was also very ill. But I had an agreement with Rachid and so out of politeness I sent him an email to run it by him. Never in a million years did I expect to cause a major marital crisis with my request. For Rachid it was already too much that I had even spoken to Said. I should have told him I was married now and hung up, he argued. The fact that I had suggested meeting another man – regardless of his age, his illness, that he was in a steady relationship or that a girlfriend was going to be there – disappointed him immensely. While he was venting his anger on the phone, I heard him stapling something – a plane ticket he told me he was printing out in order to disappear far away to Brazil for good. He intended to cancel everything, he said – our wedding celebration, our marriage and our future plans. I couldn't believe his reaction, but I immediately cancelled the invitation via Agenta. She didn't understand my decision at all, but I felt our marriage was sacred and God's answer to my prayers on the Hajj, and I wasn't going to ruin it over a lunch invitation. It took many calls to placate Rachid. Fadwa mediated and assured him that I had a pure heart. He couldn't judge me from a conservative Arabic viewpoint, she explained to him, because I was European. Eventually we made up and went ahead with our plans.

When we met at the airport in Fez in June we were both happy to be together again after the tumultuous month of separation, and all our differences seemed to be forgotten. We did some sightseeing of the ancient *medina*, and later at the festival lots of journalists recognised Rachid, but he refused to speak to any of them, proudly explaining that he was merely there to accompany his wife. I appreciated being by his side, he was protective and caring. After lunch we drove to Rabat, and Rachid happily introduced me to his mother, his sister and her husband. Rachid's family welcomed us warmly. We had some mint tea and *msemen*, a Moroccan speciality of square-shaped, layered pancakes, eaten at breakfast or for afternoon tea. His sister later gave me some lessons on how to knead, fold and fry them with a lot of butter and oil so they become crispy on the outside and chewy on the inside. Everyone was very excited about the wedding and we made all sorts of last-minute arrangements.

Over the next few days we picked up my parents and girl-friends from the airport. My family had their doubts, for even though Rachid had been living in the US for decades, our cultural differences worried them. They also felt we had married much too fast. I tried to explain to them that in Islam couples don't usually get to know their future life partners before marriage; after all, the boundaries of respect had to be preserved. Traditionally the families minutely 'research' potential candidates, and if he or she seems trustworthy and compatible – which has to be the best guarantee of a successful marriage – they begin negotiating about lifestyle, standard of living and the marriage contract, which also contains the amount of the *maher* (dowry) as the woman's security. The woman has the right to ask for whatever she wants according to the means of the husband. It could be a house, jewellery or tens of thousands of dollars, as I learned later. The wives of the Prophet are known to have asked for very little in terms of material goods, and many women want to emulate them, so they just ask for a nominal sum. Usually a family member or a Shaykh negotiates on behalf of the bride. In the Gulf it is common for fathers to insist on a hefty *maher* at the time of marriage and for husbands to sign how much they will pay on divorce. Sums such as 100,000 US dollars are not uncommon. It guarantees some protection for the wives at least in theory, because if the system is abused it can be quite easy for a man to not actually divorce his wife at all, effectively trapping her, while taking another wife. If the marriage isn't registered, as in our case, a husband just needs to say *talaq* (I divorce you) three times to divorce his wife. The first two divorces are not final and can be reconciled within a time period of three months by simply resuming marital relations. The third divorce, however, is serious: the couple can only reconcile and remarry after the woman has married another man and divorced him. Since no normal person would do this, a third divorce is considered final.

In our case none of those negotiations took place before our wedding. At our age it seemed only right to take the decision ourselves. And as a convert I was not familiar with this process anyway, and neither, of course, was my family. I agreed to a token *maher* because I felt my marriage was about love and trust, not material advancement. And also the wives of the Prophet were known to have received very little. In Rachid's family, too, he told me, there were critical voices cautioning him about marrying a European woman, especially someone who had worked in the music industry – even though I had left ten years previously. Rachid's mother and brother, however, supported us and gave us their blessing from the very beginning.

The day my parents and some of my friends arrived from London, we all visited the Roman ruins and tombs in Chellah, now home to hundreds of storks and cats. The girls went off to a *hammam,* as Moroccan women do before they get married. It was a hive of activity, with women and children washing, scrubbing or shaving their bodies without inhibition. We were showered and soaped, then we lay down on the large warm stone and relaxed for a while in the warm moist air, after which we were treated to a thorough body peeling and an excellent massage. Cleansed and regenerated, we went to dinner at Rachid's sister's house where our families met for the first time. Rachid's mother and sister had prepared a delicious chicken tagine with olives, and lamb couscous. Communication was slightly problematic because my parents didn't speak French or Arabic and Rachid's family no German and only very little English. Rachid, his sister and I did our best to translate. What mattered was a connection of hearts, and this really did develop, especially between our mothers and sisters.

The next day at our henna party, two women helped me into a fabulous green and golden Moroccan dress and together we walked upstairs to join the festivities. While Rachid entertained the guests, two professional henna artists painted exquisite flower motifs on my hands and feet. Then it was the guests' turn to be decorated. After a traditional meal of various vegetable salads, tagine and couscous, a brilliant band in long *jalabias* and red felt hats got the party going with big hand drums and long wind instruments. I had to be careful to keep the henna paste on all evening so that the print would last for a few weeks. This meant I couldn't join in with the dancing. But I was happy our guests were enjoying themselves.

The third day was the actual wedding celebration. In the afternoon Rachid's sister had arranged for me to go to a beauty salon, as all Moroccan brides do. Although I asked for very natural make-up, I hardly recognised myself after the procedure. I had never had so much hair spray and make-up pasted on me before, not even for my TV shows. Rachid and I went to the hall where the party was being held, and he took me along to the dressing room. Meanwhile the first guests had arrived, but it was apparently Moroccan tradition to let them wait forever with some rose milk and fruit juices while the bride got ready at her leisure. Two women helped me into my white Moroccan wedding dress, decorated me with costume jewellery and served delicious mint tea. A couple of hours later I stepped onto a glittering portable throne and six men carried me around the entire hall towards Rachid. The men were moving and grooving to the same live music as the day before, and the women yodelled joyfully as is customary at Arabic weddings, while I clung on tight so I wouldn't fall off the throne. My family and friends were busy taking pictures.

Rachid lifted my veil and led me to a sofa on stage. As we sat there smiling, one by one every person in the room, except for Dr Amina, came to congratulate and pose with us while the photographer captured the moment. The sofa ceremony took place twice more after every course, when I had changed into a new, bespoke dress. Traditionally the bride wears five different outfits but I thought three would do. I wanted to enjoy some of my own wedding party and not just be backstage changing the entire time. We danced until late into the night. The whole wedding was like a dream from *A Thousand and One Nights* and for three days I felt like an Arabian princess.

The next morning Rachid and I took my parents on a shopping tour. He bought them some gifts and we chose a few exquisite pieces of handicraft to take home before we sat down in a cafe to enjoy a cup of mint tea. My father asked me to pick up a handcrafted, intricately painted bowl we had bought and take it to the taxi for safekeeping. I obliged and went to hand the bowl to the driver. But when I returned to the table Rachid couldn't contain his anger. 'A wife does not go up to strange men and speak with them,' he hissed. 'It's a humiliation for the husband.' My dad had no idea what was going on and neither did I. But because I respected the customs of Rachid's culture, I apologised and promised not to do it again. Then I forgot about the incident. During those first weeks of our marriage, however, I began to realise that from now on I would be leading a very different life.

After my parents left, Rachid and I set off to visit his relatives in various parts of Morocco. Everywhere we went we were spoiled with homemade meals, pastries and gifts. When we were finished with the visits we checked in at a romantic spa outside Marrakech, where we enjoyed breakfast and dinner on a Bedouin-style terrace with a magnificent view stretching to the horizon and were pampered with rose-petal baths and face massages. Our next destination was a boutique Berber eco-hotel in the Midi Atlas, built from mud. It was simple but stylish and we liked the rustic cuisine. We relaxed against a backdrop of red-hued mountains, fertile fields and lush green meadows. Farmers were ploughing the land, donkeys pulling fully loaded carts and girls drawing water from a well. On long hiking tours Rachid and I told each other about our pasts and began to settle into married life. We were very happy together. My role now was to look after him. His was to mediate between me and the outside world. I was not even supposed to ask for salt or fetch missing cutlery – all this was his job. He explained that I would now enjoy the status of a privileged wife who didn't have to run around any more and was protected by her husband. It felt great on the one hand, but it took some time getting used to, because I had always been independent and able to look after myself. But as a convert I wanted to learn to be a good Muslim wife and I felt it was important I adapt to his ways. In the evenings we sat on the candlelit terrace enjoying the view over the mountains and listening to the *adhan,* which echoed hauntingly throughout the valley. Everything was as I had always wished it to be and I felt that we belonged together.

A few days later, back in Marrakech, something happened which I will never forget. The evening before our departure to London I insisted we stop by the tomb of Sidi Abbas Sebti, the patron saint of the town. I had frequently visited it when I was there on my own. It was a Thursday night and a group of blind people were sitting in a circle near the tomb doing *dhikr* together and chanting God's praises. I sat down on the right side, leaning against the wall, while Rachid sat on the other side behind the men. Suddenly the blind Shaykh called the name 'Sharif' and repeated it several times until Rachid finally realised that the man was referring to him. When he walked over and sat down next to the Shaykh, the man said to Rachid that it was a great honour to sense the scent of the Prophet in their midst and to have a *sharif*, a descendant of Muhammad, as a guest. Rachid's family tree allegedly shows that his lineage goes back to the Prophet. I was amazed that the blind people could see this. The Sufi scholar who had once told me about their visionary abilities was obviously right. I was impressed, for Rachid was now not only my husband but also a confirmed descendant of the noblest human being on earth, Prophet Muhammad.

Eventually we travelled to London to begin our new life together. I loved my role as wife and Rachid became my king. His wish was my command. I washed and folded his laundry and cooked and baked German, Italian and Moroccan delicacies for him, even practising making *msemen*, those square Moroccan pancakes, which sometimes turned out quite tough. Rachid didn't mind. A wife gains *ajr* (reward) when taking care of and obeying her husband, he explained. In return, Rachid would search for work, help me clear the table, wash up, carry our groceries, protect and adore me. He wrote me poems, raved to everyone about his beloved wife and was wholly focused on me – full of love and passion. I had never experienced such devotion. We worked together, laughed together and prayed together. He was the best dance partner I had ever had and helped me rewrite my website, while I assisted him when he went to castings and meetings. He would recite from the Quran in Arabic and translate Abd al-Qadir al-Gilani from the original for me, while with his help I made progress in the study of his language. He always opened the door when someone knocked and I felt safe with him. Through Rachid I experienced and grew to appreciate some of the most beautiful aspects of Arabic culture. We were both so happy. Our first Ramadan together gave us a feeling of a deep spiritual connection that neither of us had experienced before. Admittedly, the month of fasting began on a rocky note when I received a call from an ex who was now just a distant acquaintance and whose friendship I had forgotten to 'annul'. It was completely innocent, but Rachid was livid.

In the autumn of 2006 Rachid and I flew to Berlin where I presented the Inssan Festival, the first German-Muslim cultural celebration. Many great Muslim artists performed and Sami Yusuf was the headliner. I moderated a discussion on Islam with some politicians from Berlin, and many girls in the audience complained that they couldn't find jobs in Germany because they wore hijab. One even declared she had been expelled from her vocational school for wearing hijab. The politicians promised to take up her case. I hope they did. Rachid supported me brilliantly – being in the same line of business, he knew exactly what I needed and acted as my PR agent, bodyguard and co-presenter. I was thrilled to have a partner by my side who seemed to match me so well.

However, despite all these commonalities and our feelings for one another, it soon turned out that Rachid and I had very different ideas about a faith-oriented married life. Rachid said he wanted to bring me closer to Allah, and I was grateful for his Islamic guidance. He taught me the correct sequence of *wudhu* (ablution before prayer) and wrote Arabic prayers in a little book I kept. He was the born Muslim after all, and I respected that. He became my imam, leading me in prayer, and assumed religious and moral authority. After initial protests I usually ended up following his religious interpretation of whatever practical issue we were discussing in order to please God and have peace at home. This also meant that I was no longer able to go to my *dhikr* meetings because sadly Rachid had a disagreement with one of the imams there. This really was unfortunate and as a result I also lost my habit of regular practice at home.

Admittedly I had to learn certain ways of behaving that I wasn't familiar with, because I wasn't raised as a Muslim or in an Arabic environment. At the same time I wished that Rachid would be a bit more relaxed and understanding, just as I was patient with him when his behaviour was unusual by Western standards, because I believed in his good intentions. Once, he asked to attend a physiotherapy session I was having with the man who had treated my back before the Hajj. Rachid maintained that Islam taught us not to be alone in a room with someone of the opposite sex, not even a doctor. I agreed, but he ended up storming out of the session when he felt the way the physio was manipulating my back was wrong and bordered on intimacy. The physio had always been utterly professional, but still, from then on I went to a female physio because I recognised Rachid's wish that no man should touch me as a legitimate interpretation of Islam. In contrast, though, when Rachid and I had been given individual massages at a thermal bath outside Fez, his masseuse actually did cross the boundaries of professionalism, passing him a note saying he should call her later. Quite upset, Rachid had shown me the piece of paper afterwards. I was bemused at the time but just laughed it off. We obviously came from different worlds and felt differently about things, too. But I appreciate the Islamic idea that the body is sacred and that physical contact with a person of the opposite sex is exclusively reserved for the spouse, unless there are exceptional circumstances, for example when no equivalent female doctor is available. A lot of Muslims put so much emphasis on outward rules that they don't even shake hands and most would feel uncomfortable when greeted with air kisses on the cheeks by the opposite sex. A male acquaintance kissing me hello in London really annoyed Rachid, but when women planted kisses on Rachid's cheeks and he didn't immediately fend them off, which happened even in Morocco, I thought nothing of it. This European manner of greeting has become such common practice that it can be difficult to avoid without offending anyone. Although I do remember people never used to kiss like this twenty years ago. Admittedly it can sometimes feel like a bit of an invasion, especially if meeting someone for the first time or a work colleague. Still, I felt that the way forward was to try and avoid such contact and, whenever it did happen inadvertently, to put it in perspective rather than make a big fuss about it. Of course the same rules should apply to both husband and wife.

Rachid insisted he was concerned for my spiritual well-being and wanted to protect me from situations that would tarnish my purity, as he saw it. After all, I was not only his wife but also a *hajja* (a woman who has completed the Hajj). This was endearing, and I appreciated his care, but his concern also meant that I had to stop speaking to men altogether unless it was absolutely essential, whether they were work colleagues, agents, sales clerks, teachers or taxi drivers. When I explained this to my family, my father just exclaimed in disbelief: 'But men are human beings too!' Rachid's response was that he knew how men were thinking while in the presence of women and he didn't want me to be exposed to their impure thoughts. His intentions may have been good but it made life together quite difficult. Yet I so longed to be happy with Rachid that I tried to comply with his wishes and practise full segregation wherever I was. Once, at a gala evening in Monte Carlo that I was hosting at the Sporting Club, I asked the organisers to seat me between two women rather than in the customary man/woman/man/woman fashion because Rachid was adamant that I shouldn't entertain another man. Explaining the reasons for my unusual request to the conference organisers was rather awkward, and I wished Rachid would be more understanding towards my cultural and professional background. This lack of trust and the need to control every aspect of my life – he insisted on seeing my emails, sometimes even answered (men) on my behalf, and he wanted to know details of conversations with my female friends – was something I had never seen with any of my married Muslim friends.

When acquaintances, even pious Muslims, who were not aware of the situation, approached me at an event or sent an email or a text message, however respectfully, we would have problems. What made it all even harder to cope with was the fact that no man in the world could have conquered even the tiniest corner of my heart; there was only room for Rachid. He didn't seem to understand that. I loved him and really believed he was my husband for life. He in turn told me that I was his greatest love. But for him, every call, email, text message or personal approach was an attack on our marriage. Just how could we shield ourselves from the world, I wondered, especially in my position – he had seen my website before we got married.

To ease the tension I finally changed my telephone numbers and in my distress I asked some of my Muslim girlfriends how they handled interaction with the opposite sex as a married couple. Fadwa had also given up her male friends from college after her marriage and her husband had done the same with his female friends. She only maintained contact with men for religious or professional reasons; her husband didn't mind, he trusted her. The husband of one of Ruby's friends also disapproved of male friends, but she was allowed to speak to men at functions or in her daily life. Samiya and Humera, who ran the An-Nisa Society where I met Halima Krausen, continued to have a few male friends, which didn't bother their husbands as long as the boundaries of respect were maintained, and they certainly had no problems attending business meetings with men. The husbands themselves may have had former colleagues or university friends whom they occasionally saw. I suggested to Rachid that this would be a more balanced way of approaching things, but it made no difference.

My parents and friends were becoming increasingly troubled and anxious about the changes in my life, but they didn't want to stand in the way of my happiness. I asked them all to be patient, explaining that I needed to be left alone to make my marriage work, hoping everything would smooth itself out in time. A couple of times when a friend would overstep the mark and question Rachid's principles and the way I was being treated – Dr Amina or Dani, for example – Rachid would ban contact with that person. It saddened me, but I had to choose between them or my marriage. Often the only people I saw for weeks were my mender Nina, who had met Rachid and had a good way with him, and her colleague Nana. Another problem that began to haunt us was my 'past', although his far more complex past didn't count. A particular thorn in Rachid's side was Imran Khan, who had introduced me to Islam fifteen years earlier. Rachid was very upset that his wife was occasionally associated with another man in the media, even though it was an association that went back more than twelve years. I didn't understand his pain but still wanted to comfort him so I tried to erase any information I could find about my relationship with Imran in the early nineties from the Internet. I wrote to webmasters and newspaper editors around the world pleading with them to delete the ex-cricketer's name from any stories about me because I was now married and it hurt my husband. Some obliged, others didn't and most I couldn't even track down. As much as Rachid loved me, I began to wonder if, deep down, he expected to be married to a sheltered virgin who had never had much contact with the outside world. Obviously that wasn't me and I could never become that person despite my best efforts. Ruby kept telling me that a woman's past is her past and it is not for a man to ask questions. The Prophet himself had married divorced women, after all.

After we had spent six months together in London, Rachid finally found a good job – in the US. The idea was that I would follow him there when possible. At some point I prayed the *istikhara*, the prayer that Muslims use in difficult situations, asking God for guidance, as the Prophet did before he made an important decision.[1] I promptly received a bad sign in the form of an argument at five a.m. when he called from the US, but we made up again and I ignored the sign.

Our first wedding anniversary was coming up and after

some deliberation I flew out to Washington. We were very happy to see each other again and celebrated with several romantic dinners. When I told Rachid about the challenges in my new job, he was concerned they didn't treat me respectfully enough. He had also been missing me and wanted his wife by his side, so he asked me to quit. At this point I was presenting and producing an interfaith programme on a brand new channel, interviewing interesting faith-based people, from artists and scholars to community workers and psychologists. I enjoyed it tremendously despite the problems that came with it being a start-up station. And it was a legitimate way of getting out of the house. Most of my Muslim friends – apart from those with small children – were also working. Of course I wanted nothing more than to be with my husband, but I was hesitant to quit at that point because I couldn't yet leave London; the house had to be renovated before I could put it on the market to let and I also needed the income. Despite Rachid's initial promise to look after me as his wife, I was still taking care of everything by myself.

Rachid agreed to support me from now on and for the sake of our marriage, which was my absolute priority at this stage in my life, I agreed to quit. Trusting he would now keep his promise but forgetting Prophet Muhammad's advice: 'Tie your camel and then rely on God!'[2]

Back in London I spoke on the phone to Rachid every day and stayed at home most of the time as he expected – which actually did me good for a change. I renovated the house and began writing the first draft of the manuscript for my book. When I wanted to go out in the evenings I called him in Washington or sent an email asking for his permission, which reminded me a bit of my teenage years. My curfew was ten p.m., the time he usually called. Except for once, when I went to Ruby's wedding celebration and managed to negotiate time out until midnight, but only on condition that I didn't speak one word to the groom. I didn't. That night I left the women's party in full swing and dashed home from the other end of town to be back in time. He called at midnight sharp. But, even when I went out in the early evening, Rachid wasn't always pleased. Sometimes he wouldn't allow me to see a girlfriend so I had to stay home alone. Once, I told him about a fascinating lecture I had gone to about the many female *hadith* scholars in early Islam, and told him that I had asked a couple of questions, too. 'You just can't help yourself chatting to men, can you!' was his only comment. However hard I tried, with my experience of life, such segregation was simply not a viable way of living in the West.

There was a lot of pressure and tension, and I began to feel suffocated, sad and isolated. Rachid's strict emphasis on external rules was very different from the way I had been taught Islam, which was more oriented towards inward spiritual practice and good action, while naturally adhering to the Shariah. It was all so strange because when we had talked about our expectations before getting married, he had clearly spoken of an esoteric approach to the religion as opposed to an exoteric one. The reality in our marriage though was very different and eventually, I couldn't help but feel I was living in a high security prison. I prayed to God for help, to make my husband understand me better and for his heart to soften. And sometimes even Nina, Ruby or Fadwa would call Rachid for me to try and pacify him.

But even in the midst of all our problems, during a few mutual visits we still had close and loving moments and a lot of fun together. Those times always gave me the strength to carry on – to accept the enormous challenges that came with this marriage and go with him all the way – till death us did part. As a Muslim convert, newly married, and devoted to my faith and my marriage, I wanted to do the 'right thing', so I had endeavoured to 'evolve' into what Rachid wanted his wife to be. I had turned away from so much of what I knew: my friends, my familiar culture, my Sufi group and my profession. I genuinely believed that my sacrifices served a higher cause and that our differences would be resolved – bearing in mind that out of everything that was allowed in Islam, divorce was most disliked by God.[3]

From Rachid's point of view, he too had made huge sacrifices, coming to live with me in London. But that turned out to be far more difficult than either of us had imagined. Naturally, I had also made mistakes, especially at the beginning of our marriage, before we were living together, when I hadn't been able to fully implement his main rule not to speak to any men. I was sorry to have hurt Rachid unintentionally, and so I asked him – and God too, for forgiveness – many times. The Prophet taught us through his own example the importance of forgiving, he even said that whoever didn't accept the apology of his brother/sister will bear the consequences of his sin.[4]

I urged my husband that we should look at the bigger picture – our vow before God and the need to please Him. It would have been wonderful if we had been able to transcend our daily conflicts with such a spiritual attitude. But in our case it just wasn't meant to be.

Rachid had eventually found a great new job in the Middle East and the new plan was that I join him there. So I refurbished my house, put it on the market, agreed to his request to send more transfers to help him quit the US and went home to Hamburg to say goodbye to my parents, where I also destroyed the last photos that were left in the attic. Back in London, after I had arranged to switch off the electricity, Internet and water supply, and had started packing, Rachid suddenly got cold feet and told me that he no longer wanted to live with me, but that I could come out to talk. I couldn't believe it. But by now I had little will left to fight for the marriage. I thought that if he really meant it, this time he could come to me. He didn't. Instead, he divorced me on the phone – knowing that I was now relying on my husband completely to finally fulfill his original promise and without making any arrangements for my security or settling what was outstanding between us. I lay on my bed crying, unable to get up, and feeling at the lowest part of a u-turn. The divorce came as a major shock. I had trusted wholeheartedly all along but had not tied my camel.

For me it meant much more than the permanent separation from someone I had loved and sacrificed everything for. It was also a devastating personal defeat. Rachid and his family were the only Muslim family I had and with whom I could share the Islamic way of family life: breaking fast in Ramadan, celebrating Eid, praying together.

Also, by marrying a born Muslim I was hoping to show my family – who were already prejudiced against Islam and particularly Muslim men after my earlier experience – that a marriage between a Western woman and an Eastern man could work well. Sadly, that backfired completely and we became the opposite of a living example of intercultural dialogue.

For a cross-cultural marriage to work, I think both partners need to have a similar understanding of married life and they need to reflect deeply on their cultural practices and try to distinguish them from the essence of Islam. In fact, spouses can function as mirrors, and the process of discussion and discovery could even help a couple distil the essential Islamic principles and ethics from cultural colourations. In this way an intercultural marriage can draw both spouses closer to the truth and to God. Mission accomplished – or not, as in our case.

As I tried hard to pick myself up again, I prayed a lot and my family and my friends tried to console me. 'Khayr insha' Allah,' said Fadwa: may something good come out of this, God willing. And I found consolation in the wisdom of my two companions, Rumi and Gilani. The first said:

When He burns your orchard, He gifts you grapes; then in

the midst of sadness, He sends you bliss … For this reason
the friend of God never complains:
What is taken from him will be returned in another form.

In Gilani's book I found the following:

Creatures are powerless to cause you injury or bring you
benefit; in such matters they are mere instruments of the
Lord of Truth.

Therefore Gilani asks us to pay attention to God and not
to people. And that is what I wanted to do, to raise my sights
and find myself again as a European Muslim woman after my
marriage and after my Hajj so that I could be 'radiant' again,
as my name Zahra signifies.

∾

Nothing happens without God's will, and life doesn't always
go according to plan. Man proposes, God disposes. And it is
God's will that we need to surrender to. In retrospect it usually
all makes sense.

As time passed I was able to understand more about my
marriage and my faith. I had fallen in love with the beautiful, pure essence of Islam and the noble character of Prophet
Muhammad. But then reality taught me that Muslims, including those who practice, don't necessarily exemplify all those
teachings. I had wanted to submit to God and please Him by
fulfilling the wishes of my ex-husband. In reality, however, I
hadn't surrendered to God but to a man whose interpretation of Islam was very different from mine. His way to God
was not mine. His interpretation of the religion had become a
means of control and even oppression, maybe also because he
feared he would lose me. As a result I lost some of my friends,
my job and even my own self. In the long run it could never
have worked. For love to be nurtured and grow, it needs trust

and freedom (within God's limits). Happiness in marriage can only last if both partners blossom and fulfil their God-given potential, while respecting and supporting each other.

The Lebanese writer and philosopher Khalil Gibran has expressed this rather beautifully:

Love one another, but make not a bond of love
Let it rather be a moving sea between the shores of your souls.
Fill each other's cup, but drink not from one cup.
Give one another of your bread, but eat not from the same loaf.
Sing and dance together and be joyous,
but let each one of you be alone,
Even as the strings of a lute are alone
Though they quiver with the same music.
Give your hearts, but not into each other's keeping;
For only the hand of Life can contain your hearts.
And stand together yet not too near together;
For the pillars of the temple stand apart,
And the oak tree and the cypress grow not in each other's shadow.

∽

During the first few weeks of my reclaimed freedom I went out more than I had in the entire previous year. I guess I needed to make up for lost time and it was good to be amongst people again. I felt liberated and at the same time a bit strange and lonely.

Thank God it didn't take long before I managed to bounce back professionally. I threw myself into a new TV job, which took up all my energy – probably the best thing that could have happened as it prevented me from dwelling too much on the past. I liked the respectful atmosphere of that Muslim channel: it was unthinkable that a man would make a pass or flirt inappropriately as happened in other TV stations and media outlets in my experience. During Ramadan we all broke our fast together at sunset with mouth-watering Eastern meals that our boss would often organise. Many of us took short breaks for prayer in between working, and it was nice to pray with my female colleagues in the make-up room. But then, after ten months, many programmes were axed, including mine.

Fa moved into my home immediately after my divorce to support me; just when I was wondering to myself if I would ever get a break and be spoiled, she turned up with her maid and did just that – spoiled me. This is what so many Eastern people do. In times of crisis everyone comes together, no one stays alone. Fa and her maid cooked for me and took care of the house. We prayed together and she gave me many spiritual tips for dealing with the pain of separation.

I had been living in a cocoon for the past year. Now I began to slowly extend my feelers again and contacted some of my old friends. Dani was overjoyed I was back and embraced me with open arms. She had been very worried about me, having known for a long time that things were not right, but since she wasn't allowed access to me she had no idea what to do.

I visited Gai Eaton again who was happy and relieved to see me. Although he was in his late eighties and a kind of spiritual father who had taught me so much about Islam over the years, the same rule about not meeting men had applied to him. Several times during my marriage he had said that what was happening was completely un-Islamic and that I should have stood up to my husband. Before my marriage I had been visiting him once or twice a month for about ten years and I had introduced him to many of my friends and acquaintances. Without exception, everyone loved him, from Ruby, Cora and Dr Amina to Chrissie Hynde and Shaykh Hamaz Yusuf and a great number of young people who were looking for advice. During one of my visits, I asked him how it could be that some Muslims, who pray and fast and clearly have faith, can behave badly when dealing with others. I had seen this phenomenon so many times. It was neither limited to culture nor to geography, and it puzzled me. Gai told me he had always been interested in people and their frailties. His explanation was that sometimes faith was superficial and didn't penetrate the whole character, the deeper being of people.

Soon Fuad Nahdi, Humera's husband, a well-connected and active media man, asked me to bring Shaykh Habib Ali al Jifri to Gai Eaton. It was a great honour to finally meet in person the Shaykh I had heard so much about. The Shaykh presented Gai or Sidi Hasan with a lifetime achievement award for his services to Islam. The two spoke about the heart of the religion, the *ihsani* tradition, which is another term for Sufism. The word has the same roots as *hasan*, Gai's name, and means something like goodness, benevolence, inner beauty or excellence. We needed to cultivate those inner qualities in our lives, they both agreed, rather than strictly focusing on outer forms or cultural traditions. When Shaykh Habib Ali al Jifri heard about my divorce, he said: 'You've been tested.' He advised me to try and 'forgive and pardon, and this way seek to become beloved by God' without my forgiveness being tied to the one who wronged me. 'This is the Divine remedy,' he emphasised, 'remind your ego when it resists. Don't you love for God to forgive you on the day, too?' Reflecting on what the Shaykh said, his advice undid a knot in my heart and I resolved to work on my forgiveness purely for the sake of God. The Shaykh also recommended: 'Be careful about what you pray for in the future.' He promised to pray for me personally, asking God to send me a Muslim husband who would value and cherish me for who I am. *Insha' Allah*!

I also met Emma and Michael Radford again. As I told my story, shaking my head in disbelief and laughing at myself for having gone along with it all, he remarked that at least I had developed a sense of humour about my life as a Muslim. 'If I didn't laugh I'd be crying,' I countered.

I was now trying to get back into the rhythm of doing regular *dhikr* but the external pressures were still weighing heavily on me and it was not easy. I was very happy though to be able to go back to my Sufi group. I had missed the company of those gentle people and praying together in the community. They gave me a warm welcome and helped me understand what had happened from a spiritual perspective. Yet, despite everything and all the support I received I often felt sad and continued to miss Rachid, which wasn't helped by his calling me several times in tears. To overcome the pain of separation I prescribed myself homeopathic remedies and during moments of weakness I recalled key scenes from our marriage that made it clear to me in mind and heart that it was far better to be single than in the wrong relationship. And I thought about an experiment that had fascinated me during my homeopathic studies and had inspired a play by the Khayaal Theatre Company that I had seen with Fa. In the experiment, the scientist and doctor of alternative medicine Masaru Emoto froze drops of water and photographed the crystals they formed in order to document how external influences shaped the order of water molecules. He discovered that when water molecules were influenced positively, for example with classical music, prayers or words of gratitude, they formed beautiful and harmonic crystals that looked like exquisite jewels. However, water that had been subjected to aggressive music, negative emotions or verbal abuse, turned into deformed, ugly and fragmented structures. Much of the human body is composed of water – so the experiment showed how important it was for our health and well-being to avoid negativity and to surround ourselves with all that was positive.

And this is what I wanted to do. I did retain some of the lessons from my marriage, and one of the positive effects of the isolation I had experienced was that I had increased my reliance on God and learned to resolve many issues between myself and God rather than asking others for advice. And the experience taught me who my true friends were.

Gilani said something beautiful about friendship:

> The truly loyal friend (*as siddiq*) is one whom you befriend for good. His faithful friendship is always there, in private and in public, in happiness and misfortune, in hardship and ease.

I was fortunate to have a few truly loyal friends with whom I could share my ups and downs. Ruby moved into my place immediately after Fa. Her marriage had also collapsed, but she didn't want to move back in with her parents, which would have been appropriate for a 'good' Pakistani girl, no matter what age. From me she learned to cook Moroccan *tagine*, fish and Italian pasta, and I started making Pakistani omelette and *desi* curry (from the Indian subcontinent) under Ruby's supervision, even trying my hand at preparing roti, throwing the flat, soft dough quickly from one hand to the other before putting it in the *tawa*, a special flat pan. I didn't quite get the hang of it, but Ruby assured me that it takes years of experience to become proficient. But that month, aided by her sister's recipes, I managed to win the German equivalent of the TV show *Celebrity Come Dine with Me* with a menu called 'Pakistani Passion'. Ruby and I organised some fun women's evenings and relished our freedom – with God in our hearts. We were very clear that in future we would only marry a man who had similar values to our own.

I also caught up with my old friends Penny and Tony over dinner at the Groucho Club. The two of them were glowing. They were married now and had moved to the country full time, one reason we had lost touch over the last few years. One of Tony's songs with Generation X, 'Dancing with myself', had been rediscovered and now featured in several TV series. It was lovely to see them again, so happy after twenty years together, a rarity in our day and age. I visited them in the country and we spent a weekend reminiscing about the past, catching up and exchanging ideas. They, too, had a more wholesome and spiritual approach to life by now and were happy with the choices they had made. We agreed that as you get older the kind of life you lead shows on your face and in your aura.

During this time I came to understand a lot about myself, human beings, faith and the meaning of marriage and friendship. The world is not black and white, nothing is what it seems, and we are not cartoon characters that can be divided into goodies and baddies, but complex and multi-faceted beings with many weaknesses. Human beings will always disappoint. But God is there. He sometimes speaks through others and we would be wise to listen to those we trust and to our own inner voice, God's voice. No matter how difficult or painful life sometimes becomes, we must never lose faith. We may not always find justice in this world, but compassion and forgiveness are such important qualities. They help us to dissolve so much of the negativity that we hold. Practising them mostly benefits ourselves.

I wanted to let go and move on.

⁓

I realised that it was essential to deepen my knowledge of the issues concerning women in Islam. I had encountered and admired both Arab and Pakistani women who were completely fearless in dealing with their husbands or families, and relied entirely on Allah and His teachings. But I, as a strong Western woman who had always fended for herself, had not managed to stand up for my rights in marriage. So I decided to study women in the history of Islam as well as today, and I was glad to see that the number of women's movements and female Muslim theologians was on the rise.[5] I was reminded that the development of Islamic law, its interpretations and jurisprudence have for centuries been in the hands of men and that change is long overdue. The male viewpoint, like any other, could well be limited due to cultural, social and intellectual circumstances and may therefore deviate from the example of the Prophet, who always asked men to treat women with utmost kindness and respect. If Muslim men were to live Islam properly, their wives would be the happiest in the world. The point to remember is that Islam doesn't oppress women: men oppress women. But sometimes even women suppress other women or are complicit with male chauvinistic practices.

Still, after everything I had been through and having deepened my knowledge of women's issues in Islam, I sometimes wondered how much use that would be in the context of a possible future marriage with a born Muslim, who may have very different views and expectations. I must admit that I began to consider whether it would be better to be with a spiritually minded Western man after all, who may understand me far better culturally although he may not share my faith. In one way these thoughts felt like a sell-out after so many years of studying and living Islam, and I tried to banish them quickly because in my heart I always wanted a Muslim husband to share what is so dear to me, but when I examined my experiences I wondered what God had been trying to tell me.

Apart from reading about women in Islam, I also enjoyed listening to the recitation of the Quran in Arabic. For Muslims, it is a balm for the soul. Over the years I had bought a variety of different recitations, and my favourite was by the Egyptian Shaykh Abdul Basit 'Abd us-Samad who died in 1988. He was renowned for his melodic recitations, his mastery of pitch, tone and the art of *tajweed* (Quranic recitation). Even as a young man he captivated his audiences in the mosques of Cairo, and Shaykh Abdul Basit's recitations are still unsurpassed. Ruby and I decided to usher in the year 2009 with the recitation of *surah Yasin,* also called 'the heart of the Quran'. It is very beautiful and, despite its length, it is recited a lot, for example when people die or when we want to make a wish.

On New Year's Eve, we made ourselves comfortable on a few cushions in my room, put on our headscarves and silently formulated our wishes for the New Year. I thought carefully and decided to pray: 'Dear God, please give me what is good for me and bless it for me and please keep away what is bad for me. We don't know what is good for us. Only You know.' Then I pressed *play*, and a beautiful Arabic voice rang out.

Chapter 16

Coming Out as a European Muslim

And unto everyone who is conscious of God, He grants a way out, and provides for him in a manner beyond all expectation;
(65:2,3)

I have always been a survivor and, after taking some time to recover from the collapse of my marriage, 2009 turned out to be an amazing year – one that in many ways ushered in a new era for me both personally and professionally. My book had been published in Germany and I was busy travelling up and down the country doing interviews and book readings about my journey to Islam. I managed to do so much in a day that sometimes it felt as if I was being carried by angels from one appointment to another or as if God in His wisdom was bending time a little.

The book gave me the chance to meet different Muslim communities throughout Germany and find out about the challenges they faced within a climate of rising Islamophobia. I was happy nevertheless to see an Islamic culture developing, especially among second- and third-generation Muslims. One invitation came from a woman called Christiane, who was a member of the Naqshbandi Sufis in Berlin. A few months later I was there for a book reading – on the same evening the MTV Video Music Awards happened to be taking place. After the reading, Christiane took me to the Sufi centre, and to my surprise, about fifty people were waiting for me. They greeted me warmly and, as guest of honour, I was guided to a seat next to

Shaykh Effendi. He was a young man of Turkish origin who wore the typical Naqshbandi greyish floor-length robe and turban, while long locks of hair touched his shoulders. Despite his serious demeanour he had a twinkle in his eye and spoke in media-friendly sound bites even though he wasn't fluent in German. His right-hand man, who introduced himself as Metin, told me we had met before.

'I'm sorry, where would that have been?' I replied.

'I was the one who was praying in the *tekkje* in Blagaj years ago when you walked in,' he said. 'I told you at the time that we would meet again, didn't I?' he said.

And then it came back to me. This was the same young man I had met nine years ago at the Sufi *tekkje* near Mostar. '*Subhan Allah*,' (Glory be to God), I exclaimed. 'What a surprise!' Someone served us tea and Turkish sweets and the Shaykh was curious to know all about our initial meeting and asked me to recount it to the whole group. So I told them about the art exhibition and the concert I had organised in Sarajevo and then our visit to the jewel of Bosnia, the famous Naqshbandi Sufi *tekkje*. And then I remembered that incredible feeling of love I had experienced in front of one of the tombs. The Shaykh was visibly moved. 'Do you know who is buried there?' he asked me.

'No idea,' I responded.

'Sari Saltuk Baba was a great dervish, who is venerated as a saint by many. He moved some 800 years ago from Bukhara in Uzbekistan to the Balkans,' he told me. 'He had special spiritual powers and was sent by his Turkic Shaykh to open the hearts of the Western people.'

I was amazed. 'So all those centuries later, he touched my heart,' I said.

'In the spiritual world, time and space are irrelevant,' agreed the Shaykh. 'There are no coincidences and the fact that he kissed you awake means you have been given a task.'

I made many new friends in faith all over Germany and

was pleasantly surprised when news of my book even reached Turkey and the Arab world. The exposure resulted in more unexpected invitations. It seems that Muslims love converts, which is just as well. A recent survey conducted by the inter-faith organisation Faith Matters showed that more than 5,000 British people convert to Islam every year and the figures are similar in Europe. The media were quick to pick up on the trend and to recognise that the majority of converts are white, well-educated, middle-class women who embrace Islam not as converts of convenience, because they met a Muslim man they want to marry (indeed a man may marry a Christian or a Jew), but as converts of conviction. These women, like me, have done their research, believe in the truth of the message and embrace it wholeheartedly. A study conducted in Leices-ter, entitled 'A Minority within a Minority' has also revealed that despite Western portraits of Islam casting it as oppressive to women, a quarter of female converts were attracted to the religion precisely because of the status it affords them. Inter-estingly, some analysts have also argued that the 'drastic social changes in the West since the 1960s have meant that far from adopting an alien way of life, some female Muslim converts are actually re-embracing certain traditional values of mid-twentieth-century Europe such as clearer gender roles, rather than feeling expected to juggle career and family.[1]

One of the most famous male Muslim converts, Yusuf Islam, has made invaluable contributions not only to music but also to Islamic education in Britain and to a number of charitable causes. His foundation's latest project is a holistic space with a swimming pool, cafe/restaurant and performance area. I first heard about the Maqam Centre at Yusuf's comeback concert at the Royal Albert Hall, one of the most magical and memo-rable concerts I had ever been to. It was his first proper show in London since 1972 and a very emotional evening. Yusuf was warm and funny and it was great to see that the audience – mostly greying, die-hard fans and only very few Muslims

– loved the new tracks from his album *Roadsinger* just as much as the classics. Every song had a deeper meaning, and struck a special chord with me. The concert was a real treat and it was the first time I had seen Yusuf perform his Cat Stevens hits, including 'Wild World', 'Morning has broken', and 'Father and Son'. He appeared comfortable in his own skin and completely at ease with who he was and what he was doing. Here was a megastar on stage strutting his stuff and confidently showing he was filled with love for God.

The process of ageing in rock 'n' roll and in showbiz is not an easy one. Some of his contemporaries in the music business simply carry on hitting the road, peddling the same old tried and tested formulas or trying to appear cutting-edge despite their advancing years and extreme wealth. It can sometimes feel like a bit of an act. In contrast Yusuf was refreshingly authentic and inspiring, light-hearted yet profound. Watching him, I thought to myself that he could easily carry on for another hundred years. He began the show explaining that there are really only two types of story: the ones that tell of leaving home and the ones that tell of returning home. Then he quoted from T.S. Eliot's *Four Quartets* ('Little Gidding'):

We shall not cease from exploration
And the end of all our exploring
Will be to arrive where we started
And know the place for the first time.

He was back where he belonged – on stage, doing what he does best. Yusuf Islam had reconciled with Cat Stevens: the philanthropist, believer and the rock star had finally become one and arrived home. I hoped that Yusuf's return to singing might be an example to other young and talented Muslims to express themselves creatively, guided by the ethics of their faith as artists, painters, poets, writers, journalists, filmmakers or musicians, and celebrate the colourful facets of life, love and higher love in all its different forms. And seeing young Muslim artists such as Raef, Maher Zain and Mesud Kurtis recently wooing the audience with their inspirational yet groovy songs at a charity concert in London, and then shortly afterwards being transported to another realm by the fabulous Pakistani fusion orchestra Sachal Jazz, and seeing the pious yet rocking Aziz Ibrahim, who introduced his tabla player as 'the future of British drumming', fills me with hope for contemporary and traditional Islamic music to thrive. fills me with hope for contemporary and traditional Islamic music to thrive despite attempts by conservatives to squash such progress. Unfortunately, they all too often still held sway on this front, as I had also come to experience.

I was invited to speak at an Eid celebration at a Muslim community centre in Germany, which turned out to be one of the best Eids I had experienced so far. The petite Turkish-German singer Hulya Kandemir moved everyone to tears with her songs for Allah. We prayed together in between book signings and acts, and shared a homemade Moroccan meal afterwards with some of the women who had been involved in organising the event. Hulya was a talented singer-songwriter who had performed with musicians such as Joan Baez and Sheryl Crow, and the media had even compared her to Tracy Chapman and Joni Mitchell. But since she wears hijab the mainstream rejects her. Much to my surprise even some Muslim audiences in Europe gave her the cold shoulder. Conservatives think that a woman's voice could be a temptation to the lower aspects of the soul, even when she sings with emotion and love for God. It doesn't help that Hulya plays the guitar, an instrument deemed unacceptable in Islam by certain scholars. It is strange how some Muslims have a problem with Muslim women singing but at the same time don't mind going to a Lady Gaga or Madonna concert. I found such double standards objectionable, and that evening I vowed to try and help find Hulya a record deal in London and to recommend her for events. But my efforts were in vain. To my astonishment, even my suggestion she perform at a London Eid event met with a firm 'no' from the organisers, who feared upsetting conservative Muslims.

Meeting her and realising what a fine line she treads confirmed to me that the role I have chosen for myself is not an easy one either. Once I was invited by a Muslim student body to speak at a British University, only to be un-invited by the arch-conservative student committee when I objected to their request to wear hijab, knowing it would be filmed and posted on YouTube after the event. In the weeks leading up to the event I was told there would be some very conservative elements in the audience and so I had initially agreed to wear a scarf, before I knew they were going to film and despite the point of the talk being to reach out to Westerners. My hosts had even asked me to explain my stance on the scarf via email. I wrote that I had made a decision to cover in Muslim-majority societies only, in keeping with the opinion of various scholars I had consulted including my former teacher at the Muslim College, Dr Zaki Badawi, and Muhammad Asad's interpretation of the respective verses in the Quran, according to which decent dress depends on the surrounding culture. Even Shaykh Yusuf Al-Qaradawi had said to me to cover when possible, but if I have to face too many pressures in the West to leave it. Needless to say the committee was predominantly male and it was the young men who took issue with my lack of hijab. I found such intolerance amongst young British Muslims worrying. In long discussions I argued that they and society in general should respect the personal choices of women whether they agreed with them or not. Fortunately this experience was an exception and it wasn't long before the Exploring Islam Foundation contacted me to say that they would like to nominate me as their global ambassador and invited me to become one of the faces of the 'Inspired by Muhammad' PR campaign. It focused on the teachings of Muhammad, the inspiration for every living Muslim today and one of the most misunderstood religious figures in the West. For two weeks posters adorned London buses, tube stations and taxis showing different Muslims saying slogans such as 'I believe in women's rights, so did Muhammad' and 'I believe in protecting the environment, so did Muhammad' – the latter was the motto on my picture.

The 'Inspired by Muhammad' campaign was triggered by a YouGov survey that revealed some disturbing trends: more than half of British people associated Islam with extremism and terrorism and more than two thirds with the oppression of women. About sixty per cent of those questioned professed to know very little about Islam and said they obtained most of their knowledge from TV news. We hoped that the adverts and the website[2] would help convey some of Muhammad's teach-ings and their relevance today, and we were thrilled when, within hours of the posters going up, the campaign went viral around the world through social networking sites, blogs and international media coverage. I was debating whether Islam needed PR on the BBC's *Big Question* programme and was interviewed by Al Jazeera as well as several newspapers. The campaign turned out to be one of the most successful PR cam-paigns in the West.

'Islam definitely needs PR.' This is what the producer of my travel programme told me when we were on the road and he asked me about the basics of the religion. He had no idea for example that Abraham, Moses and Jesus frequently feature in the Quran along with other Prophets we know from the Bible and that Mary is celebrated in the Quran as an example for the believers (66:11–12) because of her chastity, and piety.[3] It slowly started to dawn on me that Islamic values were one of the best-kept secrets in the West. People are scared of Islam, even though they don't know what it's really about.

A recent poll showed that forty-five per cent of Britons are not ashamed to admit that they think there are 'too many' Muslims in Britain. The prejudices towards my religion at times made me feel despondent. At one dinner in London that year, an Austrian man whom I had never met before asked me about the content of my book. Given the reaction it generally elicited (a long discussion about religion), I was initially reluctant to reply as we were about to have dinner, but he was adamant that I give him a summary of my conversion – only to start attacking me the minute I had finished. Islam was violent, he insisted, ranting about terrorism and how Islam was the only religion that forced women to wear burkas. He didn't even listen to my counter-arguments. The discussion got increasingly heated and unpleasant, and I eventually went to sit at another table to eat my meal. I left the dinner early and went home feeling utterly disheartened. Would there ever be cross-cultural understanding? Would Islam ever be respected as a religion in Europe? Would people ever learn to differentiate between culture and religion? Would they one day stop blaming the majority of Muslims for the violent attacks of the extremists, who distort the teachings of Islam for their own evil goals? Were all attempts to build bridges futile? In my despair I opened the Quran and read:

> So [Prophet], put your trust in God, you are on the path of
> clear truth. You cannot make the dead hear, you cannot make
> the deaf listen to your call when they turn their backs and
> leave, you cannot guide the blind out of their error: you cannot
> make anyone hear you except those who believe in Our signs
> and submit [to Us]. (27:79–80)

I was dumbfounded. The verse was a direct answer to what had happened earlier that evening. The next day I wrote an email to the man who had harangued me, passing on some reading tips and a YouTube link which featured a speech by Cambridge academic Tim Winter, in which he cited FBI and Europol statistics claiming that Muslims were actually the group least likely to commit violence. A few hours later he got in touch to thank me and apologise for the upset caused. He promised to find out more. It gladdened my heart, and the bad feeling that had been haunting me slowly subsided. But I still felt in need of comfort because I was also disappointed by my own reaction: I had let myself be provoked and had lost my cool. So I went back to the Quran and opened the Book this time at the following verse:

> [Prophet], repel evil with what is better and your enemy will
> become as close as an old and valued friend, but only those
> who are blessed with great righteousness, will attain to such
> goodness. If a prompting from Satan should stir you, seek
> refuge with God: He is the All Hearing and the All Knowing.
> (41:33–36)

Being able to repay a bad deed with a good one, so that your foe becomes your friend, was an art I wanted to work on. The Quran gave me solace, asked me to pray to God and carry on reading. A little later I found the following:

> [Prophet] say: 'I believe in whatever Scripture God has sent
> down. I am commanded to bring justice between you. God is
> our Lord and your Lord. To us our deeds and to you yours, so
> let there be no argument between us and you. God will gather
> us together, and to Him we shall return.' (42:15)

Once again, I was amazed by how apposite the verses were. It was as if the Quran was alive and speaking to me. I discussed the whole episode with Murad Hofmann, a former German ambassador I had once interviewed. He advised me to be patient when dealing with people who completely misunderstood our religion because, when all is said and done, we all have our own experiences and who knows what might have led this Austrian man to have developed such an aggressive attitude towards Islam. For me, though, this unpleasant and painful incident ended up being a beautiful and important spiritual experience, prompting a kind of dialogue with God that only served to strengthen my faith. Recently, Matters of Faith launched a service enabling Muslims to report incidents of Islamophobia. Hopefully this monitoring and quantifying will challenge and eventually contribute to dissolving Islamophobia.[4]

∾

Only days later another encounter left me once again saddened by the negative image surrounding Islam. A friend of mine called Alexander wrote to me on Facebook saying that he wanted to produce a piece of art highlighting the violence of Islam. He asked if I was interested in helping him and giving him access to the Muslim community. 'It's a big topic,' I answered, and suggested we take some time to discuss it. I happened to have a spare ticket for a screening that day of a film that dealt with the London terrorist attacks of 7/7 and I suggested he accompany me there. He came to pick me up and on the way to the cinema Alex vented his anger at Muslim extremists and told me how he wanted to express his rage through his art.

'Muslims also feel anger about the many injustices of Western foreign policy,' I pointed out. 'Of course these issues need to be addressed at their roots, by using diplomacy and the channels of democracy, not violence.' I encouraged him to consider his responsibility as an artist for the impact of his work. 'Do you want to inspire in a positive way and bring people together with the truth?' I asked him. 'Or do you want to sensationalise prejudices and divide people even further?'

The film *London River* moved us both. Set against the backdrop of the events in the summer of 2005, it examined coexistence in London's multicultural society and looked at how Christian, or rather universal values such as neighbourly love may be a trial for some when their neighbour belongs to a different race or religion.

In a nearby Turkish restaurant we spent the rest of the evening discussing the film and the issues it raised about Islam, Christianity, philosophy and art. In the course of the conversation I sensed that Alex's attitude might be changing. At one point he recalled a Pink Floyd concert in London's Hyde Park where Roger Waters had started talking about Islam to the audience, telling them that what they read in the papers about Muslims committing atrocities in the name of Islam had nothing to do with the religion he knew. He told the audience that when he had travelled through the Middle East as a penniless student, he was always made to feel welcome by the local Muslims he met. They invited him to their homes, cooked for him and gave him a bed to sleep in. This heartfelt kindness and hospitality had affected him deeply and that was what Islam was all about, he said. I was astonished by Alex's recollection of Roger Waters' words about Muslims, spoken in the middle of a concert. He had expressed exactly what I too had always experienced.

The next day Alex emailed to thank me for the evening and promised to create an artwork that would show Islam in a more positive light, yet still attract attention. A bit later he and I began working on an interfaith art project called 'The Eye of the Needle' that symbolised the relevance today of one of the teachings found in all three Abrahamic religions. The experience reminded me how important it was to take time to respond when someone showed interest and to be patient in explaining the fundamental issues at the heart of Muslims' lives. As minorities in the West, but in fact also as majority Muslims in the East, we are ultimately all ambassadors of Islam. And we need to reach out and engage in the best possible manner, whatever the occasion.

This was something that my friend Gai Eaton had always emphasised, as well as the need to lead by example. In the fifteen years of our friendship I had asked him so many questions about different aspects of the religion. As a new Muslim

I heard many things that I felt I had to verify, and Gai would always talk me through my doubts with infinite patience, responding with his characteristic common sense, wisdom and good humour.

'Do apostates really need to be killed?' I asked him once over tea. It was a question I was often asked myself, most recently by a journalist from the *Sunday Times*, and it troubled me. 'Of course not, my dear,' he answered, explaining that 'at the time of the Prophet, it was a matter of people being either with him or against him. If they were against him they were traitors who actively fought against the young community and its religion. But when someone quietly changed their religion in private and minded their own business no one cared. Remember, the Quran says there is no compulsion in religion.' I was relieved to hear it.

In January 2010 Gai wasn't well at all. His family was on holiday and when I visited him he had no appetite, barely touching the soup I had made him. Still, as always, he gave me valuable spiritual advice. I didn't realise it would be his last. He reminded me always to carry God in my heart, in the centre of my being, and when I asked him about the *dhikr*, Gai confirmed that he did it wherever he was – while waiting in a parking lot, while walking or sitting at home. 'The continuous remembrance of God is part of our life,' he said. Then Gai told me about a dream he had had. 'I was sitting in a garden and looking at a wall while invoking. Suddenly I saw the wall dissolving, and behind it there were rolling green hills covered in flowers and trees, with birds hopping along their branches; among the hills lay a deep blue lake, and there were butterflies ablaze with colour, flapping around in the glorious sunshine.' Perhaps it was a vision of the heavenly garden, of Paradise. I asked him if he thought he was nearing the end. 'Yes, and I would welcome it, too,' he responded emphatically. Gai was ready to go to God. He had been preparing himself for this moment all his life with the invocation of God.

Not long before, I had brought some journalists over to his house and listened and took notes while they interviewed him for TV. It was a lovely day and they set up in the garden. When the camera was rolling, the journalist asked Gai how we can come closer to God. 'Through the ways He has revealed to us,' he answered. 'Islam is one such way: a rope of God and a mercy,' he said. 'If we hold on to this rope and are mindful of God, we are safe, no matter what happens. Death carries *everyone* in the stream of Divine mercy, and then our faith and our spiritual practice are the rope with which to grasp His mercy. This is why faith is so important!' he concluded the interview. Gai was grasping this rope until the last minute of his life.

One week after my visit, Margaret, his daughter-in-law, called to tell me that Gai had been admitted to hospital. I went to see him immediately but he more or less slept through my visit. I called our mutual friend Ahmed Mustafa and asked him to come and to bring a Quran. Gai's Christian family was out of depth with the Islamic requirements, so Gai had previously arranged with Ahmed that when the moment came he would ensure Gai would be washed and buried according to Islamic ritual and facing Mecca. We knew this moment could happen any minute now.

Gai briefly woke up when Ahmed came into the hospital room. He admired Gai's new book, which had just been published, and then opened his Quran to read *surah Yasin*. Gai recognised the words. He sat up a bit for the first time that day and his eyes lit up. I could see he was happy when I reminded him of my promise that one day I would go on Hajj for him – this was the one pillar of Islam he hadn't managed to fulfil. With a heavy heart I finally bid farewell to Gai. His last words to me were: 'Goodbye, my love.'

But life went on. The next day I flew to Cairo to attend the annual Islamic conference and accept an arts and sciences medal, which Gai was supposed to have received as well.

It would have been wonderful to have gone back to Cairo together, but sadly it was too late. I wasn't sure I truly deserved the medal, but perhaps it was a sign from God that I was on the right path. In *The Book of Aphorisms* by the thirteenth-century Egyptian Sufi sage Ibn Ataillah, which is said to embody the essence of spiritual life in the Islamic tradition, I found the following aphorism, which, to some extent assuaged my doubts:

> If He opens a door for you, thereby making Himself known,
> Pay no heed if your deeds do not measure up to this.
> For, in truth, He has not opened it for you
> But out of a desire to make Himself known to you.

∾

A few months later my cousin Beate invited me to visit Qatar, a region in the Islamic world that was completely unfamiliar to me. She was establishing an IT company there and told me about the International Business Women Forum taking place in Doha that May, which she thought would be a great opportunity for a visit. It was the first time I had travelled to Qatar and, although there was no ancient culture to absorb or architecture to admire except for the exhibition pieces on display in the Islamic Museum, my trip turned out to be an education of a different kind.

On my way from the airport into town I was struck by how many skyscrapers were empty but at the same time ablaze with light. It seemed like a terrible waste of electricity. The affluence of the place was overwhelming. Qatar was booming and buzzing with energy – in both senses of the word – and I had the impression that this part of the Middle East was racing towards the future at full tilt while the West was still licking its wounds in the wake of the global economic crisis. The Emir of the State of Qatar, Sheikh Hamad Bin Khalifa Al Thani, is one of the most dynamic of the Arab heads of state, while his glamorous wife Sheikha Mozah has helped establish world-class culture and education in the country with her Qatar Foundation which has attracted both the British publisher Bloomsbury and the prestigious American Georgetown University. But her number one priority seems to be the empowerment of women. As First Lady she is a role model and exerts a positive influence on the position of Qatari women. Their husbands can hardly forbid them to work when Sheikha Mozah, with the backing of the Emir, spends so much time encouraging women to do so. At the Business Forum I was surprised and delighted to see the large number of women in senior positions, not only in Qatar but also in Saudi Arabia, Sudan and Lebanon and, indeed, throughout the Arab world. They confounded even my expectations of how women in Muslim-majority countries manage the work-life balance.

One Sheikha stood out at the conference, not just for her beauty, her colourfully decorated *abaya* and her diamonds but also for the observant and insightful comments she made. When I asked her during a coffee break if I could take her picture, she smiled her agreement and we started chatting. Sheikha Dorra's English was excellent and she told me about her Tunisian roots and how she had come to marry a Prince from the Royal Family. They had many hobbies in common such as car racing and music: he plays the *oud*, she the piano. During her marriage she wrote her PhD on business philosophy at both Oxford and Harvard universities. Her husband supported her all the way and even accompanied her to England and the States for a period of time. Now she oversees his business affairs and works as communications manager at a Qatari Bank. She scuppered so many of the clichés surrounding the status of women in the Arab world that I wasn't sure I had understood her correctly, especially in the light of my own marriage to an Arab man. But she reassured me that I had.

I was impressed that the Arab women I met in Doha were both respected as businesswomen and at the same time cherished as wives and mothers. They were free to choose whether or not they wanted to work, with no pressure from their husbands. Perhaps they were still the exception to the rule but what I saw was refreshing. I also found it inspiring to see that those Arab women who had decided to pursue a career nonetheless retained their femininity and didn't resort to masculine behaviour to get ahead. Admittedly, there is still plenty of work to be done to further the rights of women in this part of the world, and many structural changes need to be implemented to improve women's opportunities in professional and social life – but at least the process has begun. Perhaps the way women will be positioned in society and their ability to contribute to it will be a measure of the success of the Arabic Awakening that followed a few months after my visit. All in all, my encounters with these strong Arab women confirmed my own wish to contribute to our global society as a European Muslim

Before I went home to start figuring out ways to channel all these thoughts into action, I checked out the headquarters of Al Jazeera in Qatar and met up on the last day with one of the star presenters of the Arabic channel, Ahmed Mansour, to discuss an interview on his show *Bela Hudood*. He took me for dinner at Les Deux Magots in the Pearl, an interesting new development still partially under construction on reclaimed land that has been hailed as one of the most beautiful and most luxurious residential and business districts in the entire Gulf region, built in an elegant fusion style of traditional Islamic and state of the art design.

∽

In Ramadan 2010, only a few months after my first visit to Qatar, I went back to Doha by invitation of Al Jazeera for the interview. It was my first time in a Muslim country during Ramadan. By day I went to meetings, and at night I explored Souq Waqif with my cousin Beate, dining al fresco, stocking up on headscarves and checking out the latest *abaya* fashion in the nearby Souq Faleh, which is something of an *abaya* heaven. There were many new and fashionable styles designed especially for Ramadan: well cut with intricate embroidery and Swarovski crystals or stretch *abayas* that looked more like loose dresses to slip on over the head.

The morning after I arrived I had an appointment at the Doha International Centre for Interfaith Dialogue with the chairman of the board, Dr Ibrahim al-Naimi, to discuss the possibility of me speaking at their next conference. Like most men in Qatar, he was dressed in a flowing white robe with a matching white headdress, held in place by a black double ring on top of his head. He gave me his card and his waiter offered me a cup of Arabic coffee, which I accepted with my left hand, as I was still holding his card in my right hand. This, it transpired, was a *faux pas*. Dr Ibrahim gently pointed out that Muslims always do everything good, including eating and drinking, with the right hand – as did Prophet Muhammad. I should have put the card down first and then accepted the cup with my right hand, he told me. After I apologised for my terrible manners, we continued our conversation about the conference, and when I asked him roughly how many people he expected to attend the session, he told me there would be about fifty. 'That's fine,' I said. 'Guess what my biggest audience has been so far?' He had no idea, so I told him. '70,000!?' he exclaimed in disbelief. I explained that I had once announced an MTV competition at a rock festival in Germany just before Prince went on stage many years ago. 'I know Prince,' he replied with a smile. 'And I met him, too.' Now it was my turn to be surprised. 'How?' I asked. When he was studying in the US, he told me, he once spotted Prince at the airport in Los Angeles. 'I was a big fan at the time and went right up to him. We chatted for a while and he was really friendly.' I haven't met many people who can say they've met and talked to Prince, and the chairman of the board of the interfaith organisation in

Doha was the last person I would have expected to have been a serious fan, but, as they say, appearances can be deceiving. We bonded over Prince and wound up our meeting agreeing that I would come back to speak at the conference.

Another interesting encounter, this time with the eminent and controversial Shaykh, Dr Yusuf Al-Qaradawi, taught me once again that Islam is so much more multi-faceted than [Western] people seem to realise. Shaykh Al-Qaradawi is seen by many Sunni Muslims as a religious authority; he had memorised the Quran before his tenth birthday and obtained his PhD at Al-Azhar University in Egypt. Al-Qaradawi has been presenting the show *Shariah and Life*, the most successful Islamic programme in the world, on Al Jazeera Arabic for over seventeen years. He has many fans in the Arab world, but not everyone supports him. In the West he is heavily criticised for condoning Palestinian suicide attacks, arguing that they are a justified form of resistance to Israeli occupation of Palestinian territory. To the best of my knowledge, he vocally condemns suicide attacks elsewhere and describes peaceful co-existence as one of the issues closest to his heart. Al-Qaradawi was one of the leading members of the Muslim Brotherhood in Egypt and went into exile in Qatar in the 1960s where he founded a Shariah faculty together with the ruling family of Qatar. He is also the President of the European Council for Fatwa & Research and has published over 100 books dealing with various aspects of Islamic life, literature and poetry.

Ahmed Mansour's assistant, Samir, took me to Dr Al-Qaradawi's villa on the outskirts of Doha in the desert. I didn't really know what to expect, but vaguely imagined I would meet a strict and imposing elderly Shaykh. Al-Qaradawi was sitting at a huge desk in front of a wall of shelves heaving with books, awards, plates and other Islamic trinkets. The Shaykh got up to greet us with a broad smile. He wore a long white gown but no headdress, his beard was relatively short and he looked friendly and kind. He invited us to sit down, and it soon became apparent that he was more open-minded than I had expected and also had a sense of humour.

I asked him how he viewed Sufism vis-à-vis Salafism.[5] 'It is commendable to purify the heart and the soul, to cultivate virtuous behaviour and do *dhikr*,' he responded. 'The great theologian Imam al-Ghazali wrote extensively about the benefits of these practices, but I don't believe in withdrawing from the world as some Sufis do. And they shouldn't introduce unwarranted innovations in the religious practice.' He continued: 'Sufis could learn from Salafis how to comply with the teachings and practices of the Prophet as promulgated in the Shariah, while Salafis could learn from the Sufis' gentle ways, good manners and affinity to the sacred.' I decided to take the opportunity to challenge the Shaykh a little more. Let's see what the good man says about women playing music. To my surprise Shaykh Qaradawi had nothing in principle against Muslim women singing, and he said that it depends on the intention. 'When the songs have a positive meaning, and especially when the lyrics are about God or the Prophet, then it is encouraged,' he said. How refreshing, I thought, and told him it was actually Sufi music that opened my heart in the first place to the religion of Islam.

After our meeting was over, he gave me an Arabic copy of his book *The Lawful and the Prohibited in Islam*, and in return, I gave him a copy of my book in German. We posed together for souvenir photographs and said our goodbyes. Back in the hotel I posted the Shaykh's opinion on Twitter and Facebook, glad about the chance to set the record straight and quote this influential figure accurately.

That evening a taxi picked me up and took me to the headquarters of Al Jazeera. I was wearing a long red Ghost dress and matching headscarf. Ahmed Mansour is known as the Jeremy Paxman of the Arab world. Many of my Facebook friends had warned me about his tough interviewing techniques and suggested I prepare myself for a grilling. I was a little nervous and didn't quite know what to expect. But Ahmed greeted me with a smile and showed me round the newsroom. The show began by Ahmed summarising my story for the audience. He was softly spoken and thankfully conducted the interview in a very friendly manner. At some point a viewer from Spain called in and suggested the station give me a show – I nearly blew him a kiss but then remembered I was wearing hijab and applauded him instead. Suddenly I saw Al Jazeera blending in my website address and, as a result, over the next few days I was flooded with thousands of sweet and touching emails and even marriage proposals from all over the world – many, to my great surprise, from twenty-somethings. Men, women and children wrote to me saying they shed tears while watching the interview. It was the warmest, most overwhelming response I had ever received to a show.

As I was sifting through the mass of emails the following day, one in particular stood out. It was from the executive office of Sheikha Jawaher Al-Qasimi, wife of the ruler of Sharjah, United Arab Emirates, saying that Her Highness was interested in meeting me, especially after the interview on Al Jazeera. I happily accepted her invitation.

∾

Back in London I kept up with news from Pakistan through friends and was concerned about developments in the country that had given me such a beautiful introduction to Eastern culture and the Muslim faith. Pakistan has long been gripped with unrest and instability due to inner political problems and foreign forces. On the one hand, we see Muslims fighting Muslims, persecution of minorities, suicide bombings even in houses of God, and the teeming millions living on the edge of poverty, while on the other the Westernised Pakistani elite live a kind of decadent high life that rivals New York and London. A sign that faith may have become weak in the hearts of many.

In May 2010, around the time of my first trip to Doha,

two places of worship of the Ahmadiyya minority in Lahore were attacked. A couple of months later, two suicide bombers struck Pakistan's most important Sufi shrine, Data Darbar, dedicated to the patron saint of Lahore, Data Ganj Bakhsh. It was a Thursday night, when the shrine was at its busiest. Almost 250 people were killed and hundreds more injured. Whoever was behind these attacks struck at the heart of Pakistan. For they deliberately targeted Muslims at prayer. It was an assault on the sacred. It had the further devastating effect of undermining the Islamic tradition of respect and acceptance of religious pluralism in Pakistan.

The shrine is the tomb of a revered *wali* Allah, a friend of God, Data Ganj Bakhsh, also known as Abul Hassan Ali Hajwiri. The great Indian mystic, Moinuddin Chishti, said of him:

> Ganj Bakhsh is a manifestation of the Light of God for people,
> a perfect guide for the imperfect ones and a guide for the perfect ones.

Hajwiri lived in the eleventh century and was a scholar of Quranic sciences and Islamic jurisprudence. His greatest gift was his famous treatise on metaphysics, *Kashf al-Mahjub*, which helps Muslims even today understand Islamic spirituality. One thousand years ago, Hajwiri wrote what has become a classic definition of Sufism:

> At the time of the Prophet Sufism was a reality without a name.
> Today, it is a name without a reality.

If those words were true then, they seem even truer now.

The suicide bombings perpetrated in Pakistan – which never happened in the days when I was regularly travelling there – are seen by many as the violent harvest of the seeds sown by what has been dubbed the 'war on terror'. This includes the endless drone attacks in the Federally Administered Tribal Areas that have been killing hundreds of civilians as collateral damage for years. Pakistan has lost more lives than any other country in Afghanistan. The sad truth is, violence only begets violence. But any kind of violence in the name of protecting the faith of Islam could not be further removed from the true message of the Prophet, the essence of which is expressed in the Arabic word *rahmah*. It denotes loving kindness and compassion, such as a mother feels towards her baby. *Al-Rahman* is one of the names of God with which every Quranic *surah* bar one begins, symbolising the feminine, caring side of God. A whole chapter in the Holy Book carries this name, *surah al-Rahman* (55), one of the most beautiful in the Quran in terms of its meaning and sound. And on the tongue of the Prophet God said, 'My mercy encompasses all things.'[6] The Quran describes the Prophet as *a mercy for all creation*,[7] not just for humans but also for animals and plants. If we revived the true essence of the Prophet's soul, and realised the spiritual and ethical values of the Quran and Prophet Muhammad, there would be no extremist violence, especially not against innocent people and the *awliya*, the friends of God.

It seems Pakistan – the land of the pure – needs to remember its spiritual roots and turn a new leaf to reclaim its soul and realise the dream for which it was created.

Chapter 17

The Journey Continues

The East and the West belong to God:
Wherever you turn, there is His face.
God is all pervading and all knowing.

Quran 2:115

My trip to Sharjah was arranged for a few months after I received the invitation. I was supposed to attend and speak at the seventh Sharjah International Forum for Muslim Women. The topic that year was 'Self Development', a subject that had featured prominently during my natural health studies in London, and I was happy to see it catching on in the Arab world. At the opening ceremony I was placed in the front row on a comfortable red velvet sofa, with a marble table in front of me. When Sheikha Jawaher arrived, everyone stood up. She greeted me with a handshake and sat down between myself and a Saudi princess who was the other speaker at the opening ceremony. They were both dressed in black *abayas* but, to my surprise, they wore their hair loose since it was a ladies-only event, while mine was neatly covered in a headscarf that matched my off-white jacket.

In her opening speech, Sheikha Jawaher called on the young ladies from all around the world to embrace their God-given roles and responsibilities in life, saying that 'women should work together with their male partners on an equal footing to develop the community, adding their special feminine touch and leaving their legacy. After all, both men and women are responsible and held accountable.' I was pleasantly surprised to hear such positive inspiration for women from the wife of a Muslim leader. Although I didn't know much about her before, I learned that Sheikha Jawaher was indeed a role model for women in the Arab world. For the last twenty-five years she had played a pivotal role in the development of the country, working tirelessly on the many projects she had founded for women, children and young people. What I liked most about these efforts to empower young women in Sharjah was the way they were linked to faith. The entire conference was about giving women the tools for self-development and self-fulfillment while strengthening their relationship with God. So often I see successful Muslims whose faith is diluted, who have sacrificed their identity in their attempt to succeed in life, have a career and fit into society. In fact eighty per cent of European Muslims are said to be non-practising.

Two young ladies helped me with all the arrangements during my stay. One was a cousin of Sheikha Jawaher, the beautiful twenty-seven-year-old Aisha, who worked in her office and looked after visitors, and the other was called Shahazade, a warm-hearted former teacher who also worked with the team and invited me for a lavish lunch. They were both incredibly helpful and lovely companions. The next day Sheikha Aisha took me to give a talk at the American University, founded in 1997 by the ruler of Sharjah. I had heard he was an intellectual and a pious, kind man, which was reflected in the way he developed the country with a focus on education rather than glass towers and glitzy malls. The university was an impressive marble building with state-of-the-art facilities and a cafe-style media lab.

I was struck by how hard my hostess the young Sheikha worked, despite being born into such privilege. In between appointments we talked about her life as a princess: 'What do you do for fun?' I asked her.

'I meet my female cousins in one of our houses – we chat,

listen to music and relax,' she replied. Of course she lived with her parents and hardly ever met men, she told me, apart from very rarely at work. How sheltered her life is and how different to mine when I was her age, I thought. 'How are you going to find a husband then?' I asked. 'I just wait,' she answered with a slight note of resignation in her voice. 'In my position, the family would never actively look for one.' I sympathised with her. God obviously tests everyone and even princesses can't always have what they want.

On one day during my trip, Sheikha Aisha had scheduled a lunch for me at the Sharjah ladies' club. It provided everything a woman and her children could wish for under one roof: from a nursery and arts centre to a gym, spa and beauty salon, two swimming pools, tennis courts, an ice-skating rink, a private beach, and a contemporary health-food restaurant. It looked amazing and I wished I could have stayed there for weeks rather than hours. Over lunch I met a group of Sheikha Jawaher's vivacious young friends. I am no stranger to the world of high society, but these beautiful girls all embodied a down-to-earth glamour that came with a heart and was quite different from what I knew in the West. They were all warm, authentic personalities, without a hint of arrogance – or indeed Botox – stylish, well-travelled and holding down jobs in various managerial positions. All were practising Muslims, and although none of them wore hijab in the ladies-only restaurant, they put it on along with their *abayas* just before stepping outside. I felt an instant bond of sisterhood with these young ladies, and we had a lot of fun talking about life and love.

The next morning, I met HRH Dr Sheikh Sultan Bin Mohammed Al-Qasimi, Member of the UAE Supreme Council and ruler of Sharjah, at his grand white palace on top of a hill. The Sheikh was waiting for me outside the front door. We walked through a white marble hall with pillars and an imposing staircase, and sat down in a huge room painted in warm terracotta tones and furnished with several seats, sofas and tables. We were offered freshly squeezed orange juice and Arabic coffee, which I accepted with my right hand, of course, and the Sheikh showed me how to shake the cup when I didn't want any more.

Sheikh Sultan Al-Qasimi proceeded to explain to me some of the history of Sharjah, from the French to the British occupation, and the formation of the UAE in 1972. He had ruled Sharjah since the very beginning. He is a historian with two PhDs, both gained at UK universities, and a prolific author – as I found out when he handed me a stack of books he had written and published. He mentioned that there were ten churches in Sharjah, which he personally looked after. And to my surprise I heard that a number of Hollywood stars had visited Sharjah, including the late American actor Patrick Swayze, who wanted to play a Sheikh in a movie and inspired Dr Al-Qasimi to write a book called *The White Sheikh*, based on the true story of a white man who lived amongst the Arabs and was made a Sheikh.

Then the Sheikh enquired about my own life, my journey, my work and the challenges I had faced since becoming a Muslim. 'May I call you sister?' he asked and suggested that I consider him as a brother. I was touched by his warmth and kindness. After one precious hour together, the Sheikh took me by jeep to the nearby stables. Sheikh Sultan is known to be in the possession of the most beautiful Arab horses, and one of them had just given birth to a foal that morning. Everyone was excited. We sat in the stands above a sand-filled arena. Mother and baby were brought in, and the beautiful little foal with a finely chiselled face took its very first faltering steps in front of us, huddling close to its mother but then actually managing to break into a little canter. It was extraordinarily moving to witness the bond between mother and foal. Marvelling at this sweet newborn creature together with its mother, I thought of God and how they were a living manifestation of our Creator's beauty. Then the Sheikh had to leave for his next appointment, and I also had to dash off for a round of interviews.

My busy schedule meant that I barely made it back to the palace in time for that evening's ceremonial dinner. We were seated in a light-blue and cream-coloured room, with a grand piano positioned in one corner, chairs and sofas placed all along the walls, and heavy chandeliers hanging from the ceiling. All the delegates wore their colourful traditional national dress, and I was glad to have bought an appropriate outfit with Shahazade, a long black Arabic dress with gold and multi-coloured embroidery. I sat next to a glamourous young woman called Ameera whom I had met at the Sharjah Ladies Club. She was a friend of the family, she told me, and worked as chairperson of the Sharjah Business Women Council and as president of the Friends of Cancer Patients Society. Compassionate and witty, she was stimulating company, and I was astonished to hear that she, too, was single. Sometimes I wonder if men are blind. But then again, in a strictly segregated society, no men outside her family would ever have seen her. Like everyone I met in Sharjah, she was full of praise for the ruling couple. They both care very much for the people, she told me, and follow their fates with their hearts.

Shortly after, Sheikha Jawaher arrived in a flowing turquoise robe and a regal diamond necklace with a large blue precious stone in the middle. Just as she had at the conference, she wore her hair loose, as did all her friends, and this time I did too. Everybody stood up as she walked in and I felt honoured when she sat down next to me. Smiling, she took the microphone and welcomed the guests in a heartwarming speech, which Ameera kindly translated for my benefit. Sheikha Jawaher reminded the young delegates that they should contribute to society and, when in the West, respect people's feelings and cultures and not frighten anyone by wearing black *niqabs*, which were not a requirement in Islam. 'We must dress modestly wherever we are, but we need to dress appropriately for the environment,' she said. In fact, most of the women I met in Sharjah told me they didn't wear their *abayas* in Europe – though in summer one sees a lot of Arab women wearing them in and around Hyde Park and Harrods. And I had noticed that 'bling' *abayas* had become quite fashionable amongst certain young Muslim women living in London these days. They may be able to get away with wearing them in London but anywhere else they do look a bit out of place. Another important point that the Sheikha made was to emphasise the need to always reach out to others no matter what their faith, and especially 'to extend friendship and hospitality to new Muslims to show them what it means to live Islam'.

It was exactly this warmth and care from fellow Muslims that had always touched me and opened my heart right from the very beginning. I wanted to cultivate this way of being in my own life, too. And as if to make a point, she then invited me to join her for dinner – or rather a banquet – in a separate room. Over the meal, she told me about her own work, and we discovered we knew some people in common. Imran did a lot of fundraising events in Sharjah for his hospital, and they used to see him frequently before he got married, she said. I did remember those trips. She wished him well for his politics. For her husband she had nothing but praise. 'He helps everyone who comes to him,' she said. 'He is accessible and people seek him out and he is always interested in their stories.' I told her how impressed I was by the love, care and sweetness that everyone I met in Sharjah had shown me.

Later I tweeted about Sharjah, the lovely ladies I had met, and the Islam from the heart I had encountered everywhere. As I was leaving I received an email from a German convert who had worked at MTV in Munich. She told me that when she saw Sheikh Sultan of Sharjah being interviewed on TV and the slogan 'Smile, you are in Sharjah', she was so touched that she decided to move to the Emirate and was very happy there. 'Your tweets have brought tears to my eyes,' she wrote.

The next day I flew to Qatar. The 8th Doha Interfaith Conference raised interesting questions about how Muslims in the West can synthesise their faith with Western culture while obeying Allah and his Messenger, and gave me plenty of food for thought. I spent the next few days resting, reading some books on Shariah and women's issues I was given at the conference and strolling with my cousin through the souqs. A former colleague of mine who had been following my Facebook updates kindly offered to organise VIP tickets for the opening of the Doha Tribeca Film Festival the night before I left for London. I went along with a female judge from the Czech Republic, a fellow revert, whom I had met at the conference, and some friends from Qatar Charity. The festival was taking place at Doha's new Cultural Village, Katara – an amazing place with lots of fabulously designed pavilions, restaurants and cafes in traditional Islamic style, an amphitheatre and a vast open-air film theatre that can seat about 2,000 and is located right beside the sea. An array of international superstars from throughout the Arab world, Hollywood and Bollywood paraded up the red carpet. Yusra and Adel Imam, Egypt's biggest stars, posed for the cameras, along with Freida Pinto of *Slumdog Millionaire* fame, Salma Hayek, Julian Schnabel and Ben Kingsley. The audience could follow every move on the red carpet via huge television screens. It was a balmy evening and the setting was beautiful.

My friends and I sat down on large, comfortable seats in the open-air theatre by the sea to enjoy the powerful opening film by Rachid Bouchareb, *Outside the Law*. There were no stars in the sky that night, but there were plenty in the audience, and I thought to myself that it would be wonderful if this new festival founded in 2009 could help boost the film industry in the region. I enjoyed all the razzmatazz from a distance, and felt transported back to the days when I reported on similar events, jostling with other journalists to get the stars to talk to my camera. However nice and familiar it felt to be there, I was glad I wasn't competing in that world any more – my heart had found another home.

∽

And that is how I keep it these days. On very rare occasions I enjoy going to concerts of musicians I know from the MTV days, such as Chrissie Hynde, and recently I saw Bob Geldof play at the Hay Literary Festival. Their shows remind me how I felt when I was younger and for two hours I have great fun, but that's it. When I bumped into Bob in my neighbourhood a few days later, he showed me his charming Chelsea studio and we had a little chat. 'Even today there are websites claiming I'm a Muslim. Thanks for that!' he laughed. I told him how bitterly I had complained to that Sufi group at the time and had never gone back. 'Well, to counterbalance the false claims that I'm a Muslim there are now several other websites claiming I am Jewish,' he said. 'Why can't anyone understand that I am neither?'

'That you're a heathen!' I interjected.

'No, not a heathen – I'm an atheist!' he responded. 'I don't deny God, because there is no God.'

'Well, we still agree to disagree on that one,' I replied. I complimented him on his latest album, which contains some very soulful songs. One way or another, Bob is definitely a spiritual person – I just wish I could inspire him to believe in God. During his talk at the Hay Festival on Africa and music, Bob described our souls as inarticulate and said that music was a kind of voice of the soul. It had the power to express our deepest feelings and convey them to the listener in a way that words cannot, he said. 'And the listener gets them,' he added. To illustrate what he meant, he painted a vivid picture: 'If you go to the incredibly beautiful Canterbury Cathedral on a Friday night and listen to the choir boys rehearse for mass on Sunday morning, you can't but weep.'

I would love to witness the soul-stirring celestial music Bob described at Canterbury Cathedral, I thought. In fact, even Shaykh Abu Bakr had recommended it once upon a time. But the Shaykh always reminded us that beauty was a manifestation of something higher – and that in beauty we recognise the Creator of beauty.

A few months later Ramadan came round again and my friends Fadwa and Samiya, who usually invite me for *iftars,* were both away. I was expecting a rather lonely, sad and difficult Ramadan with my longest fasts so far, because this year Ramadan started on the first of August and that meant the fasts lasted (initially) from just after three-thirty a.m. until eight-fifty p.m. To feel the spirit of this holy month in the company of Muslims, I decided to go for the first time for *taraweeh* prayers (the prayers after *isha*). I discovered a beautiful traditional yet modern Moroccan mosque in the area just north of Notting Hill. The ladies' section was on top in the gallery of the main mosque, and some of the women warmly welcomed me. When the imam began to recite, his voice struck me in my heart and transported me to another place. It was angelic. His singing of the Quran was so sublime it sounded like music straight from Heaven. I ended up going nearly every night and even bringing girlfriends, who also fell in love with the imam's emotional recitation. When I got to meet him at an *iftar* event I suggested he record a CD.

Over Ramadan I so enjoyed the prayers in the mosque and also signed up for a course called 'Journey through the Quran' which lasted two weekends. The fasts were initially about eighteen hours long and it was a challenge. But when you really put your mind to it, God helps. One of my fellow students told me about a fabulous app, which I downloaded on my iPad. The iQuran allowed me to listen to selected chapters and verses in Arabic while following the text in English every night before going to sleep and after *fajr* prayers. It goes to show God's blessings are infinite and unexpected.

It is wonderful to see that a British Muslim culture is flourishing, especially in London, although there is also a growing number of young people who are Muslim merely by name and don't care much about Islamic principles. Yet the increasing number of MPs in parliament, the numerous Muslim initiatives, charity and networking events, award ceremonies, Eid souks and *Iftars on the Thames* (which I got to host twice), Muslim fashion labels, musical artists and the MICA Gallery for contemporary Islamic art in the heart of Chelsea (ex-ArRum Reedah Al Sai's new venture) are all testimony to a burgeoining dynamic Muslim scene in Britain. Recently I was invited to speak at the House of Lords. After the session a few of us stayed behind and prayed *asr* together in *jamah*. It was not only a sweet moment and a spiritual conclusion to an inspiring session but felt like another milestone on my journey – praying together with fellow Muslims in the Houses of Parliament.

However I am still dismayed by the fact that in my area there is not one decent mosque. One space in particular is so small that women can't go at all and even men spill out onto the streets on Fridays, while another mosque a bit further away provides only a small and unpleasant room for women. It shows just how much still needs to be done. By chance or rather by the grace of God, I ended up attending a meeting of a committee that is planning to establish a new cultural centre in Kensington and Chelsea.[1] As long as I am part of it I will try to make sure that the space for women will be beautiful and in the mosque proper. I hope this centre will attract Muslims of all ethinicities and also wider faith communities as well as being a spiritual home for so called new Muslims. The *khutbas* (Friday sermons) could be held in English for a change, as well as Arabic, but not exclusively in Arabic or Urdu, so that everyone can understand. Our imam is Shaykh Haytham Tamim, whom I know from the Utrujj Foundation. He has been living in the UK for over a decade and knows our challenges well.

The common 'import imams' from the Middle East or

Pakistan often lack such experience and there are many mosques in the UK which women are not even allowed to attend – an appalling case of discrimination that again comes down to culture and ideology but has nothing to do with the teachings of Muhammad. I believe we also need to create institutions that provide support to help us European Muslims implement our religious principles and practices in Western society. In particular, family law and marriage are important areas, especially as there is not yet an official process to register *nikah* marriages, which leaves women in this country vulnerable to abuse and without a legal basis to claim their rights when things go wrong, as I had also experienced. With the Muslim population growing in the West such official advisory centres are essential and require staff well-versed in Muslim and Western psychology as well as Shariah and Western family law. And we definitely need another cool Muslim social club like ArRum. Such cultural and spiritual hubs would be of particular benefit to the rising number of new Muslims in the West, who often experience a degree of discrimination from both sides, mainstream society as well as the different Muslim communities. They are often left to navigate alone through a jungle of diverse ideologies and teachings with only very little support from mosques. This can leave converts confused in their identity and unstable in their practice, but also susceptible to misguided teachings. I feel blessed for having had such wonderful teachers throughout my Muslim existence who have helped me not only to find my way, answer my questions and clear my confusions, but also to encourage and strengthen me on my path. One of those teachers, Shaykh Haytham Tamim, recently inspired me during a wonderful Utrujj retreat, not only to pray *fajr* on time but also *tahajudd* (prayers before dawn) once a week – we prayed in communion at four a.m. and I felt unexpectedly exalted and energised during the days. And he suggested to all of us to purify our finances. This involves refraining from paying or accepting interest (*riba*, which is prohibited in the Quran).[2] When I consequently asked my bank to change my interest-paying account into a normal current account, the bank clerk, who used to have Muslim clients, even encouraged me: 'As we get older we tend to make different decisions based on our beliefs,' she said understandingly and advised me about my options. Incidentally I have been approached by a number of Islamic finance institutions to get involved and will look into these possibilities further because the essence of Islamic finance, which prohibits usury and financial gambling, is social and environmental stewardship in all business activities. It is a holistic approach that could offer some interesting ideas in dealing with the global economic crisis. I regard those teachings that arise from my faith, the practice and my friends in faith as some of the greatest gifts of my life.

I feel that it is only now, after a long and challenging integrative process, that my private and professional life, my Muslim and my Western identity are in harmony with one another. I carry both worlds in me and it is my wish to live and express both and to mediate between them.

Islam is a religion for all times and all worlds, says the Quran. This means it can be interpreted and lived in a variety of ways. Of course, as a European I cannot subscribe to every Muslim tradition around the world. Bosnians and Turks live differently from Afghans and Pakistanis, and the customs of Gulf Arabs are not the same as those of Syrians or Moroccans. Also Europe is home to diverse ways of practising Islam, depending on cultural or theological interpretations. Yet Muslims are united in their religion through the five pillars of Islam which are binding *(fard)* and the fundamental principles of faith *(iman)* such as the Oneness of God, *tawhid*, the Angels, the Books of Revelation, Prophethood, Divine Judgement and Destiny set out in the articles of belief, *aqidah* as well as ethical principles such as respecting parents, seeking knowledge, honesty in economic matters, and the correct etiquette in dealing with the opposite sex.

Numerous recommendations are a question of interpretation according to various established methodologies and approaches within the Islamic tradition that recognise each other's validity. There are different currents in Islam and diverse ideologies, from literalist or reformist approaches to those more focused on the inner values of the religion and the objectives of the Shariah. It is my challenge as a European Muslim to work out which interpretations to follow and how to practise my religion in the best way possible wherever I am. This requires a great deal of research, questioning, analysis and not least willpower and commitment. My goal is to find a way that does justice to the commands of the religion and its ethical principles as well as to my European understanding of life – ultimately adopting what I consider to be right and good according to the Quranic verse:

> *Those who listen to all that is said and follow what is best.*
> *These are the ones God has guided; these are the people of*
> *understanding.* (39:18)

At the same time I try to show respect and flexibility towards the culture I find myself in. But really, it is every Muslim's individual responsibility – whether new or born Muslim in the East or the West – to consciously chose Islam, as faith cannot be inherited. To ask the essential questions and find out how to adapt the universal principles of Islam in the context of our specific time and surroundings, to better ourselves from within, build on common values, and work together for the greater good.

Western principles such as democracy, the rule of law, human rights, the freedom of religious practice, education, medical care and the protection of the environment are also

Islamic values, and it is fair to say that these basic principles are often better protected in the West than in Muslim-majority countries. The scholar Muhammad Asad poignantly observed in the last century that 'there is a lot of Islam in the West but very few Muslims and there are a lot of Muslims in the East but very little Islam'. God willing, things will change for the better everywhere.

Another point to remember is that as adherents of the major world religions, we have much more uniting us than dividing us: our home countries, our sacred history, our common political responsibility, our ethical values and not least our covenant with God. We need to concentrate on these commonalities, while respecting each other's differences, which is what the Quran asks us to do:

> Say: 'O People of the Scripture! Come to a common word between us and you: that we shall worship none but God, and that we shall ascribe no partner unto Him, and that none of us shall take others for lords beside God ...' (3:64).

One such 'common word' is undoubtedly the Golden Rule: 'Treat others as you would like others to treat yourself.' It is inherent in all religions and philosophies and at the centre of the Charter of Compassion, which the British religious scholar Karen Armstrong launched in 2009. This interfaith initiative seeks to apply shared moral principles to foster global interreligious understanding and inspire people to actually practice values such as loving kindness and compassion, as well as the Golden Rule. We need to build on these essential common values and work constructively together – enjoying what is good and preventing what is evil – applying ethics in all fields: the economy, politics, science, the arts and the environment, against violence and for peace, love and justice. The future belongs to a dynamic, pluralistic society where citizens of all religions and cultural backgrounds feel at home, respect and even learn to love one another.[3] After all, love thy neighbour is also something the Bible asks us to do – no matter what race or colour.

> We have appointed a law and a practice for every one of you.
> Had God willed, He would have made you a single community,
> but He wanted to test you through that which He has given
> you. So, compete with each other in doing good. Every one of
> you will return to God, and He will inform you regarding the
> matters you differed about. (Quran 5:48)

Rumi calls us to reflect:

> On Resurrection Day God will ask,
> 'During this reprieve I gave you,
> what have you produced for Me?
> Through what work have you reached your life's end?'

As Dr Seyyed Hossein Nasr has said: 'God does not expect of us what we cannot do, but He does expect what we can do'. I was fortunate enough to hear the philosopher and scholar of Islam speak on Sufism at a spiritual retreat in Canada in the summer of 2011. I spent a wonderful few days listening to inspiring talks on metaphysics, love in the Islamic tradition and the spiritual life by a variety of speakers. Together with like-minded people I prayed, sang and contemplated God in the serene surroundings of untouched nature. The experience invigorated my spirit, re-oriented me towards the inner life and most importantly revived my regular spiritual practice, the *dhikr*, which I had never fully regained since my marriage. But now I am happy to say that I have found my peace and my felicity again in the *dhikr* and, with the help of God, I can continue to travel on my path to Him.

∽

God invites to the abode of peace and guides whoever wills [to be guided] onto a straight path. (Quran 10:25)

It took me a long time, after much searching and many detours, to find the *sirat al-mustaqim*, that straight path that leads us to our ultimate destination. It stands for surrender to God, *al-islam*, for faith in God, *al-iman*, and for *al-ihsan*, perfecting our worship of God 'as though we see Him, and if we see Him not, then verily He sees us.'[4] This also includes acting in the best possible manner, loving and doing what God loves. *Say: If you love God, then follow me; God will love you and forgive you your sins* (3:31), the Quran asks the Prophet to tell his community. The point is to follow the Prophet, not just in appearance or outward actions, but most importantly in character – and his character is said to have been magnificent. Muhammad himself even said that 'he was not sent but as a perfection of character'[5] exhibiting noble qualities such as gentleness, wisdom, tolerance, compassionate forbearance and loving mercy, avoiding conflict and seeking instead peace, justice and reconciliation.[6]

These ethical and spiritual teachings are my eternal inspiration. But having prayed to Allah for seventeen years many times a day to be guided on 'the straight path' does not mean that I have reached my goal. The journey continues, challenges never cease, and there are still moments when I am disappointed by my own shortcomings. Then I ask for forgiveness and promise to try harder. Looking back now, I can see that embracing Islam at the age of thirty was an ambitious undertaking, and one that completely changed my life. What started out as an adventure into a foreign culture motivated by love turned into an intellectual engagement with the value system and the philosophy of Islam, and then became a profound transformation that involved my entire being, heart, body and soul. My inner change was fraught with many unexpected external challenges. Once sown, the seed of faith germinated into a young plant that was blown this way and that in the wind, was hailed, rained and snowed upon while searching for the light in order to blossom. The more I watered it with spiritual practice and consciousness of God, the more my faith pulled me through my difficulties. The more I travelled on the path to God, the more I felt His blessings, and my faith grew into a strong, unshakeable tree – the fruits of which I now enjoy: contentment, direction and serenity. Anyone searching for a spiritual practice that is accessible, and seeking answers to the fundamental questions – where do we come from, what is the purpose of life, where are we going? – will find Islam to be a wonderful path, although the sacred is inherent within all religions: it has touched me deeply and never let me go. Prayer and *dhikr* connect me with my source of strength and transport me into the Divine presence. They are my stairway to Heaven – to truth, beauty, compassion peace and love. Ultimately, it is our relationship with God that counts – and that we purify our intentions and our hearts, for *the day will come when neither wealth nor children will avail anyone, except those who will come before God with a pure heart.* (26:88, 89)

The deliciousness of milk and honey is the reflection of the pure heart: from that heart the sweetness of every sweet thing is derived.

Rumi

Mathnawi, 3:2265

Key Tenets of Islam

If Islam means surrender to God,
In Islam we all live and die
Johann Wolfgang von Goethe

Muhammad

Muhammad is the final Prophet known as the 'Seal of Prophets', the last in a chain of Prophets who was sent by God to all mankind, not just a particular tribe or peoples. His mission was to restore the original monotheistic faith of Adam, Noah, Abraham, Moses and Jesus.[1]

For Muslims, Muhammad was the most perfect human being, not divine but a man of exalted and noble character, and an example to follow: *You have an excellent example in the messenger of God, for anyone who looks forward to God and the Last Day, and remembers God often* (Quran 33:21).

Muhammad was born in 570 AD in Mecca, a city of trade and pilgrimage, into the clan of the Banu Hashim, one of the leading tribes of Quraish. Orphaned at a young age – his father had died before his birth and his mother passed away a few years later – he was raised by his grandfather and later by his uncle, Abu Talib. From his early days Muhammad was known for his sincerity and reliability as Al-Amin, 'The Trusted One'. When young, he worked as a shepherd and later became a merchant, when he attracted the attention of a wealthy businesswoman, Khadija, who proposed marriage and asked him to manage her business affairs. He was twenty-five years old, she was fifteen years his senior and a widow. The two married and had four daughters together; the one most similar in character to the Prophet was Fatima al-Zahra. Khadija and Muhammad lived happily together for twenty-five years in a monogamous marriage until she died. Throughout their marriage, Muhammad often retreated to the mountains for meditation. During one of those retreats to the cave Hira near Mecca, the archangel Gabriel appeared to him and revealed the first verses of the Quran to him: *Read in the name of your Lord who created ...,* the beginning of *surah 96, al-Alaq* (The Clot). Shaken, he told Khadija about his experience and she comforted and encouraged him to accept his role as Messenger of God and Prophet. She supported his mission with all her energy and wealth. In the years after Khadija's death, Muhammad remarried several times. All the women except for one were widows and divorcees, some of them over fifty years of age. They were strong personalities who contributed to the formation of the young community and taught others what they learned from the Prophet.

In preaching God's word and uncompromising monotheism in a city that was the centre of Arabian idolatry, Muhammad faced rejection, abuse and even banishment from his own people. Two years after Khadija's death, Muhammad was taken by the angel Gabriel on a white winged horse named al-Buraq from Mecca to Jerusalem on the night journey, *al-Isra*. From there they went on a journey that transcended space and time through the seven heavens and to the Divine Presence – meeting other Prophets on the way (*al-Miraj*). It was on this journey that the five daily prayers were ordained for Muhammad's community.

Muhammad was profoundly affected by this journey, yet it was also a trial – when he recounted his experience, he suffered more scorn and insults. In order to avoid persecution he migrated in 622 with the growing number of followers to Medina, some 200 miles from Mecca. This migration, called the *hijra*, marks the major turning point in Islamic history and the beginning of the Islamic calendar. It was in Medina that the Prophet founded the first Islamic society and made treaties with Christians and Jews, who were granted freedom of religion, liberty and protection. This first community in Medina remained a model for all later Islamic societies.

Muhammad taught his companions to love God, and the Quran taught them in return to follow Muhammad (3:31). The love and respect that Muslims have for Prophet Muhammad and their desire to follow his example, then and now, is central to Islam. When Muslims mention Muhammad's name, they say the formula: *salla Llahu alaihi wa sallam* (may God's peace and blessings be with him).

Ten years after his migration to Medina accompanied by over one hundred thousand companions, Muhammad performed his final pilgrimage to the Ka'ba in Mecca. Standing on the Plain of Arafat on the Mount of Mercy, Jabal al-Rahmah, he delivered his farewell sermon outlining the key elements of the message of Islam. He spoke of the importance of following God and His messenger, the sanctity of life, the equality of mankind, human rights and in particular women's rights, justice for all and charity for the poor. And he emphasised the importance of prayer and good deeds.[2]

Still on the Mount of Mercy the last verses of the Quran were revealed: *Today I have perfected your religion for you, completed My blessing upon you, and chosen as your religion Islam (surrender to the will of God)* (5:3). A few months later aged sixty-three, Muhammad died at home in the arms of his wife Aisha in Medina.

Muhammad's successor and best friend, Abu Bakr, the father of Aisha, spoke after the death of the Prophet to the young community: 'Oh people, whoever used to worship Muhammad, verily, Muhammad is dead; and whoever worships God, verily God is the Living and Eternal.'

Prophet Muhammad's mission lasted twenty-three years during which he shaped the course of history, the effects of which we still see today. He continues to inspire millions of people fourteen centuries after he died. Muhammad tops a list, devised by the American historian Michael Hart, of the 100 most influential people in history, for being the only person ever to have been supremely successful on both the religious and secular level.

God

God is absolute and all-powerful, infinitely good, compassionate and ever forgiving. He is at the same time transcendent and immanent, that is to say: infinitely beyond all things and yet mysteriously within all things; inaccessible and yet inalienable. He is greater than anything we can imagine and closer to us than our own jugular vein, says the Quran (50:16).

The concept of God in Islam is strictly monotheistic. There is one God. He is the Creator of the heavens and the earth and all that is in between. He is totally independent and self-sufficient. All that exists and everything that happens is by God's will and He can do whatever He wishes. *When He wills a thing to be, He but says to it: Be!; and it is* (36:82). Everything in creation bears witness to His creative power and majesty. *The seven heavens and the earth and all beings therein praise God* (17:44). God has no partners in creating the universe or in maintaining it. When the Prophet was asked to describe God, the following answer was revealed to him: *He is God the One/ God the Eternal/ He begot no one nor was He begotten/ No one is comparable to Him.* This is the 112th chapter of the Quran, *al-Ikhlas* (Purity of Faith, which, after the opening chapter *al-Fatiha*, is the most recited prayer).

Associating God with other gods or forces is called *shirk*, the worst of all sins. God is never portrayed visually or personified because no depiction or image could do Him justice. According the Quran: *No (human) vision comprehends God, but God comprehends all vision* (6:103).

We learn about the nature of the Divine through the Quran which describes God in a variety of terms called 'His most beautiful names' – of which there are said to be 99, such as

Al-Ahad, 'the One', *Al-Ala,* 'the Most High', *Al-Aziz,* 'the Almighty', *Al-Haqq,* 'the Truth'/'the Reality' and *Al-Nur,* 'the Light'. The famous Throne Verse in the second chapter, *surah al-Baqarah,* which we are recommended to read daily for protection, describes God as follows:

> *God: there is no god but The God, the Ever Living, the Ever Watchful. Neither slumber nor sleep overtakes Him. To God belongs all that is in the heavens and what is on earth. Who intercedes with God except by Divine permission? God knows what is before them and what is after them, but they do not encompass anything of that knowledge except as God wills. The throne of God extends over the heavens and the earth; it does not wary God to preserve them both. He is the Most High, the Tremendous.* (2:255)

The Quran

The Quran is considered to be the direct word of God and the greatest miracle of Islam. It is the finest work of literature ever written in the Arabic language – unsurpassed in its eloquence, poetic style and content. The verses of the Quran were revealed to Prophet Muhammad, who never learned to read and write, over a time span of twenty-three years, and were memorised and written down by his companions.

The Noble Quran, as Muslims call it, is a book of *guidance and a mercy* (31:3), and the art of chanting its verses or writing them in calligraphy is considered sacred. It contains 114 chapters, consisting of varying numbers of verses.

The Quran teaches the nature of Divine reality, as well as human responsibility towards God, our fellow beings and the universe. It describes the natural world and the cosmos. And it contains the (sacred) history of earlier Prophets and their teachings, as well as laws for the individual and society. The Quran is the most important source of Islamic law, the Shariah. Ethical and spiritual principles are emphasised throughout, together with the significance of living a virtuous life as preparation for eternal life, which the Quran describes in vivid detail from the Day of Judgement to Paradise and Hell. The Quran can be understood on many different levels; the highest, however, is accessible to God alone. Every word and even every letter has a variety of meanings, and according to some contains numerological symbolism, which is said to be a science in itself.

Twenty years after the death of the Prophet the entire text was copied several times and sent to different parts of the world. There are minor variant readings of the Quran, recognised by Muslim scholars themselves, which overall don't affect the meaning of the text.

Islam
The word al-Islam is derived from *salima* (being whole, wholesome). A related verb is *aslama* (to surrender oneself, to reconcile). A derived noun is *salam* (peace). One experiences inner peace in life through complete surrender to God. This submission is a combination of love for and fear of God and encompasses the way one conducts one's entire life: 'Whoever loves God has no other religion than God.' (Rumi).

The sources of Islam
1. The Quran.
2. The *sunnah:* This comprises the Prophet's exemplary way of life and his sayings, both of which have been reported by his wives and companions and collected in the *hadith* literature. However, not everything that has been written down is authentic. In case of doubt, the Quran is always above *hadith* reports.
3. The consensus among Islamic legal scholars (*ijma*) when interpreting the Quran and the *sunnah.*
4. Development of the Shariah by scholars through analogical reasoning (*qiyas*) and other legal methods.

The five pillars of Islam
- *Shahada* – Declaration of faith: 'There is no God but God and Muhammad is God's messenger'.
- *Salah* – Five daily ritual prayers.
- *Saum* – Fasting in Ramadan.
- *Zakat* – Almsgiving.
- Hajj – Pilgrimage to Mecca, for those who can afford it.

Islamic belief

The fundamental principle of Islam is *al-tawhid* (the Oneness of God). The notion of *tawhid* is present in every sphere. The harmonious interplay of all the elements of the cosmos reflects the unity of creation in its infinite multiplicity. The belief in Prophethood (*risala*) is also essential. Muhammad is the last Prophet in a long line of messengers and Prophets of God, whose message was in essence the same[3] and whose central figure is Abraham, the 'father of monotheism'. Their task was to guide people towards God.

God is said to have sent 124,000 Prophets, of which we know only some. Muslims also believe in the earlier scriptures, the angels and life after death (*akhira*) as well as God's final judgement and destiny.

It is the aim of Islam to promote justice, fairness, moral responsibility, compassion and harmony in all aspects of life – spiritual, social and professional. Achieving these qualities enables us to live at peace with ourselves, our fellow human beings, the environment and the cosmos – and therefore in harmony with God.

Shariah

The Shariah is the ethical and juridical system of Islam encompassing all the different areas of life ranging from ritual actions such as prayer, fasting and pilgrimage to family matters and trade as well as criminal law. All aspects of Shariah are based on Quranic verses and Prophet Muhammad's traditions (*sunnah*). Almost every edict in the Shariah has a number of interpretations, which vary from liberal to conservative. The fixed and most essential part of the Shariah, however, is its objectives.

Contemporary theories surrounding the objectives of Islamic law, *maqasid al-shariah*,[4] include freedom of belief and expression as viewed in Islam, care for the family, purification of the soul, an Islamic social system, propagation of scientific thinking, the preservation of human dignity, protection of human rights, and economic and human development. These contemporary theories are in addition to the classic ones such as the preservation of faith, soul, mind, wealth and honour. It is the duty of every adult Muslim to know and fulfil the Shariah.

A Sufi saying describes the stages of the spiritual path as follows: Shariah (law), *tariqa* (way), *haqiqa* (Truth, Divine Reality). Anyone who has internalised the Shariah can embark on the spiritual path. The applications of the Shariah have to be interpreted and applied according to place and time. For Muslims in the West, following the Shariah as part of their spiritual journey means living by the law of the land. In the US this means following the American Constitution, which is compatible with the objectives of the Shariah and does not contradict Islamic rituals and rulings.

Prayer, the key to Paradise

Prayer is the foundation of the religion. It is the pillar of Islam most frequently mentioned in the Quran. According to Muhammad, 'what lies between a man and disbelief is the abandonment of prayer'.[5]

At the time of prayer, the *muezzin* traditionally calls to prayer (*adhan*) from the minaret. The faithful are asked to interrupt what they are doing in order to remember God. The five ritual prayers (*salah*) consist of different numbers of prayer units (*rakat*) depending on the time of day. In total there is a minimum of seventeen *rakat* plus some extra units the Prophet used to do. An individual supplication (*dua*) is usually added spontaneously after the ritual prayers or recited according to specific formulas. Ritual prayers are shortened when travelling and missed prayers can be made up. There are prayers for special occasions such as Eid or a funeral.

Regular prayer has a tremendous effect on the believer both spiritually and socially. In prayer we leave this world to be in the presence of the Divine. It is our most direct link with God. The more devoted and regular the prayer, the greater the impact. Prayers not only heal feelings such as depression, worry and anxiety; they also teach us virtuous behaviour, protect us from committing acts of gross misconduct, and help us to forgive instead of taking revenge and to show patience not anger. Prayers provide spiritual protection and promote contentment, confidence and courage as well as love and humility. Through prayer one often finds solutions to worldly and spiritual problems, or one remembers forgotten matters. And prayer offers an opportunity for self-reflection, repentance and forgiveness. Prayers are our spiritual refreshment.

One precondition to ritual prayer is ritual cleanliness. Depending on the situation, it is either achieved through the big washing (*ghusl*) or the small washing (*wudhu*) of hands, face, ears, nose, arms and feet. The Prophet said that Islamic prayer promotes mental and physical health.

Elements of ritual prayer: declaring our intention to pray, making physical gestures of devotion, such as standing, bowing, kneeling and prostrating, reciting Quranic verses, formulas of praise and personal prayers. We are closest to God in the position of prostration (*sajda*), when forehead and nose touch the ground. Therefore the most important personal prayers are often said in this position. God hears our prayers and promises us in the Quran that He will answer them. Sometimes it may take a while, or happen in a different way than we expected. But His answer is guaranteed:

*When My servant asks about Me, I am near. I respond to those
who call Me, so let them respond to Me, and believe in Me, so
that they may be guided.* (2:186)

∾

The Islamic year, festivals and holidays
The Islamic calendar consists of many days and nights with
special significance to Muslims. On these occasions they
recite particular prayers and/or fast voluntarily. All Muslims
are aware of these dates and mark them as they see fit.

The Islamic year
The Islamic year is based on a lunar calendar consisting of twelve
lunar months in a year of 354 or 355 days. A lunar month lasts 29
to 30 days. The Islamic year starts ten to eleven days earlier each
(Gregorian) year and therefore moves around all the seasons.
Traditionally, the first day of each month is the day of the first
sighting of the crescent moon shortly after sunset, which is
especially important in determining the beginning of Ramadan
or the pilgrimage during the last lunar month. The Islamic day
starts after sunset the evening before. Therefore the night into
Fridays, the day of the congregational prayer, *jumah* (a religious
obligation for men), is particularly significant for Muslims. Festivals also begin the evening before (just as in some countries,
Germany, for instance, Christmas begins on Christmas Eve).
    Prophet Muhammad's emigration from Mecca to Medina,
the *hijra*, marks the beginning of the Islamic calendar. It corre-
sponds to 16 July, 622 AD. The current Islamic year is therefore
1433 AH (after *hijra*), lasting from approximately 26 November 2011 (evening) to 14 November 2012 (evening).

Days
Days are traditionally divided into prayer times. The first time
for prayer begins at dawn; the second, just after the sun has

415

reached its zenith at midday, the third halfway through the afternoon, the fourth directly after sunset and the fifth after nightfall.

Months
There are twelve months:

Muharram
Safar
Rabi' al-Awwal
Rabi' al-Thani
Jumada-Ula
Jumada-al-Akhira
Rajab
Shaban
Ramadan
Shawwal
Dhul-Qada
Dhul-Hijja

Of these, Rajab, Dhul-Qada, Dhul-Hijja and Muharram are considered to be sacred (as stated in the Quran). Any form of warfare is forbidden during these periods.

The most important days and nights
Only two festivals originate with the Prophet: *Eid al-Fitr*, which marks the end of the fasting period of Ramadan and the first day of the following month, after the sighting of the new moon, and *Eid al-Adha,* the 'Festival of Sacrifice' at the end of the Hajj. All other special days and nights vary from region to region, while stricter Islamic interpretations reject them.

New Year (1st Muharram)
The Islamic year begins with Muharram, the first month of the

hijri calendar. Like all other months it is 10 to 11 days earlier every Gregorian year. The end of a year and the start of a new year is a period of contemplation for Muslims and a time when they reflect on their actions and behaviour, plans and intentions. The word Muharram derives from the same root as *haram* (forbidden, sacred), so called because it is unlawful to fight during this month.

The Day of *Ashura* (10th Muharram)

The first ten days of the New Year are voluntary days of fasting, especially the day of Ashura on the tenth day of Muharram, when Muslims remember the milestones in Islamic history, which often go hand-in-hand with suffering, oppression, resistance and liberation. It is said that on this day God accepted Adam's repentance, Noah was delivered from the flood, Abraham was born, the fire he was thrown into by Nimrod became cool and a means of safety for him, Job was healed from his illness and restored to prosperity, Moses and the Israelites were saved from Pharaoh's army, Jesus was lifted up to Heaven alive and Imam Husayn was martyred in the Battle of Karbala. It is even said that Judgement Day will be on the day of Ashura. Shia Muslims extensively mourn the martyrdom of Husayn ibn Ali, the grandson of Prophet Muhammad, in Karbala on the tenth day of Muharram in the year 61 AH.

The birthday of the Prophet *Mawlid al Nabi* (12th day of Rabi' al-Awwal)

The birthday of the Prophet, *mawlid,* is one of the highlights in the Muslim calendar. Many do extra prayers and some also fast during the day. The night before mosques are lit up and, all over the world, Muslims gather in remembrance of Prophet Muhammad, singing *nashids* (songs in praise of God and the Prophets) accompanied by *daf* (hand drums) and doing special *dhikr* in honour of Muhammad. Islamic scholars are divided on whether these birthday celebrations are necessary or even permissible in Islam. In the classical period of Islam, jurists were largely in agreement that celebrating the *mawlid* is not *bid'a* (innovation) but praiseworthy.

The night of Ascent *Laylat al-Miraj* (the 27th day of Rajab)
The *Isra* and *Miraj* are the two parts of the mysterious night journey that Muhammad undertook during a single night. The Quran refers to it at the beginning of *surah* 17:

> Glory to Him who made His servant travel by night from the sacred place of worship to the furthest place of worship, whose surroundings We have blessed.

According to tradition, Muhammad was praying at the Ka'ba in Mecca when the archangel Gabriel came to him and brought him the mythological white steed Al-Buraq, the traditional heavenly steed of the prophets. The Buraq carried Muhammad to the Masjid Al-Aqsa, the 'furthest place of worship', believed to be the site of the Al-Aqsa Mosque in modern-day Jerusalem. The Buraq then took him past Hell to tour the seven levels of Heaven and meet Allah before he returns to mankind to tell them of his experience. According to the Islamic scholar, Annemarie Schimmel, the *Miraj* is one of the most significant episodes in the life of the Prophet and has served as an inspiration even to non-Muslims. Muhammad's night journey is closely tied to the practice of ritual prayer, when believers briefly leave the earthly world behind them and bask in the presence of God. Mystics meanwhile see the night journey as an inspiration for spiritual flights. Islamic tradition says that all prayers are heard during this sacred night because it is a time when the gates of Heaven are said to be wide open. Devout Muslims therefore spend the night praying and some also fast during the day. Mosques are lit up across the Islamic world on this day, and the faithful celebrate with prayers and exchange food and treats at festive gatherings.

Mid Shaban *Laylat al-Bara'* (the 15th day of Shaban)

Shaban is said to be a month of special blessings. The Prophet Muhammed is reported to have said:

> Rajab is the month of Allah, Shaban is my month and Ramadan is the month of my *ummah* (community).[6]

Sins are said to be forgiven by Allah in Shaban while in Ramadan people are completely purified from sins.

Muhammad is also reported to have said:

> Between Rajab and Ramadan there is the blessed month of Shaban. People are not aware of it. The actions of men are presented to Allah in this month. Therefore I like to fast when my actions are presented to Allah.[7]

It is recommended to fast on the 13th, 14th and 15th of this month, but if it is not possible to fast on all three days, then to choose the 15th. Mid-Shaban is the 15th day of the eighth month and takes place two weeks before Ramadan. The preceding full moon night is known as *Laylat al-Bara'*, the Night of Salvation, or the Night of Acquittal. On this night, Muslims pray and ask God for forgiveness either at the mosque or at home.

Laylat al-Bara' is also known as the night of accountability, when destinies are fixed for the year ahead. And during this night the souls of the dead are said to visit.[8]

Muslims spend the night praying for the dead, for forgiveness, and for their wishes, setting themselves new goals and reciting specific prayers such as *surah Yasin*, also known as the heart of the Quran. Shia Muslims associate this full moon night with the birth of the 12th Imam, Muhammad al Mahdi and celebrate it with feasts and fireworks.

The Night of Power, *Laylat al-Qadr* (27th day of Ramadan)
Ramadan is the holiest month in the Islamic calendar because
it was in this month that the Quran was revealed to Prophet
Muhammad. It is a time of forgiveness, patience and compassion, and an opportunity to renew one's faith. Everyone looks
forward to this month of abstention dedicated to God, when
one can atone for sins and give up bad habits. Praying 20 *rakat
taraweeh* prayers after *isha* (evening prayers) is *sunnah*, as is
reciting the entire Quran during those prayers.

Laylat al-Qadr, also known as the Night of Destiny, is one
of the most blessed nights of the year. It marks the onset of the
Divine word into the world. On this night God revealed the
first verses of the Quran to Muhammad. *The Night of Glory is
better than a thousand months*, says the Quran in chapter 97. It
is said to be found on one of the odd nights during the last 10
days of Ramadan, most likely on the 27th night of Ramadan.[9]
For Muslims, the last 10 days of Ramadan are a time of spiritual intensity, and some remain in the mosque throughout
those days. Most Muslims spend the night of *Laylat al-Qadr*
in prayer, pleading for forgiveness, doing *dhikr* and reading
the Quran. More angels than usual are believed to be present
among mankind during this special night.

Eid al-Fitr (1st day of *Shawwal*)
The sighting of the new crescent moon marks the end of
Ramadan, and the following day Muslims celebrate *Eid al-Fitr,*
on the first day of Shawwal. This is one of the two important
Muslim holidays. Traditionally people begin the day by eating
something sweet and sharing the dish with neighbours and
friends. In their best clothes, Muslims go to the mosque to
participate in the Eid prayers after having paid *sadaqat-al-fitr*,
an obligatory amount of charity, to the poor and the needy.
The Eid celebration is a family event, children receive presents, relatives visit and share a festive meal.

Eid al-Adha (10th day of *Dhul Hijja*)

The 'Festival of Sacrifice' or *Eid kabir* (Greater Eid) is closely tied to the Hajj. After communal Eid prayers, all Muslims who can afford it sacrifice a sheep in memory of Abraham's willingness to sacrifice his son Ismael. The meat is divided into three parts to be distributed to others. The family retains one third of the share, another third is given to relatives, friends and neighbours, and the rest to the poor and needy. Muslims may also make a charitable donation worth the same amount as a sheep (*qurbani*). Children are given presents, and relatives visit one another to celebrate and enjoy a sumptiuous meal together.

If consciously marked, these special days and nights become moments of happiness that belong to eternity.[10] They are a wonderful opportunity to explore the Prophet's experience and recommendations and thereby to deepen one's consciousness of God.

> 'May all your days be as happy as the day of fast breaking and all your nights as happy as the night of the Shaban full moon.'
>
> Persian blessing

Glossary

Abd al-Qadir al-Gilani (1077–1166): theologian, jurist and Sufi, a friend of God and preacher. As founder of the Qadiriyya Sufi order, one of the greatest scholars and spiritual masters in Islam. Born in Persia, he lived in Baghdad where his tomb is found. Al-Gilani's writings breathe the spirit of compassion and charity. His key works are *Futuh al-Ghaib* (Revelations of the Unseen) and *Al-Fath ar-Rabbani* (The Sublime Revelation).

Abu Bakr: a senior companion of Prophet Muhammad, his closest friend and father-in-law. (He was the father of Aisha, Muhammad's youngest wife). Following Muhammad's death Abu Bakr was chosen as the first Caliph or successor to Muhammad.

Abu Hamid al-Ghazali (1058–1111): one of the greatest Islamic jurists, theologians and mystical thinkers, who reestablished the link between ethics, law and spirituality; his greatest work is the *Ihya' Ulum al-Din* (The Revival of the Religious Sciences), of which he wrote an abridged version in Persian: *The Alchemy of Happiness.*

Adhan: Islamic call to prayer, which is made by muezzins in mosques five times a day throughout the entire Islamic world calling the faithful to prayer.

Aisha bint Abu Bakr (613–678): Muhammad's youngest and most beloved wife after his deceased first wife Khadija. Aisha later became one of the most important scholars in early Islamic history. Over 3,000 *hadith* texts are attributed to Aisha, many of which with judicial and theological consequences. Beyond relating sayings and traditions of

Muhammad Aisha gave fatwas, interpreted the Quran and discussed theological questions with the Prophet.

Akhira: the life to come.

Al-hamdulillah: 'praise be to God', often used as a sign of gratitude towards God, regardless of good or bad fortune, for everything comes from God.

Ali ibn Abi Talib (589–661): cousin and son-in-law of the Prophet (he was married to Muhammad's daughter Fatima al-Zahra), fourth Caliph, a warrior who was known for his wisdom, justice and spirituality.

Allah: 'God', the name of the Divine (*al-ilah*), the Essence or the Absolute.

Arafat: 'realisation', 'knowledge', the name of the plain around 20 km from Mecca, one of the main stations of the Hajj, where the Mountain of Mercy, Jabal al-Rahmah is located.

Aqida: derived from *aqd*, bond, commitment. Articles of belief, derived from the statements of the Quran and *hadith*.

As-salamu-alaikum: 'peace be with you.' The greeting is answered with the reply *wa-alaikum-as-salam*, 'peace be also with you'.

Asr-prayer: consists of four *rakat*, which are prayed silently mid-afternoon.

Awliya: 'friends of God'. Men and women who are close to God, who can guide and teach in matters of faith. Firstly the Prophets and messengers. Also the many mystical teachers such as Abd al-Qadir al-Gilani, Rabia al-Basri and Jalaluddin Rumi count as God's friends.

Ayat: 'sign'. In the Arabic language the same word is used for sign (in nature) as for verse in the Quran. The Quran consists of around 6,000 *ayaat* (verses).

Ayat al-Kursi: the greatest verse in the Quran according to Prophet Muhammad, the Throne verse is found in the important second *surah* of the Quran and is often read for protection.

Baraka: a blessing, a grace or a spiritual influence sent by God which can be found in people, locations and objects; also certain good acts can bring *baraka,* just as others can avert the grace of God.

Bid'a: illegitimate innovation.

Bismillah: short formula for *bismillahi-r-rahmani-r-rahim* (in the name of God, the most Merciful, the most Compassionate), with which every *surah* of the Quran bar one begins (although the missing formula is later repeated elsewhere). Muslims say this short formula several times daily on different occasions, e.g. when offering food and drink or before beginning an action with meaning.

Caliph: leader of the community, representative of Muhammad. According to the Quran, man as such is a Caliph, and therefore vicegerent or representative of God on earth.

Chador: (from the Persian) 'cloth'. Also used as the full body veil which Persian or Pakistani women wear.

Daf: hand drum, which accompanies Eastern music.

Dervish: member of a religious brotherhood.

Whirling dervishes: the followers of the Mevlevi order, who whirl in a continuous circular motion in their *sama.* In 2005 UNESCO proclaimed the Mevlevi Sama Ceremony of Turkey as one of the Masterpieces of the Oral and Intangible Heritage of Humanity.

Dhikr: has a variety of meanings: remembrance, invocation, repetition, praise, glorification, recitation, God-consciousness. The remembrance of God with the tongue, the spirit, or the heart; *dhikru' Llah* is the goal – God-consciousness – as well as the means to reach it with the repeated invocation of God and His beautiful names. For Sufis *dhikr* is the spiritual practice *par excellence. Dhikru' Llah* in terms of God-consciousness is the purpose of all religious rites and practices. The importance of *dhikr* is mentioned several times in the Quran and *hadith.*

Deen: 'religion'.

Du'a: 'plea', 'call', a personal supplication either expressed spontaneously or recited after the Prophet's prayers or other formulas.

Eid al-Adha: the feast of sacrifice at the end of the Hajj.

Eid al-Fitr: the feast of breaking the fast at the end of Ramadan.

Fajr prayer: consists of two *rakat* and is prayed between the beginning and end of dawn.

Faqir/a (plural: fuqara): derived from *faqr* (poverty). In the religious context it relates to our need for God. In Sufism it means 'initiate' of a Sufi order. A *faqir/a* is conscious of his/her spiritual poverty and his/her need for God. He detaches himself from material things and empties his soul for the presence of God.

Fatiha: 'opening'. This *surah* consists of seven verses, it is the first in the Quran, and is called its essence, summarising our relationship with God. Muslims recite the *Fatiha* a minimum of 17 times in their daily prayers.

Fatima: usually Fatima al-Zahra (the radiant, the splendid), one of the four daughters of Prophet Muhammad from his first marriage with Khadija and married to Muhammad's cousin Ali. The Prophet praised Fatima's character, she was closest to him and he described her to be one of the four exemplary women in history.

Fatwa: a formal, legal advice from a scholar of Islamic law as an answer to a religious question posed to him/her either by a judge or a private person. Based on such legal advice, a judge can decide a case, or a private person make decisions with regards to his/her everyday life.

Five pillars of Islam: the *shahada* (profession of faith), *salah* (ritual prayer), fasting in Ramadan, *zakat* (almsgiving to the poor) and Hajj

Ghusl: the 'big' ritual washing of the entire body.

Hadith (plural: *ahadith*): the sayings of the Prophet together with his actions and habits (*sunnah*) written down by his companions and later collated by religious scholars into recognised collections of *hadith* literature.

Hajj: the great pilgrimage to Mecca, one of the pillars of Islam, which takes place annually during the twelfth month in the Islamic calendar, the *Dhul Hijja* for those who can afford it. The rites there recall the history of Abraham, Hagar and Ismael. The Hajj is a new beginning in life.

Hajji/a: one who has preformed the Hajj.

Halal: 'released' (from the prohibition), hence all that is allowed, especially food such as meat from ritually slaughtered animals.

Haqiqa: 'truth', the Reality behind the appearance of things, *Al-Haqq* is one of the names of God.

Haram: 'taboo', 'prohibited', 'inviolable'. Express Divine commands and prohibitions are inviolable.

Hijab: 'separation'. Used in the Quran in the sense of 'barrier', 'curtain' or 'veil'. In colloquial language the meaning is a head scarf.

Hijra: 'emigration'. The emigration of the Prophet from Mecca, where the young Muslim community was persecuted, to Medina. The *hijra* marks the beginning of the Islamic calendar.

Iftar: the meal with which to break the fast.

Ihram: the state of consecration on the pilgrimage to Mecca and during prayer in which certain things are not allowed. The customary white robes worn by Muslim pilgrims to Mecca, symbolising this sacred or consecrated state.

Ihsan: derives from the same root as *hasan*: benevolence, inner beauty, excellence. Traditionally the sequence in faith is: Islam (surrender or adherence to Islam); *iman* (faith, recognising the truth); *ihsan* (benevolence, beauty of the soul, excellence). To deepen both faith as well as surrender. When the Prophet was asked about the meaning of *ihsan*, he answered: 'It is to worship God as though you see Him, and while you see Him not truly He surely sees you.'

Ijtihad: 'to strive intensively', to deduce the divine laws of Shariah from authentic Islamic sources, which are relevant to time and place.

Imam: 'someone who stands in front', leader of the communal prayer at a mosque or a private gathering. An imam can also be a leading example in terms of knowledge and character, such as great scholars, the imams from the family of the Prophet or the founders of the four schools of law.

Iman: 'faith', 'trust' in the sense of certainty. Faith is no contradiction to knowledge and understanding. The Prophet said: faith is knowledge with the heart, confession with the tongue and realisation with all one's faculties.

Insan al-kamil: 'perfect human'. Amongst Muslim mystics this expression denotes the highest example of mankind, the theosophist who has realised his essential unity with God.

Insha' Allah: 'God willing' is used in the context of all future planning and expresses the dependency of our success on God's will. Also the Bible asks us to say 'God willing' when talking about future events.

Isa ibn Maryam: Arabic for 'Jesus son of Mary'. Jesus holds an exalted status in the Quran, a *rasul* (messenger). Many miracles are attributed to him, several amongst them are not mentioned in the Bible.

Isha prayer: consists of four *rakat,* which are prayed between evening and dawn, ideally before midnight. The first two are prayed aloud, the last two in silence.

Islam: 'surrender', 'submission', 'reconciliation'. Related to *salam* (wholeness, peace), the teaching of Muhammad.

Islamism: political Islam, the notion that Islam is not only a religion but also a political system, which should guide personal and social as well as political life.

Istighfar: plea for forgiveness, pronounced with the word *astaghfirullah* (I ask God for forgiveness).

Istikhara prayer: consists of two *rakat* as well as a special prayer formula. It is based on the praxis of the Prophet in order to find a solution in difficult situations.

Jabal al-Rahmah: 'Mount of Mercy'. The hill at the end of the Plain of Arafat. This is where the last verses of the Quran were revealed to the Prophet and where he held his famous farewell speech. Hajj pilgrims try to spend at least a part of the day of Arafat on Jabal al-Rahmah.

Jalaluddin Rumi (1207–1273): theologian, jurist, philosopher, Sufi master, poet and one of the greatest mystics of Islam, born in Persia, buried in Konya (Turkey). His greatest work of spiritual teachings and Sufi poetry is the *Mathnawi*.

Jahiliya: pre-Islamic time in Arabia and with that the time of ignorance. Today Muslims call the time in which they lived far away from God's decrees as their personal *jahiliya*.

Jamarat: originally three pillars, nowadays walls which symbolise the *shaytan* and are pelted with stones during a ritual on the Hajj.

Jerusalem: Arabic: *Al-Quds*, The Holy City or Sanctuary. The third holiest place in Islam after Mecca and Medina. The association with the Prophets of the Old Testament, who are also Prophets in Islam as well as the link to Jesus make the city holy for Muslims. The sanctity of it is further emphasised through the Prophet's night journey when he went accompanied by the angel Gabriel from Mecca to Jerusalem from where he ascended to Heaven (Quran 17:1).

Jihad: 'to strive', to exert oneself and to struggle in the way of God; often incorrectly translated as 'holy war'.

Jihad al-akbar: the continuous work on oneself, the inner fight against the lower tendencies of the soul and the struggle to keep up religious duties, shed faults and constantly better one's character. Also all positive efforts to earn a living, striving for knowledge, correction of wrong information and prejudices, civil protection and rebuilding after destruction and reclamation of land are all part of the *jihad al-akbar*.

Jihad al-asghar: all external struggles are part of the *jihad al-asghar*, the lesser *jihad*, which may only be conducted under strict ethical guidelines that must be carefully adhered to. It is solely permitted in defence, never as aggression; the defence and resistance against military attacks and other forms of violence such as the occupation of a country, persecution or oppression. The permission to self-defence is restricted. One is allowed to fight attackers and resist against oppressors but not non-combatants; and certainly not involve women and children, the elderly, the sick or animals. Even trees and other plants must not be destroyed during war. Limits must not be exceeded; it is prohibited to retaliate with stronger force than being attacked. Further to that a *jihad* must always be declared by a head of state. No individual has the right to declare *jihad* in a country of his choice. The most important injunction is that life is sacred. *Take not life, which God has made sacred, except by way of justice and law. Thus does He command you, so that you may learn wisdom* (6:151).

Jumah: 'congregation'. Friday symbolises the sixth day of creation and is the day of congregation when Muslims come together to remember their creation and responsibility. For men it is an obligation to pray the midday prayers in congregation in the mosque, women can voluntarily participate or pray at home.

Ka'ba: 'cube'. The house of God built by Abraham. According to Islamic belief it goes back to Adam who built the first temple at the same place, an earthly reflection of the heavenly throne. The Ka'ba as the central point of Islam is compared with the heart as the centre of man. Just as Muhammad emptied the Ka'ba of idols, we have to purify our own heart and remove the idols and everything else that prevents us from behaving worthy of God.

Kafir (plural: kafirun): 'to cover'. Someone who denies God and his ethical responsibility before God as well as being ignorant of prophetic teachings and Divine Revelations.

Khutbah: the sermon on Friday during the communal prayer, which usually deals with the explanation of a Quranic text, an ethical or spiritual topic as well as warnings and positive supplications.

Lunar calendar: Muslim calendar which in relation to the solar year moves 10 to 12 days forward each year because lunar months have only 29 to 30 days.

Masha'Allah: 'whatever God wills'. Often used in occasions where there is surprise in someone's good deeds or achievements or in relation to a compliment in order to remind oneself and others that all good is a gift from God which should not be accompanied by feelings of envy or jealousy.

Madrasa: 'place of study', religious school or college.

Maghrib: 'west', 'sunset', denotes the time of the evening prayer after sunset.

Maghrib prayers: consists of three *rakat*. The first two are recited aloud, the last one silently.

Majlis (plural: Majalis): 'place of sitting'. For Sufis the meeting for communal prayers, *dhikr*, singing of religious songs and eating.

Maryam: Arabic for 'Maria' (mother of Jesus), the only woman who is mentioned in the Quran by name. She was a role model in piety and devotion to God, in Islam she is praised as the best woman of her time.

Masjid: 'place of prostration – worship'. Mosque or meeting place for communal prayer and studies. Cleanliness and the pointing of the prayer niche towards Mecca are essential.

Masjid al-Nabi: the mosque of the Prophet in Medina, which became the prototype for all mosques.

Mawlid: birthday of the Prophet, also birthday celebrations.

Mecca (Makkah al-Mukarramah): the blessed city, also known as 'sacred city', a place of pilgrimage for over 4,000 years, in which the Ka'ba is found. This is where Prophet Muhammad was born in 570 AD and raised. Near Mecca, on the Mountain of Light, Jabal al-Noor, in the Cave of Hira, he received his first revelation. Non-Muslims generally have no access to the sacred sites in Mecca and Medina.

Medina (Al-Madinah al-Munuwwarah): 'the radiant city'. Originally the city was called Yathrib, but after the *hijra*, when the inhabitants welcomed the Prophet and his teachings as well as his companions, the city became known as Madinat al-Nabi (city of the Prophet). Muhammad is buried in the mosque, in which he was active and lived, next to the two Caliphs Abu Bakr and Umar and an empty space which is destined for Jesus.

Mihrab: prayer niche in the wall of a mosque, which points in the direction of the Ka'ba. During communal prayers the imam stands in front of the *mihrab*, facing it, while the others follow him in the ritual prayer.

Mina: an area near Mecca on the way to Arafat and with that one of the central points of the Hajj. According to Islamic tradition it was here that Abraham sacrificed a sheep instead of his son Ismael. During Hajj Mina turns into a gigantic tent city, when annually nearly three million Muslims spend a minimum of three days here in order to symbolically stone the *shaytan* and with that to ban the bad within themselves and from their lives.

Minaret: 'lighthouse', tower of a mosque, from which the *adhan* is called.

Minbar: pulpit in a mosque from which the imam gives his Friday sermon. It is usually richly decorated with intricate Islamic art such as tiling or wood carving.

Miraj: night journey of Prophet Muhammad from Jerusalem to the Divine presence.

Muhammad: the last Prophet of God, who received the religion of Islam by Divine Revelation. He is the exemplary model for all Muslims. Many Muslims believe that biblical texts such as the promise directed to Moses, 'A Prophet like you I will awaken from their brothers', in Deuteronomy or the promise of a 'comforter' in the Gospel of Johannes, refer to Muhammad.

Mu'min: a faithful and pious believer in Islam who lives according to the religious laws and principles and follows the Prophetic example. The Prophet said: 'Happy is the *mu'min* for if good befalls him, he praises and thanks God; and if misfortune befalls him, he praises God and bears it patiently.[1]

Muslim: 'one who submits to God'. A believer who follows the teachings of Muhammad. 'A Muslim is someone who harms no one with his tongue or his hand, and the believer is the one whom the people entrust their souls to', said the Prophet.[2]

Muzdalifah: a valley between Arafat and Mina where Hajj pilgrims spend the night in the open after the day of Arafat. They collect small stones, which they need for the symbolic stoning of the *shaytan*.

Nafs: 'soul', 'self'. The centre of emotions and the will and therewith the ego. Religious discipline educates and purifies the soul. Stages in the development: passion, conscience and peaceful contentment. The passionate, commanding soul follows the whims/drives of the ego without looking at the consequences, the blaming soul (accusing soul), the conscience follows reason and considers right and wrong, the contented soul has in the struggle for God reached a certainty, which gives it trust and confidence.

Nashid: Islamic song, sung a capella and often accompanied by a hand drum, the *daf*.

Nikah: marriage, marriage contract.

Nur: 'Light'. God is the source of light, from which and through which everything was created and which is mirrored in all that exists.

Purdah: a term from the Urdu language meaning 'curtain'. Signifies the segregation of the woman from the male domain through a curtain (in the home) or a veil.

Qibla: 'accepted direction'. The direction to the Ka'ba. Essential for daily prayers.

Quddus: 'very sacred', 'sanctifying'. Used exclusively for God.

Quran: the word 'quran' is derived from the Arabic verb *qaraa* (to recite or to read). Refers to the Holy Book of Islam, the direct word of God and the first source of the religion. It contains 114 *surahs* and over 6,000 verses (*ayaats*). During prayer the original Arabic is recited, love of the message is expressed in sacred arts such as calligraphy and *tajweed* – Quranic recitation.

Qurban: 'a sacrifice', the slaughtering of a sheep or cow on the tenth of the month *Dhul Hijjah,* it is a Hajj ritual commemorating Abraham's readiness to sacrifice his son.

Qutb al-Aqtab: spiritual pole of poles, highest saint.

Rahma: mercy of God, which is seen as the motive for creation; same word root as 'womb'.

Raka (plural: *rakat*): prayer unit: sequence of Quran recitation, gestures of devotion and trust as well as praise to God and blessings on the Prophet and his family. One prayer unit consists of two *rakat*; depending on the time of day an obligatory ritual prayer consists of two, three or four *rakat*, a voluntary extra prayer (*sunnah* – as the Prophet did) usually of two.

Ramadan: the ninth month in the lunar calendar in which the Islamic revelation began. Muslims fast in Ramadan from dawn to sunset.

Rasul: Messenger of God who brings a comprehensive new message.

Ruku: bowing in prayer before prostrating.

Sabr: 'patience', 'constancy'.

Sadaqa: voluntary charity, kind actions to fellow human beings.

Sakina: sacred peace experienced by a believer through being conscious of God's presence.

Salah: 'connection', 'link'; ritual prayer, usually five times daily in Arabic and with full concentration. It is considered one of the Five Pillars of Islam. The obligatory prayers consist of 17 *rakat*.

Salam: 'peace'; related to *salima* 'to be complete'.

Sama: 'listening'; a Sufi ceremony performed as *dhikr*. Rituals include prayer and poetry, sacred music and dance, and wearing symbolic attire.

Sa'y: the ritual of fast walking or running seven times between the hills Safa and Marwah in memory of Hagar after circumambulating the Ka'ba on Umrah or Hajj; Abraham's second wife did the same when searching for water for her son.

Shahada: the Islamic profession of faith; '*La ilaha illa, Llah, wa ashhadu anna Muhammadar rasul Allah*' (no god besides God, and Muhammad is God's messenger).

Shariah: 'path to the water hole'. Ethical judicial system and moral path based on the Quran and *sunnah* derived by scholars in consensus. It is the fundament of faith.

Sharif: descendent of the Prophet through Hassan or Hussain, the two sons of the Prophet's daughter Fatima and her husband Ali ibn Abi Talib.

Shaytan: 'Satan'. Said to have been created from fire and is man's arch enemy. According to the Quran he was initially with the angels in Heaven, but due to his pride and arrogance he disobeyed God when He asked all heavenly creatures to bow down before Adam. For this reason God withdrew his mercy from him.

Shaykh/a: 'old man/woman', 'elder'; a title of spiritual or worldly authority for a highly knowledgeable and honourable person. Also commonly used for a spiritual master.

Shia: 'party'; today mainly used for those who claim that they are the followers of Ali ibn Abi Talib. The Shias consider the Prophet's cousin Ali as the spiritual head (Imam) of the community, and claim that he ought to have been the first Caliph instead of Abu Bakr. Ten per cent of Muslims are Shia, their doctrines differ in certain details from those of the Sunni majority.

Shirk: the association with other deities or forces, hence with polytheism; *shirk* is the gravest sin in Islam and the only one that God does not forgive as long as it carries on.

Sufi: a Muslim who belongs to a *tariqa* and is on the spiritual path to God. One possible derivation of the word 'Sufi' is from the *ahl as-suffah* ('The People of the Bench'), a group of early Muslims who were poor and lived in the first mosque at Medina in close proximity to the Prophet Muhammad.

Sufism: Arabic: *tasawwuf*, the inner dimension of Islam or Islamic mysticism; derived from the word root *suf* (wool, early ascetics preferred woollen to luxurious garments) or *safa* (purity). The purification of the heart with *dhikr*, the ennobling of the soul and striving for perfection. The spiritual path. Inherent in Sufism are metaphysical truths which nourish our soul and gift us inner peace, train the character and promote the best in us. The aim of Sufism is the Divine. The teachings of many classical Sufi masters are universal and timeless and serve as inspiration earlier as today. Sufism made an enormous contribution to Islamic civilisation, especially to its music, philosophy, art and architecture as well as to literature and poetry.

Sujud: prostration in prayer, where forehead and nose touch the ground.

Sunnah: the exemplary practice of Prophet Muhammad including his sayings/statements, which are every Muslim's model to follow; after the Quran the second source of Islamic faith and practice.

Sunni: the adjective of *sunnah*; the majority of Muslims are Sunnis. They accept Abu Bakr as the first rightly guided

Caliph to succeed Muhammad after his death and Ali ibn Abi Talib, his cousin, as the fourth. Until today four Sunni schools of law have remained: Hanai, Shafii, Maliki and Hanbali.

Surah: a chapter of the Quran.

Protective *surahs*: the last two short chapters of the Quran, 113 *Al-Falaq* (daybreak) and 114 *An-Nas* (people), which one should say daily along with *surah* 112 for protection.

Tahajjud: night vigil – a voluntary prayer in addition to the five daily canonical prayers, for which one breaks ones sleep to devote oneself to God.

Tajwid: the act of reciting or the actual medium of a special type of recitation of the Quran. It is a beautiful recitation method that employs all the diacritics and rules of recitation in lengthening, shortening and altering sounds of letters so that it results in a wonderful sounding recitation of the Quran.

Talaq: divorce initiated by the husband. If he pronounces *talaq* once, it is revocable and becomes effective after three months but the couple can remarry; if this process has been followed three times or the *talaq* is pronounced three times in one session (although some scholars believe this counts as one *talaq* only citing examples of the Prophet's companions), it becomes final. The couple can then only remarry if the wife was married with another man.

Taqwa: often translated as 'fear of God' or 'piety', but really the consciousness of God's presence, which is linked to awe and love.

Tarawih prayers: recommended prayer after the late evening prayer in Ramadan usually consisting of up to 20 *rakat*. In Sunni practice, it is a congregational prayer.

Tariqa (plural: turuq): 'path'; in Sufism a brotherhood, a group of people guided by a Shaykh who are on the path of God. There are many *turuq*, which are all linked together and go back to the same source. They differ only marginally in doctrines and methods and are based on the Quran and the teachings of Prophet Muhammad. A *tariqa* derives its legitimacy through the chain of transmission (*silsilah*) which goes back to the Prophet.

Tasbih: praises of God, following the ritual prayer, especially on festive days or nights, but also expressed spontaneously and meditatively (with prayer beads).

Tasawwuf: Arabic for Sufism.

Tawaf: the seven circumambulations of the Ka'ba during Umrah or Hajj, which are done counter-clockwise.

Tawakkul: Trust in God.

Tawba: 'return', 'repentance'; turning away from negative thoughts, words and actions to positive ones. Whoever repents and does good receives God's forgiveness.

Tawhid: 'oneness', 'declaring or affirming One', and at the deepest level 'realising One'. The central idea of Islam is the Oneness of God.

Tekkje: Bosnian for *tekke*, a Sufi convent, where Sufis meet for communal prayers and *dhikr* and where they live at times of retreat (*i'tikaf*) during Ramadan. It usually consists of a mosque, sometimes with an attached library as well as rooms where the Sufis or occasional guests can spend the night and a kitchen for the needs of the guests and for feeding the poor.

Ummah: religious community which follows a Prophet, for example the community of Muslims. At the time of Muhammad, Jews and Christians were considered part of the *ummah* of Madinah.

Umrah: small pilgrimage, which can be performed any time during the year.

Wahabism: the ideology of Wahabis, which propagates a return to the 'unadulterated sources' of Islam and a literalist interpretation of the Quran. Great emphasis is given to the observance of rules and rituals while the spiritual dimension and the development of the soul are less emphasised. This conservative movement was founded by Muhammad ibn Abd al-Wahab whose aim it was to bring Islam back to its original state of purity.

Wakil: trustee, confidant; representative of the bride during the negotiations of the marriage contract but also a trustee in general, someone you entrust your affairs to, in this sense the word is also used in relation to God.

Wali (plural: awliya): friend of God.

Wird: a traditional sequence of meditative prayer formulas, Quran verses, and invocations of God, which are used in addition to the ritual prayers or at fixed times during the day. A *wird* is 'prescribed' by a competent teacher of a *tariqa* for either an individual or a community and passed on along that line.

Wudhu: the small washing that is required in order to reach the state of purity required for the ritual prayer.

Yasin: the 36th *surah* which the Prophet called the 'heart of the Quran'. It is recited for the dying and in order to fulfil particular wishes.

Zakat: the obligatory donation to the poor, in order to purify ones wealth, 2.5% should be paid annually. This is one of the Five Pillars of Islam.

Zamzam: the sacred source of water in Mecca near the Ka'ba, which Abraham's wife Hagar discovered with the help of an angel.

Zawiya: 'corner'; prayer room or building of religious character in which Sufis meet for prayer and *dhikr*; in North Africa also mausoleum of a saint. In the East *khanaka*, in the former Ottoman Empire *tekke* or *dirgah*.

Ziyara: 'visit'. Commonly used in the context of visit to a sacred location.

Zuhr prayer: consists of four *rakat*, which are recited silently at midday.

Notes

Chapter 1

1. Nowadays there are retirement homes for senior citizens even in Pakistan, although this is contrary to the traditional way of life where the elderly are taken care of within the families.

Chapter 3

1. After the film *Notting Hill* was released, the area was smartened up and became more expensive. Many of its original denizens moved north and wealthy businessmen and American bankers moved in.

Chapter 4

1. The region is now called Khyber Pakhtunkhwa.
2. Whenever Muslims mention a Prophet or an Angel they follow it with the formula of respect *alayhi as-salam*. A common English abbreviation of the same is 'pbuh', peace be upon him.
3. 'saw' stands for *salla Allahu alayhi wa sallam,* may God's peace and blessings be upon him. Muslims silently recite this phrase every time they mention Prophet Muhammed. For editorial reasons I have left out those formulas but I encourage the reader to recite the formulas silently.
4. (Quran 41:43, 4:163–164)
5. In fact the trinity is clearly rejected in the Quran, 4:171, 5:73, 5:116, 112.

Chapter 5

1. Musnad Ahmad, Ibn Majah.
2. Tirmidhi and Ibn Hibban.
3. See *Shamail* at-Tirmidhi.
4. r stands for *radi Allahu anha,* may God be pleased with her, a formula of respect after mentioning a female companion of the Prophet (s). For

editorial reasons I have left out these formulas but encourage the reader to pronounce them silently.

5. Abu Dawud.
6. Bukhari 4:538.
7. Musnad Ahmad.

Chapter 6

1. r stands for *radi Allahu anhu* – may God be pleased with him, which is uttered after mentioning a companion of the Prophet.
2. Bukhari.

Chapter 7

1. Nowadays this problem is largely solved with the invention of the so-called *burkini*, a full length, slightly loose two-piece Muslim bathing suit with a hood.
2. This was before the notion of 'Euro Islam' became fashionable or the concept of a European Islamic culture.
3. Bukhari.
4. The Prophet's cousin Ali's great grandson Ja'far bin Muhammad bin Ali bin Al-Husain said: If you have heard something about your brother whom you hate, seek one to seventy excuses for him. But if you can't figure it out then say: He might have had an excuse which I am not aware of. *Shu'ab Al-Iman* by Al-Bayhaqi.
5. Ali Ibn Abi Talib had famously said: 'Your cure is within, yet you do not realise it, and your disease is from you, yet you do not perceive it. You deem yourself to be an insignificant entity, and the entire universe is in you.'

Chapter 8

1. Bukhari.
2. Muslim.

Chapter 9

1. 'The example of the believers in their affection and compassion and benevolence is like the body; if one part of it becomes ill the whole body

comes to its aid with fever and sleeplessness.' (Reported by Bukhari and Muslim)

2. (Quran 3:45- 51, 5:75, 19:30–35)

3. http://www.thecubeofcubes.com/index.html

Chapter 10

1. 'Hearts become rusty as iron does when it touches water, they said to him (s) and how do we polish it? He said: much remembrance of death and the recitation of Qur'an'. *Shu'ab Al-Iman,* Al-Bayhaqi.

2. Bukhari.

3. Tirmidhi.

4. (Quran 13:4)

Chapter 11

1. Sunni Muslims hold that Islam is the culmination of all revealed religions, the most complete and the only fully valid one today. Previous religions are said to have been corrupted over time, and this means that only certain elements of the truths within their original revelations remain; Islam is the final and only true religion accepted by God. This view is based on interpretations of prophetic sayings and Quranic verses such as 3:85 *'Whoever seeks a religion other than Islam will never have it accepted from him and shall be of those who have truly failed in the next life.'* This leads to the question whether God the most merciful and compassionate would really condemn all those who worship within other religions but Islam? God says in the Quran that *'We do not punish until We send a Messenger'*. (17:15) According to traditional Islam God will show mercy to all those whom the pure message of Islam as declared by Muhammad has not reached. Most non-Muslims would be included in this category today as they have only seen a distorted image of Islam as portrayed in the media. Only those who reject the Divine message of Islam although they have fully received it, would be lost. However, scholars who expound the spiritual, metaphysical dimensions of the Quran recognise not only this interpretation but uphold a more universalist understanding of the Islamic message reconciling outwardly different religious rulings with the essential unity of underlying principles and citing Quranic verses such as 5:48, 41: 43, 42:13, 22: 67, 2:148, 2:62, 2:213, 2:285, 3:84, 4:163–165. With regard to verses 3:19 and 3:85, 'Islam' is translated as 'self- surrender or submission to God'. *In relation to God, religion is surrender* (3:19) and *If anyone seeks other*

than submission to God as a religion, it will not be accepted of him; (3:85).

Past prophets and realised souls within the religions revealed to those prophets could be called 'Muslim' as well because they had surrendered themselves to God. The Muslim believer can thus be open to the wisdom and beauty of other faiths, together with their adherents, while at the same time inviting everyone to embrace Islam based on its very inclusivity. In other words, one might consider embracing Islam not because it is the *only* true religion – and because all others are false – but because Islam is the only religion which recognises all other true religions as being revealed by God. Islam is therefore the most completely inclusive of all the religions, and this is one of the meanings of its 'universality'. (Reza Shah Kazemi: *The Other in the Light of the One*). In this light different religions are seen not only as mutually exclusive and inevitably antagonistic systems of dogmatic beliefs and ritual practices, existing on the lower slopes of the mountain of faith, but also as different paths to the summit of that mountain. The 13th century Sufi scholar Shaykh Muhyiddin Ibn al-Arabi likened all revealed religions to lights; Islam is like the light of the sun amongst the lights of the stars. When the sun appears, the light of the stars disappear, but their lights are confirmed (*muhaqqaq*) within the greater light of the sun: they do not cease to exist. Murad Hofmann compared the religion of Islam to a diamond of greater clarity and purity than others. And God knows best – *Allahu a'lam*.

2. See *Marital Discord: Recapturing Human Dignity Through the Higher Objectives of Islamic Law* by Abdul Hamid A. Abu Sulayman.

3. 'When a man marries he has fulfilled half of the religion; so let him fear Allah regarding the remaining half' (Tirmidhi).

4. Wasa'il, vol. 14, p.3.

5. *The Heart Of Islam*, Dr Seyyed Hossein Nasr.

6. Musnad Ahmad.

7. Wedding quotation from Maybudi. The Prophet even likened the husband's sperm to a charity. (Muslim)

8. Marriage quotes from Daylami.

9. Al-Mughira bin Shu'bah proposed to a woman, and the Prophet (s) said to him: have you seen her? He said: no. Muhammad replied: look at her then. (Tirmidhi).

Chapter 12

1. Bukhari.
2. Tbarani.

Chapter 13

1. See also Joseph Lumbard, *Islam, Fundamentalism and the Betrayal of Tradition*.
2. Bayhaqi.
3. Bayhaqi.
4. *Al-Jaami' al-Saghir* by Imam al-Suyuti.
5. Abu Dawud.

Chapter 14

1. Surat al-Baqara (2:201).
2. Surat al-Imran (3:193).
3. Ad-Daraqutni.

Chapter 15

1. Tirmidhi, Ibn Majah and many more report this practice of the Prophet.
2. Tirmidhi.
3. Ibn Majah.
4. 'Whoever does not accept the apology of his brother/ sister will incur the sin of one who falsely takes people's rights.' *Sunan* Ibn Majah.
5. Halima Krausen, Asma Barlas and Leila Ahmed, for example, shed light on the Quran and the practices of Prophet Muhammad from a female perspective. There is also Khaled Abu El Fadl, an Islamic jurist and scholar who teaches at UCLA in the US and is a staunch defender of women's rights. These scholars all try to promote social justice and spiritual well-being for men and women through a contemporary interpretation of the Quran. 'A comprehensive paradigm shift from within can effect a radical change for the future of Muslim women and men and can increase Islamic efficacy by shifting from coercive participation to voluntary dedication,' writes professor of Islamic studies Amina Wadud in her book *Inside the Gender Jihad*. Admittedly she is a controversial personality but her book raises some very interesting points. A lot more work needs to be done especially by female scholars.

Chapter 16

1. See the *Independent on Sunday*, 'Women & Islam: The rise and rise of the

female convert', 6 November 2011.

2. www.inspiredbymuhammad.com

3. Mary is the only female in the Quran identified by name and is mentioned far more frequently in the Quran than in the New Testament. The Prophet Muhammed called her the most virtuous woman of her time and counts her amongst the best four women of Paradise along with his first wife Khadija, his daughter Fatima, and Asia, the wife of the Pharaoh. Some scholars such as Ibn Arabi and Ibn Hazm even attribute Prophethood to Mary.

4. See: http://faith-matters.org/ and also http://www.huffingtonpost.co.uk/dr-leon-moosavi/the-fight-against-islamophobia-_b_1293441.html

5. Salafis adhere to a literalist interpretation of Islam that takes the 'pious predecessors', the first three generations of Muslims, as exemplary models to emulate.

6. Surat al-A'raaf: (7:156).

7. Surat al-Anbiya': (21:107).

Chapter 17

1. http://www.kensingtonmcc.org/

2. See verses 2:275, 276, 278, also 3:130 and 4:161.

3. Karen Armstrong concludes her second biography of the Prophet, *Muhammad: Prophet For Our Time*, with a plea to Muslims and Westerners 'not merely to tolerate but to appreciate one another'. She adds: 'A good place to start is with the figure of Muhammad ... who had profound genius and founded a religion and cultural tradition that was not based on the sword but whose name – "Islam"– signified peace and reconciliation.' (p. 214).

4. Bukhari.

5. Musnad al-Bazzar.

6. *The Spirit of Tolerance*, Reza Shah Kazemi.

Key Tenets of Islam

1. (Quran 42:13)

2. Bukhari and Muslim.

3. (Quran 4:163–164), 21:25, 41:43, 46:9

4. See one excellent treatise on the subject: *Maqasid Al-Shariah: A Beginner's Guide*, by Jasser Auda.

5. Muslim.

6. Ibn Asakir.
7. Nasa'i.
8. Other times for them to visit are the 10th of Muharram, Fridays and Eid days.
9. Bukhari.
10. *The Islamic Year.* Annemarie Schimmel.

Glossary

1. Muslim.
2. Nasa'i.

Acknowledgements

From MTV to Mecca has continued to evolve ever since its first publication in 2009 in Germany, its revision and later the Dutch edition. It is a living process as I experience new things, gain new insights, make new mistakes, and meet all different kinds of people. I am thrilled that the English edition is finally being published, because I have received so many requests for it in the last three years. This book is a product of team work, made possible only thanks to the contribution of many angels who believed in it, and who helped, inspired and supported me along the way. I am deeply grateful to every single one of you! Thank you for your support. You are in my prayers. I try to mention some of you although countless angels remain unnamed, but you know who you are.

  Bob, Jim, Tariq, Imran and Dr Nasr, thank you for your friendship and your meaningful quotes! Thank you Jane Paulick for your excellent translation from the original and your tireless edits of my rewrites – trying to adapt the book to the English market – always smiling; thank you Andy Hollis for taking the text to another level and for your attempts to teach me comma splices and other intricacies of the English grammar. Thank you both for your friendship throughout our intense year of closely working together – and beyond! Thank you Andrew Hayward for your infectious enthusiasm and faith in my book from the first moment we met at the Frankfurt book fair in 2011, which prompted Gary, director of Arcadia to publish me – agent or not. A huge thank you to my co-publishers, Gary Pulsifer and Hasan al-Banna. Thank you Hasan for wanting to publish my book ever since its first release, and thanks for your patience and understanding when I took my time … Thank you for your excellent advice whether as media mogul or Al Azhar research scholar of Islam, for proofing and correcting the Islamic passages. Thank you Angeline Rothermundt for your sharp edits, and great style! Without you the reader would have had to plough through so much more material. Thank you Toaha Qureshi MBE and Arif Anis from FIRD – for believing in this project, for your crucial contribution in making it happen and giving it international exposure through your contacts. Thank you Tony Mulliken of MIDAS PR for your generous advice and support since our first meeting long before I even had a publisher! It was so refreshing to hear about your affinity to Islam and to discover we have a few dear friends in common. Thank you Yahyia Birt for reading my manuscript, for your valuable tips, some of which I have implemented, and for your graciousness and understanding that I needed to find a mainstream publisher. Thank you Ahmed Mansour for putting me on the map in the Arab world and thank you Abu Ali, Shaykhna Bin Baya, Sheikh Sultan Dr Al Qasimi and Sheikha Jawaher for extending your friendship and kind support; thank you, Jasser Auda for clarifying essential issues in Islamic jurisprudence, by making me aware of a philosophical approach; thank you Dr Seyyed Hossein Nasr for your profound teachings of all different aspects of the religion, particularly the heart of Islam, and your invaluable spiritual and personal advice. Thank you Shaykh Haytham Tamim for your Islamic guidance and for searching the Arabic sources authenticating the *hadiths* mentioned. Thank you Dr Reza Shah Kazemi for generously sharing your knowledge and for your and your wife Nureen's encouragement and friendship in faith. Thank you Shaykh Abu Bakr Siraj ad-Din, may God be merciful to you and grant you peace, for accepting me and guiding me spiritually. Thank you Sidi Hasan or Gai Eaton, may God be merciful to you and grant you peace. During those fifteen years I was blessed to have known you as a dear friend and close adviser; you taught me so much about Islam, its spiritual and intellectual dimensions, as well as the limitations and shortcomings of not only Muslims but people at large. Your humour, wisdom and loving compassion always uplifted me and strengthened me in my identity as a European Muslim. Thank you Halima Krausen for your advice as a friend and sister in Islam as well as a Shaykha and editor of religious passages in my book; your refreshing interpretation of so many Islamic issues that made my hair stand up particularly when pertaining to women helped me to reconcile my religion with my European culture. Thank you Dr Murad Hofmann for reading and editing my previous text and patiently answering any question on Islam. Thank you to Karim Aghili for sourcing Rumi quotes in the original Farsi sources; thank you Dr William Chittick for verifying other Rumi references and for your and your wife's inspiration. Thank you to my Facebook friend Dr Amer Ahmed, whom I never met in person, for supplying me with quotes from the Quran or *hadith*. Thank you to the young *alim* Yusuf Casewit. We first met when you were a school kid, now after years of serious studies with traditional scholars in Mauritania you kindly proofed and corrected my text despite your pressures at Harvard. Thank you to my Arabic translator, Hany Beshr, who pointed out some key issues that prompted me to further research and rewrite. Thanks Edward Henry for reading and protecting me from any legal action *insha' Allah*. Thank you Dr Amina and Fadwa, my dearest sisters in faith, for your inspiration, advice and friendship always! Ruby, Dani and Fa, thank you for being there for me since the MTV days – sharing the ups and downs, the heartaches and moments of joy! Thank you Ruby for your valuable feedback and input, and Dani for editing one entire previous version. Thanks too to my other friends who have accompanied me on my long journey from MTV to Mecca or on parts or it. Thank you Imran Khan for your sincere efforts all those years ago to explain Islam to me in all its facets – in theory and in practice – when I was so far away from it. Had God chosen a long-bearded imam at that time it wouldn't have had quite the same effect. But no doubt, He knew what He was doing. Thank you also for your support in writing and helping me to remember which mountain we climbed when. And last but not least thank you to my parents and my sister for bearing with me, and for respecting my faith without fully understanding it, for not letting it come between us and for loving me all the same. Your belief in me and your love has given me the strength, courage and confidence to always follow my heart. Of course ultimately all thanks belong to God! I ask Allah to forgive my shortcomings and mistakes, and pray that He accepts this humble effort to describe what it means to be a European Muslim and try to shed some light on this so misunderstood religion, Islam, which I often don't recognise in the media as the religion I learned to love. May God bless and guide us all.